GLOBAL RESPONSIBILITY FOR
HUMAN RIGHTS

Global Responsibility for Human Rights

World Poverty and the Development
of International Law

MARGOT E SALOMON

OXFORD
UNIVERSITY PRESS

OXFORD
UNIVERSITY PRESS

Great Clarendon Street, Oxford OX2 6DP

Oxford University Press is a department of the University of Oxford.
It furthers the University's objective of excellence in research, scholarship,
and education by publishing worldwide in

Oxford New York

Auckland Cape Town Dar es Salaam Hong Kong Karachi
Kuala Lumpur Madrid Melbourne Mexico City Nairobi
New Delhi Shanghai Taipei Toronto

With offices in

Argentina Austria Brazil Chile Czech Republic France Greece
Guatemala Hungary Italy Japan Poland Portugal Singapore
South Korea Switzerland Thailand Turkey Ukraine Vietnam

Oxford is a registered trade mark of Oxford University Press
in the UK and in certain other countries

Published in the United States
by Oxford University Press Inc., New York

© M E Salomon 2007

The moral rights of the author have been asserted

Crown copyright material is reproduced under Class Licence
Number C01P0000148 with the permission of OPSI
and the Queen's Printer for Scotland

Database right Oxford University Press (maker)

First published 2007

British Library Cataloguing in Publication Data

Data available

Library of Congress Cataloging in Publication Data
Salomon, Margot E.
Global responsibility for human rights: world poverty and the
development of international law / Margot E. Salomon.
   p. cm.
Includes biliographical references and index.
   ISBN-13: 978–0–19–928442–9 (hardback: alk. paper)   1. Human
rights.   2. Civil rights.   I. Title.
   K3240.S255 2007
   341.4′8—dc22   2007030853

Typeset by Newgen Imaging Systems (P) Ltd., Chennai, India
Printed in Great Britain
on acid-free paper by
Biddles Ltd., King's Lynn.

ISBN 978–0–19–928442–9

In memory of Nathaniel H Salomon (1933–2003).

For Bubacarr Baah, and all the children of Africa.

Foreword

In this book, Dr Margot Salomon builds on and contributes to a long tradition that seeks to define the normative basis for international justice. Since ancient times and especially since Kant's *Project for a Perpetual Peace*, thinkers and activists have grappled with the conditions of international affairs under which peace is sustainable because it maximizes justice. Within this broad reflection on the conditions for the decent treatment of peoples everywhere, Margot Salomon narrows the focus to the corpus of international human rights law and more specifically to the right to development and its potential role in mitigating world poverty.

In order to assess the prospects of the right to development to contribute to global economic justice, she also focuses on a moving target, namely, the rather arcane deliberations on this right by the new United Nations Human Rights Council and its Working Group on the Right to Development. She dedicates particular attention to the Working Group's High-Level Task Force on the Implementation of the Right to Development and as chair of the task force, I welcome the opportunity to say a few words on the scope and significance of Dr Salomon's book.

Her dual objectives—a broad reflection on the contribution of international law to international justice and a narrow focus on the right to development in the United Nations institutional setting—are daunting. On the one hand, she runs the risk of preaching goodliness to hard-nosed political actors pursuing economic and security interests, and on the other hand, the equally irksome risk of interminable description of insignificant bickering over texts and working groups that have little bearing on reality. Salomon navigates these shoals well and succeeds in both enterprises.

Up to the twentieth anniversary of the adoption of the Universal Declaration of Human Rights in 1948, systematic human rights studies were few and far between; the next 20 years saw the proliferation of institutes, journals, and degree programs, resulting in the professionalization of the field. From the late 1980s to today, a third generation of scholar-activists earned degrees and became active in human rights NGOs, teaching, and publishing. Dr Salomon belongs to that third generation, and this book is the culmination of years of research, study, and participation in UN institutions on behalf of Minority Rights Group International and as Advisor to the Office of the High Commissioner for Human Rights. Her participation in the meetings of the High-Level Task Force on the Implementation of the Right to Development were the occasion for her both to provide substantive input into the task force's deliberations and to assess the broader significance

Foreword

of its work, which led to a timely and thoughtful publication.[1] She has written several other valuable pieces on the right to development,[2] including an essay in a book based on a Nobel symposium,[3] while completing the research for this book. Throughout those writings, she outlined her concern for unjust economic arrangements and posited collective duties of the international community under existing international human rights law, as interpreted by the treaty bodies.

Those ideas are considerably expanded in the present work. She makes a strong case for global justice, using the full arsenal of preferred sources of human rights law, not only in the UN Charter, human rights treaties, and political documents, but also in the pronouncements of treaty bodies, whether in general comments or in concluding observations on states parties' reports. Through the analysis of these texts and their interpretation, she argues that states have a negative duty to avoid hindering the right to development and a positive duty to ensure international enabling environments favorable to this right.

In this era of predatory globalization and the devastation wrought by the policies of neoconservative military adventures, the realist paradigm is likely to be restored with its persuasive force among powerful nations and elites in countries that are reaping the rewards of open markets and free trade. It is timely, therefore, to listen to an alternative voice, articulating a position well outside these powerful perspectives of mainstream foreign policy. Salomon stands resolutely within the movement of cooperative multilateralism, which provides a coherent justification for a human rights approach to attacking the problem of poverty and maldevelopment at their source, namely, the structural conditions that inhibit the flourishing of over a billion people for whom daily survival is their greatest challenge.

By addressing the economic injustice perpetuated by globalization, she adheres to an approach to cooperative multilateralism which should not be misunderstood as wooly idealism; on the contrary, she joins a long tradition of international jurists for whom the concept of international community and related concepts of interdependence and cooperation have operational significance in a legal regime based on the sovereign equality of states. She is returning to the basic premises of international law as they evolved in the twentieth century rather than proposing a new foundation of international justice.

Where the author is most innovative—and probably controversial—is in drawing from human rights law, specifically the right to development, the instruments

---

[1] Margot E Salomon, 'Towards a Just Institutional Order: A Commentary on the First Session of the UN Task Force on the Right to Development', *Netherlands Quarterly of Human Rights*, vol. 23, No. 3, (2005) pp. 409–438.

[2] Margot E Salomon, 'The Nature of a Right', *The Right to Development: Reflections on the First Four Reports of the Independent Expert on the Right to Development* (Franciscans International, 2003); *The Right to Development: Obligations of States and the Rights of Minorities and Indigenous Peoples* (with Arjun Sengupta, MRG, 2003).

[3] Margot E Salomon, 'International Human Rights Obligations in Context: Structural Obstacles and the Demands of Global Justice', in Bård Anders Andressen and Stephen P Marks (eds.), *Development as a Human Right* (Harvard University Press, 2006) pp. 96–118.

of redistributive justice and a strategy for dealing with the structural implications of top-down globalization. Whereas her underlying approach to the international legal order is within a highly respected tradition of the rule of law, her 'structural approach' to the realization of human rights is one of advocacy for the victims of world poverty and is all the more admirable for that bias. She is acutely aware of the conceptual deficiencies of the Declaration on the Right to Development. Therefore, she builds an extensive normative foundation on judgments and opinions of the International Court of Justice, the text of human rights treaties and their interpretations by the treaty bodies, and outcomes of international conferences and summits, culminating in the proposition that all states are bound by legal obligations to cooperate in ensuring the right to development and the universal realization of basic socio-economic rights. This proposition has its detractors, particularly donor countries who consider their efforts on behalf of poverty reduction and human rights promotion as matters of discretionary foreign policy rather than of compliance with legal obligations. It would be convenient if the legality of this obligation were moot due to the fact that recipient countries were satisfied with the voluntary and generous contribution of donor states to the realization of the right to development through assistance and cooperation. The inconvenient truth is that the recipient countries are neither satisfied with the level of aid—only five countries have met the target of 0.7 per cent of gross national income spent on official development assistance—nor do they accept that aid is the only, or principal, factor in redressing injustice in the international political economy.

Indeed, Salomon does not settle for charity as the basis for global justice through the right to development; she pushes the analysis in two critical directions, each of which has strong supporters and opponents. The first is the rejection of economic conditionality in the determination of domestic development policy by poor countries, and the second is the challenging of institutionalized advantages of the rich countries. With regard to the first, Salomon rightfully dwells on Article 2(3) of the Declaration on the Right to Development, which acknowledges the 'right and duty' of countries to formulate their own national development policies. 'Ownership' is the well-worn term for nationally established policy, free from interference by other states or institutions. In drafting criteria under MDG 8 for evaluating compliance by development partnerships with the right to development, the task force made a point of underscoring the limitation Article 2(3) placed on that otherwise free determination of policy, namely, that the policy must be aimed 'at the constant improvement of the well-being of the entire population and of all individuals, on the basis of their active, free and meaningful participation in development and in the fair distribution of the benefits resulting therefrom'. There is a fine line between conditionality—subjecting aid or loans to economic adjustment measures to please the donor or lender—and the requirement of Article 2(3), according to which only certain policies are consistent with the right to development. But it is a clear line. Participation and fair distribution are universal principles of justice in the interests of developing countries and certainly of the poor segments of their populations. They are not principles of a particular approach to macroeconomic policy of certain countries or institutions. A further requirement of the policy is that it incorporates all human rights, considered in their indivisibility and interdependence, a matter regularly stressed by Professor Arjun Sengupta in his reports as UN Independent Expert on the Right to Development. Salomon is right to shed light on this understanding of ownership of development policy.

The second challenge that Salomon poses is to treat the obligation to realize the right to development as extending beyond aid to all the domains where the cards are stacked against developing countries and where poverty is systemic. Thus, states are duty-bound to correct asymmetries in trade relations, forgive burdensome debt, remove protectionist subsidies, restrain the behavior of transnational corporations, and limit the harmful applications of intellectual property rights. This book argues that there is an international legal obligation to level the playing field in international economic relations and to take affirmative action in favour of human development. This teleological approach to international law requires her to posit an 'objective' international legal order, one that is not dependent upon consent, and a 'supra-positive character' of the obligation of international cooperation in the matter of human rights. This amounts to a legal version of moral cosmopolitanism, of which this book is perhaps the first systematic exposition.

In the middle of the twentieth century, the Universal Declaration of Human Rights expressed a revolutionary proposition in Article 28, according to which everyone has a 'right' to a social and international order in which all human rights can be assured. If one takes that proposition seriously—which Salomon does—then everyone has a right to a radical change in power relations, both domestically and internationally, for no political economy or legal system on earth today adequately ensures all human rights for everyone, and the structures of international relations often inhibit their full enjoyment. After the great ideological battles of the twentieth century, we are confronted in this century with the same unjust structures that contribute to world poverty, exacerbated by the negative impacts of globalization. Perhaps the most salient feature of Salomon's legal cosmopolitanism is that it resuscitates the revolutionary proposition of Article 28 and updates it for the twenty-first century through a thorough and well-researched argument for using the right to development to give substance to this human right to a just social and international order.

Stephen P Marks
François-Xavier Bagnoud Professor of Health and Human Rights
Harvard University, United States of America
&
Chairperson of the High-Level Task Force on the Implementation
of the Right to Development, Office of the United Nations
High Commissioner for Human Rights

Acknowledgements

This book is the product of many years of study and engagement in the worlds of academia and the United Nations, with an earlier version of this research having formed a PhD thesis successfully defended at the London School of Economics and Political Science (LSE) in December 2003. My first debt of gratitude is owed to Dr Chaloka Beyani, who encouraged me to pursue a PhD in 1999, was an erudite supervisor and continues to be a generous and invaluable colleague. He also graciously provided comments and encouragement during the writing of this book and I am extremely grateful to him for his support. My specific work on the right to development began as a research project for the NGO Minority Rights Group International (MRG), where I worked as Legal Officer during my postgraduate studies. Both the report produced for MRG and the study of the topic for my PhD thesis were greatly enriched by the scholarly insights and dedication provided by Professor Arjun Sengupta. I take this opportunity to thank him warmly. I would like also to thank sincerely Professor Paul Hunt and Professor Rein Müllerson who, having examined my thesis, recommended it for publication and provided valuable comments on turning it into a book.

The topic of world poverty, economic equity and the role of international human rights law has been an enduring interest of mine. I have published a number of pieces while preparing this monograph and have benefited greatly from the views and insights of academics and practitioners active in this area. In particular, I thank colleagues engaged with the UN High-Level Task Force on the Right to Development with whom I have worked closely: Dr Kitty Arambulo, Jean-Pierre Chauffeur, Joe Ingram, Dr Rajeev Malhotra, Professor Steve Marks, Ambassador Ibrahim Salama, and Professor Sabine von Schorlemer. My work over the years has benefited also from the experience shared and input generously provided by Professor Daniel Bradlow, Corinne Lennox, Gorik Ooms, Laure-Hélène Piron, Professor Thomas Pogge, Dr Sigrun Skogly, Dr Sivaramjani Thambisetty, Dr Arne Tostensen, Professor Peter Townsend, Dr Wouter Vandenhole, and Professor Makau wa Mutua. My appreciation is extended also to Professor Asbjørn Eide for the invitation to participate in the Nobel Symposium on the Right to Development in 2003. Additionally, I take this opportunity to thank the Harvard School of Public Health for permission to draw on the published work: M.E. Salomon, 'International Human Rights Obligations in Context: Structural Obstacles and the Demands of Global Justice', in B-A. Andreassen and S.P. Marks (eds), *Development as a Human Right: Legal, Political and Economic Dimensions* (Harvard School of Public Health—Harvard University Press, 2006).

There are a number of colleagues at the LSE that it gives me pleasure to acknowledge, not least since they have made the demanding process of writing (during term time) a more manageable and enjoyable task: everyone at the Centre for the Study of Human Rights, especially Professor Conor Gearty, Professor Francesca Klug, and Dr Claire Moon; colleagues in the Law Department, in particular Professor Christine Chinkin, as well as the members of the Research Committee for the grant awarded to complete this work. I am very grateful to Maria Bell, Ken Gibbons, and Richard Trussell at the British Library of Political and Economic Science for their vital research assistance. Jude Chillman and Azim Noorani are thanked for their wonderful and efficient work on cleaning up the manuscript. I wish also to thank Oxford University Press and the anonymous reviewers for having endorsed the publication of my PhD thesis so enthusiastically.

My final expression of gratitude is reserved for family and friends: Connie-Gail, and the late Nat Salomon, Justin, Marshal and the late Stacey Arbeiter Salomon, the families Feller, Kauffman, and van Bennekom; Anna-Maria, Atsuko, Carole, Jean, Katharine, Mishele, Richard, Simon, and Treva. Lastly, a special thanks to Stefan for sharing his expertise and knowledge, which has so benefited this work, and for his constant support during the preparation of my first book.

Margot E Salomon
LSE
June 2007

Contents

Table of Cases

National cases

World Trade Organization

Table of Legal Instruments and Documents

Introductory Note

This table sets out references to legal instruments and related documents, including World Conference Declarations and the General Comments and Concluding Observations of key Committees. References to Advisory Opinions of International Courts will be found in the Table of Cases. Documents are set out in alphabetical order by title, not including full publication data, which will be found in the Bibliography. In the case of documents with six references or more, the list of references is broken down by article or paragraph wherever possible, ordered as they appear in the document or instrument concerned. Where a document or instrument is referred to in both the body of a page and one or more footnotes, in general only the footnote references are given, as these enable the user to locate the discussion more precisely.

List of Abbreviations

GENERAL

ACHPR	African Charter on Human and Peoples' Rights
ACHR	American Convention on Human Rights
AU	African Union
CEDAW	Convention on the Elimination of All Forms of Discrimination against Women
CESCR	Committee on Economic, Social and Cultural Rights
CHR	Commission on Human Rights
Const Ct (SA)	Constitutional Court of South Africa
CRC	Convention on the Rights of the Child
DFID	(UK) Department for International Development
DRD	Declaration on the Right to Development
ECHR	European Convention on Human Rights
ECmHR	European Commission on Human Rights
ECOSOC	Economic and Social Council
ECtHR	European Court of Human Rights
EU	European Union
FAO	Food and Agricultural Organization of the United Nations
FDI	Foreign direct investment
FIDH	Fédération Internationale des Ligues des Droits de l'Homme
GA	General Assembly
GATS	General Agreement on Trade in Services
GATT	General Agreement on Tariffs and Trade
GDP	Gross domestic product
GNI	Gross national income
GRULAC	Group of Latin American and Caribbean States
HLTF RTD	High-Level Task Force on the Implementation of the Right to Development
HIPC	Heavily indebted poor countries
HRC	Human Rights Committee
HRC	Human Rights Council
IACHR	Inter-American Commission on Human Rights
IACtHR	Inter-American Court of Human Rights
ICCPR	International Covenant on Civil and Political Rights
ICERD	International Convention on the Elimination of All Forms of Racial Discrimination
ICESCR	International Covenant on Economic, Social and Cultural Rights
ICJ	International Court of Justice
IFI	International financial institution
IGO	Intergovernmental organization

ILC	International Law Commission
ILO	International Labour Organization
IMF	International Monetary Fund
LDC	Least-developed country
MDG	Millennium Development Goals
MFN	Most-favoured-nation
NAFTA	North American Free Trade Agreement
NEPAD	New Partnership for Africa's Development
NGO	Non-governmental organization
NIEO	New International Economic Order
OAS	Organization of American States
OAU	Organization of African Unity
ODA	Official development assistance
OECD	Organization for Economic Co-operation and Development
OEWG RTD	Open-ended Working Group on the Right to Development
OHCHR	Office of the High Commissioner for Human Rights
PCIJ	Permanent Court of International Justice
RTD	Right to development
TNC	Transnational corporation
TRIMS	Agreement on Trade-Related Investment Measures
TRIPS	Agreement on Trade-Related Aspects of Intellectual Property Rights
UDHR	Universal Declaration of Human Rights
UN	United Nations
UN Charter	Charter of the United Nations
UNCTAD	United Nations Conference on Trade and Development
UNDP	United Nations Development Programme
UNESCO	United Nations Educational, Scientific and Cultural Organization
UNICEF	United Nations Children's Fund
UNRISD	United Nations Research Institute for Social Development
UNTS	United Nations Treaty Series
VCLT	Vienna Convention on the Law of Treaties
WSSD	World Summit on Sustainable Development
WTO	World Trade Organization

JOURNALS

AJIL	American Journal of International Law
Am U J Int'l L and Pol'y	The American University Journal of International Law & Policy
ASIL PROC.	American Society of International Law Proceedings
Aust YBIL	Australian Yearbook of International Law
B C Int'l & Comp L Rev.	Boston College International and Comparative Law Review
BHRC	Butterworths Human Rights Cases
Brook J Int'l L	Brooklyn Journal of International Law

BYBIL	British Year Book of International Law
Cal W Int'l L J	California Western International Law Journal
CLP	Current Legal Problems
Colum J Transnat'l L	Columbia Journal of Transnational Law
DR	European Commission of Human Rights Decisions & Reports
EHRR	European Human Rights Reports
EJIL	European Journal of International Law
GYIL	German Yearbook of International Law
Harv Hum Rts J	Harvard Human Rights Journal
Harv Int'l L J	Harvard International Law Journal
How L J	Howard Law Journal
HRLJ	Human Rights Law Journal
HRQ	Human Rights Quarterly
ICJ Rep	International Court of Justice Reports
ICLQ	International and Comparative Law Quarterly
IJGLS	Indiana Journal of Global Legal Studies
IJIL	Indian Journal of International Law
ILM	International Legal Material
J Law & Soc	Journal of Law and Society
J Marshall L Rev J	John Marshall Law Review
JIEL	Journal of International Economic Law
Law & Pol	Law and Policy
LJIL	Leiden Journal of International Law
Nord J Int'l L	Nordic Journal of International Law
NQHR	Netherlands Quarterly of Human Rights
RBDI	Revue Belge de Droit International
RDH	Revue des Droits de l'Homme
Rec des Cours	Recueil des Cours
Rutgers L Rev	Rutgers Law Review

Introduction

A contemporary function of human rights is to tame the negative forces and tendencies of the current global economic system. Ethically, human rights offer a '...barrier to a worldwide, voracious, and highly divisive brand of supranational capitalism.'[1] Legally, they have the potential to humanize the global marketplace and to ensure political and economic arrangements are fair in their processes, increasing the likelihood that they will produce just outcomes. However, this will require a rigorous application of existing human rights standards and principles, and a purposive interpretation of their corresponding obligations, attuned to the nature of present-day violations.

Today, economic globalization is characterized by a particular model for the creation and distribution of wealth that is serving to enrich some, and not others. Disparities in income between nations have grown at a pace faster than ever before in recent history.[2] In its 2006 World Development Report, the World Bank concluded that unequal opportunities are 'truly staggering on a global scale.'[3] A central feature of the poverty reflected in this global divide, is that the deprivation is overwhelmingly concentrated in the 'South', with wealth and access to wealth, overwhelmingly concentrated in the 'North'.[4] The substance and direction of globalization are largely shaped by the affluent and powerful states through the institutions over which they exercise effective control. Unsurprisingly, it is these very states that benefit disproportionately from the liberalization and integration of global markets that are among the key features of economic globalization (Chapter 1). Another consequence is that governments have increasingly less control in determining the economic and social policies within their own territories, this being especially true of developing countries.[5] Although many argue

---

[1] CA Gearty, 'Human Rights' in A Kuper and J Kuper (eds), *The Social Science Encyclopedia* (3rd edn, Routledge, 2004) Vol I, 468, at 470–1.

[2] MB Steger, *Globalization: A Very Short Introduction* (Oxford University Press, 2003) 104.

[3] World Bank, *World Development Report 2006: Equity and Development* (World Bank/Oxford University Press, 2006) 6.

[4] In this book the terms 'North' and 'South' are used as shorthand to denote the affluent and poor parts of the world respectively, as are 'developed' and 'developing' countries. Where relevant to the analysis, particular terms are used, such as, 'Least-Developed Countries' (LDC), 'middle-income developing countries', and 'industrialized countries'.

[5] 'A world trade regime friendly to human development would provide domestic policy space and give developing countries flexibility to make institutional and other innovations. Such policy space should take precedence over market access considerations ....': UNDP et al, *Making Global Trade Work for the Poor* (UNDP, 2003) 41–2. 'As the recent evaluation by the IMF and World Bank demonstrates, despite considerable progress there remain question marks about the level of

that economic globalization—as currently conceived—is the only or best means by which world poverty can be reduced[6] half the people in the world still live on less than US$2 a day[7] and are not 'free from want'.[8] Any alleged contribution to a more egalitarian world order derived from this economic system, in which benefits are more widely shared, is overshadowed by the fact that it perpetuates significant global inequalities. These inequalities result in people in much of the world being denied their most basic human rights.

The figures for the past few decades on the growing gap between the global 'haves' and 'have-nots' make it clear that the international economic order is failing to satisfy the legitimate expectations of the majority of states. It is also failing to allow for the realization of fundamental human rights for a vast proportion of people. This shift in attention towards the international system 'both as the cause and perpetrator of injustice and as the locus of appropriate remedial measures'[9] was necessarily going to inform the human rights legal regime. With the centre of power globalized, so the international law of human rights must reorient and adapt itself accordingly.

This scale and concentration of deprivation exists alongside an international legal regime established in 1945 that envisioned a world order that was determined 'to reaffirm the faith in fundamental human rights, in the dignity and worth of the human person, in the equal rights of men and women and of nations large and small, and ... to promote social progress and better standards of life in larger freedom'.[10] The efforts to achieve these common ideals resulted in the drafting and adoption of a range of human rights instruments. Fundamental rights, such as the right of everyone to an adequate standard of living, including adequate food, clothing and housing, and rights to health and education, were subsequently enshrined in international law, first within the Universal Declaration of Human Rights (UDHR),[11] and then in treaty form within the

genuine autonomy that countries, especially those that depend heavily on aid, have over their own policies.': United Kingdom Department for International Development, *Partnerships for Poverty Reduction: Rethinking Conditionality*, UK Policy Paper, March 2005, para 6.1.

[6] See I Goldin and K Reinert, *Globalization for Development: Trade, Finance, Aid, Migration, and Policy* (World Bank/Palgrave MacMillan, 2006) 1, for an introduction to the debate.

[7] *Fast Facts: The Faces of Poverty*, UN Millennium Project (2005). People living on less than US$2 per day (in 1985 purchasing power parity dollars) are defined as 'poor'. See, Goldin and Reinert, *Globalization for Development*, 26.

[8] 'Whereas disregard and contempt for human rights have resulted in barbarous acts which have outraged the conscience of mankind, and the advent of a world in which human beings shall enjoy freedom of speech and belief and freedom from fear and want has been proclaimed as the highest aspiration of the common people,' Universal Declaration of Human Rights, General Assembly Resolution 217A (III), 10 December 1948, UN GAOR, 3rd Session resolutions, Pt 1, at 71, UN Doc A/810 (1948) preambular para 2.

[9] T Franck, *Fairness in International Law and Institutions* (Oxford University Press, 1995) 415, referring to the campaign for a New International Economic Order in the 1970s.

[10] Preamble, Charter of the United Nations (1945), entered into force 24 October 1945, 59 Stat 1031, TS 993, 3 Bevans 1193.

[11] UDHR, arts 25 and 26.

International Covenant on Economic, Social and Cultural Rights (ICESCR)[12] and the Convention on the Rights of the Child (CRC).[13] Then, as now, the international community recognized that an entitlement to a suitable international order,[14] and guarantees of international cooperation, may be required to give socio-economic rights meaningful effect.[15]

The strongest normative articulation of this demand, vis-à-vis the public international order, for an international environment in which human rights can be realized for all, came in the form of the right to development. Adopted in 1986 by the United Nations (UN) General Assembly,[16] the Declaration on the Right to Development[17] (DRD) places the individual at the centre of development processes.[18] At the same time, the DRD places the claims of developing countries suffering from underdevelopment at the centre of the global political economy, where their calls for a structural environment conducive to the fulfilment of human rights might be heeded. The legal instrumentation through which this change is to occur is international cooperation.

The DRD provides the various components of an 'inalienable human right'[19] to a comprehensive process of development aimed at the well-being of the entire population and of all individuals, on the basis of their meaningful participation in development, and on the fair distribution of its benefits.[20] The rights-based process for the achievement of these objectives requires suitable national, and international, environments.[21] As emphasized in the DRD, 'States have the duty to cooperate with each other in ensuring development and eliminating obstacles to development...';[22] '...As a complement to the efforts of developing countries, effective international cooperation is essential...';[23] and, 'All States should cooperate with a view to promoting, encouraging and strengthening universal respect for and observance of all human rights....'[24] In the words of Brownlie: 'the right constitutes a general affirmation of a need for a programme of international economic justice', and, as a result, '[t]here is a duty to elaborate existing human rights standards in light of the right to development, both in terms of national legal systems and at the

---

[12] International Covenant on Economic, Social and Cultural Rights (1966), entered into force 3 January 1976, GA res A/RES/2200A (XXI), 993 UNTS 3, arts 11, 12, 13.

[13] Convention on the Rights of the Child (1989), entered into force 2 September 1990, GA res A/RES/44/25, annex 44, UN GAOR Supp (No 49) at 167, UN Document A/44/49 (1989), arts 24, 27, 28, 32.

[14] UDHR, art 28.

[15] ICESCR arts 2(1), 11(1), 11(2), 15(4), and arts 22 and 23; CRC arts 4, 23(4), 24(4), 28(3).

[16] The term was coined more than a decade earlier by Senegalese jurist Kéba Mbaye. K Mbaye, 'Le Droit du Développement comme un Droit de l'Homme' *RDH* 5 (1972) 503.

[17] DRD, GA res A/RES/41/128, 4 December 1986, annex 41 UN GAOR Supplement. (no 53) 186, UN Doc A/RES/41/53 (1986).

[18] DRD, preambular para 12; art 2(1): 'The human person is the central subject of development and should be the active participant and beneficiary of the right to development.'

[19] Ibid, art 1(1).   [20] Ibid, art 2(3).

[21] Ibid, arts 3(1), 4(1), 10.   [22] Ibid, art 3(3).

[23] Ibid, art 4(2).   [24] Ibid, art 6(1).

international level. This is essentially an assertion of a standard of international economic and social justice'.[25]

While the preoccupation of the DRD is with external impediments to human-centred development, it recognizes fully the responsibilities of developing countries, including the duty to formulate appropriate development policies;[26] equality of opportunity for all in access to basic resources and in the fair distribution of income;[27] and the encouragement of popular participation.[28]

Ensuring national development policies that aim at the constant improvement in well-being of all people constitutes a duty of states acting domestically.[29] It remains an important aspect of the right to development that external factors are not used as an excuse for governments to evade their human rights responsibilities at home. However, the national duties the DRD outlines are underpinned by a complementary premise—that developing countries face certain international obstacles to reducing poverty, and furthering socio-economic rights. The DRD gives legal expression to the notion that the ability of states to develop, and to fulfil their human rights obligations, are constrained by the actions of, and structural arrangements put in place by, the powerful states of the international community. This fact caused the ambassador chairing the UN Working Group on the Right to Development to query whether the right to development could be 'the unknown saviour of globalization from its collateral injustices and dangerous turmoils.'[30]

The juridical genealogy of the right to development is found among the purposes of the United Nations, as provided for in the Charter: to achieve international cooperation in solving economic and social problems, and in promoting and encouraging respect for human rights and fundamental freedoms.[31] International economic and social cooperation forming one of the pillars of the UN system, has as its aim to ensure conditions of stability recognized as attainable through the promotion of economic and social progress and development; solutions to socio-economic problems; and the universal respect for, and observance of, human rights.[32] Article 28 of the Universal Declaration of Human Rights offers the second basis for the intellectual origins and legal claims found in the DRD. It recognizes that for human rights to be fulfilled, a suitable domestic, as well as international, order is necessary. As a result, claims on our political, economic and social arrangements, at both levels, must constitute nothing less than an actual entitlement. Today, the DRD is read in conjunction with

---

[25] I Brownlie, 'The Human Right to Development', *Commonwealth Secretariat* (1989) 1, at 8.

[26] DRD, art 2(3).   [27] Ibid, art 8(1).

[28] Ibid, art 8(2).   [29] Ibid, art 2(3).

[30] I Salama, *The Right to Development: Towards a New Approach?*, Annual Meeting of the Academic Council on the United Nations System, Ottawa, 16–18 June 2005. Unpublished at the time of publication of this book.

[31] UN Charter, art 1(3); DRD, preambular para 1.

[32] UN Charter, arts 55 and 56.

other international substantive norms for which cooperation for development, and thus for the realization of economic, social and cultural rights, is required.[33]

Through a range of human rights instruments created in the post-Cold War era, the international community has deepened this shared responsibility to advance human rights in light of the negative aspects of globalization (Chapter 2). In an age of increasing interdependence, international cooperation and shared responsibility have been entrenched as the twin principles upon which the fundamental and collective values of human rights are to be realized. There is now commanding support for the position that the Charter of the United Nations imposes binding legal obligations in the area of human rights on every Member State, including responsibilities requiring them to take joint and separate action to cooperate internationally in the respect for, and observance of, human rights (Chapter 2). The idea that human rights obligations apply to relations among states when it comes to addressing poverty and underdevelopment is not alien to the international law of human rights, notwithstanding that traditionally, the relationship focuses primarily on the regulation of the state in its conduct towards the people within its territory.

Despite decades of standard-setting in this area, economic globalization is serving to alienate rather than incorporate human rights for much of the world's population. This phenomenon is inconsistent with an international law of cooperation as the law of the international community that was both consecrated, and set in motion, under the UN Charter. The significance of an international legal regime premised on cooperation is further crystallizing within the process of globalization, with the global responsibility of states to protect human rights today based on this legal framework. Given the problem of a global order in which so many people suffer for want of their fundamental socio-economic rights, there is an urgent need to explore developments in the system of international legal safeguards. The realization of these human rights cannot be undertaken by states singly. This inquiry into the application of the international law of human rights to the manifestations of world poverty requires us to rethink human rights—as the right to development does—and, in particular, the framing of responsibilities essential to their protection.

Since the adoption of the DRD, the international community of states has sanctioned the right to development as an 'integral part of fundamental human rights',[34] with sustainable progress towards its implementation requiring not only effective national development policies, but 'equitable economic relations and a

---

[33] CESCR, General Comment no 3 on Art 2(1) (The Nature of States Parties' Obligations), (5th session, 1990) UN Doc E/1991/23, annex III (1990), para 14; CRC, General Comment no 5, General Measures of Implementation of the Convention on the Rights of the Child (arts 4, 42 and 44, para 6), (34th session, 2003) UN Doc CRC/GC/2003/5 (2003), paras 60–4.

[34] UN World Conference on Human Rights, Vienna Declaration and Programme of Action (1993) UN Doc A/CONF 157/23 Pt I, art 10.

favourable economic environment at the international level'.[35] But, while the right to development is clearly within the ambit of the post-1945 international legal order, it offers something unique to the corpus of international human rights law. The DRD demands, not merely cooperation for the achievement of human rights central to the alleviation of poverty, but also changes to the system of structural disadvantage that characterizes the current international order (Chapter 1).

Yet its innovation and strengths may also constitute its weaknesses. The right to development is a right premised on recognition of the interdependence of nations, and on an appreciation that the effects of the global political economy are a human rights issue. Its solution indicates that securing many human rights—notably socio-economic rights, those that are most affected by the inequalities at the international level, and the attendant inequalities in access to benefits domestically—will succeed only if this is made possible internationally. This focus on the 'rights' of developing states against the more powerful members of the international community in order to achieve conditions under which basic human rights can be exercised, breaks with the classical assumptions of international human rights law, which is rooted in the protection of individuals against abuse by *their* own state (Chapter 3). This is despite the fact that the realization of economic, social, and cultural rights are envisaged as giving rise to responsibilities for states other than the victim's own.

There is widespread consensus that the traditional view of human rights, which focuses solely on the individual obligations of states, is now outdated. With international law for the protection and promotion of human rights having provided considerable normative advances in this area over several decades, this newest stage of its evolution requires only that we see what it might offer regarding contemporary ills. Obligations of international cooperation for economic, social and cultural rights require something over and beyond obligations derived from the 'extraterritorial' reach of a human rights convention; they call for *proactive* steps through international cooperation in securing these rights globally, rather than obligations attached reactively (i.e. based on the potential impact of a state's activities on the people in foreign countries).

They also reinforce the existence of responsibilities of states acting collectively (Chapter 2). We cannot legally provide for the socio-economic rights of the six million children in developing countries that die annually from malnutrition,[36] or the women living in sub-Saharan Africa who have a one in 16 chance of dying in pregnancy,[37] exclusively within a legal framework that imposes obligations on states acting nationally, and even extraterritorially. Economic globalization requires also addressing the collective obligations of the international community of states to secure an institutional order that is globally just (Chapter 5).

---

[35] Ibid.
[36] *Fast Facts: The Faces of Poverty.*
[37] Ibid.

So, the novel ground covered by the DRD results in its language at times being ambiguous, even awkward. Its lack of conceptual clarity combined with the contentious nature of its core subject that effectively pits South against North—developing against developed states—has until 2004 contributed to limiting severely its operationalization. While most, if not all, states agree that the right to development has both national and international dimensions, Northern states have traditionally tended to place the emphasis primarily on good governance, anti-corruption measures, responsible economic management, and the fulfillment of human rights in developing countries. Southern countries, for their part, prioritize the need for an international economic environment conducive to economic, social, and cultural development. Their concerns revolve around inequalities in the international economic system and related institutions, the need for greater participation in global decision-making on economic policy, and promoting a fairer international trade regime (Chapter 2).

Despite the unsurprising geo-political tensions and the paucity of explicit jurisprudence on development as a right, the right to development represents an element of growth. It constitutes an outworking of the existing corpus of standards and principles of human rights providing for a procedure for which the corresponding duties engage also the international community of states.[38] At the national level, the DRD provides for this particular rights-based process to development through what has elsewhere been referred to as 'a composite right'.[39] This 'holistic' approach, incorporating all human rights—civil and political, and economic, social and cultural—as indivisible and interdependent, is particularly attentive to the implications that resource constraints have on the realization of human rights,[40] on justifications for the prioritization of certain rights functioning within a system attuned to redistribution, and in meeting the needs of the poor, i.e. 'the entire population'[41] (Chapter 3).

But whether we speak of the contribution the right to development provides in conditioning growth strategies domestically, including with regard to the influence of international institutions that tend to focus their advice and corresponding rules on currency stability, growth and market efficiency, often at the expense of human rights,[42] or with regard to international arrangements more generally, the DRD is framed in the language of responsibilities. This 'responsibilities approach' characterizing the DRD reinforces the position that this right is less about establishing a new substantive right, and more about framing a system of duties that might give better effect to existing rights (Chapter 3). It is grounded in

[38] See, Brownlie, '*The Human Right to Development*, 1, at 15.
[39] A Sengupta, *Fourth Report of the Independent Expert on the Right to Development* (Working Group on the Right to Development, 3rd session, 2002) UN Doc E/CN 4/2002/WG 18/2 para 14.
[40] DRD, arts 6(2) and 6(3), 9.
[41] Ibid, preambular para 2; art 2(3).
[42] See, SP Marks, 'Misconceptions about the Right to Development' in D Freestone and JK Ingram, *Special Report, Human Rights and Development* (guest eds), 8 *Development Outreach* (The World Bank Institute, October 2006) 9, at 10–11.

successive treaties providing for obligations of international cooperation required for the fulfilment of human rights that socio-economic underdevelopment keeps at bay. Today, it has a rich base of legal norms, and political commitments from which to draw when determining, with specificity, what constitutes international cooperation. This would include the structural content of this obligation, and thus reform of the global economic system and its institutions (Chapter 2).

Internationalization is a defining feature of globalization—the internationalization of global trade and finance, the enhanced role, and influence, of international institutions at the forefront of which are the World Bank,[43] the International Monetary Fund (IMF) and the World Trade Organization (WTO).[44] It is through these institutions that much of the agenda of economic restructuring, and of deregulated multinational capitalism, is being pursued since the end of the Cold War.[45] As Eide concludes, the 'WTO, the IMF and, to some extent the World Bank are institutional agents of globalization ...',[46] and these international organizations, while formally having their membership representative of most states, are largely influenced by those that are wealthy and powerful (Chapters 1 and 3).

To speak of an institutional order is not to disregard the fact that it is also an international order, comprised of sovereign states, making deliberate policy choices, at the international level. But it is an institutional order in that the Bretton Woods institutions, and later the General Agreement on Tariffs and Trade (GATT), and now the WTO, were established to advance economic cooperation, and together with economically powerful states, shape the global economic order. The failure to exercise those basic human rights for which international cooperation is foreseen, gives rise to legitimate claims against these institutional schemes.[47] It is not sufficient therefore to seek to advance international cooperation for human rights without interpreting that to mean a duty to cooperate

[43] The World Bank Group consists of the International Bank for Reconstruction and Development (IBRD), the International Development Association (IDA), the International Finance Corporation (IFC), the Multilateral Investment Guarantee Agency (M IGA), and the International Centre for the Settlement of Investment Disputes (ICSID). Its proclaimed mission is to fight poverty (see recently, the World Bank Independent Evaluation Group, *Annual Review of Development Effectiveness 2006: Getting Results* (World Bank, 2006)). The IBRD and IDA are lending and advisory institutions (to middle-income and poor countries respectively), as is its private sector arm, the IFC. The MIGA encourages foreign investment in developing countries in a number of ways, including by providing guarantees to foreign investors against loss caused by non-commercial risks: see <http://www.worldbank.org>. While the use of the term World Bank in this book often applies more specifically to the IBRD and IDA, many of the issues raised address concerns of general relevance.

[44] Steger, *Globalization: A Very Short Introduction*, 41.

[45] A Orford, 'Globalization and the Right to Development' in P Alston (ed), *Peoples' Rights* (Oxford University Press, 2001) 127, at 146.

[46] A Eide, *The Right to Adequate Food and to be Free from Hunger* (Sub-Commission, 51st session, 1999) UN Doc E/CN4/Sub2/1999/12, para 118.

[47] See generally, TW Pogge, 'The International Significance of Human Rights' *The Journal of Ethics* 4 (2000) 45.

in reforming the institutional economic system as a whole. From the perspective of the international law of human rights this requires consideration as to what might constitute its structural dimensions, beginning with the system of economic global governance itself (Chapter 2).

Thus, it is also the very *design* of the economic order, which contributes to the perpetuation of world poverty or, at a minimum, has failed sufficiently to relieve poverty, and the situation is worsening. And, since this poverty is a product of a system that repeated findings demonstrate benefits some by virtue of its *structure* while disadvantaging others, establishing causal relationships between harms experienced elsewhere in the world, and the actions of states acting internationally, can be extremely complex. Yet, facilitating methods of determining state responsibility for global structural impediments to the exercise of basic socio-economic rights of people in far off places is overdue, since this is essential to establishing a process of remedying existing violations manifested in world poverty, and preventing further ones (Chapter 5).

That every single state does not formally recognize socio-economic rights, or the right to development, does not detract from the fact that the international community of states as a whole has shown itself to be committed to their advancement. These rights now form an integral part of the canon of human rights, and are supported through the UN human rights machinery, with the focus on their importance continually increasing. Just as the resistance, by a minority of states, to UN multilateralism that has taken place in the first years of the twenty-first century has not undermined a general commitment to post-1945 cooperative internationalism (indeed it may have reinforced it), so too do we acknowledge detractors who challenge the project of socio-economic rights, while recognizing that their position does not alter what essentially reflects a general will of the international community to see these rights given meaningful effect universally (Chapter 1).

In fact, after decades of international law-making in this area, it can be argued that there exists a general principle of international law—legally binding on all states—to respect and observe human rights. And it can be further argued that this doctrine of basic universal rights today includes socio-economic rights. Any list of basic legal rights with customary international status would at present be considered incomplete without the inclusion of, at least, the minimum essential levels of certain rights provided for in the ICESCR (Chapter 4). The progressive development of international law has brought us to the point of recognizing obligations that transcend state consent in this area; by reason of the importance of the rights involved, the obligations are *erga omnes*, thereby engaging the legal interest of the international community. But, as Alston and Simma have pointed out, there is another powerful argument for recognizing the customary status of certain socio-economic rights: the theory of human rights and the UN doctrine demand it.[48]

---

[48] B Simma and P Alston, 'The Sources of Human Rights Law: Custom, Jus Cogens, and General Principles' 12 *Aust YBIL* (1988–1989) 82, at 95.

The United Nations has confronted world poverty through a commitment among Member States, and not merely developing countries, to give effect to the right to development. The past several years have represented important turning points in attempts at defining the terms that would facilitate its operation (Chapter 2). Most recently, this is exemplified by the established of a High-Level Task Force on the Implementation of the Right to Development by the (former) Commission on Human Rights (CHR). At its sixtieth session in 2004, the CHR created a subsidiary body to the intergovernmental Open-ended Working Group on the Right to Development.[49] This independent body, consisting of human rights experts, was convened to act as an advisory body to the Working Group, and to render operational the terms of the DRD. Its *modus operandi* is to bring together these human rights experts with representatives of the international development, finance and trade institutions to explore the evolving relationship between human rights and economic development generally, and the concerns over the marginalization of human rights in the processes, and outcomes, of global economic governance specifically.[50] The Task Force's current mandate is to develop and apply criteria for the periodic evaluation—from the perspective of the right to development—of 'global partnerships for development' as required under 'Millennium Development Goal 8'.[51] In 2006 the Working Group adopted the Task Force criteria by consensus—an unusual result in and of itself—and mandated that it be piloted to selected partnerships 'with a view to operationalizing and progressively developing these criteria, and thus contributing to mainstreaming the right to development in the policies and operational activities of relevant actors at the national, regional and international levels, including multilateral financial, trade and development institutions'.[52]

This book draws on the DRD's *travaux preparatoires*, the conclusions and recommendations of the Task Force, and the positions adopted by its intergovernmental Working Group. Among its aims are to explore what the right to development contributes conceptually, and increasingly practically, to concerns related to poverty and underdevelopment in the developing world. It also considers what the right to development offers the international human rights legal regime more generally. Notably, with its focus on a human-centred globalization, this right highlights the lack of coherence among the various branches of international law and policy, and the importance of aligning the trade regime and commonly held beliefs regarding market liberalization with human rights. Within the right to development it is individuals that constitute the central entities around which

---

[49] CHR, res 2004/7, The right to development (60th session, 2004) UN Doc E/CN4/2004/L17, para 9.

[50] See further, ME Salomon, 'Towards a Just Institutional Order: A Commentary on the First Session of the UN Task Force on the Right to Development' 23 *NQHR* 3 (2005) 409.

[51] CHR, res 2005/4, The right to development (61st session, 2005) UN Doc E/CN4/2005/L9, para 5.

[52] *Report of the Open-ended Working Group on the Right to Development* (7th session, 2006) UN Doc E/CN4/2006/26, para 77.

development evolves: it is development that serves people, and not people who serve economic development. The right to development advances this crucial premise, and seeks to reorient thinking so that people are the higher purpose— not markets, not growth, not trade. Fair processes reasonably designed to achieve just outcomes become the principal requirement for fulfilling this right.

Rights and obligations that require change to the institutional economic order are born of our interdependence. The peoples of the world today rely on the same global environment for the satisfaction of their needs, and states have a sufficient degree of contact and impact regarding their decisions to act as part of a whole.[53] Our growing interdependence conditions cooperation, mitigates sovereignty, and forms a constitutive element of the international community. There is already an international community, with common interests and values framed in the language of universal human rights. The growing interdependence of this community of states only strengthens their duty to cooperate (Chapter 1).

The current practice of economic globalization risks downgrading the centrality accorded to human rights by the UN Charter and the International Bill of Human Rights.[54] A rights-based approach to globalization seeks to place international human rights standards and principles at the centre of international economic affairs; to have them successfully inform all cooperative endeavours that may impact on their exercise. However, the international law of human rights will only provide the humanizing force that the negative trends in globalization require of it if it evolves to meet these challenges. This book is by no means exhaustive in seeking to have international law for the protection and promotion of human rights constrain contemporary forms of the use and abuse of power. The proper regulation of non-state actors, notably transnational corporations (TNCs), also requires revisiting international standards and mechanisms to ensure that their activities are consistent with human rights, and important work is being done in this area. And, although TNCs rival or even surpass certain states in their economic power, the solution still lies with states themselves;[55] effective and legitimate states still provide the best means of ensuring rights, and that the benefits of trade and investment (as well as technology and communications) will be equitably shared.[56] As such, this research can be seen as part

---

[53] K Nowrot, 'Legal Consequences of Globalization: The Status of Non-Governmental Organizations Under International Law' 6 *IJGLS* (1999) 579, at 602.

[54] CESCR, Decision on Globalization and its Impact on the Enjoyment of Economic, Social and Cultural Rights (18th session, 1998) UN Doc E/1999/22, para 3.

[55] 'Human rights law will continue to develop. We can only speculate about its contours, but states remain responsible for the activities of global companies. Some states may have trouble exercising that responsibility. They may not wish to exercise that responsibility. But as a matter of law, and as a matter of politics, states continue to be responsible'. L Henkin, 'The Universal Declaration at 50 and the Challenge of Global Markets' 25 *Brook J Int'l L* 1 (1999) 17, at 22.

[56] Report of the International Commission on Intervention and State Sovereignty, *The Responsibility to Protect* (International Development Research Centre, 2001) 7.

of a larger effort among the academic and general human rights community to address these pressing issues of our time.

After acknowledging that the International Court of Justice (ICJ) was in accordance with his views, Judge Alvarez affirmed in an individual opinion in 1949 that there are three essential factors which have to be taken into account in the development of international law: '... the general principles of the new international law, the legal conscience of the peoples and the exigencies of contemporary life'.[57] In line with this observation, this research examines the changes that are beginning to take place, and indeed must take place, if human rights law is to remain relevant.

While this work is consistently rooted in international law, and law-making processes, it is particularly attentive to what human rights law was set up to achieve, and explores the possibilities of fulfilling that vision. At its core, this book addresses the collective imperative on the international community of states to assume responsibility for world poverty. But, this demand is not based on charity or morality, or even self-interest—although these may offer other justifications. It is squarely based on the development of international law. In an era of considerable interdependence, and entrenched economic and political advantage, the particular features of world poverty give rise to important questions about the scope, evolution and application of international law, and the attribution of global responsibility for the structural obstacles that impede the realization of basic human rights, to which each and everyone one of us is entitled.

During his final address to the General Assembly, Kofi Annan, the outgoing Secretary-General of the United Nations remarked that 'Africa was in great danger of being excluded from the benefits of globalization—indeed of being left to rot on the margins of the global economy'.[58] It is the contention of this book that the international law of human rights has, and should have, something to say about this state of affairs.

---

[57] *Reparation for Injuries Suffered in the Service of the United Nations,* Judge Alvarez (ind op) Adv Op, ICJ Rep (1949) 174, at 190.

[58] K Annan, United Nations Secretary-General, Address to the General Assembly, New York, 9 September 2006.

1

Interdependence and Its Imperatives

1.1 Introduction

There exists an entity that can be called an international community. It has recognized, and entrenched, common interests and agreed values—supreme among them human rights. It is governed by the rule of law, and functions largely within commonly established institutions developed to facilitate the collaborative engagement of its members in advancing these shared interests and values. Today, it can only meaningfully give effect to these agreed values through collaborative effort. As is clear, this community of states is not a cluster of like-minded and functionally equal entities engaging harmoniously on the world stage. Self-interest persists, but this familiar tendency does so in tension with a multilateral norms-based human rights system, premised on a post-war international law of cooperation, and influenced by a general will of an organized international community of states.

As international integration has increased over the last century, so it has shaped international law, with rules guiding inter-state cooperation commensurate with the increase in their interdependence. Sovereignty has gradually given way to demands that a state under the international order comply faithfully with its international duties and obligations.[1] The changing international environment has resulted in the re-orientation of priorities: states are to act faithfully on the duties they owe to each other, and on the duties owed to a wider international community. It is no longer sovereignty, but interdependence, that shapes international law.

Nowhere is this interdependence felt more strongly than in relation to the global economic order, in which all states are reliant on an increasingly liberalized, deregulated and integrated market. Yet, a minority of affluent states enjoy a disproportionate share of the benefits of this model, and exercise an equally disproportionate degree of control over the relevant international organizations.

---

[1] The *United Nations Conference on International Organizations, San Francisco, 1945, Documents,* as cited in H Gros Espiell, 'Sovereignty, Independence and Interdependence' in A Grahl-Madsen and J Toman (eds), *The Spirit of Uppsala, Proceedings of the Joint UNITAR-Uppsala University Seminar on International Law and Organization for a New World Order* (Walter de Gruyter, 1984) 277, at 280.

The abject poverty of half the world's population, concentrated in the South, is structurally sustained through these conditions. Whether economic globalization has the potential to enrich us all and bring about equal access to its benefits, does not alter a trend that sees the persistence of 'massive global inequity'.[2] In the language of international human rights law, world poverty reflects a systemic breach of socio-economic rights.[3]

All the while, international law foresees international cooperation as essential to the realization of economic, social and cultural rights, and it remains an enduring legal basis for the framing of contemporary duties, powerfully advanced in the 1986 UN Declaration on the Right to Development (DRD). As the DRD makes clear, international cooperation is directed, not solely at the realization of socio-economic rights as was provided for in the International Covenant on Economic, Social and Cultural Rights (ICESCR), but also at the promotion of an equitable international order. Duties of international cooperation include the removal of structural impediments to that order, and give legal expression to the notion that the ability of developing states to develop, and to fulfil their human rights obligations, relies on the complementary role of the international community to create an environment conducive to those objectives.[4]

The DRD represents an evolution in international law, providing a duty to elaborate existing human rights standards both in terms of national legal systems and, at the international level, based on an assertion of international economic and social justice.[5] In recent years, the Committee on Economic, Social and Cultural Rights (CESCR), and the Committee on the Rights of the Child (CRC), have also understood that their mandates would necessarily require drawing attention to the structural deficiencies of the international order that undermine the exercise of rights codified in the respective treaties they monitor.

The suffering caused by world poverty is without modern comparator. The increasingly multilateral nature of contemporary international obligations is emerging in this area where there is a strong requirement for community action given the high degree of global economic interdependence. In order to give meaningful effect to socio-economic rights, international law for their protection and promotion is turning to address the external global environment. This development sees the continuation of the important role that international human rights has played over the decades. As Cassese notes, '... [H]uman rights doctrine has operated as a potent leaven, contributing to shift the world community from a reciprocity-based bundle of legal relations, geared to the 'private' pursuit of self-interest, and ultimately blind to collective needs, to a community hinging on a

    [2] World Bank, *World Development Report 2006: Equity and Development* (World Bank/Oxford University Press, 2006) 6.

    [3] CESCR, Statement on Poverty and the International Covenant on Economic, Social and Cultural Rights (25th session, 2001) UN Doc E/C12/2001/10, para 4.

    [4] DRD, art 4(2).

    [5] I Brownlie, 'The Human Right to Development', *Commonwealth Secretariat* (1989) 1, at 8.

core of fundamental values, strengthened by the emergence of community obligations and community rights and the gradual shaping of public interest'.[6]

1.2 Towards an International Community of States

1.2.1 Locating the international community

Since the mid-1970 the expression 'international community' has been frequently used in both political and legal instruments.[7] Despite it being an established term of art however, there is no official definition.[8] There is nonetheless general agreement among international legal and international relations scholars that there exists an international system, the actors in which have a sufficient degree of contact with each other. They also have a sufficient degree of interdependence and impact regarding their decisions, to necessitate that they act as part of a whole.[9]

The term 'international society' implies that, by being conscious of certain common interests and values, a society is formed by 'conceiving themselves to be bound by a common set of rules in relations with one another, and share in the working of common institutions'.[10] Tomuschat and other international lawyers prefer the term 'international community' to 'international society', the '[international] community being a term suitable to indicate a closer union than between members of a society'[11] and describing 'an overarching system which embodies a common interest of all States and, indirectly, of mankind'.[12] In its general usage, '"the international community" seems to be more frequently invoked to denote the repository of interests that transcend those of individual states *ut singuli* ... In this conception, the element which distinguishes a "community"

---

[6] A Cassese, *International Law* (2nd edn, Oxford University Press, 2005) 396.

[7] WD Jackson, 'Thinking about the International Community and its Alternatives' in KW Thompson (ed), *Community, Diversity and the New World Order* (University Press of America, 1994) 4. The evidence summarized by Jackson is that '[o]verall, judging by the content of the UN resolutions and the documents, uses of the expression international, global, or world community in political discourse increased only slowly until the mid-1970s, when those terms came to be used with much greater frequency.'

[8] Although the term international community has had widespread usage in United Nations Conventions and Declarations, it does not appear in the Encyclopedia of the United Nations and International Agreements (1985).

[9] K Nowrot, 'Legal Consequences of Globalization: The Status of Non-Governmental Organizations Under International Law' 6 *IJGLS* 2 (1999) 579 at 602; B Simma and AL Paulus, 'The International Community: Facing the Challenge of Globalization. General Conclusions' 9 *EJIL* 2 (1998) 266, at 269.

[10] H Bull, *The Anarchical Society: A Study of Order in World Politics* (2nd edn, MacMillan, 1995) 13.

[11] C Tomuschat, 'Obligations Arising for States Without or Against their Will', *Rec des Cours* 241 (1993 IV) 199 at 211. As discussed in this article, Allott, Charney, Franck, Dupuy, Mosler and others.

[12] Ibid, at 227.

from its components is a "higher unity", as it were, the representation and priori-tization of common interests . . .'[13]

It is its common interests and agreed values that distinguish a mere mech-anistic international system from an international community governed by the rule of law. States have built, and continue to build, 'superstructures above and between them'[14] consisting of international organizations and multilateral treaty systems. In his 1997 study aimed at defining general trends in international law, Lukashuk concluded that 'major changes are occurring in the nature of inter-State relations [and that] [t]he predominantly bilateral character of such relations is being replaced by a universal interrelationship of States and peoples . . . The inter-national community is being consolidated . . . [and] the function of protecting the interests of the international community as a whole is coming to the fore.'[15]

With value beyond the jurisprudential setting in which it was offered, Judge Bedjaoui, in a passage from his declaration in the *Nuclear Weapons* case, expounded on the existence of an international community, when he remarked that:

It scarcely needs to be said that the face of contemporary international society is markedly altered. . . . [I]ntegration and "globalization" of international society is undeniable. Witness the proliferation of international organizations, the gradual substitution of an international law of co-operation for the traditional international law of co-existence, the emergence of the concept of "international community" . . . A token of these devel-opments is the place which international law now accords to concepts such as obliga-tions *erga omnes*, rules of *jus cogens* or the common heritage of mankind. The resolutely positivist, voluntarist approach of international law still current at the beginning of the [twentieth] century . . . has been replaced by an objective conception of international law, a law more readily seeking to reflect a collective juridical conscience and respond to the social necessities of States organized as a community.[16]

The augmentation of an international community under the rule of law can be observed in the changes in the mechanisms for law-making, and the application of international legal norms, illustrated for example in the development of the concept of peremptory norms of *jus cogens,* as well as by the establishment of legal obligations *erga omnes.*[17] Although the drafters of the Vienna Convention on the Law of Treaties (VCLT),[18] in which the rule of *jus cogens* was codified in Article 53, did not identify the substantive elements of a *jus cogens* norm, nor explain the

[13] Simma and Paulus, 'The International Community', 266, at 268.
[14] Nowrot, 'Legal Consequences of Globalization', 579, at 610.
[15] II Lukashuk, 'The Law of the International Community' in *International Law on the Eve of the Twenty-First Century: Views from the International Law Commission* (United Nations, 1997) 51, at 68.
[16] *Legality of the Threat or Use of Nuclear Weapons*, Adv Op, ICJ Rep (1996) 226, at para 13.
[17] Kritsiotis points out though, that: 'Our "international community" is "deep" enough to have conceived of the idea of *jus cogens* but not deep enough to know what to do with it. It is caught in the perennial mire of something called *erga omnes* (or obligations owed to the "community as a whole") . . . .' D Kritsiotis, 'Imagining the International Community' 13 *EJIL* 4 (2002) 961, at 990.
[18] 1166 UNTS 331.

reasoning behind its higher rank, there is widespread agreement that 'the super-ior legal force of a peremptory norm must be sought in its contents, inasmuch as it reflects common values essential for upholding peace and justice in the world.'[19]

In order to define rules of *jus cogens* the term 'international community' was first applied in international law in Article 53 of the VCLT in which the con-cept of an 'international community *of States as* a whole' was introduced, not so much establishing an international community as presupposing its existence.[20] A variation of the term was applied by the International Court of Justice (ICJ) in the *Barcelona Traction* case whereby obligations concerning, inter alia, the basic rights of the human person that are 'owed towards the international community as a whole', are the 'concern of all States'.[21]

The inclusion of the reference to states in the former formulation may be to reflect the paramount role of states in the making of international law, in particu-lar with regard to the establishment of norms of a peremptory character.[22] In UN declarations and resolutions dealing specifically with human rights, it is generally the case that neither expression is used, the usual UN practice being to refer merely to the 'international community', with no specific delineation provided as to what entities, beyond state entities, comprise it, if any at all.[23] There are references at times though, explicitly to the role not only of the community of states, but of the intergovernmental organizations (IGOs) of which they are member, as well as to non-governmental organizations (NGOs) and civil society.[24] The general

[19] Tomuschat, 'Obligations Arising for States Without or Against Their Will', 199, at 223, in which he refers to the work of, among others, Hannikainen, Mosler and Simma.
[20] Emphasis added. VCLT, art 53: 'A treaty is void if, at the time of its conclusion, it conflicts with a peremptory norm of general international law. For the purposes of the present Convention, a peremptory norm of general international law is a norm accepted and recognized by the inter-national community of States as a whole as a norm from which no derogation is permitted and which can be modified only by a subsequent norm of general international law having the same character.'
[21] *Barcelona Traction, Light and Power Company Limited (Second Phase)* (Belgium v Spain) ICJ Rep (1970) 3, at paras 33–4.
[22] D Greig, '"International Community", "Interdependence" and All That ... Rhetorical Correctness?' in G Kreijan, M Brus, J Duursma, E de Vos and J Dugard (eds), *State, Sovereignty, and International Governance* (Oxford University Press, 2002) 521, at 539.
[23] Ibid, 521, at 533, 538–9 in which Greig refers, for example, to appeals to the 'international community' in a range of Security Council resolutions on Somalia. The term appears repeatedly in the Proclamation of Teheran and in the Vienna Declaration and Programme of Action of the 1993 World Conference on Human Rights. The emphasis on human rights as *universal* concerns may suggest that the corresponding responsibilities should not be limited to states but should apply to all actors. See, for example, the first preambular para of the Vienna Declaration and Programme of Action, which begins with: 'Considering that the promotion and protection of human rights is a matter of priority for the international community ...', and preambular para 14 which states that 'the international community should devise ways and means to remove the current obstacles and meet challenges to the full realization of all human rights and to prevent the continuation of human rights violations resulting thereof throughout the world.' The reference can be said to extend to all who may be in a position to help.
[24] For example, in the Declaration on the Occasion of the Fiftieth Anniversary of the UN, the General Assembly supported a broad interpretation of what constitutes the international commu-nity when it 'recognize[d] that our common work will be the more successful if it is supported by

indication then, is that fundamental norms and values are furnished by an international community of states, with the international community being defined in its narrow sense.[25] While it can be said that there exists an 'international legal community in its wider meaning,' incorporating everybody 'endowed with the capacity to take part in international legal relations' this may be distinguished, as Judge Mosler has advocated, from the international society as a legal community consisting of states, and organizations set up by states, which constitutes a community governed by law.[26]

Thus, while the exact determination as to which actors make up the wider international community may depend on the specific question posed, states are the foremost actors in the shaping of international legal norms, and currently remain the (primary) duty-bearers in protecting the common values thereby derived, although there exists a greater international community from which support needs to be drawn, and which is to be served.

Particular weight is conferred on states as the primary actors in determining rights, and under international human rights law, in guaranteeing their protection and promotion. Actors other than states, such as NGOs, and business and industry, have increasing influence on the deliberations and decisions of states in shaping the laws that regulate the international system, and in the international human rights law-making process generally.[27] Since the international

all concerned actors of the international community, including non-governmental organizations, multilateral financial institutions, regional organizations and all actors of civil society.' Declaration on the Occasion of the Fiftieth Anniversary of the United Nations, GA res A/RES/50/6 (1995), para 17. The term may extend to include private actors such as transnational corporations, particularly as the scope of their activities transcend national boundaries, affect increasing numbers of people, and impact on established universal values. See generally, Simma and Paulus, 'The International Community', 266, at 272–3.

[25] Fassbender sees the international legal community as made up of all 'subjects of international law—sovereign states, states enjoying a limited international legal personality, intergovernmental organizations, peoples and minorities, belligerent parties, individuals, as well as special entities like the Holy See.' B Fassbender, 'The United Nations Charter As Constitution of the International Community' 36 *Colum J Transnat'l L.* 3 (1998) 529, at 597. There are differing views however as to whether individuals are indeed subjects of international law. As Weiler explains, individuals have rights under international law but they are not equal actors in the shaping of those rights or in the enforcement of them. It has been argued, therefore, that they are not subjects but rather objects of international law. JHH Weiler, 'Fin-de Siècle World Law: Taking Democracy Seriously', International Law Association (British Branch), Committee on Theory and International Law, London, 25 July 2000. Notes on file with author. See similarly, M Bedjaoui, 'General Introduction' in M Bedjaoui (ed), *International Law: Achievements and Prospects* (Martinus Nijhoff, 1991) 1, at 13: '[I]n spite of an interesting evolution, due in particular to the entry of human rights into the sphere of international law, the day when we shall see individuals accepted as the *direct* objects of the norms of international law is still a long way off.'

[26] H Mosler, 'The International Society as a Legal Community' 140 *Rec des Cours* (1974 IV) xv.

[27] NGOs were very influential in the International Campaign to Ban Landmines; regarding the Convention on the Prohibition of the Use, Stockpiling, Production and Transfer of Anti-Personnel Mines and on their Destruction for which they received a Nobel Peace Prize in 1997; in strengthening the Declarations and Programmes of Actions of World Conferences, as well as, the Rome Statute of the International Criminal Court. Private sector representatives participated, for example, in the 2002 World Summit on Sustainable Development as part of official delegations.

law of human rights exists first and foremost to challenge abuse of power, the growth in power of non-state actors such as transnational corporations (TNCs)[28] will require that human rights law be made applicable to them.[29] However, 'the state remains the basic unit in the world of public international law',[30] and hence the inter-state system remains the primary structure of the world community. Significantly however, current developments in international law increasingly emphasize the interests of the international community as a whole over those of individual states.[31] Just as the modern state exists to serve its people, so the modern international community of states—created on the foundations of mutual dependency—has come together to serve a common collective end. Indeed, as Kritsiotis points out, very early on in the post war period there were 'vivid incantations of "community" as part of the rationalization for endowing international organizations with juridical personality'.[32]

The international community of states, it has been suggested, is not a reference simply to the sum total of states but rather to a 'specific system that has certain attributes, including legal attributes that are not to be found in the individual States that constitute it.'[33] As Lukashuk deduces, it is only when international law is based on the concept of a united community that it will be able to fight successfully for its own survival.[34] The world is a 'community', remarked Prime Minister Tony Blair in 2001, see 'the lesson of the financial markets, climate change, international terrorism, nuclear proliferation [and] world trade ... our self-interest and our mutual interests are today inextricably woven together'.[35] But 'the issue', as he pointed out, is:

... how we use the power of community to combine it with justice. If globalisation works only for the benefit of the few, then it will fail and will deserve to fail. But if we follow the principles that have served us so well at home—that power, wealth and opportunity must be in the hands of the many, not the few—if we make that our guiding light for the global

[28] 51 of the world's largest economies are corporations; only 49 are countries. MB Steger, *Globalization: A Very Short Introduction* (Oxford University Press, 2003) 48.

[29] See generally, J Ruggie, *Interim Report of the UN Special Representative of the Secretary-General on the issue of human rights and transnational corporations and other business enterprise,* UN Doc E/CN4/2006/97; P Alston (ed), *Non-State Actors and Human Rights* (Oxford University Press, 2005).

[30] Simma and Paulus, 'The International Community', 266, at 273.

[31] Fassbender, 'The United Nations Charter As Constitution', 529, at 553; Tomuschat, 'Obligations Arising for States Without or Against Their Will', 199, at 212.

[32] Kritsiotis, 'Imagining the International Community', 961, at 970 referring to *Reparation for Injuries Suffered in the Service of the United Nations,* Adv Op, ICJ Rep (1949).

[33] Lukashuk, 'The Law of the International Community', 51, at 53; See also, Tomuschat, 'Obligations Arising for States Without or Against Their Will', 199, at 227 where he states that '[a]lthough Article 53 of the Vienna Convention on the Law of Treaties provides that the international community is made up of States, it would be wrong to assume that States as a mere juxtaposition of individual units constitute the international community.'

[34] Lukashuk, 'The Law of the International Community', 51, at 53.

[35] T Blair, 'Let Us Re-Order this World Around Us', Address by the Prime Minister to the Labour Party Conference, Brighton, 2 October 2001.

economy, then it will be a force for good and an international movement that we should take pride in leading. [36]

This is part of the 'new doctrine of international community' to which the Prime Minister had famously referred two years earlier.[37] 'The explicit recognition that today more than ever before we are mutually dependent, that national interest is to a significant extent governed by international collaboration . . . .'[38] The creation of international enforcement machinery reflects this advent. As Cassese points out, mulilateral treaties aimed at 'protecting peace and human rights through community obligations and community rights, set up complex mechanisms for ensuring compliance with the substantive provisions they contain, and in add-ition envisage *institutionalized reactions* to breaches of those provisions. Such mechanisms prove that states share the conviction that there are important com-munity obligations, the violation of which would be inadequately met by the "private" and bilateral reaction envisaged by the legal regime of "ordinary respon-sibility" [pertaining to the reciprocal interests of States]'.[39]

In this era of multifaceted and unprecedented interdependence—an issue to which we will return—the common interests and values identified by the inter-national community demand prioritization. These today undoubtedly include higher standards of living for all, and the universal exercise of fundamental human rights. Indeed, it has been argued that 'there is *prima facie* evidence of a "community" committed to more than just the value of "sovereignty" of each of its members' seen via 'the very notion that distributive justice is put forward as a value and argued as one common denominator of states in various fields of mutual endeavour'.[40]

Even legal scholars who challenge the existence of an international community as a conceptual entity acknowledge that there have been significant developments, including the ideas of universal standards and of universal accountability.[41] The existence of a core area of agreement on the essential quality of the universality of fundamental human rights, peace, a healthy environment, economic solidarity

[36] Ibid. It is telling, perhaps, as to the real limits of renouncing power and the likelihood of a new doctrine based on sharing, that a pronouncement by an affluent and relatively powerful state on redistributing power, wealth and opportunity globally still foresees its role as one of 'leader'.

[37] T Blair, Address by the Prime Minister to the Economic Club, Chicago, 24 April 1999.

[38] Ibid.

[39] Cassese, *International Law*, 264–5. Emphasis in original. Cassese is addressing the notion of 'aggravated state responsibility' which has 'markedly distinct features. It arises when a State vio-lates a rule laying down a "community obligation"' (at 262).

[40] Kritsiotis on Thomas Franck's *Fairness in International Law and Institutions* (1995). Kritsiotis, 'Imagining the International Community', 961, at 990. For Franck's view on the limits of 'redis-tribution' (and the potency of economic interdependence) in the context of world poverty see, T Franck, *Fairness in International Law and Institutions* (Oxford University Press, 1995) 415. ('"Redistribution", in effect, is a misnomer for what must instead be recognized as investment by the affluent in the common weal').

[41] P Allott, 'The True Function of Law in the International Community' 5 *IJGLS* (1998) 391, at 411.

and sustainable development, as well as belief in the importance of democratic governance,[42] reflects a common set of universal values. The universality of these fundamental precepts is strengthened by non-Western contributions to post-war international law,[43] which include; the promotion of economic, social and cultural rights, the fight against colonialism and racism, and economic domination; which lead to the development of a range of fundamental rights including the self-determination of peoples, the right to development, as well as to the concept of a 'common heritage of mankind'.[44]

Whether one takes the view that the United Nations Charter is the constitution of the international community,[45] or an outstanding element in a 'world constitutive process of authoritative decisions,'[46] it has codified the principles and rules that are to govern states functioning as a community. The Charter took the concept of an international community from the abstract, and created from it the nearest thing to an institutional reality.[47] And, under the Charter, UN Member States relinquish a degree of their sovereignty, and in its stead accept international cooperation in the respect for, and observance of, human rights as a common purpose of their contemporary collective activities.

1.2.2　International law of cooperation as the law of the international community

The outdated law of co-existence managed separation. It had as its primary objective keeping states peacefully apart. By contrast, the law of cooperation addresses how to bring them actively together, that is, to undertake what they cannot do effectively when acting individually.[48] This is where the integral element of

---

[42] United Nations General Assembly res A/RES/55/96 (2000), Promoting and consolidating democracy 4 December 2000; CHR res 2003/36, Interdependence between democracy and human rights (59th Session, 2003); CHR res 2003/35, Strengthening of popular participation, equity, social justice, and non-discrimination as essential foundations of democracy (59th Session, 2003); Vienna Declaration and Programme of Action, Pt I, arts 8, 9, 17, 27, 34, Pt II, arts 66, 68, 74, 79, 80, 81.

[43] Judge Nelson refers to the representative contribution to international law by all states in the post World War II and post-colonial period as 'the democratization of international law'. Intervention made by Judge D Nelson, Tribunal for the Law of the Sea, at a lecture delivered by D Greig, '"International Community"—Theory or Reality?', British Institute of International and Comparative Law, London, 22 October 2001.

[44] See, Fassbender, 'The United Nations Charter As Constitution', 529, at 554. Bedjaoui suggests that the common heritage of mankind is an innovative concept and that it '… can and should be applied in the first place to human beings, the *primary* common heritage of mankind, and to humanity itself …'. M Bedjaoui, 'Are the World's Food Resources the Common Heritage of Mankind?' 24 *IJIL* (1984) 459, at 461.

[45] Fassbender, 'The United Nations Charter As Constitution', 529; JA Frowein, 'Reactions by Not Directly Affected States to Breaches of Public International Law' 274 *Rec des Cours* (1994 IV) 245, at 355 *et seq.*; Simma and Paulus, 'The International Community', 266, at 274.

[46] Tomuschat, 'Obligations Arising for States Without or Against Their Will', 199, at 299.

[47] Simma and Paulus, 'The International Community', 266, at 274.

[48] See, G Abi-Saab, 'Whither the International Community?' 9 *EJIL* 2 (1998) 248, at 249–54.

community is presumed according to Abi-Saab—in the appreciation that 'there are certain necessary things that cannot be done, or done well, unilaterally'.[49] The international law of cooperation is the result of new forms of international life which are based on the duty of states to cooperate, and on the existence of an international community ruled by law—founded on the idea and the manifestation of the interdependence of states.[50]

The fundamental tenets of the international law of cooperation are set against the anachronistic Westphalian premise of the law of co-existence.[51] The Peace of Westphalia in 1648 marked the ushering in of an international law of co-existence which ended Europe's religious wars, and established the principle of sovereignty by which each prince was free to assert his own will within his territorial domain. In order for this system to work, a form of equality among states was necessary whereby each was to respect the sovereignty of the other, allowing each omnipotent state to exercise its full powers within the ambit of its jurisdiction, and likewise therefore, to refrain from activities, such as intervention or the use of force, that would encroach on the others' domestic remit. The law of co-existence as such was predicated on 'principles of passive co-existence' which for the most part imposed obligations of abstention.[52] This international law of co-existence sought to preserve the existence, and independence, of each sovereign territorial state which recognized no superior authority, and focused the collective priority of all states on minimizing impediments to state freedom.[53] What occurred inside a state was of no concern to the international legal order,[54] and cross-border wrongful acts were deemed a private matter concerning only those affected.[55]

In his work on the subject, Abi-Saab links the early efforts at greater international cooperation to the emergence of an international economy derived of the Industrial Revolution. The establishment of the first generation of international organizations and multilateral treaties were a response to the related global problems at the end of the eighteenth century and the start of the nineteenth century.[56] Yet, despite

---

[49] Ibid, 248, at 252.

[50] See, Gros Espiell, 'Sovereignty, Independence and Interdependence', 277, at 286.

[51] W Friedmann, *The Changing Structure of International Law* (Columbia University Press, 1964) Ch 6 *passim.*

[52] Abi-Saab, 'Whither the International Community?', 248, at 252 and 254. Abi-Saab explains that where states sought to establish relations in the areas of international transactions and relations (i.e. diplomatic and consular law, the law of treaties, the law of state responsibility and state succession, and *jus in bello*) it was done according to 'legal formulae or recipes still from the perspective of the law of coexistence' (at 254–5).

[53] Steger, *Globalization: A Very Short Introduction*, 58, drawing on the work of D Held et al *Global Transformations* (2000).

[54] C Tomuschat, 'International Law: Ensuring the Survival of Mankind on the Eve of a New Century' 281 *Rec des Cours* (1999) 23, at 57–8.

[55] Steger, *Globalization: A Very Short Introduction*, 58, drawing on the work of Held et al *Global Transformations.*

[56] Examples of international organizations include the River Commissions for the Danube and Rhine, as well as the Universal Postal Union. For a comprehensive account see Abi-Saab, 'Whither the International Community?', 248, at 255.

the legal developments triggered by discrete areas of economic interdependence, active cooperation was still the exception rather than the rule. What we had, in the words of Abi-Saab, were 'mere islands of the law of cooperation in an ocean of the law of co-existence'.[57] The same could be said in the area of human rights generally. The prohibition of slavery, the laws of armed conflict (international humanitarian law), the rights of minorities, and labour rights were nineteenth and early twentieth century examples whereby the protection of select categories of individuals became the concern of international law.

After the First World War, the creation of the League of Nations furthered the shift towards a law of cooperation by turning from technical questions (such as international communications) to problems of the maintenance of international peace and security. Although the League of Nations addressed this central issue of international law with little success, (a failure marked by the Second World War), its establishment did reveal a significant shift along the continuum of legal regulation based on an awareness by states of the existence of challenges that confronted humankind in general, and an appreciation that social problems affecting their peoples might be well-served by a system of international regulation and thus a system of institutionalized cooperation.[58] While the League of Nations may not have altered the basic orientation of international law organized around the fundamental principle of sovereignty,[59] as Tomuschat notes, it brought into existence, for the first time in history the 'blueprint of a legal order not resting upon the classical doctrine of sovereign equality'.[60] Indeed, the Covenant of the League of Nations (1919) begins by codifying its aim 'to promote international cooperation and peace and security'.[61]

The acceptance of common interests and values, and the recognition that these mutually established convictions cannot be addressed unilaterally, but rather require shared effort, provided the logical and structural underpinnings of the UN and its Charter which was to follow the demise of the League of Nations. The Charter is premised on an international law of cooperation for the attainment of common goals which, following the end of the Second World War, had become an integral component of the framework of international law.[62] During the first few decades, with decolonization underway, and the demands by developing states for a New International Economic Order (NIEO), the rights of sovereign states were being reasserted, although framed within the context of their place within the wider international system.[63] There was also at this time an increase in

---

[57] Abi-Saab, 'Whither the International Community?', 248, at 255.
[58] This was reflected in the establishment of the International Labour Organization (ILO) as a permanent component of the League of Nations.
[59] C Grossman and DD Bradlow, 'Are we being Propelled Towards a People-Centred Transnational Legal Order?' 9 *Am U J Int'l L and Pol'y* 1 (1993) 1, at 2.
[60] Tomuschat, 'International Law: Ensuring the Survival of Mankind', 23, at 59.
[61] Covenant of the League of Nations, 225 Consolidated Treaty Series (CTS) 195.
[62] Tomuschat, 'International Law: Ensuring the Survival of Mankind', 23, at 60.
[63] As reflected in the debates on the NIEO of the 1970s and in the General Assembly Resolutions on the Declaration on the Establishment of a New International Economic Order,

the number of activities addressing cross-border impact. The regulation of environmental issues, nuclear proliferation, financial flows, refugees, trade, labour, and drug trafficking demanded some form of coordinated regulation.[64]

This period also saw human rights become entrenched internationally, and at present the notion of common interests is increasingly informed by the dictates of universal human rights values.[65] These universal values have been evolving in parallel to economic globalization, where national self-reliance is weak, and the need for cooperation to ensure human rights is correspondingly strengthened. Today, the world is linked by communication, disease, the environment, crime, drugs, terror, and also by the search for prosperity; these connections inform the development of international law.

The states that make up the international community rely on the same global environment for the satisfaction of their needs: this interdependence conditions their cooperation. The significance of interdependence, and the collective imperative it invites, can be seen most recently in the authoritative submissions pertaining to reform of the UN multilateral system. Effective multilateralism is deemed essential to economic development, global security, and the realization of human rights for all, as are the ways in which these interrelated aspects of the global agenda rely on each other for their achievement.[66] Yet, the equation since the founding of the UN includes not just a legal structure for the achievement of mutually beneficial solutions generally, but the formation of an international community of states to secure a just and peaceful world in which human rights are respected and realized. The principle of international cooperation repeatedly invoked in the UN Charter framed the institutional and normative evolution in the area of human rights in which the endorsement of universal values has been elevated to become a superior interest of the collective of states.

Despite considerable advances, it has been rightly noted that the incursion of international law into matters previously considered to be shielded from outside interference has not yet reached its full potential.[67] Similarly, determining and enforcing the parameters of the law of international cooperation needs to catch up with the realities of a world in which the actions and decision of states have unprecedented impact on the human rights of people in other states. The recognition

General Assembly res 3201 (S-VI) and General Assembly res 3202 (S-VI) of 1 May 1974 and the Charter on the Economic Rights and Duties of States, General Assembly res 3281 (XXIX) of 12 December 1974.

[64] Grossman and Bradlow, 'Are we Being Propelled', 1, at 6.

[65] Judge Weeramantry reminds us that: ' [T]he vast structure of internationally accepted human rights norms and standards has become part of common global consciousness today in a manner unknown before World War II ...'. *Legality of the Threat*, Judge Weeramantry (diss op) 226, at 490.

[66] See, Report of the UN Secretary-General, *In Larger Freedom: Towards Development, Security and Human Rights for All*, UN Doc A/59/2005; Report of the UN High-Level Panel on Threats, Challenges and Change, *A More Secure World: Our Shared Responsibility*, UN Doc A/59/565 (2004).

[67] Tomuschat, 'International Law: Ensuring the Survival of Mankind', 23, at 63.

of our interdependence is also not without its difficulties, as international law for the protection of human rights seeks to delineate clearly what it implies in terms of the exercise and reach of power, and of the rights and obligations effectively enforced in order to constrain excessive power. Today we can no longer rely on an inter-state system governed exclusively by the law of co-existence, and have begun to utilize the potentialities existing in the Charter, as anticipated by its drafters when they advanced principles rooted in the idea of an international community. And this duty to cooperate, as Abi-Saab remarks, 'necessarily implies a wider framework, an international community in which it can be anchored, thus being clearly situated in the logic of the law of cooperation'.[68]

The International Court of Justice, in its 1951 *Advisory Opinion Concerning Reservations to the Genocide Convention*, referred to 'common interests' and the 'accomplishment of those high purposes which are the *raison d'être* of the convention'[69] which, as has been pointed out, leads to the recognition of 'the interest of the organized international community'.[70] This concept of an organized international community under law, while known to international legal doctrine, is undergoing a process of countering the demands of vast and accelerated interactions in a global quest for mammon. Saito remarked in the early 1980 that '... State sovereignty and national interest has already become out of date; the new international law should start from the candid recognition of the interest of the organized international community and the "Bien Commun Universel"'.[71]

Changes in international society inevitably affect international law, interdependence thereby implying the need for commensurate international legal obligations. That the contemporary protection and promotion of human rights cannot but be influenced by global interdependence engenders a shared responsibility, beginning with the obligation of states to cooperate in their protection. While the doctrine of state sovereignty—the basis of which is self-interest—remains the organizing principle of our international order, it is today mitigated by the existence of global interdependence, and the shared responsibility derived of that interdependence.

1.2.3 Reconciling sovereignty and interdependence

Although the Charter is predicated on the law of cooperation, it was designed with the sovereign equality of states in mind, and hence a central feature of the law of co-existence—the all-powerful state—was still reflected as a founding

---

[68] Abi-Saab, 'Whither the International Community?', 248, at 261.
[69] *Reservations to the Convention on the Prevention and Punishment of the Crime of Genocide*, Adv Op, ICJ Rep (1951) 15, at 23.
[70] Y Saito, 'International Law as a Law of the World Community: World Law as Reality and Methodology' in Grahl-Madsen and Toman (eds), *The Spirit of Uppsala* 233, at 242.
[71] Ibid, 233, at 242–3.

principle upon which the UN would be based. While the 'purposes' enshrined in Article 1 include '… international co-operation in solving international problems of an economic, social, cultural, or humanitarian character, and in promoting and encouraging respect for human rights …',[72] Article 2(1) has the organization, and its members, pursue the purposes stated in Article 1 '… in accordance with the … principle of the sovereign equality of all its Members.' Pursuant to paragraph 1, is the prohibition in Article 2(7) disallowing intervention by the organization in matters that are essentially within the domestic jurisdiction of any UN state.[73]

The balance between these two partially competing tendencies[74] is located in the contingent nature of the concept of sovereignty. Sovereignty does not exist separately from international law, but as an element of it: it has no independent value. Its relevance is measured against its compatibility with precepts of a juridically-based international community, and the demands of international cooperation in securing, inter alia, human rights. In 1923 the Permanent Court of International Justice (PCIJ) affirmed what Judge Weeramantry felt was necessary to reaffirm in 1996, and that is that the 'sovereignty of states would be proportionally diminished and restricted as international law developed'.[75] Wilfred Jenks similarly concluded, in line with the view of the Permanent Court of International Justice, that 'sovereignty is essentially a relative concept, subject to a process of erosion by the assumption of new obligations.'[76]

Sovereignty can refer to the legal authority or competence of a state 'limited or limitable only by international law and not by the national law of another State';[77] this external sovereignty or independence, as Judge Anzilotti of the PCIJ elaborated in addressing the concept of sovereignty, provides that the state has over it no *other* authority than that of international law.[78] The concept of the reserved domain of sovereign states, which prohibits intervention in matters

[72] UN Charter, art 1(3).

[73] See further, A Randelzhofer, 'Chapter I: Purposes and Principles, Article 2' in B Simma (ed), *The Charter of the United Nations: A Commentary* (2nd edn, Oxford University Press, 2002) Vol I, 64, at 65.

[74] Partially, in that the recognition that states regardless of size, wealth or power are legally equal is a particularly constructive doctrine in the context of world poverty.

[75] As cited in *Legality of the Threat*, Judge Weeramantry (diss op) 226, at 495. 'The questions whether a certain matter is or is not solely within the jurisdiction of a State is an essentially relative question; it depends upon the developments of international relations'. *Nationality Decrees Issued in Tunis and Morocco* (1923) PCIJ, Adv Op (Series B) No 4, 27.

[76] CW Jenks, 'Law in the World Community, (1967) as cited in E Ustor, 'Independence and Interdependence' (Report of the Working Group II) in Grahl-Madsen and Toman (eds), *The Spirit of Uppsala* 52, at 53.

[77] JN Saxena, 'Sovereignty, Independence and Interdependence of Nations' in Grahl-Madsen and Toman (eds), *The Spirit of Uppsala* 289, at 290.

[78] *Advisory Opinion Concerning the Customs Regime between Germany and Austria*, PCIJ (1931) Judge Anzilotti (sep op) as cited in Saxena, 'Sovereignty, Independence and Interdependence of Nations' 289, at 290. 'Internal' sovereignty applies to the capacity of a population freely to effect and express choices about the identities and policies of its governors See, WM Reisman, 'Sovereignty and Human Rights in Contemporary International Law' 84 *AJIL* (1990) 866' at 872.

that are essentially within the domestic jurisdiction of any state, does not today imply the superiority of the internal juridical order over the international order. As Gros Espiell explained in the early 1980s, a point universally reaffirmed with regards to human rights in the Vienna Declaration and Programme of Action in 1993,[79] the content of the reserved domain is essentially relative and changing, contingent and evolving, the exclusive domain is thus derived from international law, the changing content of which depends on whether or not there is an appropriate international norm.[80] All states have recognized international norms, and the responsibility to share in the objective of securing basic human rights.[81] It is possible therefore to arrive at a current concept of state sovereignty in this area which '... is compatible with the demand that the state under the international legal order should comply faithfully with its international duties and obligations.'[82]

Notably, Article 2(1) of the Charter does not use the term sovereignty in isolation, but refers to this principle in affirming the equality of all members of the UN. While this may indicate that all states are equal in legal status, it does not endow them with functional equality on the international plane.[83] The differential in functional equality equates to differences in the scope and content of international (i.e. external) obligations. In the context of world poverty, developed states will have particular responsibilities for addressing poverty, commensurate with their power, and the economic advantages derived of that power.[84]

State sovereignty is not the tool it once was—providing a justification for protecting the actions of states as seems good to them without restraints on their freedoms.[85] Today sovereignty, to the extent that it has come to imply that there is something inherent in the nature of states that makes it impossible for them to be subject to law, as Brierly points out, is a false doctrine.[86] As Judge Alvarez noted in 1948, 'States no longer have an absolute sovereignty but are interdependent, they have not only rights but duties towards each other and this society', and he termed this new international law 'the International Law of Interdependence'[87]

---

[79] Vienna Declaration and Programme of Action, Pt I, art 4.

[80] Gros Espiell, 'Sovereignty, Independence and Interdependence', 277, at 282.

[81] See further, ch 2.

[82] *The United Nations Conference on International Organizations, San Francisco, 1945* as cited in Gros Espiell, 'Sovereignty, Independence and Interdependence', 277, at 280; see also 282.

[83] GG Schram, 'Independence and Interdependence (Interventions at Plenary and Group Sessions) in Grahl-Madsen and Toman (eds), *The Spirit of Uppsala*, 351, at 358–359.

[84] See further, ch 2 and 5.

[85] See, JL Brierly, *The Law of Nations: An Introduction to the International Law of Peace* (6th edn, Oxford University Press, 1963) as cited in RB Lillich, 'Sovereignty and Humanity: Can they Converge?' in Grahl-Madsen and Toman (eds), *The Spirit of Uppsala*, 406, at 408.

[86] As Brierly further explains, it is a false doctrine 'which the facts of international relations do not support'. Brierly, *The Law of Nations* as cited in Lillich, 'Sovereignty and Humanity', 406, at 413, fn 30.

[87] *Conditions of Admission of a State to Membership in the United Nations*, ICJ (1948), Judge Alvarez (sep op) as cited in Saxena, 'Sovereignty, Independence and Interdependence of Nations', 289, at 292–33.

which, as Gros Espiell noted, 'is today what the doctrine calls the International Law of Cooperation'.[88] The safeguards afforded states under the UN Charter are based not on any intrinsic worth that they possess, but on the idea that they may be necessary to achieve the dignity, justice, rights, well-being and safety of their own people, and increasingly of people found elsewhere.[89] State sovereignty today 'clearly carries with it the obligation of a State to protect the welfare of its own peoples and meet its obligations to the wider international community'.[90]

Extending what was taking shape 60 years ago to contemporary international law in which the protection of human rights forms an integral component, sovereignty is only a legitimate claim insofar as it seeks to guarantee the basic rights, and satisfy the basic needs, of humanity in line with universally agreed principles and standards. This holds as true for the weak as for the strong; by adding human rights into the mix there has been fashioned over time a doctrine of objective state sovereignty.

1.2.4 The influence of interdependence on international law

In considering the influence of interdependence on public international law generally, a point of departure is provided by the international law of neighbourliness developed during the inter-war period. The premise propounded by the Yugoslav jurist Juraj Andrassy drew on '[c]oexistence, community and integrity which he saw as legally limiting the power of states in situations that provoked direct effects on the territory of neighbouring states ...'.[91] Geographical proximity, according to Andrassy, which had direct implications on, for example, shared resources of air, land and water, required, and resulted in, the development of laws of co-existence in line with the symbiotic relationship among neighbouring states. Andrassy recognized that the notion of co-existence and community necessarily impinged on accepted thinking in relation to territorial sovereignty, but that this special body of law was expressed in customary law, treaties, and case law, as well as emerging general principles of international law.[92] Andrassy's central thesis, 'that the objective physical facts of the neighbour relation between two or more States *logically implied the existence of international law obligations* flowing from those societal facts irrespective of the will of the parties'[93] retains cogency. The ability to affect another state (or in the case of human rights law, the people within a state) creates corresponding legal obligations.

---

[88] Gros Espiell, 'Sovereignty, Independence and Interdependence', 277, at 286.
[89] *Report of the UN High-Level Panel on Threats, Challenges and Change*, para 30.
[90] Ibid, para 29.
[91] E McWhinney, 'The Concept of Co-operation' in Bedjaoui (ed), *International Law: Achievements and Prospects* 425, at 430; See also, O Schachter, *International Law in Theory and Practice* (Martinus Nijhoff, 1991) 363.
[92] McWhinney, 'The Concept of Co-operation', 425, at 430.
[93] Ibid (emphasis added).

Nowadays the approach to environmental transboundary concerns, and their international legal regulation, is not, and cannot, be limited to geographical neighbours *inter se,* since activities undertaken in one place have an impact on people in far-off places.[94] In the 1996 ICJ Advisory Opinion on the *Legality of the Threat or Use of Nuclear Weapons,* Judge Weeramantry remarked that '[the principle] of good neighbourliness ... is one of the bases of modern international law, which has seen the demise of the principle that sovereign States could pursue their own interests in splendid isolation from each other'.[95] This reasoning is equally apposite to the protection of socio-economic rights in a world characterized by global proximity—marked by the sheer inability to exist isolated from the decisions and actions of other states acting in various formations. Judge Weeramantry further deduces that: 'A world order in which every sovereign State depends on the same global environment generates a mutual interdependence which can only be implemented by co-operation and good neighborliness'.[96]

The United Nations Charter, in Article 74, enshrined the principle of good-neighbourliness. In addressing UN Member States with administrative responsibility for 'non-self governing territories', the article expressed agreement that their policies must be based on 'the general principle of good-neighbourliness, [as] due account being taken of the interests and well-being of the rest of the world, in social, economic, and commercial matters'. Judge Weeramantry concludes that '[t]he Charter's express recognition of such a general duty of good neighbourliness makes this an essential part of international law'.[97] Indeed, the language of the inter-war period which still spoke of 'co-existing independent communities'[98] was, as Judge Shahabudden pointed out, 'an idea subsequently improved upon by the Charter, a noticeable emphasis on co-operation having been added'.[99]

International trade and foreign investment, worldwide flows of goods and services, global financial markets, and the international institutions that direct global economic policy have virtually eliminated physical proximity as a prerequisite to being a 'neighbour'. Andrassy's premise that the relations between neighbouring states logically imply the existence of suitable international law

---

[94] As per the Declaration of the United Nations Conference on the Human Environment, principle 21: states have the responsibility 'to ensure that activities within their jurisdiction or control do not cause damage to the environment of other States or of areas beyond the limits of national jurisdiction'. UN Doc A/CONF48/14/Rev1 (1973); In *Legality of the Threat,* the ICJ noted that: 'The existence of the general obligation of States to ensure that activities within their jurisdiction and control respect the environment of other States or of areas beyond national control is now part of the corpus of international law relating to the environment'. *Legality of the Threat,* 226, at 241–2.

[95] *Legality of the Threat,* Judge Weeramantry (diss op) 226, at 505. See also, *Case Concerning the Gabčikovo-Nagymaros Project* (Hungary v Slovakia) Judge Weeramantry (sep op) ICJ Rep (1997) 88, at 95.

[96] *Legality of the Threat,* Judge Weeramantry (diss op) 226, at 505.

[97] Ibid.

[98] '*Lotus' Case,* PCIJ, Series A, No 10 (1927) 4, at 18.

[99] *Legality of the Threat* , Judge Shahbudden (diss op) 226, at 393.

obligations is equally true today—the distinction is in the definition of the term neighbour. With economic globalization functioning as it does on a vast and global matrix we are called upon to recognize, and respond to, '[t]he reality of the human neighbourhood'.[100]

While the term interdependence is not found in the language employed by the UN Charter, interdependence nevertheless forms one of the constitutive elements of the international community, and its significance flows from the principle of international cooperation which has been repeatedly invoked by the UN Charter.[101] Recognizing the importance of interdependence in the development of international law, back in 1963 Jenks asserted that '[i]nterdependence can no longer be regarded as a political, economic or sociological concept too general or imprecise to be of any substantial value to the lawyer; it is in the process of crystallizing into a legal concept which lies at the heart of contemporary international law'.[102] Over two decades before Judge Weeramantry remarked that the global environment generates mutual dependencies,[103] Jenks noted that the co-existence of communities depends on the full recognition of their mutual dependencies, stating that 'interdependence ... [has] superseded sovereignty as the seedbed of the law'.[104]

Interdependence characterizes globalization, and is a defining feature of it, not only in terms of economic interdependence, but also in relation to peace and security, human rights, including development, and environmental sustainability. There exists an economic, political and social interdependence of the world community,[105] a world community in which human rights considerations need apply to decisions and activities of states that may have negative impact beyond their borders, including when acting collectively in endeavours that directly or

[100] S Ramphal, 'Globalism and Meaningful Peace: A New World Order Rooted in International Community' 23 *Security Dialogue* (1992) 81, at 83.
[101] Ustor, 'Independence and Interdependence' (Report of the Working Group II) 52 at 53.
[102] CW Jenks, *Law, Freedom and Welfare* (Longman, 1963) 71.
[103] *Legality of the Threat*, Judge Weeramantry (diss op) 226, at 505.
[104] Jenks, *Law, Freedom and Welfare*, 71. There has been some discussion as to whether interdependence can be understood as a principle or whether it is descriptive of a de facto situation (in which independence is the principle) (see, 'Independence and Interdependence' (Interventions at Plenary and Group Sessions) in Grahl-Madsen and Toman (eds), *The Spirit of Uppsala* 351, at 352-3). Tesón suggests that the Jenkian vision which sees interdependence as an 'interpretive principle' for deriving legal obligations is flawed and rather that interdependence while 'incapable of providing a test for identifying binding rules and principles of international law, is still an important concept, a building block, for the scheme of ideal rationality suggested as the normative basis of the law of nations'. FR Tesón, 'Interdependence, Consent, and the Basis of International Obligation' 83 *American Society of International Law Proceedings* (1989) 558, at 559 and 565.
[105] E Suy, 'A New International Law for a New World Order' in Grahl-Madsen and Toman (eds), *The Spirit of Uppsala* 92, at 93. Suy links economic interdependence to the finite and unbalanced distribution of natural resources, the steadily more insistent demands of people for a better and more prosperous life, and the realization by prosperous states that their economies depend on events occurring in other countries. Political interdependence refers to the events of one country altering the internal and social processes of another country—crisis is not necessarily contained within the state or region where it has occurred.

indirectly impinge on the most basic requirements for life of people unknown. Müllerson has rightly remarked that the most important task of this post-modern era is the management of global issues.[106] The most important task of contemporary international law is to evolve in a way that ensures their regulation, including with regard to the protection and promotion of human rights, a centrepiece of the post-1945 international system.

Human rights standards form part of the international community's agreed common values, now entrenched as universal. Contemporary international law does not offer a neutral field for states to use according to their will and power; it is rather common objective values that orient its process.[107] The emergence of human rights in 1945, and their subsequent development within this reconstituted international law, enhanced their place within the new world order.[108] In the early 1980s, Suy observed what today presents an even greater truism, that justice has been increasingly asserting itself as a highly important objective of international law, the absence of which would impact on the legitimacy and thus the validity of any legal system.[109]

Events in one part of the world have repercussions elsewhere in the world, the impact of which is widening in terms of both scale and scope. Our understanding of interdependence then, is not limited merely to relying on each other in various ways, but rather that the relationship between countries is such that if interdependence is not respected then damage may be felt by others countries.[110] Ustor designated this the 'systems approach' the basic tenet being that the unity of the contemporary world is understood as a system of interrelated parts, and as soon as one part is touched other parts are effected.[111] Notably, interdependence is not coterminous with symmetry, interdependence can, and indeed does, exist without all countries wielding similar power or being affected equally by the exercise of power. As we will see later in 1.3 of this chapter, the current management

---

[106] R Müllerson, *Ordering Anarchy: International Law in International Society* (Martinus Nijhoff, 2000) 280.

[107] H Montealegre, 'Sovereignty and Humanity', (Report of Working Group III) in Grahl-Madsen and Toman (eds), *The Spirit of Uppsala*, 58, at 58–9. 'These commonly held values are not only related to matters such as the prohibition of the use of force, the distribution of wealth in the world, ecological imperatives, but also to the conditions of personal human dignity'.

[108] See, Suy, 'A New International Law' at 92 where he responds to the question 'do we have a new world order?' by explaining that: 'An objective survey of the international scene would indicate that we are indeed witnessing the emergence of a new world order which differs in many respects from the old one. One important difference is the universal character of the present world community, as compared to what it was prior to, or even immediately following 1945. The new world order is universal in membership, in outlook and in purpose .... The aims of the new order are global and its attention is turned beyond the traditional objectives of peace and security, to such questions of universal concern as cooperation, development and environmental control, to mention only a few'.

[109] Ibid, 92, at 95.

[110] RH Cassen, 'Mutual Interests' in the Brandt Commission papers, Selected Background Papers prepared for the Independent Commission on International Development Issues (1978–9) as cited in Saxena, 'Sovereignty, Independence and Interdependence of Nations' 289, at 293.

[111] E Ustor, 'Independence and Interdependence' (Oral presentation of the Report of the Working Group II) in Grahl-Madsen and Toman (eds), *The Spirit of Uppsala*, 375, at 377.

of our economic interdependence is flawed, and our failure to regulate justly in a manner that can secure the exercise by all of basic socio-economic rights is all the more unacceptable since it is underpinned by an international legal regime that anticipated the growth and merits of global interdependence.[112] Joseph Stiglitz, a former Chief Economist and Senior Vice-President of the World Bank reminds us what this interdependence requires:

… We are a global community, and like all communities have to follow some rules so that we can live together. These rules must be—and must be seen to be—fair and just, must pay due attention to the poor as well as the powerful, must reflect a basic sense of decency and social justice. In today's world, those rules have to be arrived at through democratic processes; the rules under which the governing bodies and authorities work must ensure that they will heed and respond to the desires and needs of all those affected by policies and decisions made in distant places.[113]

1.2.5 The continued predominance of cooperative internationalism in the twenty-first century

It is legitimate to question whether this project of an international community cooperating under the international rule of law has suffered particularly glaring setbacks in recent years. Although there has been concern over the advent of a 'lawless world' in which some global rules are routinely flouted,[114] there have also been innumerable examples of the multilateral project being alive,[115] if not well, despite the tendency towards exceptionalism exercised by the world's (current) 'hyperpower'.[116] With many examples of United States exceptionalism to, or dismissal of, human-centred multilateralism (its rejection of the Millennium Development Goals at the General Assembly Summit 2005;[117] its use

---

[112] See Ch 2.

[113] J Stiglitz, *Globalization and its Discontents* (Penguin Press, 2002) xv.

[114] P Sands, *Lawless World: America and the Making and Breaking of Global Rules* (Penguin Books, 2005).

[115] On the web of multilateral initiatives, see J Alvarez, 'The Promise and Perils of International Organizations', London School of Economics, London, 6 December 2006.

[116] Kagan explains that the now familiar term was coined by former French foreign minister Hubert Védrine who referred to a *hyperpuissance* to describe 'an American behemoth too worryingly powerful to be designated merely a superpower.' R Kagan, *Paradise and Power: America and Europe in the New World Order* (Atlantic Books, 2003) 43.

[117] During the negotiations at the 2005 World Summit, United States ambassador Bolton offered an endorsement of the Millennium Declaration but not the Millennium Development Goals, and explicitly rejected the universally supported MDG target that donor countries seek to reach 0.7% gross national income in official development assistance. See *Letter from the Representative of the United States of America on the Millennium Development Goals*, 13 August 2005. In the *Letter from the Representative of the United States of America to the General Assembly (Development Chapter)* 30 August 2005, ambassador Bolton wrote: 'In this section as in others [draft Outcome document, paras 16–17], the US proposes using the phrase internationally agreed development goals rather than the term Millennium Development Goals in order to be clear that we are referring to goals agreed among governments—not the subsequent more elaborate framework of goals, targets and indicators prepared by the UN secretariat.' <http://www.unreform.org>. The European

of 'extraordinary rendition'; its rejection of the Kyoto treaty on climate change; its general hostility towards the Rome Statute establishing an International Criminal Court; its controversial use of force in Iraq in 2003; its flouting of international humanitarian law in the treatment of prisoners of war in Guantanamo Bay and Abu Ghraib detention facilities), they remain just that, the disregard of rules that thrive, and continue to thrive, through the *general* endorsement of the international community.[118] The US, acting outside the boundaries of acceptable self-interest, sits in stark contrast to the collective will of the majority of states.[119]

The more pressing issue then, is not whether US action and inaction represents the death of multilateral cooperation, but whether an equitable form of multilateralism, that better represents the concerns of all the world community, is possible.[120] A critical test to these ends, would be in advancing a cooperative

Union members of the G8 donor states meeting in July 2005 at Gleneagles saw announcements by France and the United Kingdom of timetables to reach 0.7% ODA/GNI by 2012 and 2013 respectively and reaffirmed the recent EU agreement to reach 0.7% ODA/GNI by 2015 with an interim target of 0.56% ODA/GNI by 2010—a doubling of EU ODA between 2004 and 2010: 'G8 Finance Ministers' Conclusions on Development', Press Release, UK Government, 11 June 2005. Despite the United States objection, the continued support for the 0.7% GNI target was reaffirmed by the General Assembly at its 2005 Summit, *2005 World Summit Outcome*, UN Doc A/60/L1, 15 September 2005, para 23(b).

[118] It is worth being reminded here of Rosalyn Higgins' point that non-compliance with a rule of international law, even by the majority of states—and she provides the example of the use of torture—does not necessarily weaken its normative quality if the conduct of non-compliance is defended by appealing to exceptions or justifications: R Higgins, *Problems and Process: International Law and How we Use It* (Clarendon Press, 1998) 20; see also *Military and Paramilitary Activities in and against Nicaragua* (Merits) (Nicaragua v United States of America) ICJ Rep (1986) 14, at 98. It is beyond the scope of this work to look in any detail at the many nuances of United States exceptionalism. Views suggest though, that some US exceptionalism is positive (Koh, at 118–9), that some exclusionary treaty practices are less problematic than others (Koh, at 115), and in any event, the US's current track record should be considered in light of its strong record of compliance with the underlying norms even of non-ratified treaties (Ruggie, at 334). In addressing this issue, attention has also been given to the pressures on the US to seek international support for its actions, and the costs to it, including to its corporate sector, of non-compliance with shared international norms. (Ruggie, at 336–8). The US nonetheless maintains double standards applying more permissive criteria in judging its friends than its enemies (Ignatieff, at 3), and US exceptionalism in the area of human rights offers an 'embarrassing record of late' (Ruggie, at 334). HK Koh, 'America's Jekyll and Hyde Exceptionalism'; JG Ruggie, 'American Exceptionalism, Exemptionalism and Global Governance'; M Ignatieff, 'Introduction: American Exceptionalism and Human Rights'. All in M Ignatieff (ed), *American Exceptionalism and Human Rights* (Princeton University Press, 2005).

[119] A rare example of the willingness of the current US administration under George W Bush to yield to the opinion of the international community was reflected in its abstention rather than veto on the referral by the UN Security Council of Sudan to the International Criminal Court for atrocities in Darfur.

[120] After a count of the various editors, bureau chiefs and reporters who cover trade for the Financial Times (UK), the Trade Minister for Zambia, serving also as coordinator for the 50 Least-Developed Countries (LDCs) at the 2005 WTO Ministerial Meeting in Hong Kong, easily concluded that the Financial Times has more capacity to do trade than the LDCs. A Beattie, 'Dipak and the Goliaths', *Financial Times Magazine*, 10–11 December 2005. On the disadvantages developing countries face within the WTO system, see, N Udombana, 'A Question of Justice: The

system that confronts the global gap between rich and poor. Thus, a central challenge to the realization of many human rights in the twenty-first century, is the failure to allow for any meaningful cross-fertilization of international legal regimes or mandates and the intergovernmental institutions that drive them.[121] Bringing the focus on economic development closer to the UN, where *human* development is advocated, the *High-Level Panel on Threats, Challenges and Change* which addressed UN reform, offered some recommendations aimed at integrating human rights concerns and global economics under a restructured Economic and Social Council.[122] In so doing however, the Report had to attest at the outset to the limitations of the proposal by conceding that: '... decision-making on international economic matters, particularly in the areas of finance and trade, has long left the United Nations and no amount of institutional reform will bring it back'.[123] While human rights considerations would seem to be increasingly relevant to some at the World Bank, and gaining a public profile,[124] the IMF is so far largely impenetrable on

WTO, Africa and Countermeasures for Breaches of International Trade Obligations' 38 *J Marshall L Rev J* (2005) 1153. The General Assembly's failure at its 60th session to advance a reform agenda for the Security Council provides a different, but similarly telling, example of disadvantage.

[121] A noteworthy observation by one commentator proposes that the current United States commitment to the WTO rules may wither should the Appellate Body allow other social values, such as human rights to influence trade rules. See Sands, *Lawless World*, 113. Questioning whether various sets of international rules and commitments are counterproductive one to the other, such as the Millennium Development Goals and the intellectual property regime in the areas of health, food, traditional knowledge, education and the environment: see, ME Salomon, 'Addressing Structural Obstacles and Advancing Accountability for Human Rights: A Contribution of the Right to Development to MDG8', Briefing Note to the 2nd session of the UN High-Level Task Force on the Right to Development (November 2005) 7 <http://www.ohchr.org/english/issues/development/taskforce.htm>. See further, ch 3: The Current Incongruence of International Legal Regimes.

[122] The Report suggests that ECOSOC transform itself into a 'development cooperation forum', where it can provide a regular venue for engaging the development community at the highest level. *Report of the UN High-Level Panel on Threats, Challenges and Change*, para 274.

[123] Ibid. The recommendation for a development cooperation forum was endorsed by the Secretary-General in his report to the 59th session of the General Assembly. Report of the UN Secretary-General, *In Larger Freedom*, 171–80. At its 60th session the General Assembly agreed, in the most general terms, that ECOSOC should 'serve as a quality platform for high-level engagement among Member States and with the international financial institutions, the private sector and civil society on emerging global trends, policies and action and develop its ability to respond better and more rapidly to developments in the international economic, environmental and social fields' (2005 World Summit Outcome), and it should ' hold a biennial High-Level Development Cooperation Forum to review trends in international development ... .' (para 155(b)). See also *Report of the High-Level Task Force on the Implementation of the Right to Development* (1st session, 2004) UN Doc E/CN4/2005/WG18/2, para 27.

[124] The Task Force on the Right to Development agreed at its first session that a number of principles underlying the Declaration on the Right to Development guided the work of international development and financial institutions, the agreed tenets being drawn from the formal presentation made by the representative of the World Bank. These included: 'the indivisibility and interdependence of all human rights; a holistic view of human rights and development; the multidimensional nature of development strategies, including poverty elimination; the importance of empowering people as active agents in the development process, with rights and duties; and the centrality of the individual as the subject of human rights and the beneficiary of development ... .' *Report of the High-Level Task Force* (2005, 1st), para 30; ME Salomon, 'Towards a Just Institutional Order: A Commentary on the First Session of the UN Task Force on the Right to Development' 23 *NQHR*

the subject of human rights, if not outright revisionist in its selection and chosen reading of rights.[125] And, while there may be cracks in the WTOs 'self-contained regime',[126] there is still a concerted effort to keep it a forum discrete from human rights considerations.[127] In sum, there are insufficient responses to the fact that the objectives underpinning international cooperation in those organizations serve an instrumental role in relation to the realization of human rights.

The world today sees the pursuit of the individual interests of states channelled through multilateral institutions, and through lobbying blocs within those institutions.[128] Yet, are these attempts at rules-based multilateralism serving our needs

---

(2005) 409, at 415. The World Bank has established a human rights working group in the Legal Vice-Presidency and various research projects are underway on human rights indicators and on economic justifications for human rights, including consideration of economic, social and cultural rights. L-H Piron and T O'Neil, *Integrating Human Rights into Development: A Synthesis of Donor Approaches and Experiences* (Overseas Development Institute, 2005) 8 <http://www.odi.org.uk/rights>. See further, D Freestone and JK Ingram (guest eds), *Human Rights and Development*, 8 *Development Outreach* (The World Bank Institute, October 2006).

[125] Speaking in his personal capacity on the topic of human rights policies, the IMF representative to the UN remarked that: '[I]t would be ... helpful to look at the economic, social and cultural rights that would be relevant from an economic development perspective, focused first and foremost on the protection of economic, social and cultural freedoms. The key ingredients of economic freedom would include personal choice, voluntary exchange, freedom to compete, and the protection of personal property.' J Bengoa, *Report of the Chairperson/Rapporteur*, UN Social Forum (Sub-Commission, 57th session 2005) UN Doc E/CN4/Sub2/2005/21, para 35. Similar remarks were made during the subsequent 2005 session of the Task Force on the Right to Development. From this perspective human rights become mere instrumental means for achieving economic policy objectives, and what were once framed as *human* rights risk becoming rights of other actors, serving different objectives, such as the protection of business and corporate interest and investments. Alston has coined this 'epistemological misappropriation'. P Alston, 'Resisting the Merger and Acquisition of Human Rights by Trade Law: A Reply to Petersmann' 13 *EJIL* 4 (2002) 815, at 842. On the issue of prioritizing human rights, see, Salomon, 'Towards a Just Institutional Order', 409, at 428.

[126] '[T]he basic interpretive technique of the Appellate Body is one that rejects the notion of WTO as a self-contained regime ... and is in principle open to interconnectedness in the interpretation of "development"'. R Howse, *Mainstreaming the Right to Development into International Trade Law and Policy at the World Trade Organization*, UN Doc. E/CN.4/Sub.2/2004/17, para 21.

[127] During the 2nd session of the Task Force on the Right to Development, which was *mandated* by the intergovernmental Working Group on the Right to Development to consider ways of strengthening MDG8 on the Global Partnerships for Development, the United Kingdom representative, speaking on behalf of the European Union, remarked in her opening statement to the Task Force: 'Issues of trade and development are under negotiation in other, dedicated fora. We will not comment here on those processes.' *Statement by the Representative of the United Kingdom of Great Britain and Northern Ireland, on behalf of the European Union* (High-Level Task Force on the Right to Development, 2nd session, 2005).

[128] For example, in the WTO there is the Group of 20 (G20) constituting a coalition of developing country agriculture exporters lead by Brazil, the G90 comprised of African, Caribbean and Pacific states and other poor economies, and the recently formed G6 which consists of the US, EU, Brazil, India, Japan and Australia. 'Making Sense of WTO's Bewildering Variety', *Financial Times*, 15 December 2005. The UN has its own cleavages, including, for example, the African Group, the Group of Latin American and Caribbean States (GRULAC) and the Non-Aligned Movement, a mix of developing countries from various geographical regions.

for global justice?[129] International cooperation possesses no inherently objective value unless, and until, it pursues objectives consistent with our *agreed* values and *common* interests. Fundamental among them are the UN Charter's international legal obligation to cooperate for clearly defined purposes—the promotion of social progress and higher standards of living, and universal respect for, and observance of, human rights and fundamental freedoms.

Economic policies and institutions aimed at the creation of wealth are meant to be consistent with the international normative framework that, through human rights, has codified the *minimum* content of human dignity. Economic globalization associated with liberalization of trade and industry, privatization of public enterprises, deregulation of the economy, the expansion of international financial markets, a shrinking role of the state and its budget, and a growing rich-poor global divide, rely on the integration of the legal regime for the protection and promotion of human rights to render it just, to hold the 'invisible' hand of the free market.[130] Highlighting these priorities, the UN Working Group on the Right to Development recognized that development had to be grounded in policies that fostered economic growth with equity and social justice,[131] and that human rights impact assessment of trade and development rules and policies at the national and international levels were 'critical for the realization of the right to development',[132] and should be used in 'all the relevant trade forums'.[133] Similarly, the United Nations Development Programme (UNDP) reminds us that '... greater openness to trade, like economic growth, is not an end in itself: it is a means to expanding human capabilities. Indicators for increased openness— such as export growth and rising trade to GDP ratios—are important, but they are not proxies for human development.'[134]

Multilateralism, we know, is not a perfect tool, it is subject to the follies, preferences, interests, greed, and power differentials that have characterized every phase of globalization from colonial imperialism to the predatory capitalism we see today. Its imperfections as a tool at the service of justice are evident in a

---

[129] Speaking on International Trade and Development, Georges Abi-Saab, Chair of the WTO Appellate Body, told a UN seminar on the right to development that if we choose to abide by a neoliberal model then it must be general and not partial; what is needed is a level playing field. UN High-Level Seminar on the Right to Development: Global Partnership for Development, Geneva, 9–10 February 2004. Notes on file with author. Udombana provides a critique of trade liberalization under the WTO and its failures at positively including or impacting on Africa. Udombana, 'A Question of Justice', 1153.

[130] This is descriptive of a neoliberal agenda, which has dominated contemporary economic globalization. UN Research Institute for Social Development (UNRISD), 'The Sources of Neoliberal Globalization', *Report of UNRISD Seminar on Improving Knowledge on Social Development in International Organizations* II (2002) 3.

[131] *Report of the Open-ended Working Group on the Right to Development* (6th session, 2005) UN Doc E/CN4/2005/25, para 42.

[132] Ibid, para 52; see also para 53.

[133] Ibid, para 54(e).

[134] UNDP, *Human Development Report 2005: International Cooperation at a Crossroads: Aid, Trade and Security in an Unequal World* (Oxford University Press, 2005) Ch 4, at 113.

world system that continues daily to struggle with its conflicting tendencies—the self-interests of states, their agreed fundamental values, their contemporary reliance on collective endeavour. Even among believers, the case for 'cooperative internationalism', is not overstated,[135] but as Simma and Paulus query: 'Perhaps the cup is half full ... After all, who would have cared—and how—a hundred years ago?'.[136]

Far from fully matured or insulated from abuse of power, multilateralism in the twenty-first century nonetheless continues to reflect the humane, and some of the more civilized, tendencies of a global community shaped by a post-1945 system rooted in the new international law of cooperation. Multilateralism understood as institutional, norms-based international cooperation continues to underpin our international order because the international community of states *as a whole* regards it as critically important. Community is not synonymous with unanimity; it is constructed from a general will.[137]

Despite US denunciation of key human rights, notably economic, social and cultural rights, and the right to development, these issues have long remained important parts of the UN human rights agenda, and continue to gain significance.[138] The general support for the establishment, in the last decade, of UN special procedures on human rights and extreme poverty, on the right to development, on the rights to education, food and housing, on the effects of foreign debt, and on the right to the highest attainable standard of health, attests to this collective will and value system.[139]

---

[135] See, G Evans, '2005: Make or Break for Global Governance', London School of Economics, London, 18 February 2005. (Member of the UN Secretary-General's High-Level Panel on Threats, Challenges and Change).

[136] Simma and Paulus, 'The International Community', 266, at 272.

[137] *Case Concerning the Gabčíkovo-Nagymaros Project*, Judge Weeramantry (sep op) 88, at 95. 'The general support of the international community does not of course mean that each and every member of the community of nations has given its express and specific support to the principle. ...' D Kritsiotis, 'Imagining the International Community', 961, at 990.

[138] See, for example, the establishment by the Commission on Human Rights in 2004 of the High-Level Task Force on the Implementation of the Right to Development (CHR res 2004/7, 60th session, 2004) and the on-going work of the Open-ended Working Group to Consider Options Regarding an Optional Protocol to the International Covenant on Economic, Social and Cultural Rights (CHR Res 2003/18, 59th session, 2003).

[139] Resolution establishing the post of Independent Expert on the question of human rights and extreme poverty, CHR res 1998/25, 51 votes to one with no abstentions, United States voted against; Resolution establishing the post of Independent Expert on the right to development, CHR res 1998/72, adopted without a vote (United States voted against every subsequent annual resolution, including 2004/7 establishing the Task Force on the Right to Development); Resolution establishing the post of Special Rapporteur on the right to education, CHR res 1998/33, 52 votes to one with no abstentions, United States voted against; Resolution establishing the post of a Special Rapporteur on the right to food, CHR res 2000/10, 49 votes to one, with two abstentions, United States voted against; Resolution establishing the post of Special Rapporteur on adequate housing as a component of the right to an adequate standard of living, CHR res 2000/9, adopted without a vote; CHR res 2003/27 renewing the mandate was adopted without a vote. Resolution establishing the post of Independent Expert on the effects of economic reform policies and foreign debt, CHR res 2000/9, 30 votes to 15, with seven abstentions, United States voted against; Resolution establishing

When it comes to the formation of norms, being powerful but wrong does not undermine the collective and accumulated will of the majority, and the strengthening of international standards that are meant to guide their actions. The past several decades reflect the most intensive efforts at global governance, and now we *need* to act together to sustain human progress;[140] applied today, 'power-based internationalism'[141] will erode our collective well-being; it is only through our shared responsibility that we can effectively provide for our common survival. At the 2005 Montreal talks on climate change, the then Prime Minister of the host state said his message to 'reticent nations, including the US is this: there is such a thing as a global conscience and now is the time to listen to it'.[142] The notion of interdependence underpinning developments in international law is derived from the fact that the global community has travelled far down the path of being interdependent in the satisfaction of its needs; and whether in the area of trade, environment, security or human rights, or at their points of intersection, draws on the same global environment in order to have them met.

To be sure, the first years of the twenty-first century have shown themselves in many ways to be dark and worrying, and the United States's selective engagement with the rules in the international context may frustrate our collective enterprise, and undermine morale; but it has also ignited a backlash against exceptionalism. Paradoxically, it has strengthened the demands for a rigorous application of the fundamental standards of legitimacy, acceptable behaviour of the international community, and a more democratic process of global governance. In an editorial entitled 'International Law: Alive and Kicking', Sands concluded that while 'there remains much that is of serious concern [with regard to the US] it is striking that the Bush administration has not succeeded in killing off Kyoto [the climate change treaty] or the International Criminal Court, or rewriting the Geneva Conventions [on international humanitarian law] or the torture convention, or

---

the post of a Special Rapporteur on the right of everyone to the enjoyment of the highest attainable standard of physical and mental health, CHR res. 2002/31, adopted without a vote; CHR res 2005/24 extending the mandate, 52 votes to one with no abstentions, United States voted against.

[140] S Ramphal, Panellist, 'Lawless World: The US, Britain and the Making and Breaking of Global Rules', The Royal Institute of International Affairs (Chatham House), London, 9 March 2005.

[141] As Koh see it, the post-September choice for the US is no longer between being isolationist or internationalist, but rather what type of internationalist it will be. Will it rely on a 'power-based internationalism in which the United States gets its way because of its willingness to exercise power whatever the rules? Or will it be a norm-based internationalism ... .'. HK Koh, 'America's Jekyll and Hyde Exceptionalism' in Ignatieff (ed), *American Exceptionalism and Human,* 111, at 142. It is interesting to note that even unilateral, coercive power is cast today as a form of internationalism. More recently, America has sought to re-establish itself as a team player. As the Economist points out, 'America has rediscovered merit in multilateralism after its Mesopotamian Adventure'. 'The Future of Nato: The Test in Afghanistan', *The Economist,* 25 November 2006.

[142] 'Mind the Gap between the US and its Allies: Today's Differences Turn on Values instead of Geopolitics', *Financial Times,* 10 December 2005.

building any sort of consensus to support its revised approach to the international rules governing the use of force. Quite the contrary'.[143]

Having laid out the pillars that inform our international order—interdependence, community, cooperation—and the place of human rights in providing a system of common values and community obligations that underpin it, we will now turn to examine the features of the global economy and their particular relevance to our subject of enquiry.

1.3 Globalization in an Era of Human Rights

1.3.1 Economic globalization as a structural impediment to the exercise of human rights

Economic globalization has considerable implications for the realization of socio-economic rights in developing countries. Whether one endorses the view that 'globalization is the only means by which global poverty can be reduced', or rather that it is 'an important cause of global poverty',[144] there is no disagreement on the fact that poverty on a massive scale continues to plague the people of many developing countries. Second, wealthy states, whether acting bilaterally, or with other states, including as part of multilateral institutions,[145] are largely responsible for decisions, policies and rules that impact on the ability of people the world over to exercise their human rights.[146] The World Bank, the International Monetary Fund and the World Trade Organization, guided by the preferences of the rich countries,[147] make and advance the rules of the global economy that

[143] P Sands, 'International Law: Alive and Kicking', *The Guardian*, 17 May 2005.

[144] I Goldin and K Reinert, *Globalization for Development: Trade, Finance, Aid, Migration, and Policy* (World Bank/Palgrave MacMillan, 2006) 1.

[145] Following on from the G8 decision at its summit in July 2005, the World Bank and IMF annual meeting, 24–25 September 2005, concluded that 18 countries stand to have their debts cancelled by the end of 2005. While this could free up money to invest towards meeting the MDGs, existing IFI imposed economic conditionality limiting countries' spending on social goods could counter these objectives. On the decision to cancel multilateral debt, see IMF Press Release, no 05/210, 24 September 2005 and 'World Bank, IMF Strike Debt Deal, Shift Sights to WTO', *Bridges Weekly Trade News Digest*, 28 September 2005. 'Extrapolating from UNICEF data, as many as 5,000,000 children and vulnerable adults may have lost their lives as a result of the debt crunch since the late 1980s'. I Manokha, 'Terrorism and Poverty: Is there a Causal Relationship?', in ME Salomon, A Tostensen, and W Vandenhole (eds), *Casting the Net Wider: Human Rights, Development and New Duty-Bearers* (forthcoming, Intersentia, 2007).

[146] The existence of poverty signifies that human rights are not being realized. See, P Hunt, M Nowak and S Osmani, *Principles and Guidelines for a Human Rights Approach to Poverty Reduction Strategies* (OHCHR, 2005), para 19.

[147] 'One of the main arguments in the concluding chapter of this report is that the rules and processes in global markets can be unfair to developing countries. A country's power in decision-making in multilateral banks is usually correlated with its economic strength.' At the WTO, '[i]n practice, the ability of countries to influence the agenda and decisions depends crucially on their capacity to be present, to follow negotiations, to be informed, and to understand fully the

are a result of by the power differentials between developed and developing countries.[148] Economic globalization and world poverty are linked through the existence of these structural determinants.[149] The identifiable shift towards international cooperation need also be directed at addressing the structural impediments characteristic of the contemporary coercive global order—the rules and institutions of the system as a whole—through those states that uphold the order from which they so greatly benefit.

The term globalization often refers to the realms of international trade, finance and investment.[150] The three most significant developments related to economic globalization that have gained ground with the fall of Communism in the late 1980s and early 1990s have been the internationalization of trade and finance, the increasing power of transnational corporations, and the enhanced role of international economic institutions at the forefront of which are the World Bank, the IMF and the WTO.[151] The UN Committee on Economic, Social and Cultural Rights, notes that this globalization:

has come to be closely associated with increasing reliance on the free market, a significant growth in the influence of international financial markets and institutions in determining the viability of national policy priorities, a diminution in the role of the state and size of its budget, the privatization of various functions previously considered to be the exclusive domain of the state, the deregulation of a range of activities with a view to facilitating investment and rewarding individual initiative, and a corresponding increase in the role and even responsibilities attributed to private actors, both in the corporate sector, in particular to the transnational corporations, and in civil society.[152]

impact of the complex issues at hand.' World Bank, *World Development Report 2006: Equity and Development* 67.

[148] 'We judge that the problems we have identified are not due to globalization as such but to deficiencies in its governance ... There is concern about the unfairness of key global rules on trade and finance and their asymmetric effects on rich and poor countries.' *A Fair Globalization, Report of the World Commission on the Social Dimension of Globalization*, (Geneva, ILO, 2004) xi. 'At the global level, the present system of governance is based on rules and policies that generate unbalanced and often unfair outcomes. Global governance needs to be reformed ...'. *A Fair Globalization*, annex 1: Guide to Proposals and Recommendations, at 143. Referring to the ILO World Commission report Joseph Stiglitz remarks: '... the emerging consensus [is] that globalization—despite its positive potential—has not only failed to live up to that potential, but has actually contributed to social distress'. *The Guardian*, 12 March 2004.

[149] 'The core message ... is that many of the world's poorest countries and regions face structural impediments that have made it very difficult to achieve sustained economic growth. Thus it is not an accident that they are the poorest.' UNDP, *Human Development Report 2003: Millennium Development Goals: A Compact Among Nations to End Human Poverty* (Oxford University Press, 2003) Ch 3.

[150] CESCR, Statement to the Third Ministerial Conference of the World Trade Organization (21st session, 1999) UN Doc E/C12/1999/9, para 2.

[151] See generally MB Steger, *Globalization: A Very Short Introduction* (Oxford University Press, 2003).

[152] CESCR, Decision on Globalization and its Impact on the Enjoyment of Economic, Social and Cultural Rights (18th session, 1998) UN Doc E/1999/22, para 2.

In its broader sense it is not uncommon to hear references to 'globalizations', which include not only international trade and investment, but information technology, communication and culture, the globalization of standards, and the burgeoning of an international civil society.[153] A tripartite model outlines the historical process of globalization in which two stages, one consisting of the age of late capitalism, and the other of the internationalization of human rights principles and the growth of a global civil society run concurrently.[154] These two strains have been referred to as 'globalization-from-above' and 'globalization-from-below', respectively.[155] Globalization-from-above 'concerns the activities of transnational corporations, international economic organizations'[156] and 'reflects the collaboration between leading states...',[157] whereas globalization-from-below includes 'popular participation at the local levels, the building of civil societies and the enhancement of non-governmental organizations...'.[158] A similar system of categorization refers to 'top down' and 'bottom up' globalization,[159] in which 'top down' globalization is criticized for exposing local communities to the negative impact of international trade, corporate imperialism and globalized communications.

Bottom-up globalization, for its part, is attributed with having encouraged the communication of ideas around conceptions of justice and equity, the notion of a human global agenda, and facilitated the globalization of standards.[160] Conversely, the dominance of capitalism and the muscle of the market place today gives rise to grave concerns that profit is being put before people; as one commentator remarked, it is 'a world where there are no citizens just customers'.[161] The South African political economist Patrick Bond, describes this system quite

---

[153] See for example, J Bengoa, *The Relationship Between the Enjoyment of Human Rights, in particular Economic, Social And Cultural Rights, and Income Distribution/Poverty, Income Distribution and Globalization: A Challenge For Human Rights*, Addendum to the Final Report, (Sub-Commission, 50th session, 1998) UN Doc E/CN4/Sub2/1998/8, para 22, where he suggests 'we must speak of globalizations' given that there are 'various simultaneous processes of globalization'.

[154] J Oloka-Onyango, *Globalization in the Context of Increased Incidents of Racism, Racial Discrimination and Xenophobia* (Sub-Commission, 51st session, 1999) UN Doc E/CN4/Sub2/1999/8, para 11. The first era Oloka-Onyango outlines in the coverage of the historical processes of globalization is that of colonial imperialism.

[155] R Falk, 'The Making of Global Citizenship', in J Brecher et al (eds), *Global Visions: Beyond the New World Order* (South End Press, 1993) 39.

[156] R McCorquodale with R Fairbrother, 'Globalization and Human Rights' 21 *HRQ* 3 (1999) 735, at 739.

[157] R Falk, *Predatory Globalization: A Critique* (Polity Press, 1999) 128.

[158] McCorquodale with Fairbrother, 'Globalization and Human Rights', 735 at 739.

[159] J Bengoa, *The Relationships between the Enjoyment of Human Rights, in particular Economic, Social and Cultural Rights, and Income Distribution*, Final Report, (Sub-Commission, 49th session 1997) UN Doc E/CN4/Sub2/1997/9, paras 42–44.

[160] Ibid, para 44.

[161] In addressing 'The Future of Human Rights in a Globalized World', Rein Müllerson refers to the work of two commentators who welcome globalization without qualification and 'especially

simply as providing for the 'commoditization of everything'.[162] While human rights as articulated in international law are indigenous to both orders, they are so far only meaningfully reflected in the globalization of the bottom-up variety.

The international policy framework that informs economic management may be growing increasingly sensitive to the social consequences of liberalization, privatization, and deregulation—perhaps representing a shift from the 'Washington Consensus' to a 'post-Washington Consensus'[163] or beyond.[164] Yet it remains an economically driven process that proceeds on the primary principles of private property and uninhibited market forces,[165] on a strange mix of a doctrine of liberalized markets, protectionism[166] and vastly unequal power.[167] While the goal of bilateral and multilateral development agencies is now being expressed in terms

welcome those aspects of it that other commentators usually believe to constitute its most negative effects'. Müllerson, *Ordering Anarchy*, 278.

[162] P Bond, 'NEPAD: Breaking or Shining the Chains of Global Apartheid?' *NEPAD Political-Economic Speaker Series*, Columbia University, New York, 22 April 2003.

[163] Bond advances the view that this neoliberal agenda which endorses liberalization of the economy, rapid privatization and deregulation, known as the 'Washington Consensus', is endorsed by, among other agencies and governments: the UNDP, UN Global Compact, WTO, World Bank, IMF, the European Union and Japan. Those who support a 'post-Washington Consensus' approach to economic management which poses the need for greater state intervention and more attention to sustainable development, equity and environmental protection, are said to include UNCTAD, UNICEF, Canada, Germany, the Scandinavian countries, the Rockefeller Foundation, George Soros, Kofi Annan and Joseph Stiglitz. The latter he distinguishes from what he refers to as 'Third World Nationalism' which calls for increased market access, however, with reform of the way in which it is currently managed. Lastly, he refers to the 'Global Justice Movement' which calls for the 'deglobalization of capital, decommodification and expanded human rights'. Bond, 'NEPAD: Breaking or Shining the Chains of Global Apartheid?'. Notes on file with author.

[164] Maxwell refers to a 'current meta-narrative' that has replaced the post-Washington Consensus. 'It emphasises the Millennium Development Goals, as an over-arching framework, and lays out the link between the MDGs, nationally owned poverty reduction strategies, macro-economic policy (including trade), effective public expenditure management, and harmonised aid in support of good governance and good policies. It also recognises the concern for security and poorly performing countries, as well as the international trade and finance agenda. The current meta-narrative can be improved, by paying more attention to rights, equity and social justice, to the problems of "infant economies", and to issues of aid policy and aid architecture'. S Maxwell, *The Washington Consensus is Dead! Long Live the Meta-Narrative*, Overseas Development Institute, Working Paper 243 (2005) v.

[165] UNRISD, 'The Sources of Neoliberal Globalization', 4.

[166] 'What are the costs of trade protectionism for the developing world? A number of studies have tried to assess this. To take one example, the World Bank has considered the impact of a 'pro-poor' trade liberalization scenario. This scenario involves *only* tariff reductions and agricultural subsidies reform. The welfare gains to developing countries of this liberalization scenario are estimated to be over US$250 billion in 2003 prices. This is *four times* the value of foreign aid. ... The possibility of exports helping to alleviate poverty is significantly curtailed by trade protectionism in rich countries. This occurs in the form of tariffs, subsidies, quotas, standards, and regulations. ... Rich-country protectionism poses a significant barrier to poverty alleviation, not to mention the overall participation of the developing world in the global economy.' Goldin and Reinert, *Globalization for Development*, 66 and 75.

[167] 'Developing countries face massive challenges in influencing the global rules and processes that determine outcomes, which matter greatly to the well-being of their citizens'. World Bank, *World Development Report 2006: Equity and Development*, 68.

of poverty reduction[168] and 'pro-poor' growth,[169] serious concerns that economic efficiency is prioritized over social equity remain.[170] Contemporary strategies for reducing poverty and inequality exist in tension with the poverty and inequality logically implied by free market forces. Globalization may be a positive sum game in the aggregate, but it is one that produces both winners and losers. This idea of aggregate benefit (a rising tide that lifts all boats), and collective good, that the free market espouses works against greater equality, benefiting those who have skills valued by the market, while further marginalizing the poorest, and those already politically disadvantaged.[171] Models based on notions of aggregate benefit would seem to work to the disadvantage of the poor whether we talk of states or people within states.

While national autonomy has become constrained generally, scope for man-oeuvring in terms of policy options is particularly limited for developing states. They have weaker international influence in the areas of trade[172] and finance,[173] and

---

[168] See, AM Jerve, 'Social Consequences of Development in a Human Rights Perspective: Lessons from the World Bank', in I Kolstad and H Stokke (eds) *Writing Rights* (Fagbokforlaget, 2005) 98, at 100.

[169] See for example, *Pro-Poor Growth in the 1990's: Lessons and Insights from 14 Countries* (World Bank, 2005).

[170] 'The World Bank's own auditing arm [the Independent Evaluation Group] has confirmed what many anti-poverty campaigners have long been saying: the Bank's projects did not adequately reduce poverty levels in borrowing nations over the past five years. ... [T]he report pointed out how export-oriented and privatisation dependent economies tend to suffer when growth does occur because the gains go to very few people'. A commentator remarked that: 'Language [in the report] is couched carefully so as not to address directly the failures of the now much-discredited poverty-creating, "Washington Consensus" structural adjustment policies, as liberalisation, privatisation and other adjustment measures are still being placed on loans by these institutions'. 'Bank Focuses on Growth often Leaves Poor Behind', *Inter-Press Service*, 7 December 2006.

[171] J Donnelly, *Universal Human Rights: Theory and Practice* (Cornell University Press, 2003) 201; UNRISD, 'The Sources of Neoliberal Globalization', 3. Jeffrey Sachs similarly notes, that 'if you start poor ... the market is trained to ignore you': J Sachs, *The End of Poverty: Economic Possibilities for Our Time*, Transcript, Carnegie Council on Ethics and International Affairs, 30 March 2005 <http://www.carnegiecouncil.org>.

[172] 96% of the world's farmers (1.3 billion people) live in developing countries yet are unable to trade their way out of poverty due to protection in developed countries in the form of tariffs, quotas, anti-dumping duties and subsidies to European and American domestic producers. Rich world farmers are protected in different forms to the tune of about 300 billion US dollars a year. Developed countries protect their markets at a loss to developing countries of US$700 billion annually in export revenues. The G8 industrialized countries meeting in July 2005 failed to agree to any changes in the current system of trade distorting practices. See, TW Pogge, '"Assisting" the Global Poor', in DK Chatterjee (ed), *The Ethics of Assistance Morality and the Distant Needy* (Cambridge University Press, 2004) 260, at 275; I Goldin, '*Meeting the Challenge of Development: An Action Agenda to Achieve the MDGs*', London School of Economics, 3 February 2005; *EU Heroes and Villains: Which Countries are Living up to their Promises on Aid, Trade, and Debt?* Joint NGO Briefing Paper, ActionAid, Eurodad and Oxfam (2005).

[173] For example, 46 sub-Saharan African member countries together control just 5.2% of the World Bank's Board of Directors total voting power and among them have only two directors on the executive boards of both the World Bank and IMF. Together the EU states account for 28% of voting power and the United States accounts for over 16%—the highest share of any one state. Country influence in setting the agenda is not limited to board membership, however, two-thirds of senior management-level positions at the World Bank are occupied by the citizens of mainly

are subject to the interests,[174] charity[175] and conditions of more powerful states.[176] They are often working from a position of disadvantage in terms of infrastructure and institutions,[177] and may be shackled with the legacy of unsustainable debt.[178]

OECD countries, even though these countries account for less than one-fifth of the global population. World Bank, *World Development Report 2006: Equity and Development* 67.

[174] Woods concludes that rich countries on the World Bank board are most interested in ensuring that their companies get the valuable contracts: N Woods, Programme in Global Governance, University of Oxford, Speaker, 'What Kind of Banker Does the World Need?', London School of Economics, London, 4 May 2005.

[175] If members of the OECD's Development Assistance Committee (the world's 23 largest donors) actually delivered official development assistance equal to 0.7% of their GNI as per internationally agreed targets, aid would be $165 billion a year—three times the current level and well above current estimates of what is needed to achieve the Millennium Development Goals. UNDP, *Human Development Report 2003: Millennium Development Goals*, Ch 8.

[176] It was only in 2005 that the British government adopted a policy stating that 'the UK will not make our aid conditional on specific policy decisions by partner governments or attempt to impose policy choices on them (including in sensitive economic areas such as privatisation or trade liberalisation)': *Partnerships for Poverty Reduction: Rethinking Conditionality*, UK Policy Paper, March 2005, para 5.13.

[177] While bad governance, including corruption, is a factor in keeping certain poor countries poor, Sachs suggests that this is only part of the explanation, with insufficient food production, insufficient disease control and economic isolation providing key reasons for Africa's impoverishment: Sachs, *The End of Poverty*. As Pogge notes however, while there will be international variations in the evolution of severe poverty caused by country-specific factors, it does not follow that these must be the only causally relevant factors, nor that global factors are irrelevant. TW Pogge, 'The First UN Millennium Development Goal: A Cause for Celebration?' 5 *Journal of Human Development* 3 (2004) 377, at 391.

[178] Greater debt relief is required for sustainable development and in order to release resources that could finance additional social spending and contribute to the realization of human rights in developing countries. While there has been agreement to cancel the majority of bilateral debt, action has not systematically followed pledges. Moreover, the majority of developing country debt is owed to multilateral institutions and this type of debt is not being cancelled systematically. In a 2005 report, the World Bank concluded that debt reduction remains highly concentrated in a few countries: *Global Development Finance 2005: Mobilizing Finance and Managing Vulnerability* (World Bank 2005). While the G8 Summit in July 2005 agreed to cancel 100% of the multilateral debt of 18 Heavily Indebted Poor Countries (HIPC), amounting to a total of US$55 billion in relief, it remains unclear as to whether this will be additional funds or will come from diverting money from existing aid budgets, and, what potentially harmful economic reforms will be imposed on the countries being granted debt relief. Further, there are currently 23 other HIPC countries—which are among the poorest of the poor. The UN Independent Expert on foreign debt and human rights noted that between 1990–2002 external debt as a percentage of developing countries' gross national income increased from 34% to 39%. B Mudho, *Report of the Independent Expert on the Effects of Structural Adjustment Policies and Foreign Debt on the full Enjoyment of Human Rights, particularly Economic, Social and Cultural Rights*, UN Doc E/CN4/2005/42, paras 6 and 11. An UNCTAD representative remarked that debt, which is fundamentally an African problem, was accumulated between 1985–1995 when those countries were under the tutelage of the Washington institutions. First session of the UN Task-Force on the Right to Development, 13–17 December 2004. Notes on file with author. Pogge reminds us that newly elected governments that break with corrupt, brutal and undemocratic preceding governments are compelled to pay off the debts incurred by those regimes sapping the capacity of such democratic governments to implement reforms and other political programs: See Pogge, '"Assisting" the Global Poor.'

Further, the escaped accountability of transnational corporations continues to plague the people of developing countries.[179]

Forty-six per cent of the world's people, concentrated in the South, live below the World Bank's US$2 a day poverty line,[180] and have an aggregate global income of 1.2 per cent.[181] 2.7 billion people—half of all people living in the South—live in poverty on less than US$2 a day,[182] while developed countries protect their markets at a loss to developing countries of US$700 billion annually in export revenues.[183] These figures translate into a human cost: almost half of the 10.5 million deaths a year of children under five occur in the poorest region, sub-Saharan Africa.[184] While there are a number of factors that contribute to this statistic, at the root of these unpardonable figures on child mortality lies poverty.[185]

The prevailing global order favours a small number of wealthy countries that hold sway over an institutionalized system that sees these divisions entrenched. The substance and direction of economic globalization are shaped by the richest and most powerful states to their particular benefit. The concentration of power among certain states that design, and give effect to, this economic system, and the relative insulation from democratic processes among the relevant international organizations, have not allowed for alternative models that may favour more redistributive approaches to take hold,[186] or for the concentration of power to be effectively challenged. A just system of globalization for sharing the benefits of cooperative efforts is not being realized,[187] and the negative repercussions of

---

[179] On the need to regulate transnational corporations in relation to their impact on the exercise of human rights see, *Report of the United Nations High Commissioner for Human Rights on the Responsibilities of Transnational Corporations and related Business Enterprises with regard to Human Rights*, UN Doc E/CN4/2005/91. Note also the recent establishment of a UN Special Representative to the Secretary-General on Human Rights and Transnational Corporations and other Business Enterprises, CHR res 2005/69.

[180] Moreover the figure of US$2 a day has been criticized as being wholly without value as a measure by which to assess the scale of world poverty. A more accurately derived figure, it has been argued, would reflect a substantially higher degree of poverty and less favourable trends in (what is already modest) improvement as presented by the World Bank. TW Pogge and SG Reddy, *How Not to Count the Poor* (2003). <http://www.columbia.edu/~sr793/techpapers.html>.

[181] TW Pogge, *World Poverty and Human Rights* (Polity Press, 2002) 2.

[182] *Fast Facts: The Faces of Poverty*, UN Millennium Project (2005).

[183] Pogge, '*Assisting' the Global Poor*. Protection comes in the form of tariffs, quotas, anti-dumping duties and subsidies to domestic producers. See further, UNDP, *Human Development Report 2005: International Cooperation at a Crossroads*, Ch 4, at 126–32.

[184] UNICEF *Statistics: Child Mortality* (May 2006). <http://childinfo.org/areas/childmortality>.

[185] 'Child mortality is closely linked to poverty: advances in infant and child survival have come more slowly in poor countries and to the poorest people in wealthier countries.' UNICEF *Statistics: Child Mortality*.

[186] UNRISD, 'The Sources of Neoliberal Globalization' 3; see generally, P Townsend and D Gordon (eds), *World Poverty: New Policies to Defeat an Old Enemy* (The Policy Press, 2002).

[187] '… [T]he most fundamental criticism of globalization as it has been practiced [is] that it is unfair and that its benefits have disproportionately gone to rich people'. J Stiglitz, 'Poverty, Globalization and Growth: Perspectives on Some of the Statistical Links' in UNDP, *Human Development Report 2003: Millennium Development Goals*, Ch 3, 80.

economic globalization, most profoundly felt in countries of the developing world, impact on the ability of the people in those countries to exercise their fundamental human rights. And where there are rights, there are obligations.

As one aspect of redressing global inequality, the UN Secretary-General's Task Force Report on the MDGs calls for the democratization of international institutions;[188] in the run-up to the United Kingdom's presidencies of the G8 and the European Union in the second half of 2005, its report by the independent Commission on Africa called for African countries to have greater representation on the IMF and World Bank boards;[189] there are ongoing calls for a true democratization of the WTO, and better access for developing countries, as well as observers.[190] Some call for a shift towards an international welfare state, and a 'more civilized form of economic development';[191] all recognize that the benefits of globalization are unevenly shared, while its costs are unevenly distributed,[192] with the people in developing countries suffering most, and the people in the North benefiting most.[193] Gordon and Townsend provided a cogent summary of this state of affairs when they noted that 'what has been neglected is not so much the conditions of poverty or of exclusion, but rather those of acquisition and affluence at the other extreme of the population experience, and the mechanics or agents of the entire distribution'.[194]

This research, however, is not an analysis of global economic policy aimed at providing an assessment of the successes and failures of the current model. Having left this to, among others, the economists and philosophers to assess,[195] it takes as its starting point that there remains a vastly unequal distribution of wealth in the world; that those suffering from 'unfreedoms',[196] including impoverishment as a

---

[188] *The Millennium Project Report 2005, Investing in Development: A Practical Plan to Achieve the Millennium Development Goals* (UNDP, 2005) <http://www.unmillenniumproject.org/reports/fullreport.htm>.

[189] *Our Common Interest, Report of the Commission for Africa* (2005) <http://www.commissionforafrica.org>

[190] *A Fair Globalization*, para 347; *EU Heroes and Villains*.

[191] P Townsend, 'Poverty, Social Exclusion and Social Polarisation: The Need to Construct an International Welfare State', in Townsend and Gordon (eds), *World Poverty*, 3, at 19.

[192] UN Millennium Declaration (2000) UN Doc A/55/2, arts 5 and 6, Solidarity.

[193] 'This pattern of distribution is not accidental. Inequality in wealth mirrors a deep inequity in the rules governing world trade and finance, which have been structured around the interests of the most developed countries': K Watkins, *Globalisation and Liberalization: Implications for Poverty, Distribution and Inequality* (UNDP Occasional paper 12, 1997) <http://hdr.undp.org/publications/papers.cfm>.

[194] P Townsend and D Gordon, 'The Human Condition is Structurally Unequal' in Townsend and Gordon (eds), *World Poverty*, xi, at xv.

[195] See for example, Reddy and Pogge, *How Not to Count the Poor*; A Sengupta, *Preliminary Study of the Independent Expert on the Right to Development, on the Impact of International Economic and Financial Issues on the Enjoyment of Human Rights* (Working Group on the Right to Development, 4th session, 2003) UN Doc E/CN4/2003/WG18/2, para 13.

[196] Sen provides a non-exhaustive list of what he has referred to as 'unfreedoms' which are essentially what is left when rights are violated, arguing that 'development requires the removal of major sources of unfreedoms'. A Sen, *Development as Freedom* (Oxford University Press, 1999) 3–4.

result of the existing structure of global wealth accumulation and distribution, do so at the hands of a minority of others who largely gain from this very system. While our interdependence is characterized by the contemporary requirement that all people draw from the same global environment for their survival, vast numbers of people concentrated in the South are unable to reap that which is necessary to secure their basic human rights.

The world poverty figures are evidence that key aspects of the existing political-economic order severely undermine the creation of an environment conducive to justice being served, and in which human rights for all have a greater chance of being realized. Globalization as practiced today may have the potential to be a force for good across the world, with the litmus test for successful economic globalization increasingly seen as the speeding up of development, and the reduction of absolute poverty in a manner that ensures economic, social and environmental sustainability.[197] But this alternative scenario will require a radical reconceptualization of the way in which it is managed.[198]

In light of these circumstances, typified by interdependence and external influences on well-being, international law for the protection of human rights is undergoing its own evolution. It is informed by the search for global equity impeded by structural deficiencies in our international arrangements. World poverty reflects not merely injustice and misfortune, but a violation of international human rights standards, and therefore its remedying engages the international human rights legal regime.

1.3.2 Poverty as a human rights issue

In referring to 'freedom from want' in its preamble, the Universal Declaration of Human Rights (UDHR) established that poverty is a human rights issue.[199] At the Vienna World Conference on Human Rights, the international community acknowledged that '[t]he existence of widespread extreme poverty inhibits the full and effective enjoyment of human rights',[200] and affirmed that 'extreme poverty and social exclusion constitute a violation of human dignity'.[201] In the pointed words of the Committee on Economic, Social and Cultural Rights, poverty reflects 'a massive and systemic breach' of international human rights law.[202]

While the term 'poverty' is not explicitly used in the Covenant, the exercise of the range of rights articulated in ICESCR have a 'direct and immediate' bearing on the eradication of poverty, the rights to work, and an adequate standard of

---

[197] *A Fair Globalization*, para 172.
[198] See, Stiglitz, *Globalization and its Discontents*, ix–x.
[199] UDHR, preambular para 2; CESCR, Statement on Poverty, para 1 *et seq.*
[200] Vienna Declaration and Programme of Action, Pt I, art 14.
[201] Ibid, Pt I, art 25. The position has been reaffirmed by the General Assembly in its biennial resolutions on Human Rights and Extreme Poverty ever since.
[202] CESCR, Statement on Poverty, para 4.

living, housing, food, health and education, having been referred to particularly by the Committee in this context.[203] There are also aspects of poverty characterized not solely by lack of income, but by qualitative deprivations, such as lack of power, choice and capability.[204] Although there is no conclusive definition of the term poverty,[205] from a human rights perspective it is widely accepted as transcending sheer economic deprivation. As Chinkin points out, poverty includes deprivation of conditions that are fundamental to life, incorporating social and economic exclusion, deprivation of human dignity, erosion of individual freedoms such as participation rights, expression and family life. It has the potential to expose people to violence and exploitation; it is 'the antithesis of the human right to development'; and is often linked to the violation of land rights central to the protection of indigenous peoples.[206] From a human rights perspective, others frame poverty as consisting of 'the non-fulfilment of a person's human rights to a range of basic capabilities. Capability failure is thus the defining attribute of poverty'.[207] Despouy suggests that extreme poverty denies human rights as a whole, providing a clear example of the interdependence and indivisibility of human

---

[203] Ibid, para 1.

[204] Drawing on the seminal work of Nobel prize-winning economist Amartya Sen, the Committee on Economic, Social and Cultural Rights has defined poverty as '... a human condition characterized by sustained or chronic deprivation of the resources, capabilities, choices, security and power necessary for the enjoyment of an adequate standard of living and other civil, cultural, economic, political and social rights ...': CESCR, Statement on Poverty, para 8. Sen distinguishes between income poverty and capability poverty, arguing that development is not the acquisition of more goods and services but the enhanced freedom—that is the capability—to lead the kind of life one values. Poverty is the deprivation of basic capabilities: Sen, *Development as Freedom*, Ch 4.

[205] For an authoritative compilation of definitions on poverty from a human rights perspective, see OHCHR *Definitions on Poverty*, UN Doc HR/GVA/POVERTY/SEM/2001/2 (2001). The OHCHR Guidelines on poverty reduction propose that: 'Since poverty denotes an extreme form of deprivation, only those capability failures should count as poverty that are deemed to be basic in some order of priority. As different societies may have different orders of priority, the list of basic capabilities may differ from one society to another. However, empirical observation suggests a common set of capabilities that are considered basic in most societies. They include the capabilities of being adequately nourished, avoiding preventable morbidity and premature mortality, being adequately sheltered, having basic education, being able to ensure security of the person, having equitable access to justice, being able to live in dignity, being able to earn a livelihood and being able to take part in the life of a community. The present *Guidelines* deal with this common set. But in each country, it must be ascertained, through a participatory process, which other capabilities its people consider basic enough for their failure to count as poverty.': Hunt, Nowak and Osmani, *Principles and Guidelines for a Human Rights Approach to Poverty Reduction Strategies*, paras 31–2.

[206] C Chinkin, 'The UN Decade on the Elimination of Poverty: What Role for International Law', *Current Problems in International Law Series*, University College, London, 22 February 2001. Notes on file with author. Published in, C Chinkin, 'The United Nations Decade for the Elimination of Poverty: What Role for International Law?' 54 *CLP* (2001) 553.

[207] Hunt, Nowak and Osmani, *Principles and Guidelines for a Human Rights Approach to Poverty Reduction Strategies*, para 30. 'From a human rights perspective, poverty can be described as the denial of a person's rights to a range of basic capabilities—such as the capability to be adequately nourished, to live in good health, and to take part in decision-making processes and in the social and cultural life of the community. In the language of rights, one may say that a person living in poverty is one for whom a number of human rights remain unfulfilled—such as the rights to food, health, political participation and so on' (para 7).

rights.[208] Human rights figure prominently in much of the current preoccupation with poverty, providing an important perspective when we recognize that the 'denial of human rights is both a cause and consequence of poverty'.[209]

A current danger is that the legal regime reflecting human rights principles and standards is being inadequately integrated into the way in which the global economy is directed. Any international system must be consistent with, at least, minimum conditions cast in terms of the fundamental respect for and observance of human rights. The Committee on Economic, Social and Cultural Rights has shown its concern that insufficient effort is being made by governments to devise complementary approaches which would enhance the compatibility of globalization trends with full respect for human rights. In this regard, the Committee states that '[c]ompetitiveness, efficiency and economic rationalism must not be permitted to become the primary or exclusive criteria against which governmental and inter-governmental policies are evaluated'.[210]

Agreement as to the influence the external environment has on the perpetuation or reduction of poverty is widespread. While failures of the global system reflected in world poverty do not provide justification for breaches by the governments of developing countries of their international human rights obligations domestically, for example, to realize progressively economic, social and cultural rights, an international environment conducive to the realization of human rights is necessary as a complement to the human rights obligations of states acting at the domestic level.[211] As acknowledged also by the World Bank, '[g]lobal inequities are massive. ... But global action can change external conditions and affect the impact of domestic policies. In this sense, global and domestic actions are complementary'.[212]

Human rights are concerned primarily with challenging abuse of power at all levels—preventing it, ensuring a system of accountability, and remedying the violations brought about by its occurrence. The requirement of establishing an

---

[208] L Despouy, former UN Special Rapporteur on human rights and extreme poverty, in OHCHR *Definitions on Poverty*.

[209] Chinkin, 'The United Nations Decade for the Elimination of Poverty', 553, at 556. Further, explicit reference to human rights within poverty alleviation policies and programmes—as advanced within 'human rights-based approaches' to poverty reduction—brings with it an extensive international normative framework, as well as a claim on the fulfilment of rights allowing for development (and not just goals or objectives) within a system of accountability. See, UNDP, *Human Development Report 2000: Human Rights and Human Development* (Oxford University Press, 2000) Ch 1.

[210] CESCR, Decision on Globalization, para 4.

[211] See, DRD, art 4(2): 'Sustained action is required to promote more rapid development of developing countries. As a complement to the efforts of developing countries, effective international co-operation is essential in providing these countries with appropriate means and facilities to foster their comprehensive development'; DRD, art 10: 'Steps should be taken to ensure the full exercise and progressive enhancement of the right to development, including the formulation, adoption and implementation of policy, legislative and other measures at the national and international levels'.

[212] World Bank, *World Development Report 2006: Equity and Development*, 16.

enabling international environment conducive to the exercise of rights by all people follows from this fundamental premise. Accordingly, international law for the protection of human rights has an important contribution to make in addressing the structural obstacles that contribute to world poverty. As the areas of human rights law based on international cooperation have begun to reflect, this particular approach is increasingly understood as essential to curtailing human rights abuses as exist today.

1.4 The Structural Approach to the Realization of Human Rights

1.4.1 The right to development

The Declaration on the Right to Development, adopted in 1986 by the United Nations General Assembly, emerged in large part as a response to the call by developing countries for an international order in which effective international cooperation would reduce the perceived unfairness of the prevailing economic order. The Declaration gave legal expression to the notion that the ability of states to develop, and to fulfil their human rights obligations, are constrained by the structural arrangements and actions of the international community. In addressing the right to development, the international community is to 'bear in mind' the purposes and principles of the UN as established in its Charter, notably, the achievement of international cooperation in solving international problems of an economic and social nature, and in promoting respect for human rights. Reference to these Charter objectives were reproduced verbatim in the very first paragraph of the DRD.[213] The universal entitlement to a human rights-based international order as articulated in the Universal Declaration of Human Rights at Article 28, further substantiates the rationale that underpins the Declaration, and was reproduced in the final DRD at preambular para 3.[214] Indeed, as a draft of the DRD and the consensus of the drafting committee of intergovernmental experts reflect, the right to development is *'based upon* Article 28 of the Universal Declaration of Human Rights.'[215] An intricate system of

[213] Ibid, preambular para 1; UN Charter, art 1(3).

[214] DRD, preambular para 3 states: 'Everyone is entitled to a social and international order in which the rights and freedoms set forth in this Declaration can be fully realized'.

[215] *Report of the Working Group of Governmental Experts on the Right to Development* (4th session, 9 December 1982) UN Doc E/CN4/1983/11 annex IV, Pt I, Section II, art 1, (emphasis added). A point reaffirmed by the expert from the USA, *Report of the Working Group of Governmental Experts on the Right to Development* (8th session, 24 January 1985) UN Doc E/CN4/1985/11 annex VIII (Compilation of proposals) 3. Following 'in-depth discussions' in the working group of governmental experts mandated to elaborate the draft Declaration, 'a general understanding was reached with respect to the following provisions of the draft declaration dealing with the preamble [including those reaffirming Charter article 1(3) and UDHR article 28]'. *Report of the Working Group of Governmental Experts on the Right to Development* (6th and 7th sessions, 14 November 1983) UN Doc E/CN4/1984/13, para 9.

obligations necessary for the realization of human rights was foreseen in Article 28 of the UDHR, which established the principle that respect for human rights is not about narrowly focused obligations limited to relations between individuals and their states, but rather presents a multi-layered system of obligations which attach themselves to all societal relations at the national and international levels.[216] In the words of Marks, Article 28 'implies a holistic framework in which the cumulative effect of realizing all types of human rights is a structural change in both national societies and international society'.[217] And as Alston noted: '[I] n many respects the right to development is an endeavour to give greater operational context to [Article 28].'[218]

With the adoption of the DRD, the General Assembly recognized the right to development as an 'inalienable human right'.[219] By casting development as a human right, the Declaration brought to the fore an appreciation that development does not occur solely as a result of economic growth or development planning; it is a process aimed at the creation of an international environment, and national environments, conducive to the realization of human rights, and it is through the exercise of their human rights that people will be able to develop in ways that are meaningful to them. The DRD provides the framework required to give meaning to this right. By clearly defining development as a human right, it recognizes people as right-holders, as active subjects in their development. Article 2(1) of the DRD holds that '[t]he human person is the central subject of development and should be the active participant and beneficiary of the right to development.' It also recognizes states, acting at the national level,[220] and cooperating at the international level,[221] as duty-bearers.[222]

The language of the Declaration reflects that states acting at the national level have the 'duty' to formulate national development policies, devised in a participatory manner, and aimed at improving the situation of the entire population through the equitable distribution of its benefits. However Article 2(3) also provides that states acting at the national level possess this same 'right'.[223] This 'right' of states can be understood as exercisable against the international community in its ability structurally to constrain developing states from implementing policies that

---

[216] P Alston, 'The Shortcomings of a "Garfield the Cat" Approach to the Right to Development' 15 *Cal W Int'l L J* (1985) 510, at 515.

[217] SP Marks, *The Human Rights Framework for Development: Seven Approaches* (2003) 3 <http://www.hsph.harvard.edu/fxbcenter>.

[218] Alston, 'The Shortcomings of a "Garfield the Cat" Approach', 510, at 515.

[219] DRD, art 1(1).

[220] Ibid, arts 2(3), 3(1), 5, 6(3), 8(1), 8(2), 10.

[221] Ibid, arts 2(3) 3, 4, 5, 6, 7, 8, 10.

[222] Ibid, arts 2(3), 3(1), 3(2), 3(3), 4(1), 4(2), 5, 6(1), 7, 10.

[223] 'States have the right and the duty to formulate appropriate national development policies that aim at the constant improvement of the well-being of the entire population and of all individuals, on the basis of their active, free and meaningful participation in development and in the fair distribution of the benefits resulting therefrom.'

further the realization of human rights.[224] Similarly, 'equality of opportunity' is recognized in the DRD as a 'prerogative both of nations and the individuals who make up nations.'[225]

While work towards its operationalization is now underway,[226] the DRD lacks a certain conceptual clarity, and is so far void of empirical application to date that might help refine it.[227] It is not surprising then, that over the years the right has received its share of criticism.[228] Yet despite some problems of identity, its motivation is noteworthy. Soon after its adoption, Brownlie remarked that: 'The significance of questions of form should not be over-estimated and there is no doubt that the DRD, with other instruments, forms part of a persistent political drive to obtain legitimacy (in the broad sense) for particular goals and principles in the conduct of international affairs'.[229] The DRD saw the calls of developing countries for a new international economic order[230] evolve into a demand for international cooperation to ensure the realization of human rights. Development was placed within the framework of rights and duties, thus inviting corresponding claims, including against the international community for structural obstacles to human rights. While its provisions are somewhat unconventionally framed for a human rights instrument, its assertions are made possible due to the existence of an international community of states organized on a juridical basis, as such, the right to development offers an abiding example of a human right that requires a high degree of cooperation among states for its fulfilment. The concept of development may not be clearly defined in the DRD, yet the debates and negotiations

---

[224] See, A Orford, 'Globalization and the Right to Development', in P Alston (ed), *Peoples' Rights* (Oxford University Press, 2001) 127, at 137.

[225] DRD, preambular para 17. At the national level, states should undertake 'all necessary measures for the realization of the right to development and shall ensure, inter alia, equality of opportunity for all in their access to basic resources, education, health services, food, housing, employment and the fair distribution of income. Effective measures should be undertaken to ensure that women have an active role in the development process. Appropriate economic and social reforms should be carried out with a view to eradicating all social injustices'. DRD, art 8(1).

[226] As exemplified, in particular, by the work of the UN High-Level Task Force on the Implementation of the Right to Development, addressed herein.

[227] In considering methods of overcoming obstacles to the RTD, the Chair of the Working Group on the Right to Development identified these two key obstacles. I Salama, *The Right to Development: Towards a New Approach?* Annual Meeting of the Academic Council on the United Nations System, Ottawa, 16–18 June 2005. Unpublished at the time of publication of this book.

[228] 'Who or what is to be developed and who or what is to do the developing?'. See questions raised in the work of some panellists at the discussion on 'Beyond Rhetoric: Implementing the Right to Development', Annual Meeting of the Law and Society Association in Toronto, June 1995, as referred to in RW Perry, 'Rethinking the Right to Development: After the Critique of Development, After the Critique of Rights' 18 *Law & Pol* 3–4 (1996) Special Issue on the Right to Development, M wa Mutua, LA Obiora and RJ Krotoszynski Jr (eds), 225, at 229; 'it confuses rights with moral claims and is unclear as to right-holders and duty-bearers': J Donnelly, 'In Search of the Unicorn: The Jurisprudence and Politics of the Right to Development' 15 *Cal W Int'l L J* (1985) 473, at 482.

[229] Brownlie, 'The Human Right to Development', 1, at 10.

[230] See, K Hossain (ed), *Legal Aspects of the New International Economic Order* (Frances Pinter Publishers, 1980).

that took place during its drafting and adoption reflect that the central element the proponents of this right were seeking to advance was an economic and social order based on equity and justice.[231] Its imperfections notwithstanding, there is little doubt that at the heart of the right to development lies the demand that global structural disadvantage be addressed.

The right to development was proclaimed by the international community on the premise of a shared responsibility, (although the term only entered the human rights lexicon 14 years later),[232] recognizing that the ability of a state to formulate and execute policies that will allow for rights to be delivered to the people in the country cannot be disassociated from the influence and cooperative role of the international community of states. A range of proposals from both Northern and Southern states provided during the drafting of the DRD reflect this key component, found repeatedly in its drafts, notably by stating that 'the right to development implies that states and the international community as a whole should aim at the creation of local and national conditions whereby everyone may enjoy the rights set forth in the Universal Declaration of Human Rights and the International Covenants on Human Rights'.[233] Senegal, for example, proposed a preambular paragraph noting that '... in an increasingly interdependent world, the economic fortunes and political stability of both developed and developing countries are more and more intertwined',[234] with the United States '[a]ware that there should be efforts at the international level, both to promote and to protect human rights and to establish a new international economic order'.[235]

Consistent with human rights instruments generally, there is an assumption that the primary responsibility for the realization of the right to development lies with the state acting domestically.[236] However, integral to the logic of this right, is the recognition that its implementation domestically may be undermined by global structural disadvantage that developing countries face in their dual role as both claimants and duty-bearers of the right to development. Even developed states that today can be cautious about endorsing international aspects of the right to development:[237] proposed language during the final stages of the drafting of the DRD suggesting that '[t]he right to development as a human right involves

---

[231] *Report of the Working Group of Governmental Experts on the Right to Development* (4th session, 9 December 1982) UN Doc E/CN4/1983/11. See also, A Sengupta, 'On the Theory and Practice of the Right to Development' 24 *HRQ* 4 (2002) 837, at 849–50; and, Brownlie, 'The Human Right to Development', 1, at 8.

[232] Millennium Declaration, Pt I Values and Principles, art 6. Shared responsibility.

[233] *Report of the Working Group of Governmental Experts on the Right to Development* (4th session, 9 December 1982) UN Doc E/CN4/1983/11 annex IV, Compilation of Proposals Made by the Experts, Pt I, Section II, art 6; see similarly, art 7.

[234] *Report of the Working Group of Governmental Experts on the Right to Development* (8th session, 24 January 1985) UN Doc E/CN4/1985/11 annex VII, Proposal by Senegal, 1 October 1984, at 4.

[235] Ibid, Proposal by the USA, 3 October 1984 at 4.

[236] DRD, preambular para 15: *'Recognizing* that the creation of conditions favourable to the development of peoples and individuals is the primary responsibility of their States'.

[237] See Ch 2.

an international order which is properly attuned to the encouragement of every nation's full and active participation ...'.[238] The right to development is, by its very nature, structural in its approach to human rights, locating the principle obstacle to the realization of economic, social and cultural rights of people in developing countries (the rights foreseen as requiring international cooperation) to an inequitable global order.[239] This obstacle persists to date, and in an era of unparalleled economic interdependence herein lies the right to development's greatest potential for furthering the realization of human rights, as well as its most conceptually challenging juridical contribution.

In their external dimension collective rights belonging to society as a whole (such as the right to development) are largely exercised by the state on behalf of the people.[240] While the international legal system has yet to allow for the full participation of all international actors in the processes that affect them,[241] or provide for affected parties to hold to account those who make and implement the policies,[242] the right to development articulated and endorsed as a human right, as in the case of all human rights, implies the requirement of a system of corresponding responsibility. It is indeed this binary relation which distinguishes human rights from the general valuing of freedom that exists without a correlated obligation to help bring about that freedom.[243]

In the case of the right to development whereby the duty-bearers include the states of the international community, the focus is on those states that are to cooperate in order to provide the 'essential complement' to the efforts of developing countries.[244] That the parameters of this duty of international cooperation

---

[238] *Report of the Working Group of Governmental Experts on the Right to Development* (8th session, 24 January 1985) UN Doc E/CN4/1985/11 annex III, Draft Declaration on the Right to Development, submitted by France and the Netherlands, at 2.

[239] On this point, see also the coverage on the right to development and the international order in, F Ouguergouz, *The African Charter on Human and Peoples' Rights: A Comprehensive Agenda for Human Dignity and Sustainable Democracy in Africa* (Martinus Nijhoff, 2003) 308–16.

[240] See, Donnelly, 'In Search of the Unicorn', 473, at 498–9.

[241] On the 'powerful normative messages' conveyed by the right to development including participation, and its 'concrete agenda for transformation of practice and structure' of the WTO, see, Howse, *Mainstreaming the Right to Development*. See further, Ch 3.

[242] See, Grossman and Bradlow, 'Are we Being Propelled', 1, at 22–5. See also, *Analytical Study of the High Commissioner for Human Rights on the Fundamental Principle of Participation and its Application in the Context of Globalization*, UN Doc E/CN4/2005/41. The World Bank's Inspection Panel is an accountability mechanism that allows for claims to be filed by people directly affected or potentially affected by a violation of the World Bank's policies and procedures. While innovative insofar as it is the first independent complaints mechanism to assist in compliance with an IGO's operational procedures, it falls short of providing for a system of human rights accountability in a number of areas, including, being limited to the consideration of breaches of the Bank's own policies, and excluding alleged violations of international human rights standards.

[243] A Sen, 'Consequential Evaluation and Practical Reason' 27 *The Journal of Philosophy* (2000) 477; Marks, *The Human Rights Framework for Development*, 18–20; A Sengupta, *First Report of the Independent Expert on the Right to Development* (General Assembly, 55th session, 2000) UN Doc A/55/306, para 8; and A Sengupta, *Fourth Report of the Independent Expert on the Right to Development*, UN Doc E/CN4/2002/WG18/2, paras 15, 31, 35.

[244] DRD, art 4(2).

are only beginning to be more clearly delineated[245] does not determine the *status* of the right, but rather demands a rigorous consideration, and application, of the nature of corresponding duties. 'Imperfect obligations' of the international community of states do not easily lend themselves to specifying exact duties of particular agents, that is, rights for which the right-duty correspondence is not clear-cut, does not determine their status as rights. As Sen points out: 'Certainly, a perfect obligation [an obligation that entails specified duties of particular agents] would help a great deal toward the realization of rights, but why cannot there be unrealized rights, even rights that are hard to realize?'.[246] We cannot conclude from the fact that some countries cannot ensure that their people can be fed or guarantee food security, that those people have no right to food.[247] While we consider the scope of state obligations generally under a reoriented international law made relevant to the configurations of world poverty, we need to recognize that having imperfect obligations are not the same as having no obligations at all.

The ideas provided for in the right to development are located on the threshold of where international law is headed in order to be made relevant to the form, and exercise, of state power today.[248] The duties of the international community of states are triggered on the basis of grounds that cannot be limited to the traditional human rights correlation between a state and the people within its territory; interdependence has resulted in the blurring of the boundaries between the domestic and the international, including when it comes to the nature of duties. Decisions taken at the highest level are felt down at the smallest unit. The rich states hold in their hands the food that would fill the stomachs of the 'global poor', and the roofs that would shelter them. International law for the protection and promotion of human rights, if it is to continue to be relevant, must adapt to regulate effectively this very twenty-first century relationship.

Consistent with the International Covenant on Economic, Social and Cultural Rights which preceded it, and followed by the entry into force of the Convention on the Rights of the Child (CRC) a few years later, the Declaration on the Right to Development likewise entrenches the notion that states are duty-bearers not only at the national level, but at the international level as well. But the Declaration perhaps takes the scope of duties a step further in seeking to provide a juridical framework for oft-repeated claims against the public international order, for the failure of our international economic arrangements to allow for an environment

---

[245] However, see further chs 2 and 5.

[246] Sen, 'Consequential Evaluation and Practical Reason', 477, at 496. On imperfect obligations and the right to development see, A Sengupta, *Second Report of the Independent Expert on the Right to Development*, UN Doc. E/CN4/2000/WG18/CRP1, paras 8–9.

[247] A Sen, 'Law and Human Rights', The Paul Sieghart Memorial Lecture, British Institute of Human Rights, London, 6 July 2005. Unpublished at the time of publication of this book.

[248] The deficiencies of the present international legal regime to regulate effectively and fairly is by no means limited to the coverage provided in this book. Grossman and Bradlow, for example, address the need for international law to recognize and incorporate into its jurisdiction all international (private) actors. See, Grossman and Bradlow, 'Are we Being Propelled', 1.

in which the human rights of all people can be met.[249] Treaty-bodies dealing with economic, social and cultural rights have indicated that the treaties they oversee must also evolve to meet this reality.

1.4.2 The position of treaty-bodies

The idea that the sovereign equality of states precludes them from having varied human rights obligations has no merit today, if it ever did.[250] While the level of national wealth does not modify the nature of a state's domestic obligations to realize progressively economic, social and cultural rights under the Covenant,[251] at the international level, the differential in power and influence among states, suggests there can be no legitimate expectation that they will be subject to the same obligations.

A requirement for each state party to take steps through 'international assistance and cooperation' was foreseen as a necessary element in the realization of Covenant rights, as several articles reflect, most notably Article 2(1) which pertains to the rights enumerated in the Covenant.[252] The Convention on the Rights of the Child provides for a similar obligation in relation to the economic, social and cultural rights found among its provisions,[253] and articulates

---

[249] See, ME Salomon, 'International Human Rights Obligations in Context: Structural Obstacles and the Demands of Global Justice' in B-A Andreassen and SP Marks (eds), *Development as a Human Right: Legal, Political and Economic Dimensions* (Harvard School of Public Health-Harvard University Press, 2006) 96.

[250] That all states are not to the same extent subject to rights and obligations 'is proven by the privileged status of the permanent members of the Security Council as laid down in the Charter': Randelzhofer, 'Chapter I: Purposes and Principles, Article 2', 64, at 65. The traditional view of development and 'international development law' has opponents of the NIEO maintain that, at least from a legal perspective, all states are equal and their rights and duties thus do not vary according to their level of development. See, DD Bradlow: 'Development Decision-Making and the Content of International Development Law' 27 *BCInt'l & CompLRev* 2 (2004) 195, at 203–7. On differentiated responsibilities in the context of international cooperation, see Ch 5.

[251] Steps towards progressively realizing economic, social and cultural rights are to be taken within a 'reasonably short time' and should be 'deliberate, concrete and targeted' toward fulfilling the rights (CESCR, General Comment no 3 on Art 2(1) (The Nature of States Parties' Obligations), (5th session, 1990) UN Doc E/1991/23 annex III, para 2). The duty in question obliges all state parties to the ICESCR, regardless of their level of national wealth, to move towards the realization of the Covenant rights. See generally paras 9 and 10.

[252] ICESCR, art 2(1): 'Each State Party to the present Covenant undertakes to take steps, individually and through international assistance and co-operation, especially economic and technical, to the maximum of its available resources, with a view to achieving progressively the full realization of the rights recognized in the present Covenant by all appropriate means, including particularly the adoption of legislative measures.' ICESCR, on the right of everyone to an adequate standard of living, including adequate food, clothing and housing, and to the continuous improvement of living conditions, reaffirms 'the essential importance of international cooperation in ensuring the realization of this right (art 11(1)). Art 11(2) imposes an obligation on states parties to take measures 'individually and through international cooperation regarding the fundamental right to be free from hunger'. See also procedural arts 22 and 23.

[253] CRC, art 4: 'States Parties shall undertake all appropriate legislative, administrative, and other measures for the implementation of the rights recognized in the present Convention. With

a particular 'need of developing countries' for international cooperation in achieving progressively the full realization of certain rights in the Convention.[254] Yet unlike the Declaration on the Right to Development, these international human rights treaties that provide for international obligations based on cooperation, are geared towards violations against individuals (and groups),[255] and do not have as their underlying logic the remedying of global structural disadvantage.

Today however, the Committee on Economic, Social and Cultural Rights (CESCR) emphasizes the structural deficiencies of the international order, and has begun to consider how states parties, and indeed states *generally*, should address them. The Committee has begun to interpret the obligation of international assistance and cooperation in light of contemporary human rights violations which are linked—be it by omission or commission—to this order. We see a similar trend in the work of the Committee on the Rights of the Child exemplified by its position in 2003 that the 'implementation of the Convention [on the Rights of the Child] is a cooperative exercise for the states of the world.'[256] Such a reference to the 'states of the world' is all the more significant for a claim to a collective global obligation since all but two states have ratified the CRC.

The CESCR recognizes that 'formidable structural . . . obstacles resulting from international . . . factors beyond the control of [developing] states impede the realization of the right to health'[257] with '. . . the existing gross inequality in the health status of people, particularly between developed and developing countries . . . [as] unacceptable and therefore *a common concern to all countries*'.[258] An interpretation as to the collective nature of obligations is also seen in the Committee's reference to the Member States of international financial institutions, notably the World Bank, International Monetary Fund and regional development banks,[259] and to the international financial institutions themselves and their ability to have an impact on the right to health through their lending policies, credit agreements and structural adjustment programmes.[260] Similar references are made with

regard to economic, social and cultural rights, States Parties shall undertake such measures to the maximum extent of their available resources and, where needed, within the framework of international co-operation'.

[254] CRC, preambular para 12, arts 23(4), 24(4), 28(3).

[255] 'Regardless of whether groups as such can seek remedies as distinct holders of rights, States parties are bound by both the collective and individual dimensions of art 12. Collective rights are critical in the field of health; modern public health policy relies heavily on prevention and promotion which are approaches directed primarily to groups.' CESCR, General Comment no 14, The Right to the Highest Attainable Standard of Health (art 12), (22nd session, 2000) UN Doc E/C12/2000/4 fn 30.

[256] CRC, General Comment no 5, General Measures of Implementation of the Convention on the Rights of the Child (arts 4, 42 and 44, para 6), (34th session, 2003) UN Doc CRC/GC/2003/5, para 60.

[257] CESCR, General Comment no 14, The Right Health, para 5.

[258] Ibid, para 38 (emphasis added).

[259] Ibid, para 39.

[260] Ibid, para 64.

regard to the right to food[261] and the right to water.[262] The Committee on the Rights of the Child, in its general comment on the Implementation of the CRC, refers to the need for the activities of the World Trade Organization in relation to international cooperation and economic development, to promote the full implementation of the Convention.[263]

In 1998, when the CESCR discussed the issue of globalization in the context of realizing economic, social and cultural rights, it emphasized that 'international organizations, as well as the Governments that have created and manage them, have a strong and continuous responsibility ... .'[264] The Committee further directed its calls to the World Bank and IMF to give explicit recognition to economic, social and cultural rights, and to the World Trade Organization to devise methods that would facilitate a more systematic consideration of the impact upon human rights of particular trade and investment policies.[265] In its *Statement to the Third Ministerial Conference of the World Trade Organization* in 1999, the Committee considered trade liberalization as a means of contributing to human well-being (defined legally through international human rights standards), and not as an end in itself.[266] In 2001, the Committee reflected the view that actors other than states, including international organizations, 'carry obligations, which must be subject to scrutiny'. Then, departing quite considerably from a traditional understanding as to the duty-bearers in international law, it went on to remark that '... all actors [must be] held to account for their obligations under international human rights law'.[267]

In 2002, the CESCR issued a joint statement with Special Rapporteurs, mandated by the UN Commission on Human Rights, on *The Millennium Development Goals and Economic, Social and Cultural Rights*, in which it emphasized the importance and added-value of integrating human rights into the Millennium Development Goals (MDGs),[268] a set of goals, targets and indicators that reflect a globally endorsed strategy for poverty reduction and sustainable

---

[261] CESCR, General Comment no 12, The Right to Adequate Food (art 11), (20th session, 1999) UN Doc E/C12/1999/5 para 41.

[262] CESCR, General Comment no 15, The Right to Water (arts 11 and 12), (29th session, 2002) UN Doc E/C12/2002/11, para 60.

[263] CRC, General Comment no 5, General Measures of Implementation, para 64.

[264] CESCR, Decision on Globalization, para 5.

[265] Ibid, para 7.

[266] CESCR, Statement to the Third Ministerial Conference, para 6. Back in 1990, the Committee emphasized the importance of having international agencies contribute '... not only to economic growth or other broadly defined objectives, but also to enhanced enjoyment of human rights'. CESCR, General Comment no 2, International Technical Assistance Measures (art 22), (4th session, 1990) UN Doc E/1990/23, annex III at 86, para 6.

[267] CESCR, Statement on Human Rights and Intellectual Property (27th session, 2001) UN Doc E/C12/2001/15, at para 10 (Accountability).

[268] *The Millennium Development Goals and Economic, Social and Cultural Rights*, A Joint Statement by the UN Committee on Economic, Social and Cultural Rights and the UN Commission on Human Rights' Special Rapporteurs on Economic, Social and Cultural Rights, 29 November 2002, para 9.

human development. Just as for the CESCR, the Committee on the Rights of the Child also interprets international cooperation to include meeting the internationally agreed targets for official development assistance of 0.7 per cent of gross national income which form the basis of the MDGs.[269] The Committee on the Rights of the Child reads the Millennium Declaration 'pledge' to cooperate internationally in the elimination of poverty with the universally applicable 'pledge' in Article 56 of the UN Charter 'to take joint and separate action in cooperation with the Organization' to achieve purposes defined at Charter Article 55 to which international economic and social cooperation will be directed.[270]

The CESCR's concern with global inequality can also be found in the first paragraph of its general comment on the right to water, where it notes that 'the Committee has been confronted continually with the widespread denial of the right to water in developing countries. Over one billion persons lack access to a basic water supply, while several billion do not have access to adequate sanitation ... the continuing contamination, depletion and unequal distribution of water is exacerbating existing poverty....'.[271] The international responsibilities of developed states, remarks the CESCR, are engaged as a result of 'the structural obstacles confronting developing countries' that inhibit them from providing sustainable anti-poverty strategies; effective poverty reduction strategies by developing states 'lie beyond their control in the contemporary international order.'[272] 'In the Committee's view, it is imperative that measures be urgently taken to remove these global structural obstacles, such as, unsustainable foreign debt and ... the absence of an equitable multilateral trade, investment and financial system'.[273] The centrality of the role of the international community in fulfilling human rights today is reinforced by the Committee's explicit reference in this regard to both Article 28 of the UDHR, which refers to the entitlement of all to a just social and international order in which human rights can be realized,[274] and to the Declaration on the Right to Development, Article 3(3), which provides that 'States have the duty to cooperate with each other in ensuring development and eliminating obstacles to development ...'.[275]

These examples suggest an emerging trend in the jurisprudential work of the Committee on Economic, Social and Cultural Rights, and of the Committee

---

[269] CRC, General Comment no 5, General Measures of Implementation, para 61. The CRC has also remarked on the obligation to move quickly in meeting the goal. CRC, Concluding Observations: Germany (35th session, 2004) UN Doc CRC/C/15/Add226 (2004), para 21.

[270] CRC, General Comment no 5, General Measures of Implementation, para 60. These include higher standards of living, full employment, economic and social progress and development, solutions of international economic and related problems, and respect for and observance of human rights. See further, Ch 2.

[271] CESCR, General Comment no 15, The Right to Water, para 1.

[272] CESCR, Statement on Poverty, para 21.

[273] CESCR, Statement on Human Rights and Intellectual Property, para 21.

[274] CESCR, Statement on Poverty, para 21; similarly see, CESCR, Statement on Human Rights and Intellectual Property, para 14.

[275] CESCR, Statement on Human Rights and Intellectual Property, para 21 and fn 17.

on the Rights of the Child, towards an appreciation of the substantial influence on the fulfilment of human rights posed by the external environment, and the decisions taken under the auspices of the lead states and the institutions they direct. The positions of the Committees underscore the expectation that human rights will be integral to international decision-making where those decisions may impact on them, and whether explicit or implied, that they give rise to corresponding collective international obligations.

1.5 Conclusion

International law has undergone profound changes in the past century matched by developments in international human rights law. Both have been informed by developments in the world outside. The shift is noticeable in the appreciation that while international law still preserves sovereignty, attention is on the people's sovereignty rather than the sovereign's sovereignty.[276]

The concept of sovereignty is a relative one, and while reaffirmed in the UN Charter, the principle has been eroded by the assumption of new obligations—by universal human rights standards, and by the principle of international cooperation which is necessary for their realization. Under the Charter sovereignty is relinquished for a system of cooperation in which state sovereignty is meant to be fully compatible with the international duties and obligations under a community legal order.[277]

The recognition that a balance must now be struck between these two opposing structures—that of state sovereignty and that of the duty to cooperate—in the words of Tomuschat, 'denotes an important shift in the general orientation of the international legal order'.[278] While sovereign equality prioritizes the interests of the individual state, a system of international cooperation prioritizes the general interests and values of the international community.[279] This new legal

---

[276] Reisman, 'Sovereignty and Human Rights', 866, at 869.

[277] While it is an accepted premise that state sovereignty today must be compatible with human rights obligations, some maintain that the language of sovereignty is a hindrance altogether. Reisman, for example, remarked that 'it is curious that a discussion about the design and construction of a new world order should rely on a term drafted centuries ago in a different context and for purposes quite different from ours [designing an international system which can best achieve the goals expressed in the United Nations and other authoritative fora]': W M Reisman, 'Sovereignty, Interdependence and Independence', Interventions at Plenary Session, in Grahl-Madsen and Toman (eds), *The Spirit of Uppsala*, 351, at 354.

[278] Tomuschat, 'International Law: Ensuring the Survival of Mankind', 23, at 262.

[279] Koskenniemi deduces in fact, that: 'Neither community nor autonomy can be exclusive goals. To think of community as the ultimate goal seems utopian: as there is no agreement on the character of a desirable community, attempts to impose it seem like imperialism in disguise. To think of autonomy as the normative aim seems apologist: it strengthens the absolutist claims of national power-elites and supports their pursuits at international dominance. ... An acceptable world order seems to be one which can construct community without falling into totalitarianism and which provides for autonomy without degenerating into furthering egoism': M Koskenniemi,

framework has replaced the primary rule of state sovereignty with a rule requiring the accommodation of the promotion of the welfare of humankind.[280]

The international system premised on co-existence has evolved as the need for cooperation has intensified. As Wolfgang Friedmann explained in his renowned work *The Changing Structure of International Law*, we have shifted along the continuum from an outdated international law of coexistence of the seventeenth and eighteenth centuries, where the primary objective of international law was to impose passive obligations of abstention on sovereign states, to the international law of cooperation of the twentieth and twenty-first centuries, which provides the modalities for their cooperation, in the form of positive obligations, to realize common values and achieve common ends.[281]

This new legal order was entrenched in the UN Charter, and while inspired by the League of Nations' blueprint, is qualitatively distinct from that which had gone before it. The Charter established the structure for a legal community of states governed by the rule of law, pursuant to and in pursuit of common interests and universal values, the furtherance of which was recognized as only being possible through international cooperation. The prioritization of the interests and values of the international community distinguishes it from the individual states that comprise it, and as a community, mandate it to secure the promotion and management of a global order in which social justice can prevail.

The *raison d'être* of this philosophy of cooperation was rooted in the concept of human dignity, and the approach was informed by an appreciation that creating better conditions of life for every human being would diminish the risks of political tensions and armed conflict.[282] Today, we have moved beyond the need merely to diminish global risks (e.g. security, climate change), towards the essential requirement to refine the entire system that manages our economic, social and political interdependence. It is this interdependence which currently enriches so few and deprives so many, in which costs and burdens are unequally distributed, and in which states acting separately and collectively can impact so profoundly on the ability of people half-way across the globe to secure their most basic rights.

To what degree the existing system of economic globalization contributes to the greater good, or has the potential to do so, does not challenge the empirical fact that globalization—a process that is characterized by the development of interdependencies among states—has institutionally embedded a system that tends to favour the rich and powerful states. The World Bank acknowledges that while most external policy advice given to poor countries over the last several decades—including by the Bank—has emphasized the advantages of

---

From Apology to Utopia: The Structure of International Legal Argumentation (Finnish Lawyer's Publishing Company, 1989) 424.

[280] Tomuschat, 'International Law: Ensuring the Survival of Mankind', 23, at 263.

[281] See, Friedmann, *The Changing Structure of International Law*, Ch 6.

[282] Tomuschat, 'International Law: Ensuring the Survival of Mankind', 23, at 61.

participating in the global economy, the 'global markets are far from equitable, and the rules governing their functioning have a disproportionately negative effect on developing countries'.[283] This is set against unpalatable figures on world poverty that reflect sharp and enduring divisions between North and South.[284]

This state of affairs prevails despite the existence of an international community of states informed by a law of cooperation meant to guide the achievement of what the individual members of that community cannot do, or do well, individually. And it is despite the recognition by the international community of their function to protect the common interests and values of the international community as a whole, exemplified in its professed resolve to 'take all measures within its power to secure a democratic and equitable international order ... [which] fosters the full realization of human rights for all ... [based on] [t]he right to an international economic order, on equal participation in the decision-making process, interdependence, mutual interest, solidarity and cooperation among all States'.[285]

The sanctioning of the right to development by the international community of states has placed human rights clearly within the ambit of 'the international law of cooperation'. While the treaties that address economic, social and cultural rights are being interpreted to include requirements of international cooperation also to address structural obstacles to the realization of human rights, the right to development was conceived with that very objective in mind. For a human rights instrument, the Declaration on the Right to Development is unconventional in its language, yet it is unequivocal in its message. It sets out a duty of international cooperation to remove structural obstacles to development, and to realize the human rights that the directors of the institutional order so effectively deny the poor. The Declaration refocuses the international law of human rights, seeking to make it relevant to twenty-first century violations.

The international community has moved passed the 'the hostile environment of classical international law'[286] and, in the past 60 years, has begun to elaborate an

---

[283] World Bank, *World Development Report 2006: Equity and Development*, 16.

[284] The UNDP concludes in its most recent *Human Development Report* that 'costs and benefits have been unevenly distributed across and within countries, perpetuating a pattern of globalization that builds prosperity for some amid mass poverty and deepening inequality for others': UNDP, *Human Development Report 2005: International Cooperation at a Crossroads*, Ch 4, at 113. The aggregate decline in international inequality, as the World Bank points out, 'is largely due to the fast growth in China and South Asia': World Bank, *World Development Report 2006: Equity and Development*, 68.

[285] CHR res 2003/63, (59th session, 2003), paras 2 and 4(e) on the Promotion of a democratic and equitable international order, has drawn from art 3(3) of the Declaration on the Right of Development which states: 'States have the duty to cooperate with each other in ensuring development and eliminating obstacles to development. States should realize their rights and fulfil their duties in such a manner as to promote a new international economic order based on sovereign equality, interdependence, mutual interest and co-operation among all States, as well as to encourage the observance and realization of human rights'.

[286] Dimitrijevic, 'A Natural or Moral Basis for International Law' as cited by Lillich, 'Sovereignty and Humanity', 406, at 407.

international legal framework premised on an appreciation that interdependence is a condition that affects each state's independence.[287] Without doubt, the accelerated pace of global developments, and the international legal response to them, have added complexity to both the theory and practice of international law in the defence of human rights. But as Reisman reminds us:

Because human rights considerations introduce so many more variables into the determination of lawfulness, an even heavier burden of deliberation devolves upon international lawyers in assessing the lawfulness of actions. Matters becomes more complex and uncertain than they were in an international legal system that was composed of a few binary rules applied to a checkerboard of monarchical states and, most particularly, that lacked an international code of human rights ... No one is entitled to complain that things are getting too complicated. If complexity of decision is the price for increased human dignity on the planet, it is worth it ... .[288]

Human rights were included in the Charter of the United Nations in 1945 as part of the international legal framework designed to advance a just international order. At present, economic globalization is part of the global system, the priorities of which are relegating human rights to the sidelines. Global justice—reflected in an arrangement integrating equity, fairness, and redress underpinned by an international legal regime for the protection and promotion of human rights has a claim on this order. The quest for global justice in international law is a search for legal obligations that are anchored in global institutional arrangements that are fair to impoverished nations and peoples. As Ramphal remarks: 'We are now at the stage where we have an international community, and we need the rule of law there as badly as we do at home'.[289] It is to the establishment and content of the critical obligation of international cooperation for human rights under law that we will now turn.

---

[287] Saxena, 'Sovereignty, Independence and Interdependence of Nations', 289, at 296.
[288] Reisman, 'Sovereignty and Human Rights', 866, at 876.
[289] Ramphal, Panellist, 'Lawless World: The US, Britain and the Making and Breaking of Global Rules'.

2

Sources and Content of an International Responsibility to Cooperate for Human Rights

2.1 Introduction

This chapter addresses the sources of cooperation for economic, social and cultural rights in international law, and explores the contemporary content of this obligation. Drawing on a broad range of hard and soft law instruments, the centrality of international cooperation for addressing the deprivations of poverty is reaffirmed legally, and given shape operationally. The complementary principle of a shared responsibility for human rights, recently pronounced by the international community, strengthens this legal obligation to cooperate internationally.

Cooperative engagement for finding solutions to economic and social problems, and in promoting human rights was foreseen in the United Nations Charter (UN Charter), and has been consistently advanced in subsequent articulations. Notably, the Declaration on the Right to Development (DRD) sets out that effective international cooperation is essential to providing developing countries with international conditions, and appropriate means and facilities, to foster their comprehensive development.[1] The Declaration's normative force has been buttressed through frequent reaffirmations in UN resolutions and declarations, and via the establishment of machinery to advance its implementation.

Today, international cooperation for the protection and promotion of human rights is a precondition for any effective action on world poverty. International cooperation both precludes obstructive international endeavours that would undermine the realization of economic, social and cultural rights, and requires proactive measures by states acting both individually and collectively. Frequent declarations by the UN General Assembly addressing human rights and related concerns in the context of economic globalization, and a purposive interpretation of international cooperation in this regard, suggest that the legal duty is not confined to the human rights-based policies and programs of multilateral

---

[1] DRD, arts 2(3), 3(1), 3(2), 3(3), 4(1), 4(2), 5, 6(1), 7, 10.

and bilateral agencies, but also to the very structures of the international political economy as a whole.[2] Considering the content of the human rights obligation of international cooperation in the context of such structural impediments,
serves to reveal a range of fundamental requirements necessary to the reform of
those aspects of the international economic order that undermine the ability of so
many people to exercise their human rights.

Needless to say, international cooperation is not the exclusive privilege of the
international legal regime for human rights. It was central to the post war establishment of economic and financial organizations that were generally created to
fulfil the vision of the UN Charter in solving social and humanitarian problems.
But we are yet to see whether these various areas of international activity can
better complement each other. And it remains to be established to what degree
external human rights obligations will be honoured when states are faced with
seemingly conflicting international legal commitments. What is clear though,
is that compliance with international human rights obligations in the pursuit
by states of cooperation in other areas, is increasingly emphasized as a legal
responsibility.

2.2 The Sources of Cooperation for Human Rights in International Law

Prior to 1945, international law was, for the most part, a system of law governing
relations between states. While there were certain significant developments in
the protection of the rights of people, the classical doctrine of state sovereignty,
which held that a state's treatment of its own nationals is a matter exclusively
within its own domestic jurisdiction, remained paramount. Early forms of international standard-setting in the area of human rights—the prohibition of slavery,
the protection of victims of war and national minorities, 'were linked to implementation by States; only sovereign States were recognized as the bearers of rights
and duties'.[3]

While concern for certain individual human beings were reflected in the programmes under the League of Nations, it only addressed human rights from an
ad hoc perspective.[4] The language of human rights was not provided for in the
Covenant of the League of Nations which preceded the UN Charter, and only

[2] B-A Andreassen and SP Marks, 'Conclusions', in B-A Andreassen and SP Marks (eds),
Development as a Human Right: Legal, Political and Economic Dimensions (Harvard School of
Public Health—Harvard University Press, 2006) 304, at 307.

[3] E Riedel, 'Chapter IX: International Economic and Social Co-operation, Article 55(c)', in
B Simma (ed), *The Charter of the United Nations: A Commentary* (2nd edn, Oxford University Press,
2002) Vol II, 917, at 919; PR Ghandhi, 'The Universal Declaration of Human Rights at Fifty Years:
Its Origins, Significance and Impact' 41 *GYIL* (1998) 207, at 220.

[4] See, Ghandhi, 'The Universal Declaration', 207, at 214.

two articles within the Covenant made reference to what were later to be recognized as human rights under the Charter.[5] The League's approach was aimed at protecting specific categories of people, and to these ends it set up several Advisory Committees (namely on The Traffic in Women and Children and on the Traffic in Opium and other Dangerous Drugs), as well as a refugee organization in 1921. These bodies were established because of their evident cross-border element or their relevance to the system of mandated territories which necessitated a response among those states affected, and not due to an appreciation that human rights should be universally applicable. The predecessor to the United Nations did, however, recognize the need for international cooperation and transnational regulation in a select number of areas where regulation could not be meaningfully undertaken by any one state.

The internationalization of human rights, including cooperation as essential to its global advance, began in the period immediately following World War Two when the United Nations came into being. The UN Charter elevated the human rights ideal by bringing it into the international arena, giving it prominence, and declaring it both an interest, and the basis for obligations, of the entire international community. In the words of Lauterpacht, the Charter provided a 'landmark in the recognition of the status of the individual and his protection by international society'.[6]

The Charter of the United Nations was adopted at San Francisco on 26 June 1945, and was the first multilateral treaty to articulate the promotion of respect for, and observance of, human rights as an international standard. On 24 October 1945, when the Charter came into force, a new era in which an internationally recognized need for a unified front of states against future tyrannies, and the development of an international legal regime for the protection of human rights, came with it. And unlike its predecessor The League of Nations, the United Nations aspired to universal membership. Over time it has achieved this objective.[7]

Emphasizing the importance of social justice and human rights, the Charter indicates the centrality of these elements to the foundation of a stable

---

[5] The Covenant of the League of Nations, Art 22(5) referred to 'freedom of conscience and religion', and with regard to 'mandated territories' to 'the prohibition of abuses such as the slave trade'. Art 23 referred, inter alia, to (a) 'fair and humane conditions of labour for men, women and children both in their own countries and in all countries to which their commercial and industrial relations extend, ...'; (b) 'undertake to secure just treatment of the native inhabitants of territories under their control'; and, (c) 'will entrust the League with the general supervision of the execution of agreements with regard to the traffic in women and children ...': 225 Consolidated Treaty Series 195.

[6] H Lauterpacht, *Human Rights, the Charter of the United Nations, and the International Bill of Rights Report* (1948), as cited by Riedel, 'Chapter IX: International Economic and Social Co-operation', 917, at 919.

[7] Fifty-one states comprised the original members of the UN. At 28 June 2006, there were 192 UN Member States, the most recent to join being East Timor (2002), Switzerland (2002), and Montenegro (2006). <http://www.un.org/Overview/growth.htm>.

international order. The realization of these common goals is linked to cooperation among states, and it is this tenet that constitutes the essence of the treaty. Among the purposes of the UN as Article 1(2) proclaims is: 'To develop friendly relations among nations based on respect for the principle of equal rights and self-determination of peoples'. This is followed by Article 1(3) which states that a main purpose of the United Nations is:

To achieve international co-operation in solving international problems of an economic, social, cultural, or humanitarian character, and in promoting and encouraging respect for human rights and for fundamental freedoms for all without distinction as to race, sex, language, or religion;[8]

Article 55, located in Chapter IX of the Charter, which addresses International Economic and Social Cooperation, was regarded by the drafters of the Charter as 'the provision that would implement Article 1, stressing the necessity of UN action'.[9] It states that:

With a view to the creation of conditions of stability and well-being which are necessary for peaceful and friendly relations among nations based on respect for the principle of equal rights and self-determination of peoples, The United Nations shall promote:

(a) higher standards of living, full employment, and conditions of economic and social progress and development;

(b) solutions of international economic, social, health, and related problems; and international cultural and educational co-operation; and

(c) universal respect for, and observance of, human rights and fundamental freedoms for all without distinction as to race, sex, language, or religion.

The interpretation by the UN of Articles 55(a) and 55(b) has been, as Wolfrum points out, '. . . to concentrate mainly on the economic and social development of developing countries, with the concept of "development" in Article 55(a) having become a keyword in the practice of the UN. It is the basis of all the measures taken by the UN for the establishment of a "new international economic order"'.[10] And, while noting certain opposing scholarly views, Riedel concludes in his commentary to Article 55(c), that 'there can be no doubt that responsibility exists for any substantial infringement of the provisions, and that Articles 55 and

---

[8] The other purposes include: 'To maintain international peace and security, and to that end: to take effective collective measures for the prevention and removal of threats to the peace, and for the suppression of acts of aggression or other breaches of the peace, and to bring about by peaceful means, and in conformity with the principles of justice and international law, adjustment or settlement of international disputes or situations which might lead to a breach of the peace' (art 1(1)), and, 'To be a centre for harmonizing the actions of nations in the attainment of these common ends' (art 1(4)).

[9] R Wolfrum, 'Chapter IX: International Economic and Social Co-operation, Article 55(a) and 55(b)', in Simma (ed), *The Charter of the United Nations: A Commentary*, Vol II, 897, at 898.

[10] Ibid, 897, at 901.

56 impose legal obligations on members States singly or jointly to stand up for respecting human rights'.[11]

These provisions provide the general source of human rights in international law, and are tied to a solemn pledge to uphold them through cooperation by all those who have ratified the Charter. Article 56 thus provides that:

All Members pledge themselves to take joint and separate action in co-operation with the Organization for the achievement of the purposes set forth in Article 55.

Article 56 creates a clear legal obligation requiring states to cooperate constructively with the UN,[12] and precludes them from adopting policies that are obstructive of those ends.[13] The duty of the international community to cooperate in realizing the right to development as articulated in the 1986 Declaration was built upon Articles 56 and 57 of the Charter of the United Nations.[14] The adoption of the Charter reflects the beginning of an international movement in which formal and authoritative recognition is given to the need for cooperative engagement in finding solutions to socio-economic underdevelopment, and in promoting respect for and observance of human rights. The principles of equality and self-determination among states provided their motivation, and their achievement is recognized as instrumental to international peace.

Hersch Lauterpacht has ardently supported the view that Article 55 implies a 'mandatory obligation'[15] in stating that the UN 'shall promote respect for, and observance of, human rights and fundamental freedoms'; with Article 56 expressing a distinct 'element of a legal duty in the undertaking'.[16] Unlike Henkin, who in 1965 depicted the Charter provisions on human rights as 'hortatory phrases',[17] Lauterpacht warned against 'facile generalizations',[18] which invited the flawed

---

[11] Riedel, 'Chapter IX: International Economic and Social Co-operation', 917, at 922 (footnotes removed).

[12] Note also, art 2(2): 'All Members, in order to ensure to all of them the rights and benefits resulting from membership, shall fulfill in good faith the obligations assumed by them in accordance with the present Charter'.

[13] Wolfrum, 'Chapter IX: International Economic and Social Co-operation', 897, at 942.

[14] A Sengupta, *Report of the Independent Expert on the Right to Development*, UN Doc A/55/306 (2000), para 11. Art 57 requires that specialized agencies with international responsibilities in the economic, social, cultural, educational, health, and related fields be brought into a relationship with the UN.

[15] H Lauterpacht, *International Law and Human Rights* (Stevens & Sons, 1950) Ch 9, at 148.

[16] Ibid.

[17] L Henkin, 'The United Nations and Human Rights' *International Organization* 19 (1965) 504, at 510: 'Political realities and national reluctances are protected by lack of definiteness and definition [in the Charter], by hortatory phrases instead of commitment ...'. See also, M Hudson, 'Integrity of International Instruments' 42 *AJIL* (1948) 105; and L Henkin, *The Age of Rights* (Columbia University Press, 1990) 19, in which he suggests that: '[i]t continues to be debated whether a violation of human rights by a member of the United Nations is a violation of the Charter pledge'. The question as to whether the UN Charter's human rights provisions create binding obligations upon Member States has divided scholars, particularly in the years following its inception.

[18] Lauterpacht, *International Law and Human Rights*, Ch 9, at 147.

conclusion that the human rights provisions were mere declarations of principle, and supported the position that:

> the provisions of the Charter on the subject figure prominently in the statement of the Purposes of the United Nations. Members of the United Nations are under a legal obligation to act in accordance with these Purposes. It is their legal duty to respect and observe fundamental human rights and freedoms ... They were adopted, with deliberation and after prolonged discussion before and during the San Francisco Conference, as part of the philosophy of the new international system ... Nothing but the most the explicit terms of the Charter would justify the conclusion that these Articles were contemplated as being devoid of any effect from the point of view of either legal obligations resting upon the Members or the duty incumbent upon the United Nations as a whole.[19]

In the decades following Lauterpacht's pronouncements as to the legal force of the human rights provisions of the UN Charter, the International Court of Justice (ICJ) handed down several judgments which supported this position.[20] And, although the Charter does not confer direct rights on private individuals, it recognizes the rights of individuals in international law as conferred by states.[21] In the 1970 *Barcelona Traction* case, the Court addressed the rights of individuals in international law, referring to the human rights obligations intrinsic to the Charter, including the prohibition of genocide, and principles and rules concerning the basic rights of the human person.[22]

All states are bound to uphold obligations as reflected in the Charter's provisions, and in so doing recognize that ensuring respect for fundamental human rights is no longer to be understood as the exclusive concern of each individual state. In the wake of the Second World War human rights, and the dignity and worth of the human person, had become internationally valued, and were endorsed as a matter of legitimate concern for every Member State of the UN. While Article 2(7) of the Charter was intended to provide a legal buffer against incursions into the domestic affairs of states,[23] it has been 'eroded and emptied of substance' because increasingly 'matters are no longer recognized as belonging to

---

[19] Ibid.

[20] *Legal Consequences for States of the Continued Presence of South Africa in Namibia (South-West Africa) notwithstanding Security Council Resolution 276 (1970)*, Adv Op, ICJ Rep (1971) 16, at paras 52 and 131; *United States Diplomatic and Consular Staff in Tehran* (Merits) (United States of America v Iran) ICJ Rep (1980) 3, at para 42.

[21] I Brownlie, *Principles of Public International Law* (5th edn, Clarendon Press, 1998) 558–589. In the words of Lauterpacht: '[the provisions of the UN Charter in the matter of human rights and fundamental freedoms] transfer the inalienable and natural rights of the individual from the venerable but controversial orbit of the law of nature to the province of positive law, of international law.' Lauterpacht, *International Law and Human Rights*, Ch 9, at 159.

[22] *Barcelona Traction, Light and Power Company Limited (Second Phase)* (Belgium v Spain) ICJ Rep (1970) 3, at para 34.

[23] UN Charter, art 2(7): 'Nothing contained in the present Charter shall authorize the United Nations to intervene in matters which are essentially within the domestic jurisdiction of any state or shall require the Members to submit such matters to settlement under the present Charter; but this principle shall not prejudice the application of enforcement measures under Chapter VII.'

the domestic jurisdiction of states'.[24] By the 1960s (in relation to apartheid), the problems relating to human rights had become the interest of all nations, premised on the Charter's designation that they constituted a matter of international concern.[25] If sovereignty implies legal autonomy, and thus freedom of action of a state, then among the Charter's greatest contributions was its codification of the principle that where human rights are concerned state sovereignty provides no right of exclusivity.

The international community of states set, as among its goals, the reaffirmation of the faith of humankind in fundamental rights, in the dignity and worth of the human person, in the equal rights of men and women, and of nations large and small. It also professed its determination to promote social progress and better standards of life.[26] The Charter provided the basis for the elaboration of the standards, and machinery for implementing the protection of human rights, clearly mapping the place of prominence human rights was meant to have in the new post-war international order.[27] It was upon the Charter's foundation that a world system premised on the duty of international cooperation regarding the respect for and observance of human rights would take shape, and a legal doctrine of international responsibility for the protection of human rights would be built.

The fact that the human rights and fundamental freedoms are not defined within the Charter (other than the principle of non-discrimination) may have given rise— due to a lack of clarity and precision—to circumstances that could impair their juridical application. While Lauterpacht suggested, with authority, that the legal nature of the obligations in the Charter on the matter of human rights are not decisively influenced by that fact,[28] the point is largely moot today. The Universal Declaration of Human Rights (UDHR) provided the initial content to the Charter's human rights provisions,[29] and is accepted as an authoritative interpretation of the human rights provisions of the UN Charter.[30] In recent

---

[24] G Nolte, 'Chapter 1, Article 2(7)' in Simma (ed), *The Charter of the United Nations: A Commentary*, Vol 1, at 171.

[25] Ibid, 161.   [26] UN Charter, preamble.

[27] See arts 13, 62, and 68.

[28] H Lauterpacht's view as cited in Ghandhi, 'The Universal Declaration', 207, at 231.

[29] See, for example, C Beyani, 'The Legal Premises for the International Protection of Human Rights' in GS Goodwin-Gill and S Talmon (eds), *The Reality of International Law: Essays in Honour of Ian Brownlie* (Oxford University Press, 1999) 21, at 24; Henkin, 'The United Nations and Human Rights', 504, at 506.

[30] B Simma and P Alston, 'The Sources of Human Rights Law: Custom, Jus Cogens, and General Principles' 12 *Aust YBIL* (1988–1989) 82, at 90–3 and 100; See also, J Humphrey, 'The Universal Declaration of Human Rights: Its History, Impact and Juridical Character' in BG Ramcharan (ed), *Human Rights: Thirty Years After the Universal Declaration* (Martinus Nijhoff, 1979) 21, at 33–4 in which he refers to General Assembly res 285 (III) of 25 April 1949 which assesses measures adopted in relation to UDHR provisions against whether or not they are in conformity with the UN Charter. Humphrey goes on to explain that '[s]ince the Charter neither catalogues nor defines human rights, the logical and inescapable conclusion is that the states which voted for the resolution were using the Declaration to interpret the Charter. This was the first of many times that the

decades, specialized international treaties have filled any lacunae. These include treaties against racial discrimination, in defence of a range of civil and political rights, and economic, social and cultural rights; against discrimination aimed at women; prohibiting torture and other crimes against humanity; and in defence of the rights of the child. Diverse declarations adopted under the auspices of the UN pronouncing on the right to development and of minorities, to name but a few, as well as the jurisprudence and authoritative comments of the treaty monitoring bodies, have further enriched the Charter's content in this area. Rather than providing for substantive rights, the UN Charter's focus on human rights was by way of describing the organization's purposes, with international cooperation providing the method by which those purposes would be achieved.

2.3 Cooperation and Shared Responsibility in International Human Rights Instruments

The principle of international cooperation in the protection of human rights established in the UN Charter is found throughout human rights instruments within which a variety of rights are elaborated. While international cooperation implies shared responsibility, this latter term is now explicitly articulated in soft law; and in the last decade, as the concerns of globalization have become more apparent, these twin principles have come to occupy a defining place within international human rights instruments that address economic, social, cultural, and development rights. In the section below, an overview of international cooperation and shared responsibility within hard and soft law instruments is provided, substantiating their significance within the human rights legal framework, and their importance in contributing to a just economic globalization.

2.3.1 International cooperation in human rights conventions and declarations

Instead of including a Bill of Rights within the UN Charter, it was agreed that a drafting committee would be set up and would present an International Bill of Rights to the General Assembly.[31] On 10 December 1948, three years

General Assembly used the Declaration—as certain delegations said in 1948 it should be used—as an authentic interpretation of the Charter'. In the words of Louis Sohn, '[m]embers can no longer contend that they do not know what human rights they promised in the Charter to promote.' LB Sohn, *A Short History of the United Nations Documents on Human Rights* (Report of the 18th Commission to Study the Organization of Peace, 1968) as cited in MGK Nayer, 'Human Rights: United Nations and United States Foreign Policy' 19 *Harv Int'l LJ* (1978) 813, at 816.

[31] Art 68 of the UN Charter mandates the setting up of a commission on human rights by the Economic and Social Council. It is the only commission within the United Nations system the establishment of which is mandated by the Charter. Although the Charter requires a human

after the Charter came into force, the General Assembly adopted the Universal Declaration of Human Rights. The UDHR is an explication of the Charter; its status was that of an authoritative guide to the interpretation of the Charter, produced by the General Assembly.[32] The preamble to the Declaration refers to the pledge contained in Article 56 of the Charter which entails cooperative action to ensure the achievement of the purposes provided in Article 55, which include, inter alia, the promotion of conditions for economic and social progress, and universal observance of human rights.

The drafting was done in a post-war climate wrought with revulsion at the horrors of the Second World War. Common moral outrage united delegates in their pursuit, enabling a sufficient disregard for competing political and philosophical positions which may have otherwise proven insurmountable. The UDHR was adopted not by consensus but by vote. Forty-eight of the 56 UN Member States voted in favour, none voted against, and eight abstained.[33] As a declaration, the UDHR was not meant to create binding obligations. It was meant to stand as 'the first complete and detailed catalogue of human rights and fundamental freedoms to be recognized and solemnly declared by the international community of sovereign states'.[34] The Declaration contains a total of 30 operative articles encompassing civil and political rights and economic, social and cultural rights.[35]

rights commission be set up, it does not explicitly mention that it will undertake the drafting of an International Bill of Rights. This is nonetheless implied as the Charter's *travaux préparatoires* demonstrates. Art 68 states: 'The Economic and Social Council *shall* set up commissions in economic and social fields and for the promotion of human rights, and such other commissions as may be required for the performance of its functions', (emphasis added).

[32] I Brownlie (ed), *Basic Documents on Human Rights* (3rd edn, Oxford University Press, 1997) 21.

[33] Abstentions were lodged by: Byelorussia, Czechoslovakia, Poland, Saudi Arabia, South Africa, Ukraine, the USSR and Yugoslavia.

[34] P Sieghart, *The Lawful Rights of Mankind: An Introduction to the International Legal Code of Human Rights* (Oxford University Press, 1985) 63.

[35] The arts as they appear in the UDHR are not ranked in any particular order of priority nor are they divided into categories pertaining to civil and political rights and economic social and cultural rights. And although now there is widespread recognition as to the indivisibility and interdependence of rights—a position most recently reinforced in the Vienna Declaration on Human Rights—the case has been made that for a great majority of the drafters the distinction between these categories of rights was a benign one. According to Morsink, '[a]lmost all of [the drafters] seem to have believed that there is a fundamental unity to all human rights, which they expressed in what they called the 'organic unity' of their document.': J Morsink, *Universal Declaration of Human Rights: Origins, Drafting and Intent* (University of Pennsylvania Press, 1999) xiv. Art 2 is a non-discrimination clause. The grounds enumerated apply to the rest of the Declaration. Articles 3–27 address a range of civil, and political rights and economic, social and cultural rights. The enumerated rights are: the right to life, liberty and security; freedom from slavery and slave labour in all their forms; freedom from torture, cruel inhuman or degrading treatment or punishment; the right to juridical personality; the right to equal protection, without discrimination, of the law; the right to an effective remedy by a competent national tribunal; freedom from arbitrary arrest, detention or exile; the right to a fair trial; the right to presumption of innocence until proved guilty, and freedom from *ex post facto* laws; freedom from arbitrary interference with privacy, family, home or correspondence; the right to freedom of movement and residence, to leave any country and to return to one's country; the right to seek and enjoy in other countries asylum from persecution; the right to a nationality; the right of adults to consensual marriage; the right to own property and

International cooperation is recognized within it as necessary for the achievement of economic, social and cultural rights (Article 22), and as an entitlement underpinning the entire Declaration, since it is understood as essential to the creation of an international order conducive to the realization of the human rights as set out in the Declaration (Article 28).

The UDHR Article 22 has been referred to as an 'umbrella article', in that it refers not only to international cooperation in the context of a somewhat vague notion of social security, but also to both national effort and international cooperation in the realization of economic, social and cultural rights generally. It states that: 'Everyone, as a member of society, has the right to social security and is entitled to realization, through national effort and international co-operation and in accordance with the organization and resources of each State, of the economic, social and cultural rights indispensable for his dignity and the free development of his personality'.

A study on the origins of this article explains that while the issue of fulfilling economic, social and cultural rights beyond national borders within the context of globalization was addressed by the Commission on Human Rights (CHR), (where the drafting was taking place), and anticipated in Article 22 of the UDHR, at the time of drafting the questions of a fair division of income and wealth among citizens of different societies, and issues related to international distributive justice, did not in fact inspire much debate in the CHR.[36]

The catalogue of rights outlined in Articles 3–27 is followed by Article 28 which, despite its brevity, addresses the instrumental responsibility posited at the centre of an effective international human rights regime, the discharging of which is necessary for the exercise of the other rights. Article 28 of the UDHR states that: 'Everyone is entitled to a social and international order in which the rights and freedoms set forth in this Declaration can be fully realized'. International cooperation thereby constitutes an implied prerequisite to the attainment of this entitlement.

Article 28 reflects a view that is now widely endorsed—that methods for the meaningful protection and promotion of human rights cannot be disassociated from the wider global environment. This position was advanced in the Proclamation of Teheran produced at the UN Conference on Human Rights in 1968. The Conference was the first major review of progress and obstacles

---

freedom from arbitrary deprivation of one's property; freedom of thought, conscience and religion; freedom of opinion and expression; freedom of peaceful assembly and association; the right to participate in government; the right to social security and of economic, social and cultural rights; the right to work, to equal pay for equal work without discrimination, to favourable remuneration, and the right to form and join trade unions; the right to leisure; the right to a standard of living adequate for the health and well-being of the person and his family (including food, clothing, housing, necessary medical care and financial security in the event of circumstances beyond the person's control); the right of all children to special care and assistance, as well as to their mothers during pregnancy and nurturing; the right to education; and the right to participate in cultural life, enjoy the arts and share in scientific advancement, and rights related to the protection of the moral and material interests of authors.

[36] B-A Andreasson, 'Article 22' in G Alfredsson and A Eide (eds), *The Universal Declaration of Human Rights: A Common Standard of Achievement* (Martinus Nijhoff, 1999) 453, at 476 and 488.

since the adoption of the UDHR, and aimed 'to formulate a programme for the future'.[37] The Proclamation calls for cooperation from the international community to, inter alia: implement the principle of non-discrimination at the international, as well as at national levels; address the widening gap between the economically developed and developing countries which impedes human rights; eradicate illiteracy; and pay attention to the possibility that although scientific discoveries and technological advances have opened vast prospects for economic, social and cultural progress, such progress may endanger the rights and freedoms of individuals. The Proclamation of Teheran also declared human rights to be indivisible stating that 'the full realization of civil and political rights without economic social and cultural rights is impossible,'[38] a tenet that would be echoed decades later in the Declaration and Programme of Action adopted at the UN World Conference on Human Rights in Vienna in 1993.

More recent references to Article 28 in standard-setting instruments suggest that the article does not apply only to states, but is addressed to all actors of the wider international community. The Declaration on the Rights of Human Rights Defenders (1998),[39] states in its preamble that: 'individuals, groups, institutions and non-governmental organizations also have an important role and responsibility in contributing, as appropriate, to the promotion of the right of everyone to a social and international order in which the rights and freedoms set forth in the Universal Declaration of Human Rights and other human rights instruments can be fully realized'. The General Assembly would seem to have advanced this expansive interpretation that makes duty-bearers of us all, when it proclaimed the UDHR 'as a common standard of achievement for all peoples and all nations, to the end that *every individual* and *every organ of society*, keeping this Declaration constantly in mind, shall strive by teaching and education to promote respect for these rights and freedoms and by progressive measures, national and international, to secure their universal and effective recognition and observance, both among the peoples of Member States themselves and among the peoples of territories under their jurisdiction'.[40] Noting the contemporary relevance of having human rights impose duties on non-state actors, Henkin emphasized at the 50th anniversary of the UDHR that:

Every individual includes juridical persons. *Every individual and every organ of society* excludes no one, no company, no market, no cyberspace. The Universal Declaration applies to them all.[41]

---

[37] Proclamation of Teheran (1968) UN Doc A/CONF32/41, preamble para 1.

[38] Ibid, art 13.

[39] Declaration on the Right and Responsibility of Individuals, Groups and Organs of Society to Promote and Protect Universally Recognized Human Rights and Fundamental Freedoms, General Assembly res A/RES/53/144, 53 UN GAOR Supp UN Doc A/RES/53/144 (1999).

[40] UDHR, preamble.

[41] L Henkin, 'The Universal Declaration at 50 and the Challenge of Global Markets' *Brook J Int'l L* 1 (1999) 17, at 25 (emphasis in the original).

Emphasizing the role of developed states in the creation of a just international order, Pogge suggests that Article 28 extends a request to 'the citizens and governments of developed states ... to support the emergence and stability of democratic, rights-respecting and peaceful regimes [...] that would also tend to reduce radical economic deprivations and inequalities, which now engender great vulnerabilities to civil rights violations as well as massive premature mortality from malnutrition and easily curable diseases'.[42] Article 29(1) which follows, refers to duties that one owes to the community. These duties are not elaborated in the UDHR, but by reference to the *travaux préparatoires* they can be understood to reflect general legal and ethical duties that might form part of, for example, an individual's contribution to the common good.[43] Elsewhere it has been suggested that perhaps the inclusion of Article 29(1) rested largely on the moral and political appeal of the idea.[44]

The steadily-emerging international law of cooperation is rooted in Article 28—an early formal expression by the international community that human rights involve claims on our global order; that our global order is to be assessed, developed and reformed principally by reference to its relative impact on human rights fulfilment.[45] The United Nations Development Programme (UNDP) Human Development Report of 2000 aptly noted in this regard that 'human rights are ... claims on the behaviour of individual and collective agents, and on the design of social arrangements'.[46]

2.3.1.1 *The International Covenant on Economic, Social and Cultural Rights, the Convention on the Rights of the Child and other Human Rights Conventions*

The International Covenant on Economic, Social and Cultural Rights (ICESCR) does not contain a jurisdictional clause. Instead, it defines obligations under the Covenant in the context of international cooperation, including at times international assistance. While the jurisdictional competence of states in the area of human rights is primarily territorial[47]—and the ICESCR is no exception in this regard[48]—a state's jurisdiction also extends to acts outside its

---

[42] TW Pogge, 'The International Significance of Human Rights' 4 *The Journal of Ethics* (2000) 45, at 56–7.

[43] 'Taking Duties Seriously: Individual Duties in International Human Rights Law' (International Council on Human Rights Policy, 1999) 24–6.

[44] T Opsahl and V Dimitrijevic, 'Article 29 and 30' in Alfredsson and Eide (eds), *The Universal Declaration of Human Rights*, 633, at 641.

[45] Pogge, 'The International Significance of Human Rights', 45, at 55.

[46] UNDP, *Human Development Report 2000: Human Rights and Human Development* (Oxford University Press, 2000) 25.

[47] For example, case of *Bankovic, Stojanovic, Stoimenovski, Joksimovic and Sukovic* v *Belgium, the Czech Republic, Denmark, France, Germany, Greece, Hungary, Iceland, Italy, Luxembourg, the Netherlands, Norway, Poland, Portugal, Spain, Turkey and the United Kingdom*. ECtHR App no 52207/99, admissibility decision of 12 December 2001, para 59.

[48] CESCR, General Comment no 1 (Reporting by States parties), (3rd session, 1989) UN Doc E/1989/22 annex III at 87, para 3.

territory, wherever it exercises effective control.[49] Yet the obligations of international cooperation for economic, social and cultural rights require something beyond obligations derived from the 'extraterritorial' reach of a human rights convention. They call for *proactive* steps through international cooperation in securing economic, social and cultural rights globally rather than obligations attached reactively, i.e. based on the potential impact of a state's activities on the people in foreign countries. They also reinforce the existence of responsibilities of states acting collectively.[50]

International cooperation is addressed in six articles within the ICESCR,[51] beginning with Article 2(1), which applies to the provisions of the Covenant in their entirety, and obliges states parties to: '... undertake[s] steps, individually and through international assistance and co-operation, especially economic and technical, to the maximum of its available resources with a view to achieving progressively the full realization of the rights recognized in the present Covenant by all appropriate means, including particularly the adoption of legislative measures'.

'International assistance' appears in Article 2(1) along with international cooperation, and are meant to be provided to the 'maximum of states parties' available resources'. Article 22 for its part addresses international technical assistance,[52] and Article 23 provides a non-exhaustive list of necessary international action.[53] Since both the terms international assistance and international cooperation were used in the Covenant, the presumption is that the drafters considered them to be distinct, although the *travaux préparatoires* shed little light

---

[49] HRC, General Comment no 31 on Article 2 (The Nature of the General Legal Obligation Imposed on States Parties to the Covenant), (80th session, 2004) UN Doc CCPR/C/21/Rev1/Add13 (2004), para 10; HRC, Concluding Observations: USA (53rd session, 1995) UN Doc CCPR/C/79/Add50 (1995), para 284; HRC, Concluding Observations: Israel (63rd session, 1998) UN Doc CCPR/C/79/Add93 (1998), para 10; HRC, Concluding Observations: Israel (78th session, 2003) UN Doc CCPR/CO/78/ISR (2003), para 11; HRC, Concluding Observations: Belgium (81st session, 2004) UN Doc CCPR/CO/81/BEL (2004), para 6; CESCR, Concluding Observations: Israel (19th session, 1998) UN Doc E/C12/1/Add27 (1998), para 8; CESCR, Concluding Observations: Israel (30th session, 2003) UN Doc E/C12/1/Add9 (2003), para 31; *Loizidou* v *Turkey*, (Preliminary Objections) ECtHR App no 15318/89 Grand Chamber, 23 March 1995.

[50] See further, Ch 5.

[51] Arts 2(1), 11(1), 11(2), 15(4), and arts 22 and 23.

[52] ICESCR, art 22: 'The Economic and Social Council may bring to the attention of other organs of the United Nations, their subsidiary organs and specialized agencies concerned with furnishing technical assistance any matters arising out of the reports referred to in this part of the present Covenant which may assist such bodies in deciding, each within its field of competence, on the advisability of international measures likely to contribute to the effective progressive implementation of the present Covenant.'

[53] ICESCR, art 23: 'The States Parties to the present Covenant agree that international action for the achievement of the rights recognized in the present Covenant includes such methods as the conclusion of conventions, the adoption of recommendations, the furnishing of technical assistance and the holding of regional meetings and technical meetings for the purpose of consultation and study organized in conjunction with the Governments concerned.'

on the matter.[54] While the Committee itself has not formally elaborated any distinction between the terms, international assistance might more readily apply to technical support; for example, aiding developing countries effectively to monitor public policy,[55] or in their relations with specialized agencies.[56] When used in conjunction with international cooperation, the term is employed expansively by CESCR to apply to 'a programme of international cooperation and assistance' that will give effect to Articles 55 and 56 of the Charter, and to the principles recognized in the Declaration on the Right to Development.[57] The Committee on the Rights of the Child would seem to read assistance into the obligation of international cooperation enshrined in the Convention on the Rights of the Child (CRC),[58] pertaining most notably, to technical assistance provided by UN agencies.[59] Generally then, as Craven suggests, international cooperation may be broader than international assistance, 'providing for mutual action directed towards a common goal .... Whereas "assistance" implies the provision or transfer of some "good" from one state to another'[60] including, but not limited to, economic and technical cooperation.[61] The language found in succeeding instruments may also be instructive on this matter: a reference to international assistance in a draft of the Declaration on the Right to Development was dropped from the final Declaration of 1986, which relied instead on the language of international cooperation.[62] The Convention on the Rights of the Child, adopted

[54] M Craven, *The International Covenant on Economic, Social and Cultural Rights: A Perspective on its Development* (Oxford University Press, 2002) 146–7; S Skogly, *Beyond National Borders: States' Human Rights Obligations in International Cooperation* (Intersentia, 2006) 84–9.

[55] CESCR, General Comment no 1, Reporting by States parties, para 3.

[56] CESCR, Concluding Observations: Solomon Islands (29th session, 2002) UN Doc E/C12/1/Add84 (2002), paras 25, 28 and 33.

[57] CESCR, General Comment no 3 on Art 2(1) (The Nature of States Parties' Obligations), (5th session, 1990) UN Doc E/1991/23 annex III, para 14. The Committee refers only to 'international cooperation for development' earlier in the statement when linking Covenant obligations in this area to the comparable Charter obligations.

[58] On international cooperation the Committee concludes that: 'Article 4 emphasizes that implementation of the Convention is a cooperative exercise for the States of the world. ... The Charter of the United Nations (arts 55 and 56) identifies the overall purposes of international economic and social cooperation, and members pledge themselves under the Charter "to take joint and separate action in cooperation with the Organization" to achieve these purposes. ... [and recently] States have pledged themselves, in particular, to international cooperation to eliminate poverty'. CRC, General Comment no 5, General Measures of Implementation of the Convention on the Rights of the Child (arts 4, 42 and 44, para 6), (34th session, 2003) UN Doc CRC/GC/2003/5, para 60. Articles pertaining to international cooperation in the CRC are: 4, 11(2), 17(b), 21(e), 22(2), 23(4), 24(4), 27(4), 28(3), 34, 35.

[59] CRC, General Comment no 5, General Measures of Implementation, paras 63–4.

[60] Craven, *The International Covenant on Economic, Social and Cultural Rights*, 147.

[61] On the limits of the concept of international 'assistance' see Ch 5.

[62] Report of the Working Group of Governmental Experts on the Right to Development, (6th and 7th sessions, 14 November 1983) UN Doc E/CN4/1984/13, annex II, p 4, art 4(2). The draft article reads: 'Sustained action is required to ensure more rapid progress of developing countries. As a complement to the efforts that developing countries make, individually and collectively for their development, it is essential to provide them with effective international assistance'. DRD, art 4(2) reads: 'Sustained action is required to promote more rapid development of

in 1989, in which international cooperation to address the needs of developing countries figures prominently, also relied only on the language of international cooperation, with no mention of an obligation of international assistance in this regard. Since neither international assistance nor international cooperation (taken together as it appears in Article 2(1)) ICESCR) should be understood as encompassing only financial and technical assistance,[63] a conclusion can be drawn to the effect that international cooperation encompasses all relevant measures. The more heated question currently being debated intergovernmentally, is whether there exists in fact a *legal* obligation of international cooperation (and assistance) and what the content of this obligation might be. We return to this issue in section 2.4 below.

While international assistance and cooperation is an obligation corresponding to all rights in the Covenant, the obligation of international cooperation is reaffirmed in several articles, serving to emphasize historically its importance with regards to these particular rights. In ICESCR Article 11(1) states parties agree to 'take appropriate steps to ensure the realization of this right of everyone [to an adequate standard of living including adequate food, clothing and housing, and to the continuous improvement of living conditions] recognizing to this effect the essential importance of international co-operation based on free consent'. In Article 11(2), states parties are obligated to take 'individually and through international co-operation' relevant measures to fulfil the 'fundamental right of everyone to be free from hunger'. While the reference to international cooperation based on *free consent* at Article 11(1) might today be relied on to advance the preferred position of many affluent states that there can be no binding obligation to transfer resources to poorer countries, at the time of the Covenant's drafting and adoption this contemporary preoccupation received little attention in the UN General Assembly's 3rd Committee.[64] In today's world of mass starvation, and the continuation of a systemic global divide between the 'haves' and the 'have-nots', the notion that attending to world poverty should rest on 'free consent' lacks legitimacy. International commitments to address world hunger, and to lift people out of abject poverty, such as the Millennium Development Goals (MDG), would seem to support this view.

Article 15(4) of the Covenant also explicitly refers to international cooperation, including international c6ontacts, as (potentially)[65] important to derive benefits in the scientific and cultural fields. Focused on cross-border collaboration,

developing countries As a complement to the efforts of developing countries, effective international co-operation is essential in providing these countries with appropriate means and facilities to foster their comprehensive development'.

[63] See section 2.4 below.

[64] Skogly, *Beyond National Borders*, 90.

[65] As has been noted earlier, international cooperation does not represent a value in and of itself and, as Skogly points out, 'from a quality perspective, it may be possible to identify situations where international contact and cooperation may be harmful to people's enjoyment of their scientific and cultural life ... '. Skogly, *Beyond National Borders*, 95.

here the language is more tailored and narrow than elsewhere, but touches on a broader issue of increasing concern to the Committee and others: the protection of a variety of economic, social and cultural rights under the international regulation of intellectual property.[66] The effect of these international trade rules is to protect disproportionately business and corporate interests over the human rights of people, and this gives rise to grave concerns by CESCR in a range of areas including, food security, indigenous knowledge, bio-safety, and access to health care.[67] In addressing the right to health of people in developing countries CESCR has repeatedly voiced its apprehension as to whether the WTO Agreement on Trade-Related Aspects of Intellectual Property Rights (TRIPS) provides a framework that is consistent, inter alia, with the right of everyone to the enjoyment of the highest attainable standard of health, and whether TRIPS is being applied in a manner that ensures the exercise of this right.[68] The Committee on the Rights of the Child has raised similar issues in relation to bilateral and regional trade deals (TRIPS Plus), and the realization of the right to health of children.[69] TRIPS establishes a global regime for intellectual property based on the level of protection provided in the most developed countries. This one-size-fits-all for intellectual property protection is criticized for failing to take adequately into account the needs of developing countries, and for undermining

---

[66] CESCR, General Comment no 17, The Right of Everyone to Benefit from the Protection of the Moral and Material Interests Resulting from any Scientific, Literary or Artistic Production of which he is the Author (Art 15(1)(c)), (35th session, 2005) UN Doc E/C12/GC/17 (2005); CESCR, Statement on Human Rights and Intellectual Property (27th session, 2001) UN Doc E/C12/2001/15; see also J Bueno de Mesquita, *International Covenant on Economic, Social and Cultural Rights: Obligations of International Assistance and Cooperation,* Background briefing submitted to CESCR (2003). Unpublished at the time of publication of this book; and, AR Chapman, *Approaching Intellectual Property as a Human Right Obligations Related to Article 15(1)(c),* Discussion paper submitted by the American Association for the Advancement of Science to the CESCR General Day of Discussion on: *Substantive issues arising out of the implementation of the ICESCR on the Right of Everyone to Benefit from the Protection of the Moral and Material Interests Resulting from any Scientific, Literary or Artistic Production of which he is the Author, Article 15(1)(c),* (24th session, 2000) UN Doc E/C12/2000/12.

[67] CESCR, Statement to the Third Ministerial Conference of the World Trade Organization (21st session, 1999) UN Doc E/C12/1999/9, para 4; see also CESCR, Statement on Human Rights and Intellectual Property Ch 3.

[68] 'The Committee strongly urges the State party to conduct an assessment of the effect of international trade rules on the right to health for all and to make extensive use of the flexibility clauses permitted in the WTO Agreement on Trade-Related Aspects of Intellectual Property Rights in order to ensure access to generic medicine and more broadly the enjoyment of the right to health for everyone in Ecuador.': CESCR, Concluding Observations: Ecuador (32nd session, 2004) UN Doc E/C12/1/Add.100 (2004), para 55.

[69] 'In this regard the Committee also recommends that the State Party ensure that regional and other free trade agreements do not have a negative impact on the implementation of children's rights and, more specifically, that these will not affect the possibility of providing children and other victims of HIV/AIDS with effective medicines for free or at the lowest price.' CRC, Concluding Observations: Botswana (37th session, 2004) UN Doc CRC/C/15/Add242 (2004), para 20; see also CRC, Concluding Observations: Philippines (39th session, 2005) UN Doc CRC/C/15/Add258 (2005), para 59(f).

poverty reduction.[70] Notably, firms in developed countries currently account for 96 per cent of royalties from patents, or US$71 billion a year.[71]

The Committee on Economic, Social and Cultural Rights has also gone some way in elaborating the content of the obligations of international assistance and cooperation as they apply to Covenant provisions generally. Thus, with regard to implementing obligations pertaining to the right of everyone to adequate food, CESCR highlights the requirement that states parties ensure the right to food in countries other than their own. Referring to the UN Charter and to the Declaration of the World Food Summit of 1996 in this regard,[72] the Committee affirmed:

In the spirit of Article 56 of the Charter of the United Nations, the specific provisions contained in articles 11, 2.1, and 23 of the Covenant and the Rome Declaration of the World Food Summit, States parties should recognize the essential role of international cooperation and comply with their commitment to take joint and separate action to achieve the full realization of the right to adequate food. In implementing this commitment, States parties should take steps to respect the enjoyment of the right to food in other countries, to protect that right, to facilitate access to food and to provide the necessary aid when required . . .[73]

In the context of the right to health, the Committee has taken the view that:

To comply with their international obligations in relation to article 2(1), States parties have to respect the enjoyment of the right to health in other countries, and to prevent third parties from violating the right in other countries, if they are able to influence these third parties by way of legal or political means, in accordance with the Charter of the United Nations and applicable international law. Depending on the availability of resources, States should facilitate access to essential facilities, goods and services in other countries, wherever possible and provide the necessary aid when required . . . .[74]

In interpreting the term 'the right of everyone' in Article 12 of the ICESCR, Judge Weeramantry, in his dissenting opinion in the Advisory Opinion of the International Court of Justice on the *Legality of the Use by a State of Nuclear Weapons in Armed Conflict*, quoted Article 12 by which 'States parties to the

---

[70] *Report of the Commission on Intellectual Property Rights UK: Integrating Intellectual Property Rights and Development Policy* (2002).

[71] UNDP, *Human Development Report 2005: International Cooperation at a Crossroads: Aid, Trade and Security in an Unequal World* (Oxford University Press, 2005) Ch 4, at 135.

[72] And more recently, Declaration of the World Food Summit: Five Years Later, WSF: fyl2002/3 (FAO, 2002); and, the *FAO Voluntary Guidelines to Support the Progressive Realization of the Right to Adequate Food in the Context of National Food Security* (127th session, FAO Council, 2004) Section III, International Measures, Actions and Commitments.

[73] CESCR, General Comment no 12, The Right to Adequate Food (art 11), (20th session, 1999) UN Doc E/C12/1999/5, para 36.

[74] CESCR, General Comment no 14, The Right to the Highest Attainable Standard of Health (Art 12), (22nd session, 2000) UN Doc E/C12/2000/4, para 39.

present Covenant recognize the right of everyone to the highest attainable standard of physical and mental health'. He then went on to proclaim:

It will be noted here that the recognition by States of the right to health is … that they
recognize the right of "everyone" and not merely of their own subjects. Consequently
each state is under an obligation to respect the right to health of all members of the international community.[75]

The CESCR continues to remark on the scope of the obligation of international
cooperation with regard to Covenant rights noting recently in its General
Comment on the Right to Work:

To comply with their international obligations in relation to article 6, States parties
should endeavour to promote the right to work in other countries as well as in bilateral and multilateral negotiations. In negotiations with international financial institutions, States parties should ensure protection of the right to work of their population.
States parties that are members of international financial institutions, in particular the
International Monetary Fund, the World Bank and regional development banks, should
pay greater attention to the protection of the right to work in influencing the lending policies, credit agreements, structural adjustment programmes and international measures
of these institutions. The strategies, programmes and policies adopted by States parties
under structural adjustment programmes should not interfere with their core obligations
in relation to the right to work and impact negatively on the right to work of women,
young persons and the disadvantaged and marginalized individuals and groups.[76]

The Convention on the Rights of the Child, which reflects in its provisions the
greatest awareness of the inequity between developed and developing countries,
and addresses the need for international cooperation in the realization of economic, social and cultural rights most frequently, is also among the most recent
of the human rights treaties. It was drafted and adopted when the potential repercussions of economic globalization on the enjoyment of human rights had begun
to capture the attention of the international community. The preamble to the
CRC attests to the need for '[r]ecognizing the importance of international co-operation for improving the living conditions of children in every country, in particular in the developing countries.'[77] This is followed by several articles in which
obligations of international cooperation are articulated. CRC Article 4 obliges
states parties to undertake appropriate measures 'to the maximum extent of
their available resources and, where needed, within the framework of international co-operation'.[78] International cooperation is also encouraged with regard

---

[75] *Legality of the Use by a State of Nuclear Weapons in Armed Conflict*, Judge Weeramantry (diss op) ICJ Rep (1996) 66, at 144.
[76] CESCR, General Comment no 18, The Right to Work (art 6), (35th session, 2005) UN Doc E/C12/GC/18 (2005), para 30.
[77] CRC, preambular para 13.
[78] While the language here tends towards an obligation to *seek* international cooperation when necessary in order to fulfil the rights as provided, the implication is that there is an equal or

to: accessing information from a range of national and international sources as is necessary for the well-being and health of the child;[79] the international exchange of information required in order to care for the health of children, with particular emphasis on the needs, in this context, of developing countries;[80] and, the progressive realization of the right to health of children, and their right to education in relation to the elimination of ignorance, illiteracy and the development of teaching methods.[81] With regard to international cooperation and both the right to health and to education of children, 'particular account shall be taken of the needs of developing countries'.[82]

The Convention on the Elimination of All Forms of Discrimination Against Women (CEDAW),[83] refers in preambular paragraph 9 to the need for a '... new international economic order based on equity and justice ...', which would contribute to the realization of equality between men and women. Considering that the figures on the 'feminization of world poverty' demonstrate that the majority of the 1.5 billion people living on US$1 a day or less are women,[84] attests to the contemporary significance of this instructive claim.[85]

The first substantive paragraph of the general comment on the Nature of the General Legal Obligation Imposed on States Parties to the International Covenant on Civil and Political Rights (ICCPR),[86] begins by remarking that '[w]hile article 2 is couched in terms of the obligations of States Parties towards individuals as the right-holders under the Covenant, every State Party has a legal interest in the performance by every other State Party of its obligations'. Drawing from the *Barcelona Traction* case[87] and the UN Charter, the Human Rights

---

corresponding obligation upon those states in a position to cooperate to these ends. This would reasonably entail an obligation to countenance the request—that is, to discuss, consider, and respond satisfactorily.

[79] See generally, CRC, art 17.   [80] Ibid, art 23(4).

[81] Ibid, arts 24(4) and 28(3).   [82] Ibid, arts 24(4) and 28(3).

[83] Convention on the Elimination of All Forms of Discrimination Against Women (1979), entered into force 3 September 1981, General Assembly res A/RES/34/180, 1249 UNTS 20378.

[84] The 'extremely poor' are defined as those people living on less than US$1 per day (in 1985 purchasing power parity dollars). I Goldin and K Reinert, *Globalization for Development: Trade, Finance, Aid, Migration, and Policy* (World Bank/Palgrave MacMillan, 2006) 26.

[85] UN Division for the Advancement of Women, The Feminization of Poverty <http://www.un.org/womenwatch/daw/>; see further, UN Fourth World Conference on Women: Action for Equality, Development and Peace, Women and Poverty Diagnosis. Strategic Objective A1. In particular, CEDAW Art 14(1) states: 'States Parties shall take into account the particular problems faced by rural women and the significant roles which rural women play in the economic survival of their families, including their work in the non-monetized sectors of the economy, and shall take all appropriate measures to ensure the application of the provisions of the present Convention to women in rural areas'.

[86] HRC, General Comment no 31, The Nature of the Legal Obligation.

[87] The ICJ in its renowned *obiter dictum* in the *Barcelona Traction* case of 1970 referred to the obligations a State owed towards the international community as whole, obligations that are as such the concern of all States. In the view of the importance of the rights involved, every State can be held to have a legal interest in their protection. These obligations owed by every state towards all (*erga omnes*) are derived from, inter alia, principles and rules concerning the basic rights of the human person: *Barcelona Traction*, paras 33–4. See further Ch 4.

Committee remarks that this follows from the fact, that the:

rules concerning the basic rights of the human person are *erga omnes* obligations, and that, as indicated in the fourth preambular paragraph of the Covenant, there is a United Nations Charter obligation to promote universal respect for, and observance of, human rights and fundamental freedoms.[88]

While civil and political rights are not subject to 'obligations of international cooperation', the HRC advances a general appreciation of the need for an ethos of international cooperation when it comes to human rights. It does this by affirming that for each state party to 'assert their interest in the performance of other States Parties' on possible breaches of the Covenant under the inter-state complaint mechanism at Article 41 'should not be regarded as an unfriendly act but as a reflection of legitimate community interest'.[89] Reference to community interests reaffirms a general awareness of the shift from a largely bilateral international legal system to one where the fundamental rules must be honoured by every member of that community, and in which common interests are to be prioritized.[90]

2.3.1.2 Declarations

The 1969 Declaration on Social Progress and Development is not directly cast in the language of human rights (i.e. rights-holders and duty-bearers), but emphasizes inter-state responsibility in the achievement of certain related objectives.[91] Moreover, it reaffirms in its second preambular paragraph the 'faith in human rights and fundamental freedoms and in the principles of peace, of the dignity and worth of the human person, and of social justice proclaimed in the Charter'.[92] The Declaration makes clear that the objectives of social progress and development addressed within it are directed towards 'meeting the needs common to all humanity,'[93] and recalls in its preamble major human rights conventions and declarations.[94] Article 2 further claims that social progress and development is founded on 'respect for the dignity and value of the human person and shall ensure the promotion of human rights and social justice,' followed by a subsequent reference to the aim of continuously 'raising the material and spiritual

---

[88] HRC, General Comment no 31, The Nature of the Legal Obligation, para 2.
[89] Ibid.
[90] On the extraterritorial application of the ICCPR and the relevance of legal developments in this area to that of international cooperation for economic, social and cultural rights, see, ME Salomon, 'International Human Rights Obligations in Context: Structural Obstacles and the Demands of Global Justice' in B-A Andreassen and SP Marks (eds), *Development as a Human Right: Legal, Political and Economic Dimensions* (Harvard School of Public Health—Harvard University Press, 2006) 96 at 107–11.
[91] Declaration on Social Progress and Development, General Assembly res A/RES/2542 (XXIV), 11 December 1969, 24 UN GAOR Supp (no 30) at 49, UN Doc A/7630 (1969).
[92] Ibid, preambular para 2.   [93] Ibid, preambular para 12.
[94] Ibid, preambular para 3.

standards of living of all members of society with respect for and in compliance with human rights . . '.[95] The aim of protecting and improving the human environment is stated twice.[96] The Declaration calls for national and international action,[97] and refers, inter alia, to social progress and development as the common concerns of the international community directed at raising the living standards of peoples,[98] as well as the mobilization of international resources.[99] It also addresses the importance of equity in its international dimension with regard to favourable terms of trade, and of equitable and remunerative prices,[100] and emphasizes the importance of the expansion of the principles of equality and non-discrimination in the international trading system,[101] and rectifying the position of developing countries by, inter alia, fairer terms of trade.[102]

The importance of international cooperation can also be found in the UN Educational, Scientific and Cultural Organization's (UNESCO) Declaration of the Principles of International Cultural Cooperation,[103] and in the Declaration on the Use of Scientific and Technological Progress in the Interests of Peace and for the Benefit of Mankind. The first article holds that: 'All States shall promote international co-operation to ensure that the results of scientific and technological developments are used in the interests of strengthening international peace and security, freedom and independence (of states), and also for the purpose of the economic and social development of peoples and the realization of human rights and freedoms in accordance with the Charter of the United Nations.'[104]

The Declaration on the Right to Development, which was adopted by the General Assembly in 1986, reflects an important shift from an international legal discourse centred on international equity and development as giving rise to rights and duties largely among states,[105] to the explicit recognition of development as a *human* right. The first preambular paragraph of the DRD refers to the purpose of the United Nations relating to the achievement of international cooperation in solving international problems of an economic, social, cultural or humanitarian nature, and in promoting and encouraging respect for human rights as per Article 1(3) of the UN Charter. Preambular paragraph 3 of the DRD provides a

---

[95] Ibid, Pt II, Objectives.   [96] Ibid, arts 13(c) and 25(a).

[97] Ibid, preambular para 15.   [98] Ibid, art 9.

[99] Ibid, Pt III, Means and Methods.   [100] Ibid, art 7.

[101] On the importance of reconciling the principle of non-discrimination in international trade law with the application of the principle of non-discrimination and substantive equality in international human rights law, see: *Analytical Study of the High Commissioner for Human Rights on the Fundamental Principle of Non-Discrimination in the Context of Globalization*, UN Doc E/CN4/2004/40, paras 28–50.

[102] Declaration on Social Progress and Development, art 23; see also *The Right to Development: The Importance and Application of the Principle of Equity at Both the National and International Levels*, OHCHR, UN Doc E/CN4/2003/25, para 19.

[103] UNESCO, General Conference, 4 November 1966.

[104] General Assembly res 3384 (XXX), 10 November 1975, art 1.

[105] Exemplified by the Charter on the Economic Rights and Duties of States, General Assembly res A/RES/3281 (XXIX), 12 December 1974.

further assertion through which the operative paragraphs of the DRD should be interpreted,[106] stating that: '... under the provisions of the Universal Declaration of Human Rights everyone is entitled to a social and international order in which the rights and freedoms set forth in that Declaration can be fully realized'. The Preamble sets the tone for a Declaration that articulates, inter alia, the duties placed upon states to cooperate internationally in creating conditions favourable for the realization of the right to development.[107] This human right to development is one in which 'the human person is the central subject of development and should be the active participant and beneficiary of the right to development';[108] which is aimed at the 'constant improvement of the well-being of the entire population and of all individuals on the basis of their active, free and meaningful participation in development and in the fair distribution of benefits resulting therefrom'[109] and in which 'all human rights and fundamental freedoms can be fully realized'.[110] The international component of the right to development is addressed in four of its ten articles all of which aim at a comprehensive process[111] of realizing the inalienable human right to development,[112] via the essential need to provide developing countries with appropriate means and facilities to foster their comprehensive development.[113]

2.3.1.3 *The legal basis of international cooperation in the right to development*

Article 3(1) of the Declaration on the Right to Development makes clear that states have the primary responsibility for the creation of national and international conditions favourable to the realization of the right to development. This includes all necessary measures at the national level for the realization of this right as further reflected in the DRD Article 8,[114] with the Declaration at Article 3(3) recognizing the duty of all states to cooperate with each other in ensuring development and eliminating obstacles to development. This is followed by Article 4(1) which refers to the duty of all states to take steps individually and collectively to formulate international development policies. Then, at Article 4(2), the

---

[106] The Preamble defines the object and the purpose of the instrument and provides the basis for interpreting the operative paragraphs: R Jennings and A Watts (eds), *Oppenheim's International Law* (9th edn, Longman, 1992), 1273.

[107] DRD art 3(1).   [108] Ibid, art 2(1).

[109] Ibid, preambular para 2; art 2(3).

[110] Ibid, art 1(1).   [111] Ibid, preambular para 2.

[112] Ibid, art 1(1).   [113] Ibid, art 4(2).

[114] Ibid, art 8(1): 'States should undertake, at the national level, all necessary measures for the realization of the right to development and shall ensure, inter alia, equality of opportunity for all in their access to basic resources, education, health services, food, housing, employment and the fair distribution of income. Effective measures should be undertaken to ensure that women have an active role in the development process. Appropriate economic and social reforms should be carried out with a view to eradicating all social injustices'; art 8(2): 'States should encourage popular participation in all spheres as an important factor in development and in the full realization of all human rights.'

DRD unambiguously accepts—as previously noted—that effective international cooperation is essential '[a]s a *complement* to the efforts of developing countries [and] in providing these countries with appropriate means and facilities to foster their comprehensive development'.[115] The Declaration also calls upon states to cooperate in promoting, encouraging and strengthening universal respect for human rights and fundamental freedoms for all.[116]

However, the role of international cooperation of states in facilitating the right to development is not derived uniquely from the Declaration itself, but may be considered an imperative borne of the UN Charter. That development falls not only to states acting nationally, but also to the international community of states to address, can be seen in Articles 1(3), and 55 of the Charter with full recognition of cooperation to ensure equitable socio-economic development as part and parcel of respecting human rights. These central principles of the UN are matched by an explicit pledge; as Schwelb concludes: '[t]he Charter itself provides ... an obligation of member states in [the] field [of human rights]. It sets forth not only a "principle" but contains, in Article 56, the pledge of all members to take joint and separate action in cooperation with the organization for the achievement of the purposes set forth in Article 55'.[117]

There is authoritative support, including from the International Court of Justice, resolutions of the General Assembly and the writings of scholars, for the position that the UN Charter imposes binding obligations in the area of human rights on every Member State,[118] reinforced by the mandatory obligation implied in Article 55, and a distinct 'element of a legal duty in the undertaking' expressed in Article 56.[119] Moreover, the General Assembly in its resolutions has repeatedly referred to the responsibilities and obligations which devolve upon it under Articles 55 and 56, and which place on it the duty to cooperate in the promotion of development specifically.[120] Citing a string of resolutions, including the DRD, Brownlie asserts that:

The United Nations Charter, in Chapters IX and X, recognizes the urgent need to deal with economic and social problems, and certain of its provisions create binding obligations for governments to maintain human rights. There is probably also a collective duty

---

[115] Emphasis added.

[116] DRD, art 6(1).

[117] E Schwelb, 'The Law of Treaties and Human Rights' in WM Reisman and BH Weston, *Towards World Order and Human Dignity: Essays in Honour of Myres S McDougal* (Collier MacMillan, 1976) 262, at 265.

[118] *Tehran Hostages* case, 3, at para 91; *Legal Consequences*, 16, at para 131; res 616 A and B (VII) of 5 December 1952 on apartheid as inconsistent with the pledges of the Members under Art 56 of the UN Charter; Lauterpacht, *International Law and Human Rights*, especially Ch 9; Ghandhi, 'The Universal Declaration', 207, at 229–31; MT Kamminga, *Inter-State Accountability for Violations of Human Rights* (Penn Press, 1992) 74–7.

[119] Lauterpacht, *International Law and Human Rights*, Ch 9, at 148.

[120] M Bedjaoui, 'The Right to Development' in M Bedjaoui (ed), *International Law: Achievements and Prospects* (Martinus Nijhoff, 1991) 1177, at 1186.

of member states to take responsible action to create reasonable living standards both for their own peoples and for those of other states.[121]

The Committee on Economic, Social and Cultural Rights emphatically endorsed the existence of an obligation to cooperate internationally for development when it stated in its General Comment no 3:

The Committee wishes to emphasize that in accordance with Articles 55 and 56 of the Charter of the United Nations, with well-established principles of international law, and with the provisions of the Covenant itself, international cooperation for development and thus for the realization of economic, social and cultural rights is an obligation of all States. It is particularly incumbent upon those States which are in a position to assist others in this regard. The Committee notes in particular the importance of the Declaration on the Right to Development adopted by the General Assembly in its resolution 41/128 of 4 December 1986 and the need for States parties to take full account of all the principles recognized herein. It emphasizes that, in the absence of an active programme of international assistance and cooperation on the part of all those States that are in a position to undertake one, the full realization of economic, social and cultural rights will remain an unfulfilled aspiration in many countries . . . .[122]

International cooperation in the realization of the right to development can thus be said to provide an authoritative interpretation and elaboration of principles within the UN Charter binding all states even though the Declaration on the Right to Development itself cannot be said to bind states. This obligation is further strengthened, and its scope elaborated, by human rights jurisprudence in this, and related, areas.

While the Charter did not explicitly define the human rights and fundamental freedoms to which it referred, it outlined the purposes behind its creation, including international cooperation in the solving of international problems and in the promotion of human rights, and provided the structure by which the content was expected to be elaborated.[123] Moreover, although at one time there may have been some debate as to whether the human rights provisions of the Charter were sufficiently clear and precise to give rise to specific obligations of Member States, in the decades since the birth of the UN, universal standards have been elaborated in a range of treaties and declarations strengthening the Charter's normative content, and hence substantiating the obligations that underscore its purposes and pledges. Indeed, the ICJ has accepted that the provisions of the Charter

---

[121] Brownlie, *Principles of Public International Law*, 256.

[122] CESCR, General Comment no 3, The Nature of States Parties' Obligations, para 14.

[123] For example, Art 68, which mandates the setting up of a commission in economic and social fields and for the promotion of human rights, and Art 13 in which the General Assembly is charged with the duty to 'initiate studies and make recommendations for the purpose of: (a) promoting international co-operation in the political fields and encouraging the progressive development of international law and its codification; (b) promoting international co-operation in the economic, social, cultural, educational and health fields . . . and in the realization of human rights and fundamental freedoms for all . . .'.

contain binding obligations, and that they may be interpreted in light of subsequent human rights instruments adopted by the United Nations.[124]

Although recognition of the role that international cooperation plays in the creation of an enabling environment—in which all people can be free from want and be able fully to develop in ways that are meaningful to them—had always been implicit in international human rights instruments, the DRD explicitly recognized collective development as a human right, and identified corresponding duties. The DRD contributed significantly to this area of human rights by offering a reformulation of the imperative of international cooperation through a demand for structural reform of economic, social and political international arrangements.

Since the adoption of the DRD, the role of the international community in cooperating in the realization of the right to development has been reinforced in subsequent declarations adopted at representative world conferences, including in the 1993 Vienna Declaration and Programme of Action of the World Conference on Human Rights.[125] The normative status of the right to development as a right existing within an international law of cooperation should now be beyond doubt.

2.3.1.4 *The normative force of the Declaration on the Right to Development*

Some commentators have referred to the Declaration on the Right to Development as providing a suitable example in law of 'what ought to be' as opposed to 'what is'. These authors emphasized the need to distinguish between moral claims and legal assertions, and concluded that the DRD provides a 'broad framework yet to crystallize into substantive law'.[126] The vast majority of commentators nonetheless

---

[124] *Tehran Hostages* case, 3, at para 91 in which the ICJ held: 'Wrongfully to deprive human beings of their freedom and to subject them to physical constraint in conditions of hardship is in itself manifestly incompatible with the principles of the Charter of the United Nations, as well as with the fundamental principles enunciated in the Universal Declaration of Human Rights.' Significantly, the ICJ interpreted the human rights provisions of the UN Charter on the basis of the UDHR regarding human rights that were not explicitly contained in the Charter. See further, Kamminga, *Inter-State Accountability*, 76.

[125] Pt I, art 10: 'The World Conference on Human Rights reaffirms the right to development, as established in the Declaration on the Right to Development, as a universal and inalienable right and an integral part of fundamental human rights. As stated in the Declaration on the Right to Development, the human person is the central subject of development. While development facilitates the enjoyment of all human rights, the lack of development may not be invoked to justify the abridgement of internationally recognized human rights. States should cooperate with each other in ensuring development and eliminating obstacles to development. The international community should promote an effective international cooperation for the realization of the right to development and the elimination of obstacles to development. Lasting progress towards the implementation of the right to development requires effective development policies at the national level, as well as equitable economic relations and a favourable economic environment at the international level.'

[126] See L A Obiora, 'Beyond the Rhetoric of a Right to Development' 18 *Law & Pol* 3–4 (1996) in M wa Mutua, LA Obiora and RJ Krotoszynski Jr. (eds), Special Issue on the Right to Development, 366, at 378; J Donnelly, 'In Search of the Unicorn: The Jurisprudence and Politics of the Right to Development' 15 *CalWInt'lLJ* (1985) 473.

agree that certain General Assembly resolutions or declarations may indeed set in motion, influence or become part of the process of custom-building,[127] that they play a pivotal role in the international law-making process, and that by embodying the convictions of adopting states, they may create expectations on the part of other states.[128] Thus it has been noted that 'the mere recognition of a rule and the conditions for its execution in a resolution give it the beginning of legal force'.[129] Taken together, these views suggest that General Assembly resolutions can become a critical means of standard-setting.

The process that moves a General Assembly declaration from 'provid[ing] evidence of the state of the law and also the meaning of texts, and ha[ving] considerable legal significance', to attaining full normative maturity is typically determined by a host of factors.[130] Assessing these factors as they apply to the DRD serves to reinforce the potency of its normative force. First, the language is mandatory, signifying the intent of the parties to provide certain legal assurances.[131] This is exemplified in Article 1, which states that 'the right to development is an inalienable human right' and then refers to the 'entitlement of every human person and all peoples'. It is direct, unambiguous in this regard, and, as has been argued, 'leaves little scope for debate as to whether the intention of the General Assembly was to declare the existence of a legally guaranteed right to development'.[132] Second, the DRD, having been adopted with only one state having cast a vote against it,[133] and six abstentions, can be said to have created a presumption that the rules and principles embodied in it are law.[134] At a minimum, as Dixon has noted, 'a vote in favour of a resolution infers that the state will act according to its terms, even if it is not legally bound to do so'.[135] Third, a considerable number of procedures have been established to advance the implementation of the right to development, suggesting a willingness on behalf of the international community of states to see its tenets given practical effect. In 1996 the General

---

[127] Simma and Alston, 'The Sources of Human Rights Law', 82, at 90.

[128] Obiora, 'Beyond the Rhetoric of a Right to Development', 366, at 379.

[129] Ibid.

[130] Brownlie, *Principles of Public International Law*, 695.

[131] On intent in the interpretation the force of a declaration see, B Sloan, 'General Assembly Resolutions Revisited (Forty Years Later)' 58 *BYBIL* (1987) 39, at 128–9 and 138. See also, I Sarnoff (ed), *International Instruments of the United Nations: A Compilation of Agreements, Charters, Conventions, Declarations, Principles, Proclamations, Protocols, Treaties adopted by the General Assembly of the United Nations, 1945–95* (United Nations, 1997) xii.

[132] W Mansell and J Scott, 'Why Bother about the Right to Development?' 21 *J Law & Soc* (1994) 171, at 174.

[133] The USA cast the only vote against its adoption. The right to development has since been endorsed by all states including the USA through the adoption of the Vienna Declaration and Programme of Action. The USA, however, remains vocal in its rejection of economic, social and cultural rights. For a detailed analysis of the USA's objection to the RTD and examples of its de facto implementation of the right in practice, see, SP Marks, 'The Human Right to Development: Between Rhetoric and Reality' 17 *Harv Hum Rts J* (2004) 137.

[134] Sloan, 'General Assembly Resolutions Revisited', 39, at 140.

[135] M Dixon, *Textbook on International Law* (3rd edn, Blackstone Press, 1990) 43–4.

Assembly established a Branch within the Office of the High Commissioner for Human Rights, '... the primary responsibilities of which would include the promotion and protection of the right to development';[136] the UN Commission on Human Rights established an Open-ended Working Group on the Right to Development as a follow-up mechanism aimed at furthering methods by which the right to development may be implemented, and to report on the progress of said implementation;[137] and in 1998 the Commission created the mandate of an Independent Expert on the Right to Development:[138]

in view of the urgent need to make further progress towards the realization of the right to development as elaborated in the Declaration on the Right to Development ... [and] to present to the working group on the right to development at each of its sessions, a study on the current state of progress in the implementation of the right to development.[139]

In 2004, a subsidiary body of the intergovernmental Working Group on the Right to Development was established by the Commission at its 60th session.[140] The High-Level Task Force on the Implementation of the Right to Development is an independent expert body with semi-operational responsibilities. The Task Force is an innovative construct, since it brings together, under the formal auspices of a UN human rights mechanism, human rights experts and representatives of the international development, finance and trade institutions.[141] Its primary objective is to strengthen international cooperation for development by bridging diverse ideological perspectives on the problems and solutions of world poverty and underdevelopment. Its first session was intended to produce a shared vision and approach to advancing human rights, in the relevant areas, through collective international action.[142] At the 2005 World Summit, the General Assembly reaffirmed its commitment to providing the machinery necessary to ensure the effective enjoyment of the right to development.[143]

---

[136] General Assembly res A/Res/50/214, 23 December 1995, para 37.

[137] The Working Group on the Right to Development was set up by the Economic and Social Council decision 1998/269. It held its first session in September 2000.

[138] CHR res 1998/72, 22 April 1998.

[139] Note by the Secretary-General on the Right to Development accompanying the report of the Independent Expert to the General Assembly, UN Doc A/55/306 (2000), para 1.

[140] CHR res 2004/7, para 9.

[141] Notably, but not limited to, the World Bank, IMF and the WTO. See further, ME Salomon, 'The Significance of the Task Force on the Right to Development', Special Report, Human Rights and Development, (guest eds) D Freestone and JK Ingram, 8 *Development Outreach* (The World Bank Institute, October 2006) 27–9.

[142] For a detailed consideration of the work of the Task Force at its first session, see, ME Salomon, 'Towards a Just Institutional Order: A Commentary on the First Session of the UN Task Force on the Right to Development' 23 *NQHR* 3 (2005) 409.

[143] 'We resolve further to strengthen the United Nations human rights machinery with the aim of ensuring effective enjoyment by all of all human rights and civil, political, economic, social and cultural rights, including the right to development.' 2005 World Summit Outcome, UN Doc A/60/L1 (2005), para 123.

The status of the right to development has been elevated through the adoption of annual resolutions by the General Assembly and the Commission on Human Rights, and through declarations emanating from representative world conferences, including: the 1992 Rio Conference on Environment and Development;[144] 1993 Vienna World Conference on Human Rights;[145] the 1995 World Summit for Social Development;[146] 1995 Fourth World Conference on Women;[147] 2000 Millennium Summit;[148] 2001 World Conference on Racism, Racial Discrimination, Xenophobia and Related Intolerance;[149] and, the 2002 World Summit on Sustainable Development.[150] The international community

[144] United Nations Conference on Environment and Development (1992), Rio Declaration on Environment and Development, UN Doc A/CONF151/26, Principle 3: 'The right to development must be fulfilled so as to meet developmental and environmental needs of present and future generations'.

[145] Vienna Declaration and Programme of Action, art 10: 'The World Conference on Human Rights reaffirms the right to development, as established in the Declaration on the Right to Development as a universal and inalienable right and an integral part of the fundamental human rights.'

[146] United Nations World Summit for Social Development, Copenhagen Declaration and Programme of Action (1995) UN Doc A/CONF166/9, Commitment 1(f): 'at the national level we will: Reaffirm, promote and strive to ensure the realization of the rights set out in relevant international instruments and declarations, such as, the Universal Declaration of Human Rights, the International Covenant on Economic, Social and Cultural Rights, and the Declaration on the Right to Development ...'; Commitment 1(n): 'At the international level we will: Reaffirm and promote all human rights which are universal, indivisible, interdependent and interrelated, including development as a universal and inalienable right and an integral part of fundamental human rights, and strive to ensure that they are respected, protected and observed.'

[147] United Nations Fourth World Conference on Women: Action for Equality, Development and Peace, Beijing Declaration and Platform for Action (1995) UN Doc A/Conf177/29 and A/Conf177/20/add1; the Declaration at art 8 states: 'We, the Governments, participating in the Fourth World Conference on Women, reaffirm our commitment to: The equal rights and inherent human dignity of women and men and other purposes and principles enshrined in the Charter of the United Nations, the Universal Declaration of Human Rights and other international human rights instruments, in particular the Convention on the Elimination of All Forms of Discrimination against Women and the Convention on the Rights of the Child, as well as the Declaration on the Elimination of Violence against Women and the Declaration on the Right to Development'.

[148] Millennium Declaration, art 11 states: 'We will spare no effort to free our fellow men, women and children from the abject and dehumanizing conditions of extreme poverty, to which more than a billion of them are currently subjected. We are committed to making the right to development a reality for everyone and to freeing the entire human race from want'; Art 24 states: 'We will spare no effort to promote democracy and strengthen the rule of law, as well as respect for all internationally recognized human rights and fundamental freedoms, including the right to development.'

[149] United Nations World Conference Against Racism, Racial Discrimination, Xenophobia and Related Intolerance, Durban Declaration and Programme of Action (2001) UN Doc A/CONF189/12; the Declaration at Art 78 states: 'We affirm the solemn commitment of all States to promote universal respect for, and observance and protection of, all human rights, economic, social, cultural, civil and political, including the right to development, as a fundamental factor in the prevention and elimination of racism, racial discrimination, xenophobia and related intolerance'.

[150] The Plan of Implementation of the WSSD refers to the right to development several times (although an ideological slant in favour of market solutions can be evidenced). At para 5: Peace, security, stability and respect for human rights and fundamental freedoms, including the right to development, as well as respect for cultural diversity, are essential for achieving sustainable development and ensuring that sustainable development benefits all; para 62(a): Create an enabling

has recognized repeatedly a right to development, the fulfilment of which would see advanced international economic equity. Widespread examples of non-compliance—while contributing to egregious human rights violations—do not negate the existence of a norm,[151] while the support of the international community as a whole gives rise to reasonable expectations that states will fulfil their requisite duties.[152]

The DRD can be understood as enshrining and elaborating the values of the international community. The references in the Declaration to the right to self-determination, sovereignty over natural resources, and international peace and security, reflect a relationship with existing principles of international law, placing the right to development among those key principles central to a just and secure international order.

2.3.1.5 *International cooperation and shared responsibility in world conferences*

Recognition by the international community that cooperation in addressing a range of human rights concerns has become a necessity is evidenced by the number, and focuses, of World Conferences convened in the post Cold War period, and in the content of their final documents. The conferences are organized under the auspices of the UN, subject to a decision by the General Assembly. They are often preceded by regional intergovernmental conferences and NGO fora, and conclude with universal declarations and programmes of action on their areas of focus. A review of the conference declarations highlights the widespread acceptance among the international community of states of the centrality of the principle of international cooperation, and of shared responsibility, in the realization of human rights today, and the requirement of global equity as reflected therein.

---

environment at the regional, sub-regional, national and local levels in order to achieve sustained economic growth and sustainable development and support African efforts for peace, stability and security, the resolution and prevention of conflicts, democracy, good governance, respect for human rights and fundamental freedoms, including the right to development and gender equality; para 138: Good governance is essential for sustainable development. Sound economic policies, solid democratic institutions responsive to the needs of the people and improved infrastructure are the basis for sustained economic growth, poverty eradication, and employment creation. Freedom, peace and security, domestic stability, respect for human rights, including the right to development, and the rule of law, gender equality, market-oriented policies, and an overall commitment to just and democratic societies are also essential and mutually reinforcing; para 169: Acknowledge the consideration being given to the possible relationship between environment and human rights, including the right to development, with full and transparent participation of Member States of the United Nations and observer States. UN Doc A/CONF199/20 (2002).

[151] See, R Higgins, *Problems and Process, Problems and Process: International Law and How We Use it* (Oxford University Press, 1998) 20; *Military and Paramilitary Activities in and against Nicaragua* (Merits) (Nicaragua v United States of America) ICJ Rep (1986) 14, at para 186.

[152] McDougal, Lasswell and Reisman, among others, defend the source of 'community expectation' as a jurisprudential basis underlying all obligations.

The number of World Conferences held in the past decade illustrates the internationalization of human rights generally, addressing themes which may have once sat more commonly within the realm of domestic consideration only. The subject matter of some these conferences, although not specifically that of human rights, concern human rights related areas, and often require, in order that the agreed plans may be effectively promoted, the mainstreaming of human rights. These post Cold War global conferences at which the international community has committed themselves to take action, have dealt with the areas of: children (New York, 1990); the environment and development (Rio de Janeiro, 1992); human rights (Vienna, 1993); population and development (Cairo, 1994); social development (Copenhagen, 1995); women (Beijing, 1995); human settlements (Istanbul, 1996); food (Rome, 1996); earth (New York, 1997); the establishment of an international criminal court (Rome, 1998); peace, development and human rights (Millennium Declaration, 2000); racism, racial discrimination, xenophobia and related intolerance (Durban, 2001); and sustainable development (Johannesburg, 2002).

On 25 June 1993 in Vienna, the World Conference on Human Rights adopted a Declaration and Programme of Action which solemnly sanctioned the obligation to cooperate internationally in the achievement of human rights for all. This conference reflected the first international consensus in the post-Cold War era on the importance of promoting effective cooperation among the international community of states. The preamble reaffirms, inter alia, the commitment undertaken by UN Member States by virtue of Articles 55 and 56 of the UN Charter to 'take joint and separate action placing proper emphasis on developing effective international cooperation for the realization of the purposes set out in Article 55, including universal respect for, and observance of, human rights and fundamental freedoms for all'. The Declaration reflects on 'the major changes taking place on the international scene', and the relevance these changes have on encouraging respect for human rights.[153] This Conference gave clear recognition of the essential need for international cooperation in protecting human rights and in so doing are:

Invoking the spirit of our age and the realities of our time which call upon the peoples of the world and all States Members of the United Nations to rededicate themselves to the global task of promoting and protecting all human rights and fundamental freedoms so as to secure full and universal enjoyment of these right,[154] [and are]

Determined to take new steps forward in the commitment of the international community with a view to achieving substantial progress in human rights endeavours by an increased and sustained effort of international cooperation and solidarity.[155]

The principle that the promotion and protection of human rights is the legitimate concern of the international community was given recognition with the

---

[153] Vienna Declaration and Programme of Action, preambular para 9.
[154] Ibid, preambular para 15.   [155] Ibid, preambular para 16.

founding of the UN, and has gained credence and scope with the evolution of human rights standard-setting ever since. It was the Vienna Declaration, however, which stated this unequivocally thereby revalidating its transformative capacity. Human rights as forming a legitimate concern of the international community, provides a starting point from which a broad legal duty of international cooperation and shared responsibility are derived. In this regard, paragraph 4 of the Vienna Declaration states that:

The promotion and protection of all human rights and fundamental freedoms must be considered as a priority objective of the United Nations in accordance with its purposes and principles, *in particular the purpose of international cooperation.* In the framework of these purposes and principles, the promotion and protection of all human rights is a legitimate concern of the international community. The organs and specialized agencies related to human rights should therefore further enhance the coordination of their activities based on the consistent and objective application of international human rights instruments.

The Declaration and Programme of Action stresses that '[t]he international community must treat human rights globally in a fair and equal manner';[156] that 'the international community should promote an effective international cooperation for the realization of the right to development and the elimination of obstacles to development,'[157] including the 'developmental and environmental needs of present and future generations'.[158] The international community is called upon 'to make all efforts to help alleviate the external debt burden of developing countries,'[159] and to prioritize 'the immediate alleviation and eventual elimination' of extreme poverty.[160] International cooperation is further referred to in the context of child rights, particular priority to be given to, inter alia, 'reducing infant and maternal mortality rates, reducing malnutrition and illiteracy rates and providing access to safe drinking water and to basic education'.[161] Thus the Vienna Declaration and Programme of Action repeatedly calls for international cooperation in fulfilling human rights, and recognizes the impact of certain external conditions on their exercise.

The Declaration and Programme of Action adopted at the World Summit for Social Development held in Copenhagen in 1995 sets out commitments in terms of those to be undertaken at the national level, and those at the international level.[162] The Declaration fully recognizes the interdependence of the economies and societies of the world, the relationship between national and international responsibilities, and international cooperation as necessary to achieving social development and justice.

---

[156] Ibid, Pt I, art 5.   [157] Ibid, Pt I, art 10.
[158] Ibid, Pt I, art 11.   [159] Ibid, Pt I, art 12.
[160] Ibid, Pt I, art 14.   [161] Ibid, Pt II, art 47.
[162] United Nations World Summit for Social Development, Copenhagen Declaration and Programme of Action (1995), UN Doc A/CONF166/9.

In the section highlighting the current social situation, and reasons for convening the Summit, key elements of globalization, such as increased human mobility, enhanced communications, increased trade and capital flows, and technological developments, are cited in the context of the need urgently to enhance their benefits, while mitigating the negative effects of the poverty brought to bear on so many people.[163] Continued threats and consequences which have been 'globalized' were detailed, including intensified poverty, unemployment, social disintegration, and threats to human beings such as environmental risks.[164] The Declaration also refers to the need to give priority to coordination and cooperation—especially at the regional and international levels—to the fight against 'world-wide conditions', that pose severe threats to health, safety, peace and security, and well-being; including chronic hunger and malnutrition.[165]

In addition to national responsibilities the Declaration is clear that the principles and goals pledged by heads of states and government, integral to a viable framework for action, cannot be reached 'without the collective commitment and efforts of the international community'.[166] Indeed, the vision for social development professed by the state delegations was one based on inter alia, 'human dignity, human rights, equality, respect, peace, democracy, *mutual responsibility and cooperation* . . . .'[167]

Five years after the adoption of the Declaration on Social Development the General Assembly met to appraise the outcome of the Summit, and to decide on further initiatives for social development. This special session of the General Assembly entitled 'World Summit for Social Development in A Globalizing World' (Copenhagen +5) resulted in the adoption of 'Further Initiatives for Social Development'.[168] As the General Assembly noted, both documents '[e]mphasize the vital importance of placing the goals of social development . . . at the centre of economic policy-making, including policies that influence domestic and global market forces and the global economy.'[169] The resolution on Further Initiatives for Social Development reiterates that enhanced international cooperation is essential to address the challenges of globalization,[170] and the implementation of social development programmes and actions,[171] reaffirming its commitment to the rights set out in international instruments and declarations, including the UDHR, the two Covenants, and the Declaration on the Right

---

[163] Ibid, arts 13–4.   [164] Ibid, art 14.
[165] Ibid, art 20.   [166] Ibid, art 26 (c).
[167] Ibid, art 25. Emphasis added.
[168] Development for All in a Globalizing World (Copenhagen +5, 2000), General Assembly res A/RES/S-24/2 (24th special session, 1 July 2000).
[169] Implementation of the outcome of the World Summit for Social Development and of the special session of the General Assembly in this regard, General Assembly res A/RES/55/4, 29 November 2000, art 3.
[170] Copenhagen +5, Pt I, para 11.
[171] Ibid, Pt III, Commitment 1, para 2.

to Development.[172] The document addresses the requirement of international cooperation in the eradication of poverty throughout the world,[173] in relation to resource allocation for social development,[174] including official development assistance,[175] and in the context of equitable, development-oriented and durable solutions to the external debt and debt-servicing burdens of developing countries.[176] The General Assembly underscores its position that social development requires not only economic activity, but also a reduction in the inequality in the distribution of wealth, and more equitable distribution of the benefits of economic growth within, and among, nations.[177] As has been elsewhere suggested, this would necessitate an open, equitable, secure, non-discriminatory, predictable, transparent and multilateral rule-based international trading system which maximizes opportunities, guarantees social justice, and recognizes the interrelationship between social development and economic growth.[178] The special session document also refers to the requirement that the Bretton Woods institutions—the World Bank and IMF—give due consideration to the objectives and policy approaches of the United Nations conferences and summits,[179] and to the need for these institutions to 'promote the full realization of the right to development through, inter alia, the implementation of the provisions of the Declaration on the Right to Development . . .'.[180]

The Copenhagen +5 political declaration came on the heels of the United Nations Millennium Declaration,[181] which brought together heads of state and government to adopt a declaration that takes as its starting point the vital importance of international cooperation in addressing the ills of globalization. It also affirms the grand objective of global equity and the role of shared responsibility to these ends. The Declaration, adopted by the General Assembly, recognizes in addition to the responsibilities of states to their individual societies, that 'we [the Member States] have a *collective responsibility* to uphold the principles of human dignity, equality and equity at the global levels. As leaders we have a duty therefore to all the world's peoples . . .'.[182] In this regard, the Declaration refers to the timelessness of the purposes and principles of the UN Charter, including respect for human rights, and international cooperation in solving international problems

---

[172] Ibid, Pt III, Commitment 1, para 5.

[173] Ibid, Pt III, Commitment 2; Commitment 8 aims to ensure that when structural adjustment programmes are agreed that they include social development goals, in particular in relation to the eradication of poverty.

[174] Ibid, Pt III, Commitment 9.

[175] Ibid, Pt III, Commitment 9, para 143(d).

[176] Ibid, Pt I, para 7.

[177] Ibid, Pt I, para 4.

[178] *The Right to Development: The Importance and Application of the Principle of Equity at Both the National and International Levels*, para 23.

[179] Copenhagen +5, Pt III, Commitment 10, para 149(b).

[180] Ibid, Pt III, Commitment 10, para 151.

[181] GA res A/55/2, 8 September 2000.

[182] Millennium Declaration, art 2 (emphasis added).

of an economic, social, cultural or humanitarian character as per Charter Article 1(3),[183] and notes that its relevance and capacity has increased due to the interconnection and interdependence of nations and peoples.[184] The Millennium Declaration explicitly recognizes the trouble with economic globalization, noting that 'the central challenge we face today is to ensure that globalization becomes a positive force for all the world's peoples ... at present the benefits [of globalization] are unevenly shared, while its costs are unevenly distributed ...[185] the global challenge must be managed in a way that distributes the costs and burdens fairly in accordance with basic principles of equity and social justice'.[186] It subsequently declares that these basic principles of equity and social justice require 'solidarity' which is a 'fundamental value[s] ... essential to international relations in the twenty-first century'.[187]

Other fundamental values recognized in the Declaration as essential to contemporary international relations include: the right to live in dignity, free from hunger, from the fear of violence and oppression, and within a system of democratic participatory governance based on the will of the people;[188] equality of opportunity to benefit from development for both people and nations;[189] respect for nature in accordance with the precepts of sustainable development;[190] and shared responsibility for managing, inter alia, worldwide economic and social development.[191] The Declaration then provides key objectives to which are assigned 'special significance' in order to implement these shared values, making particular demands on developed countries. These include: a fair and equitable multilateral trading and financial system;[192] debt relief;[193] more generous development assistance;[194] and encouraging the pharmaceutical industry to make essential drugs more widely available and affordable to people who need them in developing countries.[195] To these ends, and in addition to ensuring respect for internationally recognized human rights by means of 'fully uphold[ing] the Universal Declaration of Human Rights',[196] the UN Member States solemnly reaffirm that they will seek to realize their 'universal aspirations for peace, cooperation and development.'[197]

The Monterrey Consensus, adopted in 2002 at the International Conference on Financing for Development, while placing the primary responsibility for tackling poverty on national governments, calls for greater international cooperation

---

183 Ibid, art 4.   184 Ibid, art 3.   185 Ibid, art 5.
186 Ibid, art 6, Solidarity.
187 Ibid, Pt I Values and Principles, art 6, Solidarity.
188 Ibid, art 6, Freedom.   189 Ibid, art 6, Equality.
190 Ibid, art 6, Respect for Nature.
191 Ibid, art 6, Shared responsibility.
192 Ibid, Pt III Development and Poverty Eradication, art 13.
193 Ibid, art 15.   194 Ibid.
195 Ibid, Pt III Development and Poverty Eradication, art 20.
196 Ibid, Pt V Human Rights, Democracy and Good Governance, art 25.
197 Ibid, Pt VIII Strengthening the United Nations, art 32.

in financing for development, noting that: '... domestic economies are now interwoven with the global economic system ... [national] efforts need to be supported by an enabling international economic environment.'[198]

It is apparent from the overview just provided that there is widespread recognition, at the highest level, that international action is required in order to fulfil a range of fundamental human rights today. Although the obligation to avoid violating human rights, as well as to promote human rights, rests also with states acting domestically, there is a clear responsibility incumbent upon states to cooperate at the international level. The Universal Declaration of Human Rights, and the normative human rights framework developed since, has been strengthened by the common positions articulated as a result of the declarations of a range of World Conferences over the past decade. These representative gatherings, derived as they are from public discourse in fora open to all states, strengthen the legal force of these demands for global justice. Delbrück notes in this regard that 'similar requirements apply to the accelerated creation of rules of international customary law that articulate public interests'.[199]

2.4 The Content of International Cooperation

There would seem to be a certain accord—at least among the affluent and powerful states—as to what a duty of international cooperation for human rights does not entail. Most vociferously the affluent states tend to claim that it does not provide for a binding obligation to transfer resources from North to South.[200] Yet clearly it is not limited to international development cooperation. While there may be some uncertainty as to what international cooperation in this area can be said legally to require, the latest phase of economic globalization, covering the last 15 years or so, has done much to refine the content of this pivotal obligation.

2.4.1 The position of Northern states

The United Nations Working Group on the Right to Development is the principal international forum for debate on characterizing the right to development *as* a right. In this forum, Northern states tend to place considerable emphasis on

---

[198] UN International Conference on Financing for Development, Outcome of the International Conference on Financing for Development (Monterrey Consensus), (2000), UN Doc A/CONF 198/3, Pt I, para 6.

[199] J Delbrück, 'Prospects for a "World (Internal) Law"? Legal Developments in a Changing International System' 9 *IJGLS* (2002) 401, at 430.

[200] The view of Southern states tends to be very different: 'The representative of Egypt stressed that article 2(1) [of the ICESCR] recognized a legal obligation of international assistance which should be reflected in the text of an optional protocol.' *Report of the Open-ended working group to consider options regarding the elaboration of an optional protocol to the International Covenant on Economic, Social and Cultural Rights* (2nd session, 2005) UN Doc E/CN4/2005/52, para 77.

duties at the national level, particularly as they pertain to the South, while the Southern states tend to focus on specific elements in relation to the international dimension of the right to development. Thus the direction of discussion set by the South is usually towards issues such as inequalities in the international financial system, greater participation of developing countries in global decision-making on economic policy, and promoting a fairer international trade regime. The Northern states tend to draw more on the importance of suitable domestic conditions in the South, with good governance, democracy, responsible economic management and human rights receiving considerable attention.[201]

Although some Northern (read: donor) governments call for the strengthening of human rights principles in the processes of addressing poverty, most notably that of mutual accountability,[202] there is little readiness to embrace a notion that there exists a legal duty of international cooperation for addressing poverty elsewhere under the Declaration on the Right to Development,[203] nor with regard to international cooperation under ICESCR.[204] Concerns centre almost exclusively on the fear of being locked into resource transfers, or of suggesting a diminished set of responsibilities belonging to developing states at the domestic level for fulfilling economic and social rights. Indeed, the numerous public pronouncements by Northern states on this single aspect of international cooperation (equated with development cooperation) leaves little doubt that they recognize no binding obligation to transfer aid, however, this is not the whole story regarding international cooperation. While developed states are loathe to acknowledge any legal obligation to transfer resources, there is agreement that an international enabling

---

[201] C Lennox and ME Salomon, 'Negotiating the Right to Development for Minorities' 4 *McGill International Review* 1(Winter 2003) 4, at 5–6.

[202] See the EU statement to the 2004 Working Group on the Right to Development: 'The EU is of the view that another issue that merits consideration following the [UN High-Level Seminar on the Right to Development] is that of accountability of all involved, based on human rights principles. That means accountability of multilateral donors, including the World Bank and International Monetary Fund, bilateral donors and recipient governments. All should ensure that they are adopting a human rights approach.' Statement on behalf of the European Union, Working Group on the Right to Development, (5th session, 2004), agenda item 4(a): Consideration of the ideas and proposals raised at the High-Level Seminar.

[203] *Report of the Open-ended Working Group on the Right to Development* (1st and 2nd sessions 2001), annex III, Comments Submitted by Japan, para 46, denying the existence of any consensus as to a duty of international cooperation for the realization of the right to development. At the first session of the Task Force on the Right to Development in 2004, Sweden, a country that remains among the most progressive on the notion of shared responsibility for development, remarked that: 'Our position is no secret, there is no legal obligation of international cooperation we do it out of a sense of international solidarity . . . we have a moral obligation . . .'. Notes on file with author.

[204] 'The representatives of the United Kingdom, the Czech Republic, Canada, France and Portugal believed that international cooperation and assistance was an important moral obligation but not a legal entitlement, and did not interpret the Covenant to impose a legal obligation to provide development assistance or give a legal title to receive such aid.' *Report of the Open-ended working group to consider options regarding the elaboration of an optional protocol to the International Covenant on Economic, Social and Cultural Rights* (2nd session, 2005) UN Doc E/CN4/2005/52, para 76.

environment is required to give effect to the right to development and to socio-economic rights. The support shown through the reiteration of commitments in the Millennium Development Goals, including Goal 8, reflects this consensus.

The Millennium Development Goal 8 on a Global Partnership for Development reflects the important role of developed countries in the realization of the MDGs. It constitutes a political commitment on behalf of rich countries in the areas of aid, trade, debt relief and implicitly, global governance.[205] While MDG 8 relates to developing a global partnership between rich and poor countries, the weight of the responsibility for giving effect to the partnership is understood to rest with developed countries, and it is those countries that report against it.[206] Goal 8 is focused on action to be taken at the international level and is essential to advancing the other seven Goals.[207]

The significance attached to Goal 8 in making possible the achievement of the MDGs confirms the importance given today to international cooperation and shared responsibility in the creation of an international environment conducive to having the people of developing countries secure food, water, housing, sustainable livelihoods, access to healthcare and education; in sum, to emerge from conditions of terrible poverty. This informs the content of an obligation of international cooperation. Moreover, as Alston notes, the repeated formal commitments to mobilize resources to fulfil the MDGs and meaningfully to counter poverty as found in the Millennium Declaration, the Plan of Implementation of the World Summit on Sustainable Development, and the Monterrey Consensus:

provide a strong argument that some such obligation has crystallized into customary law. It will be difficult for countries to insist that they have persistently objected to such an evolution if they continue to affirm in so many contexts their commitment to assisting developing country governments to achieve targets as tangible and clearly achievable as the MDGs ... the [developing country] would have a plausible claim against wealthy countries as group ....[208]

---

[205] The targets under MDG 8 address: developing further a rules-based trading and financial system; the needs of least developed countries, focusing on aspects of the international trading system (tariffs and market access), enhancing debt relief, cancellation and sustainability, and, increasing official development assistance; strategies for productive work for youth in developing countries; the provision of affordable essential drugs in developing countries in cooperation with pharmaceutical companies; and furthering the availability of new technologies in the areas of communication and information in cooperation with the private sector.

[206] <http://www.undp.org/mdg/donorcountryreports.html>.

[207] The MDGs are: a reduction by half of the proportion of people living in extreme poverty; achieving universal primary education; promoting gender equality; reducing the child mortality rate; improving maternal health; combating HIV/AIDS and other diseases; furthering sustainable development which includes reducing by half the proportion of people without access to safe drinking water and improving the lives of slum dwellers; and developing a global partnership for development.

[208] P Alston, 'Ships Passing in the Night: The Current State of the Human Rights and Development Debate Seen Through the Lens of the Millennium Development Goals' 27 *HRQ* 3 (2005) 755, at 778. Alston remarks that the arrangement would depend on the developing country

2.4.2 'Maximum available resources'

The emphasis in the Declaration on the Right to Development is on cooperation and collective action. The International Covenant on Economic, Social and Cultural Rights entrenches both substantive obligations of international cooperation in the progressive realization of Covenant rights, as at Articles 2(1), 11 and 15, and procedural obligations, as at Articles 22 and 23. This international assistance and cooperation (under the Covenant) is required 'to the maximum of [a states parties] available resources':

> The Committee notes that the phrase "to the maximum of its available resources" was intended by the drafters of the Covenant to refer to both the resources existing within a State and those available from the international community through international cooperation and assistance. Moreover, the essential role of such cooperation in facilitating the full realization of the relevant rights is further underlined by the specific provisions contained in articles 11, 15, 22 and 23. With respect to article 22 the Committee has already drawn attention, in General Comment 2 (1990), to some of the opportunities and responsibilities that exist in relation to international cooperation. Article 23 also specifically identifies "the furnishing of technical assistance" as well as other activities, as being among the means of "international action for the achievement of the rights recognized ...". [209]

Jurisprudentially, few advances have been made in determining specifically that which constitutes a state's maximum available resources for the purposes of meeting its obligation of international assistance and cooperation. Moreover, it would seem that the very approach enshrined in the Covenant presents a perverse (albeit predictable) logic; it is concerned with what a state can afford to do by its own estimation[210] rather than what needs to be done to secure the minimum essential levels of economic, social and cultural rights globally.[211] To recognize, for example, that 44 per cent of the world's population lives below a World Bank poverty line of US$2 a day yet consumes only 1.3 per cent of the global product,[212] is also to presume liability on the part of the affluent members of the international community of states for failing to undertake steps to their maximum available resources. Maximum available resources at the international level are equated

meeting its correlative obligation by demonstrating its best efforts to meet the MDGs and its inability to do so because of lack of financial resources (but cf Ch 5).

[209] CESCR, General Comment no 3, The Nature of States Parties' Obligations, para 13.

[210] This might be distinguished from the evaluation of what resources are considered to be available at the domestic level, which Craven concludes is an objective one providing for non-absolute state discretion, 'a point underscored by the Committee's willingness to consider issues of government expenditure'. Craven, *The International Covenant on Economic, Social and Cultural Rights*, 137.

[211] See further Ch 5.

[212] As revisited in Ch 5, high-income countries, with far less people, together consume 81% of the global product. Pogge draws his figures from the World Bank, *World Development Report 2003*. See, TW Pogge, 'World Poverty and Human Rights' 19 *Ethics and International Affairs* 1 (2005) 1, at 1.

with the globally endorsed 0.7 per cent GNI in official development assistance, which now represents an objective standard and its phased achievement is used by the Committee as a yardstick to measure whether a developed country is taking steps to the maximum of its available resources. Its use as an objective form of evaluation does not address the fact that it has been set in order to lift only half, and not all, of the world's poor from extreme poverty by 2015.[213]

2.4.3 The structural content of international cooperation

It may be true then, that to a certain degree, the parameters of the obligation to cooperate internationally in the realization of socio-economic rights are not yet clearly drawn. But perhaps this aphorism pertains to the limited success in embedding global constraints and effecting reform, rather than any paucity of criteria as to what might constitute the structural dimensions of international cooperation for human rights.

International cooperation favours obligations of conduct: process over outcome, conduct over result, assurances of best effort over guarantees of success.[214] While the foreseeable impact of arrangements at the international level are undermining the exercise of human rights, increasing consensus on steps needed to address this situation is serving to strengthen the range of recommendations in this area.

Political commitments towards international cooperation have been recently articulated as 'global partnerships for development', provided for in the 8th Millennium Development Goal. These political commitments, in so far as they are consistent procedurally and advance substantively human rights, may contribute to the content of defining obligations of international cooperation. Consistent with global partnership requirements, international cooperation for human rights includes then, ensuring an international economic system geared towards poverty reduction,[215] and participatory international multilateral trading investment and financial systems that are conducive to the elimination of poverty.[216] It would include improved access to markets by the least developed countries, as well as a comprehensive approach to addressing the problem of debt

---

[213] If affluent countries all honoured this commitment Pogge deduces that world poverty could be eliminated: TW Pogge, 'The First UN Millennium Development Goal: A Cause for Celebration?' 5 *Journal of Human Development* 3 (2004) 377, at 388. We might thus assume that the figure of 0.7% GNI in official development assistance was endorsed based on the assumption that many developed states would not meet it, or would meet it over a long period of time and therefore the corresponding commitment should realistically be to lifting only half those that need it from poverty rather than all.

[214] See Ch 3.

[215] Millennium Development Goal 8, Target 1 <http://www.un.org/millenniumgoals>.

[216] P Hunt, M Nowak and S Osmani, *Principles and Guidelines for a Human Rights Approach to Poverty Reduction Strategies* (OHCHR, 2005), para 102. These Guidelines draw on consultations with various stakeholders including UN Member States, intergovernmental and non-governmental organizations.

faced by developing countries.[217] The international community of states has also recognized the need for 'cooperation' with pharmaceutical companies to provide access to essential drugs at affordable prices in developing countries.[218] Giving effect to the obligation of international cooperation may require, but is not limited to, the international transfer of resources.[219] Other methods by which this obligation could be complied with is through, for example, supplying technology, and creating new international mechanisms to meet the specific requirements of developing countries.[220]

Yet, requirements to address in particular the *structural* aspects of international cooperation in these areas might look quite different. These demands might entail strengthening the role of developing countries in global governance so as to be able to assert the economic rights of their people, imposing nothing short of a duty to reform the existing institutional economic system; establishing an independent and transparent debt arbitration mechanism;[221] and dramatically reworking the way in which pharmaceutical innovation is encouraged and rewarded to create incentives for pharmaceutical companies to address the global disease burden.[222] There are many other global configurations that have been identified as being in urgent need of revisiting if we are to see effect given to the realization of basic socio-economic rights in the South: they would include international arms control that would halt a trade that sustains oppression in developing countries;[223] addressing international tax evasion that represent losses to developing countries equivalent to that which are required to meet the MDGs;[224] and compensating

---

[217] Millennium Development Goal 8, Targets 2 and 3 <http://www.un.org/millenniumgoals>.
[218] Ibid, Target 6.
[219] For example, the international commitment of developed states to providing 0.7% GNI to poverty reduction under the Millennium Development Goals.
[220] A Sengupta, *Third Report of the Independent Expert on the Right to Development* (Working Group on the Right to Development, 2nd session, 2001) UN Doc E/CN4/2001/WG18/2, para 34.
[221] *Europe: A True Global Partnership for Development? CIDSE Shadow Report on European Progress towards Millennium Development Goal*, (Coopération Internationale pour le Développement et la Solidarité, 2005) 5.1; B Mudho, *Report of the Independent Expert on the Effects of Structural Adjustment Policies and Foreign Debt on the Full Enjoyment of all Human Rights, particularly Economic, Social and Cultural Rights*, UN Doc E/CN4/2005/42, para 45.
[222] For policy suggestions, see for example, TW Pogge, 'Human Rights and Global Health: A Research Program' in C Barry and TW Pogge (eds), *Global Institutions and Responsibilities: Achieving Global Justice* (Blackwell, 2005) 190.
[223] 'The international community must ... adopt more effective and legally binding agreements on territorial and extra-territorial arms brokering, and common standards on monitoring and enforcement.' This UK Government commissioned report further notes that several of the largest manufacturers, exporters, and brokers of arms to Africa are to be found in the G8 and EU countries. *Our Common Interest*, Report of the Commission for Africa (2005) 5.2.2.
[224] *Group de Travail sur Les Nouvelles Contributions Financières Internationales* (Landau Report, 2004) 38. Researchers credit the UK with launching the Extractive Industries Transparency Initiative at the World Summit on Sustainable Development in 2002, while noting that 'the UK also bears a key responsibility in the development of tax evasion and money laundering with its Crown sheltering half of the world's tax havens.': *Europe: A True Global Partnership for Development?* at 3.2.1.

developing countries for the skills drain that effectively leave them subsidizing the healthcare systems of developed countries.[225] The UN Special Rapporteur on the Right to Health drew the attention of the General Assembly to his conclusion that this 'perverse subsidy' was inconsistent with the human rights responsibilities of developed countries derived of international assistance and cooperation.[226] A thread common to all these various areas is the focus on international reform and regulation. Domestic, bilateral and regional initiatives may well serve particular ends,[227] but cannot replace harmonized standards, practices and enforcement at the global level. This is a demand born of our interdependence.

Part of this duty to reform the current institutional order that allows for 18 million deaths annually due to avoidable poverty-related causes[228] might entail a duty to negotiate internationally. This would include a serious attempt to reach a multilateral solution informed by an appreciation that the views and obligations of others matter. Referring to the WTO's landmark *Shrimp/Turtle* decision (which addressed the import ban by the US on shrimp farmed in a manner that did not protect sea turtles as required by US environmental laws), Alvarez notes that while we may disagree with the ruling, the Appellate Body made the important point that the United States erred in not negotiating multilaterally, and that it was important for the Appellate Body to have made this point and to have directed it to the hyper-power.[229] Sands, in his analysis of the same case, noted that 'in effect, a state cannot act on its own until it has engaged in good faith, in efforts to achieve a negotiated and consensual solution'.[230] In light of the concern regarding the impact of certain WTO agreements on the exercise of human rights,[231] the scope of an emerging duty to negotiate might reach back to

---

[225] P Hunt, *Report of the Special Rapporteur on the Right of Everyone to the Highest Attainable Standard of Health*, UN Doc. A/60/348 (2005), paras 82–5. The Special Rapporteur reports to the General Assembly that some 30–50% of health graduates leave South Africa for the USA or UK each year and in 1999, Ghana lost more nurses than it trained. During the 1990s, two thirds of Jamaica's nurses left the country permanently. P Hunt, Special Rapporteur on the Right of Everyone to the Enjoyment of the Highest Attainable Standard of Physical and Mental Health, *Statement to the Third Committee of the General Assembly*, 8 October 2005.

[226] 'As well as being ethically indefensible, this flow of resources from poor to rich is inconsistent with developed countries' human rights responsibility of international assistance and cooperation, as well as other international commitments, including the Millennium Declaration and Goal 8. There is a compelling case that this perverse subsidy should be redressed by the payment of compensation, restitution or reparation to those developing countries of origin where the skills drain reduces their capacity to fulfil the right to health obligations that they owe their citizens.': Hunt, *Report of the Special Rapporteur on the Right of Everyone to the Highest Attainable Standard of Health* (2005), para 83.

[227] See, for example, the UN's Special Unit for South-South Cooperation <http://tcdc1.undp.org>.

[228] TW Pogge, *Reward Pharmaceutical Innovators in Proportion to the Health Impact of their Invention* (Carnegie Council on Ethics and International Affairs, Policy Innovations, 2006) <http://www.policyinnovations.org>.

[229] J Alvarez, 'The Rule (and Role) of Law in the International Community', 72nd International Law Association Conference, Toronto, 4–8 June 2006. Notes on file with author.

[230] P Sands, *Lawless World: America and the Making and Breaking of Global Rules* (Penguin, 2005) 112.

[231] See Ch 3.

the point of evaluating the existing negotiating positions of developing countries in order to ascertain whether their positions are sufficiently strong to ensure the fulfilment of their human rights obligations, and thus prevent negative social impact domestically.[232] The premise that there is a duty to negotiate in order to secure compliance with human rights obligations presupposes a capacity of developing states to undertake meaningful negotiations (including when negotiating with TNCs),[233] (as well as their willingness to honour those obligations within the decision-making process[234]). A recent UN report reflecting the views of experts, states, relevant IGOs, and NGOs draws attention to the fact that 'international assistance and cooperation' aimed at poverty reduction requires that 'all bilateral and multilateral decision-making processes are fair, equitable and transparent, and sensitive to the needs of developing States, especially their disadvantaged and marginalized individuals and groups, including the poor'.[235] In order for, inter alia, the socio-economic rights of the poor not to be undermined, the report seeks assurances that 'before adopting relevant international agreements or policies there is an independent, objective and publicly available assessment of its impact on the poor' and that the findings of the assessment give rise to the adoption of effective measures.[236]

To negotiate in a manner consistent with the obligation of international cooperation for human rights, developed states must ensure that their external human rights obligations are both understood and respected by those in finance and trade who represent the government in international negotiations on those issues, as well as those representatives responsible for the policies and projects of the Bretton Woods institutions.[237] Compliance with international obligations under ICESCR requires that states parties seek to promote (and respect) economic, social and cultural rights in countries other than their own, as well as in their bilateral and multilateral negotiations.[238] This highlights the

---

[232] R Howse, *Social Impact Assessment in the Areas of Trade and Development at the National and International Levels* (OHCHR, 2004) 12. An indication of a country's capacity to negotiate is the size of its representation. A recent study has found that 'only 8 of the 38 Sub-Saharan countries had close to five (the WTO average) resident delegates .... Worse, 19 of the 38 countries—half of the Sub-Saharan WTO membership—had no delegate resident in Geneva. Only Nigeria had a delegation that deals solely with the WTO': World Bank, *World Development Report 2006: Equity and Development* (World Bank/Oxford University Press, 2006) 67.

[233] 'When formulating a national poverty reduction strategy, developing States should: ... Endeavour to strengthen their negotiating capacity in relation to their dealings with TNCs, the operations of which may have a significant impact on poverty'. Hunt, Nowak and Osmani, *Principles and Guidelines*, para 105(c).

[234] For example, there is a disinclination among developing states towards regulatory frameworks that would seem to compromise their comparative advantage.

[235] Hunt, Nowak and Osmani, *Principles and Guidelines*, para 104(c).

[236] Ibid, para 105(b).

[237] Ibid, para 104(b); CESCR, General Comment no 15, The Right to Water (arts 11 and 12), (29th session, 2002) UN Doc E/C12/2002/11, para 35: 'Agreements concerning trade liberalization should not curtail or inhibit a country's capacity to ensure the full realization of the right to water'.

[238] For example, CESCR, General Comment no 18, The Right to Work (art 6), (35th session, 2005) UN Doc E/C12/GC/18, para 30.

issue of policy coherence required across government departments in order to ensure the consistent application of human rights obligations in all international policy-making processes.[239] The pressing need for international policy coherence is receiving increasing attention,[240] including by some developed states,[241] advancing its significance as a criterion for the fulfilment of the obligation of international cooperation.

States determine the policies of intergovernmental organizations such as the World Bank, the International Monetary Fund, and the World Trade Organization. They bring to these prescribed cooperative engagements their existing external human rights obligations, compliance with which must be retained as they go about their mandated activities.[242] The Member States of international organizations are compelled to ensure that the transfer of competences to the organization does not allow them to avoid their responsibilities under international human rights law.[243] As concluded by Sands and Klein:

[M]embers of international organisations may be responsible not for the consequences of the latter's illegal acts, but for their own participation in that act, or for their failure

[239] Hunt, Nowak and Osmani, *Principles and Guidelines*, para 104(b).

[240] See J Ziegler, *Report of the UN Special Rapporteur on the Right to Food*, UN Doc E/CN4/2005/47; P, Hunt, *Report of the UN Special Rapporteur on the Highest Attainable Standard of Health, Mission to the WTO*, UN Doc E/CN4/2004/49/Add1; *A Fair Globalization*, Report of the World Commission on the Social Dimension of Globalization, (ILO, 2004); and the ILO follow-up regarding a 'Policy Coherence Initiative', see ILO Governing Body, 292nd session, Working Party on the Social Dimension of Globalization, GB 292/WP/SDG/1, March 2005; and the *Report of the Working Party on the Social Dimension of Globalization*, GB292/15 March 2005.

[241] See, *Finland's Report on the MDGs* (2004), <http://www.undp.org/mdg/donorcountryreports.html>; *Report of the High-Level Task Force on the Implementation of the Right to Development* (1st session, 2004) UN Doc E/CN4/2005/WG18/2, para 18. Sweden reported to the Task Force that: 'The objective of [its new development cooperation] policy was to contribute to an equitable development and the achievement of the Millennium Development Goals by applying human rights perspectives based on conventions and by viewing development from the perspectives of the poor in the partner developing countries. It was pointed out that through this new policy, Sweden was not only aiming to empower partner countries with increased budget support *but was also promoting overall coherence among policies within its own boundaries* as well as in the recipient countries with a view to contribute to the promotion and protection of human rights both domestically and internationally.' (emphasis added).

[242] See, *Matthews v United Kingdom* ECtHR App no 24833/94, Grand Chamber judgement of 18 February 1999, para 32: 'The European Convention on Human Rights does not exclude the transfer of competences to international organisations provided that the Convention rights continue to be "secured". Member States' responsibility therefore continues even after such a transfer.'; ECmHR, *M & Co v Germany*, 9 February 1990, 64 *DR* 138; Hunt, Nowak and Osmani, *Principles and Guidelines*, para 95: 'States determine the policies of some global actors, including the World Bank, the International Monetary Fund and the World Trade Organization. When determining the policies of such global actors, a State must conform to its international human rights duties and must be respectful of other States' international human rights obligations. How a State discharges its duties when determining the policies of global actors must be subject to monitoring and accountability procedures.' See, further, the consideration of accountability at 3.3.4.

[243] P Sands and P Klein, *Bowett's Law of International Institutions* (5th edn, Sweet & Maxwell Ltd, 2001) 521–6.

to ensure that the powers they have transferred to an organisation have been exercised in conformity with their own international obligations.[244]

In the case of *Waite and Kennedy* v *Germany*, the European Court of Human Rights had this to say on the matter:

The Court is of the opinion that where States establish international organisations in order to pursue or strengthen their cooperation in certain fields of activities, and where they attribute to these organisations certain competences and accord them immunities, there may be implications as to the protection of fundamental rights. It would be incompatible with the purpose and object of the Convention, however, if the Contracting States were thereby absolved from their responsibility under the Convention in relation to the field of activity covered by such attribution. It should be recalled that the Convention is intended to guarantee not theoretical or illusory rights, but rights that are practical and effective.[245]

That states are to comply with their human rights obligations when pursuing international cooperation in other areas is emerging as an incontrovertible principle.[246] To make this effective, they must ensure that their representatives have the knowledge, and instructions, to provide this assurance. A related matter is that of the accountability of international organizations for human rights violations, an area receiving increasing attention.[247] For its part, the OHCHR has issued guidelines providing that: 'In their own capacity global actors must be subject to accessible, transparent and effective monitoring and accountability procedures'.[248]

International cooperation in the area of socio-economic rights includes monitoring and evaluation that lead to corrective measures; monitoring the impact of aid and trade on the exercise of rights by people in other countries;[249]

---

[244] Ibid, 525.

[245] *Waite and Kennedy* v *Germany*, ECtHR App no 26083/94, Grand Chamber judgement of 18 February 1999, para 67.

[246] *Bosphorus Airways* v *Ireland*, ECtHR App no 45036/98, Grand Chamber judgment of 30 June 2005, para 156. During CESCR's dialogues with States parties, both developed and developing states are regularly questioned on their adherence to the Covenant obligations in the context of world trade and international finance and development. See, for example, CESCR, Concluding Observations: United Kingdom of Great Britain and Northern Ireland—Dependent Territories (28th session, 2002) UN Doc E/C12/1/Add79 (2002) para 26; CESCR, Concluding Observations: Ireland (28th session, 2002) UN Doc E/C12/1/Add77 (2002), para 37; CESCR, Concluding Observations: Ecuador (32nd session, 2004) UN Doc E/C12/1/Add100 (2004), para 56; CESCR, Concluding Observations: Chile (33rd session, 2004) UN Doc E/C12/1/Add105 (2004), para 60.

[247] *Accountability of International Organizations*, Final Report (International Law Association, 2004); the responsibility of international organizations is currently a topic under consideration by the International Law Commission.

[248] Hunt, Nowak and Osmani, *Principles and Guidelines*, para 96. Sands and Klein, *Bowett's Law of International Institutions*, 459: 'It has been suggested that, for example, the World Bank is not subject to general international norms for the protection of fundamental human rights. In our view that conclusion is without merit, on legal or policy grounds.'

[249] A Eide, *Report on the Right to Adequate Food and to be Free from Hunger* (Sub-Commission, 51st session, 1999) UN Doc E/CN4/Sub2/1999/12, para 131(c).

and, developing and using social and human rights impact assessments in the trade and development fields,[250] as well as in relation to the business activities of transnational enterprises.[251] The latter point would form part of a state's preliminary responsibility to protect people from human rights violations by companies headquartered in its jurisdiction and operating overseas.[252] When it comes to foreign direct investment, impact-analysis should not remain limited to 'an examination of the impact of a particular investment or project on the human rights of the population concerned ["micro-analysis"] ... [rather] the human rights perspective should and can be applied at the "macro-level" of analysis ... to its structural dimensions', in particular, to the legal framework of FDI.[253] International cooperation towards the proper regulation of foreign direct investment would require the integration of human rights and environmental standards into multilateral rules on investment,[254] and that the commercial activities for which a state has direct responsibility conform to international human rights standards.[255]

Pogge observes that: 'The relevant governments are clearly quite active in formulating the global economic rules they want, in pressing for their acceptance, and in prosecuting their enforcement.'[256] It is time that international cooperation for the realization of human rights takes its rightful place in the international order so that food, water, access to essential healthcare and education, and a decent and secure place to live become tangible for the world's poor. With 2.7 billion people living in poverty, what is called for in the face of such serious breaches of international standards, is a joint and coordinated effort by all states to counter the effects of these breaches: both under treaty law and under general international law there is a positive obligation to cooperate in order to

---

[250] 'The Task Force agreed that social impact assessments provide important methodological tools to promote evidence-based policy formulation by including distributional and social effects in the *ex ante* analysis of policy reforms and agreements ... .' *Report of the High-Level Task Force* (2005, 1st), para 41.

[251] *Report of the United Nations High Commissioner on Human Rights on the responsibilities of transnational corporations and related business enterprises with regard to human rights*, UN Doc E/CN4/2005/91, para 52(f).

[252] CESCR, General Comment no 15, The Right to Water, paras 33–4: 'Steps should be taken by States parties to prevent their own citizens and companies from violating the right to water of individuals and communities in other countries. ... Depending on the availability of resources, States should facilitate the realization of the right to water in other countries, for example through provision of water resources, financial and technical assistance, and provide the necessary aid when required.'

[253] O De Schutter, 'Transnational Corporations as Instruments of Development' in P Alston and M Robinson, *Human Rights and Development: Towards Mutual Reinforcement* (Oxford University Press, 2005) 403, at 405–406. Structural dimensions such as 'the pressure under which developing states are to attract FDI and the concessions they make to ensure that foreign capital flows in, or the consequences of FDI on the situation of local producers and investors or on the relative wages'.

[254] SD Amarasinha and J Kokott, 'The Long and Winding Road towards Multilateral Investment Rules' in P Muchlinski and F Ortino (eds), *Oxford Handbook of International Law of Foreign Investment* (forthcoming, Oxford University Press, 2008).

[255] Hunt, Nowak and Osmani, *Principles and Guidelines*, para 104(e).

[256] TW Pogge, *Severe Poverty as a Human Rights Violation* (2003) 20 <http://www.etikk.no/globaljustice>.

bring an end to these transgressions. Since international cooperation is often the only way of remedying effectively these violations, the requirement to do so is strengthened.[257] However, cooperation for ensuring human rights can only be meaningful if it targets the very way in which our international economic order is arranged, and thus the distribution of, and access to, that which is necessary to sustain and have flourish, each and every one of us.

2.5 Conclusion

Starting with the UN Charter, through the relevant human rights treaties and declarations, to the collective voice of the international community derived of World Conferences, international cooperation for ensuring human rights constitutes an essential component of the obligations of states. It was understood in 1945, and resonates today with renewed urgency, that international cooperation is necessary to advance solutions to poverty and underdevelopment, and to realize human rights. Given the rich sources of international law from which state responsibility can be derived in this area, the existence of this obligation should by now be beyond question.

The requirement to cooperate in securing human rights has been repeatedly recognized and reaffirmed in the provisions of various international human rights instruments for over a half a century, recently complemented by the principle of shared responsibility. This system entrenches the broadest set of standards and 'contractual' commitments in existence. It reflects a universal consensus attained for the defence of human beings[258]—with the fulfilment of these human rights reliant also on collective action. As awareness of the adverse effects of economic globalization has increased over the past decade, the standard applied to the international community regarding its role in the realization of economic, social and cultural rights has shifted. The lesser trigger of human rights being of mere 'legitimate international concern' has become one of international implication, where relevant states are able to hinder the exercise of human rights in many parts of the world. This fact is necessitating a reconsideration of the precise content of the obligation of international cooperation. The progressive development of international law in this area is providing the basis for claims of global economic equity, representing a necessary turn towards having international law address particular injustices of the contemporary human condition.

Over the past several years, judicial, quasi-judicial, political and expert views have provided some clarification as to what this obligation of international

---

[257] See generally, Articles on the Responsibility of States for Internationally Wrongful Acts with commentaries (2001) Commentary to art 41, 286–287.

[258] J Bengoa, *The Relationships between the Enjoyment of Human Rights, in particular Economic, Social and Cultural Rights, and Income Distribution*, Final Report (Sub-Commission, 49th session, 1997) UN Doc E/CN4/Sub2/1997/9, para 43.

cooperation entails. Beyond obligations that extend to decisions and acts of a state having negative impact on people outside of its territory (extraterritoriality), this chapter has shown that the obligation of international cooperation requires that states proactively address the structural causes of world poverty, including when acting under the auspices of relevant international organizations. This would include ensuring compliance with human rights obligations when seeking to advance cooperation in other areas that may have a bearing on the realization of human rights. With its focus on duties of international cooperation, the Declaration on the Right to Development epitomizes this legal evolution, and has now been endorsed to the point of creating considerable legal expectations. This Declaration speaks to the collective rights of the hungry, thirsty, ailing and unsheltered, but its terms offer something more: in the words of Hunt, the Declaration on the Right to Development 'not only permits addressing structural disadvantage, but demands'.[259]

A vital aspect of giving effect to obligations of international cooperation, and a duty of shared responsibility, would be for developed countries to dismantle the structural obstacles over which they have influence—the range of barriers that impede the ability of people in developing countries to realize their fundamental human rights.[260] In setting out what might today represent the structural content of the obligation of international cooperation, it becomes clear that there is no replacement for reform of the way in which our international economic order is negotiated and arranged, and access and benefits are secured. In a world of plenty the figures on global inequality and deprivation remain astounding.[261] Yet international economic arrangements and policies detrimental to poverty alleviation and to the exercise of basic human rights are maintained by those states that reap its advantages, just as the institutional order that facilitates and produces the factors that perpetuate these conditions remains firmly in place.[262] This gap between rich and poor can only but offer a presumption of 'liability' on the part of the affluent states of the international community. In his 2005 statement to the Third Committee of the General Assembly, the Ambassador of Egypt and Chair of the Working Group on the Right to Development, recounted

[259] Paul Hunt, oral comment at *The Nobel Symposium on the Right to Development and Human Rights in Development,* Oslo, October 2003. Notes on file with author.

[260] 'We judge that the problems we have identified are not due to globalization as such but to deficiencies in its governance ... There is concern about the unfairness of key global rules on trade and finance and their asymmetric effects on rich and poor countries.' *A Fair Globalization,* at xi.

[261] In developing countries more than 850 million people, 300 million of whom are children, go to bed hungry every night. Of these 300 million children, 90% are suffering long-term malnourishment and 6 million children die annually of malnourishment. More than 40% of Africans do not even have the ability to obtain sufficient food on a day to day basis. All the while, the international trading system is 'rigged' in favour of the rich countries. *Fast Facts: The Faces of Poverty,* UN Millennium Project (2005); UNDP, *Human Development Report 2005: International Cooperation at a Crossroads,* Ch 1.

[262] On the 'rigged system' see, UNDP, *Human Development Report 2005: International Cooperation at a Crossroads,* at Ch 4.

a response he offered the CESCR while having his country's report considered. Committee members had asked the Ambassador if Egypt was making the argument during its negotiations with IFI's, and in relation to international trade, that its obligations under the Covenant constituted a minimum international threshold which it had a commitment to guarantee. The Ambassador told the General Assembly: 'Politically speaking, and I remember having said it bluntly, in a negotiating context individual developing states can hardly raise the issue of incoherence of norms ...'.[263] While still tentative, this duty to negotiate in order to achieve mutually beneficial solutions is part of a broader trend towards international cooperation aimed at limiting the negative impact of international rules and policies that serve to contravene the human rights of some of the most marginalized people in the world.

In this increasingly interdependent world, it is has become a legal requirement that the protection of human beings, and hence the application of international law aimed at ensuring human rights for all, takes its rightful place among the many systems of cooperation of which globalization is comprised. Moreover, these other forms of cooperative engagement must be tested for their compatibility with the exercise of human rights, lest they risk running counter to international law and to modern standards of legitimacy. Dimitrijevic expressed it well:

The essence of the international human rights complex is a cluster of universally held values, related to the entire international community, which exist because they are felt by our contemporaries .... [I]n the sphere of public conscience the ideals of humanism have been victorious in the second half of our century [and] all ideologies competing for human minds and broad support have a chance only if they show that they aim to the liberation, self-attainment and fulfillment of the human being in a just society ... no claim to legitimacy can be based on the rejection of the humanist ideal.[264]

Today, the right to development offers a highly pertinent standard against which the legitimacy of the current model of economic globalization might be tested. The following chapter is devoted to the unravelling and application of the various aspects of this right to our subject of concern.

---

[263] HE Ambassador I Salama, Chair, Working Group on the Right to Development, *Statement to the Third Committee of the General Assembly*, 25 October 2005, 12.
[264] V Dimitrijevic, 'A Natural or Moral Basis for International Law' in A Grahl-Madsen and J Toman (eds), *The Spirit of Uppsala, Proceedings of the Joint UNITAR-Uppsala University Seminar on International Law and Organization for a New World Order* (Walter de Gruyter, 1984) 383, at 395.

3

The Right to Development and Human-centred Globalization

3.1 Introduction

This chapter examines dominant ideologies and practices related to international economic activities, through the lens of the various elements that constitute the right to development. Like the collective right of self-determination that came before it, the right to development has both external and internal dimensions.[1] Externally, on the international stage, it is a right invoked by a state on behalf of its people for international and institutional arrangements conducive to the exercise of fundamental socio-economic rights. Similarities in its evolution can be seen with the principle of self-determination as provided for in the United Nations Charter (UN Charter), which had its status elevated to that of a right in the Covenants only once 'the agitation in context of decolonization raised both the stakes and the normative aspirations of the proponents'.[2] A similar trajectory is found with regard to the right to development, which began to take shape as a result of this most recent wave of economic globalization, and the remonstrations by developing states against its particular forms of subjugation.

The Declaration on the Right to Development (DRD) emphasizes the integrated nature of these two rights, both of which have their roots in struggles for liberation from external power and control. Article 1(2) of the Declaration holds that the right to development 'implies the full realization of the right of

---

[1] 'In respect of the self-determination of peoples two aspects have to be distinguished. The right to self-determination of peoples has an internal aspect, that is to say, the rights of all peoples to pursue freely their economic, social and cultural development without outside interference. ... The external aspect of self-determination implies that all peoples have the right to determine freely their political status and their place in the international community based upon the principle of equal rights and exemplified by the liberation of peoples from colonialism and by the prohibition to subject peoples to alien subjugation, domination and exploitation.': CERD, General Recommendation no 21 (Right to self-determination), (48th session, 1996) UN Doc A/51/18 annex VIII at 125, 1996, para 4.

[2] P Alston, 'Peoples' Rights: Their Rise and Fall' in P Alston (ed), *Peoples' Rights* (Oxford University Press, 2001) 259, at 261.

peoples to self-determination …',[3] advocating nothing short of a demand for 'self-determined development',[4] and a place that allows for functional equality of developing states on the international stage. Addressing poverty in developing countries is an international affair, a fact affirmed by the diminished domestic autonomy in decision-making that characterizes globalization in this area. With the prevailing market-based ideology being translated into domestic economic policies however, the right to development also has an important contribution to make in conditioning orthodox growth strategies at home (i.e. internal dimension), through its stipulation of a 'particular process' of development that favours the human rights of every person.

As we have seen in previous chapters, the human person is the subject of development, the participant, and the beneficiary, under the Declaration.[5] This is consistent with international human rights law, and despite its unusual formulation, the Declaration on the Right to Development is no exception in this regard. Within the right to development, the human person constitutes the centre piece around which development evolves. It is development that serves people, and not people who serve economic development. The right to development advances this crucial premise, and seeks to reorient thinking so that people are the higher purpose—not markets, nor growth, nor trade. Fair processes reasonably designed to achieve just outcomes become the principal requirement for fulfilling this right. While results conducive to the realization of economic, social and cultural rights are anticipated, it is conduct—including at the international level—that lies at the centre of determining the nature of the human rights obligations in this area. That 'everyone' has the right to an adequate standard of living, including adequate food, clothing and housing, and to the continuous improvement of living conditions,[6] is not a reference to everyone in the aggregate globally or domestically, but rather to each and every person, beginning with the poor.

Drawing on the recent work of the expert UN High-Level Task Force on the Implementation of the Right to Development, and the intergovernmental Working Group on the Right to Development to which its recommendations are reported, detailed consideration is given to what the right to development indicates about deficiencies in our international economic order, and how its precepts might be instructive of change. Most notably, greater coherence among the various strands of international law and policy are necessary to allow for the exercise of human rights, which the international community has concluded, is first among the responsibilities of governments.[7]

---

[3] DRD provisions on self-determination are found at preambular para 6: '*Recalling* the right of peoples to self-determination, by virtue of which they have the right freely to determine their political status and to pursue their economic, social and cultural development', and arts 1(2), and 5.

[4] UNDP Policy Note, *UNDP and Indigenous Peoples: A Policy of Engagement*, UNDP, August 2001, 8.

[5] DRD, art 2(1).

[6] ICESCR, art 11(1).

[7] Vienna Declaration and Programme of Action, Pt I, art 1.

3.2 The 'Right-holder' of the Right to Development

As was briefly addressed in Chapters 1 and 2, the right to development is concerned with the collective development of all people within a given state. While individuals remain the right-holders and intended beneficiaries of the right to development, in its external dimension it is a right claimed by the state on behalf of the people; states acting within the existing inter-state system are the entity through which the international component of the right is asserted. The role of developing states in seeking to invoke the right to development of their people internationally does not, however, render the right to development a right of states, as some commentators and representatives of several developing states insist on arguing. The *travaux préparatoires* to the Declaration on the Right to Development support this shift to development understood as a *human* right. A 1983 version of the draft Declaration defined the right as '. . . a right of all states and peoples for peaceful, free and independent development'.[8] However, the reference to the right of states was dropped from the final Declaration, with only individuals and peoples identified as right-holders. Distinguishing between the state as the entity through which the right is asserted internationally, yet recognizing that it is only people that hold the right, may offer only a subtle distinction, but it is a significant one nonetheless.

The debate on the right to development began with developing countries propounding that the right to development was distinct from civil, political, economic, social and cultural rights, and instead should be understood as a right of developing countries seeking to build a new international economic order. Bedjaoui is among those who advocated that the right to development is a right of states.[9] Yet, while he defended the view that the right to development is primarily a right belonging to developing states in claiming their entitlement 'to receive a fair share of what belongs to all', he recognized that the beneficiaries should be individuals, as well as the state.[10] The DRD consciously casts the right to development as a human right at the centre of which is 'the constant improvement and . . . well-being of the entire population and of all individuals.[11] At Article 1, the Declaration affirms that 'the right to development is an inalienable human right'.[12]

The primary concern of those who defend the right to development as a right of states is to extend the human rights principles of equality, non-discrimination,

---

[8] *Report of the Working Group of Governmental Experts on the Right to Development* (4th session, 9 December 1982) UN Doc E/CN4/1983/11 annex IV, para 2.

[9] Bedjaoui is a former judge and president of the ICJ (1982–2001).

[10] M Bedjaoui, 'The Right to Development' in M Bedjaoui (ed), *International Law: Achievements and Prospects* (Martinus Nijhoff, 1991) 1177, at 1192 and 1179–80.

[11] DRD, preambular para 2; art 2(3).

[12] And at DRD preambular para 16.

participation and accountability, as well as democratic decision-making, to international relations. This, it is felt, would facilitate the development of their countries thwarted by the unequal relationships of the international economic systems that govern trade and finance. While developing countries—then as now—emphasize the need for equity and participation in international relations, in the debates on a New International Economic Order of the 1970s, little attention was given to the human rights implications domestically.[13] Although there is little doubt that it is reasonable for developing states to expect equitable treatment that mirrors universally agreed human rights principles within the scope of their international interactions, in order for a right to development of people to be fulfilled, representation must be established as genuine and democratic. The need for legitimate democratic structures is part of the right to development, which, as the DRD makes clear, includes respect for civil and political rights.[14] The duty placed upon states to cooperate with each other in ensuring development, and in eliminating obstacles to development,[15] is meaningful only if the benefits of that cooperation further the rights of people, including the most marginalized.[16] To suggest the right belongs to the state is to fail fully to appreciate that which is distinctive about human rights: the beneficiaries are people; mechanisms must exist to ensure that their rights are protected; and therefore any benefits derived of international cooperation must be accrued accordingly.

The views of some detractors notwithstanding, the international community has repeatedly endorsed the idea of a human right to development, as we saw in Chapter 2. The Vienna Declaration and Programme of Action, adopted by consensus, reaffirmed support for this 'integral part of fundamental human rights',[17] as did the Millennium Declaration seven years later, which lay the foundation for a global movement aimed at addressing world poverty. Its recognition and acceptance as a human right, at least from the adoption of the DRD onwards, implies the existence of a binary relationship between right-holders and duty-bearers—where there are human rights there are duties.

Now if human beings are the right-holders, who are the duty-bearers of the right to development? The duty-bearers are both the state, and the international community of states. It is at both these levels that the obligation to realize the human right to development exists. As public international law and policy is still a system that operates largely within an inter-state paradigm, at the international

---

[13] The Charter on the Economic Rights and Duties of States, General Assembly res 3281 (XXIX) of 12 December 1974. 'The Charter of Economic Rights and Duties of States was conceived of as "a kind of basic code" containing fundamental principles in different spheres of international economic relations.' K Hossupta, 'Introduction' in K Hossain (ed), *Legal Aspects of the New International Economic Order* (Frances Pinter Publishers, 1980) 1, at 5.

[14] DRD, preambular para 10, arts 6(2), 6(3).

[15] Ibid, art 3(3).

[16] See, ME Salomon with A Sengupta, *The Right to Development: Obligations of States and the Rights of Minorities and Indigenous Peoples* (MRG, 2003).

[17] Vienna Declaration and Programme of Action, Pt I, art 10.

level it is for the state to claim the right to development from the international community on behalf of its people. It follows that it is for the state to deliver the right to development to the people, within a framework that respects existing human rights standards. The duty is thus owed to the people who are meant to benefit from a just process of development.

Notably, international bodies have been established to develop policy in this area and to issue recommendations, the most recent being the UN Task Force on the Implementation of the Right to Development. This nascent mechanism will assess compliance with the principles enumerated in the DRD.[18] For its part, the Committee on Economic, Social and Cultural Rights (CESCR) is providing guidance in terms of the content of obligations under the International Covenant on Economic, Social and Cultural Rights (ICESCR), both nationally and internationally. An optional protocol allowing for a system of complaints under the Covenant could contribute to strengthening accountability in this area, although the prospect of having international cooperation form the basis of complaints under the ICESCR invites contention.[19]

So, while the international community of states has human rights obligations to all people, the fulfilment of these obligations is often made possible through the state. When certain states assert that the right to development is a right of states, their argument can only be understood as another way of remarking on their role as a vehicle in the realization of the human right to development. Although a state may need to claim the right to development from the international community before it can be realized by the people to whom it is owed, this does not make the right to development a right of states. It simply reflects the role of the state in an inter-state system. The government may be the agent through which the right can be vindicated; however, it will be acting in a secondary capacity, rather

---

[18] The Task Force has been mandated recently by the Working Group to apply criteria for assessing global partnerships from the perspective of the right to development '... on a pilot basis, to selected partnerships, with a view to operationalizing and progressively developing these criteria, and thus contributing to mainstreaming the right to development in the policies and operational activities of relevant actors at the national, regional and international levels, including multilateral financial, trade and development institutions': *Report of the Open-ended Working Group on the Right to Development* (7th session, 2006) UN Doc E/CN4/2006/26, para 77. As the Task Force's work at its second session reflects, there are conceptual and practical links between MDG 8 requiring a global partnership for development and the right to development. See, *Report of the High-Level Task Force on the Implementation of the Right to Development* (2nd session, 2005) UN Doc E/CN4/2005/WG18/TF/3, para 82.

[19] Certain Northern states oppose the idea of allowing for communications alleging a violation of the obligation of 'international assistance and cooperation', emphasizing the moral character of the obligation over the legal (particularly when the duty is construed in terms of transfer of resources—see Ch 2). Questions also surround whether petitioners could make claims alleging a failure of their own state to *seek* international assistance. While the specifics are yet to be decided: 'On the issue of whether an optional protocol should cover the international dimension of States' obligations including the issue of international cooperation, Committee experts noted that in theory such cases might arise': *Report of the Open-ended Working Group to consider options regarding the elaboration of an optional protocol to the International Covenant on Economic, Social and Cultural Rights* (1st session, 2004) UN Doc E/CN4/2004/44, para 45.

than as the holder of the right.[20] This idea that states may play multiple roles in fulfilling the right to development is reflected in the *travaux préparatoires* to the Declaration. The rationale of several contributors that subsequently went some-way to informing the logic of the Declaration held that: 'States and organizations had rights and obligations as far as the realization of human rights was concerned and in relation to the right to development as a human right, although that did not mean that they possessed human rights as such'.[21] Following the adoption of the Declaration, the Indian delegate summarized the matter in these cogent terms:

The Government of India is of the view that the Declaration adopting the right to devel-opment as a human right implies the growing recognition by the international commu-nity of a new conceptual scheme which seeks to integrate human rights and human needs. The Declaration implies that a certain prerogative is given to States and to human beings. However, the implementation of this right does not in any sense imply that the right of a State to development transcends the human rights of its citizens.[22]

The Convention on the Rights of the Child in which a relatively recent bind-ing articulation of the obligation of international cooperation for the realization of economic, social and cultural rights is found, similarly refers to the 'special needs of developing countries' without making them rights-holders under the Convention.[23] Obiora provides a clear synopsis of the point:

Where LDCs [Least Developed Countries] become the subject of the right to develop-ment at the international level, their citizens and subjects are endowed with the right at the national level as individuals and/or as members of relevant ... groups. In this mode, development constitutes a collective process and the individual, while not able to assert the right per se, may claim the establishment of conditions necessary for her or his development in interaction with others. In turn the state becomes the plenipotentiary or international dimension of peoples ... .[24]

Thus while the state can invoke the human right on behalf of its people, the con-dition of this claim must be that a procedure is established for the delivery of the human right in question. As previously mentioned, this procedure must be democratic, and representative, in order to ensure that the rights of individuals,

---

[20] J Crawford, 'Some Conclusions', in J Crawford (ed), *The Rights of Peoples* (Clarendon Press, 1988) 159, at 167.

[21] *Report of the Working Group of Governmental Experts on the Right to Development* (8th session, 24 January 1985) UN Doc E/CN4/1985/11, para 20.

[22] *Analytical compilation of comments and views on the implementation and further enhance-ment of the Declaration on the Right to Development prepared by the Secretary-General* (12th session, Working Group of Governmental Experts on the Right to Development, 21 December 1988) UN Doc E/CN4/AC39/1989/1, at 6.

[23] CRC, arts 23(4), 24(4), 28(3).

[24] LA Obiora, 'Beyond the Rhetoric of a Right to Development' 18 *Law & Pol* 3–4 (1996) Special Issue on the Right to Development, M wa Mutua, LA Obiora and RJ Krotoszynski Jr (eds), 366, at 369.

and of groups, are met in the processes, and in the outcomes, and that the checks and balances are in place to ensure that rights aren't arbitrarily limited in the name of development.

The drive of developing states to participate as equals in international economic affairs, and to invoke this prerogative in relation to the international community in order to allow for their sustainable economic development, is by no means without merit, and is reflected in the DRD. The Preamble confirms that 'the right to development is an inalienable human right and that equality of opportunity for development is a *prerogative* both of nations and of individuals who make up nations'.[25] While the reference to the prerogative of nations emphasizes the international dimension of the right to development, there is a greater objective to be met. In the words of Ustor, '[s]tates have a function within the world community, which they do not exercise on their own behalf—for the State is not an aim in itself—but on behalf of an order for the community of the human race, in accordance with given principles.'[26]

The language in Article 2(3) of the DRD is particularly instructive in this regard, it provides that:

States have the right and the duty to formulate appropriate national development policies that aim at the constant improvement of the well-being of the entire population and of all individuals, on the basis of their active, free and meaningful participation in development and in the fair distribution of the benefits resulting therefrom.

The formulation implies that the state can assert the right of its people to development against other states and the international community.[27] In the current globalized world the insistence on international cooperation being directed at the human-centred development articulated in Article 2(3) is strengthened in light of the prevalent loss of domestic autonomy experienced by individual states; a loss that characterizes the contemporary global economy, and impacts disproportionately on poorer, weaker countries. The right to development entails freedom from external manipulation, a clear indication of which is found in the draft Declaration which noted in forceful terms that 'the right to development includes within its content a right of every state to choose its economic ... and social system ... without outside interference or coercion and its right to pursue

---

[25] DRD, preambular para 16 (emphasis added).

[26] E Ustor, 'Independence and Interdependence' (Report of the Working Group II) in A Grahl-Madsen and J Toman (eds), *The Spirit of Uppsala, Proceedings of the Joint UNITAR-Uppsala University Seminar on International Law and Organization for a New World Order* (Walter de Gruyter, 1984) 52, at 54.

[27] This formulation reflects language left over from the NIEO debates of the 1970s which propelled onto the international stage 'the growing dissatisfaction felt by developing countries with the working of the international economic system in general, and that of the rules governing international trade in particular'.: Hossain, 'Introduction' at 2. Indeed, reference to the need to promote a new international economic order is made in the DRD at preambular para 15 and at art 3(3).

its proper path of development based on the will of its people'.[28] Softer language found its way into the final Declaration with the same points being advanced: that the ability of a (developing) state to fulfil its domestic obligations, including the duty to formulate appropriate policies to deliver the right to development, may be constrained by the actions and arrangements of the international community. Thus not only does the international community have a vital positive role to play in giving effect to the right to development, but developing states have a right to be free from negative impositions that inhibit the human development of their people at the hands of more powerful states. In its 2005 work on establishing criteria for assessing global partnerships for development under MDG 8 from a right to development perspective, the Task Force on the Right to Development relied on DRD Article 2(3) in recommending an assessment of 'the extent to which the partnership respects the right of each State to determine its own development policies, in accordance with its obligations to ensure that the policies are aimed at the constant improvement of the well-being of the entire population and of all individuals ... .'[29] The criterion was subsequently endorsed, by consensus, by the Working Group on the Right to Development.[30]

In light of this reasoning, the proper interpretation of the right referred to in Article 2(3) is that the right of states is the 'right to develop human rights-based development policies in the interests of their people'[31] made possible, where necessary, through international cooperation. The role of the state acting nationally, then, is not as a holder of the right to development, but as a conduit through which the right can be realized by its people.[32] The international community of states, for its part, has a duty to cooperate in order to enable the realization of the right, and to contribute to the ability of the developing state to fulfil the right. Perhaps Kéba Mbaye, former Vice-President of the International Court of Justice and among the first advocates of a right to development, best explained the distinction when he wrote:

Admittedly, it is usually States, as representatives ... that exercise the [human] rights accorded to [individuals considered jointly]. But it in no way alters the basic legal fact that these rights are accorded to peoples and nations ... The State itself plays the role of the equivalent of legal trustee.[33]

---

[28] *Report of the Working Group of Governmental Experts on the Right to Development* (4th session, 9 December 1982) annex IV, para 11(a).
[29] *Report of the High-Level Task Force* (2005, 2nd), para 82(b).
[30] *Report of the Working Group* (2006), para 67(b) and (d).
[31] A Orford, 'Globalization and the Right to Development' in Alston (ed), *Peoples' Rights*, 127, at 137.
[32] Writing in 1985, Alston framed the state as a 'medium' through which the rights of people could be effectively asserted against the international community. P Alston, 'The Shortcomings of a "Garfield the Cat" Approach' 15 *CalWInt'lLJ* (1985) 510, at 512. Orford refers to the state as the 'agent' of the 'entire population and of all individuals'. Orford, 'Globalization and the Right to Development', 127, at 137.
[33] K Mbaye, 'Introduction' to (Part Four) 'Human Rights and Rights of Peoples' in M Bedjaoui (ed), *International Law: Achievements and Prospects* (Martinus Nijhoff, 1991) 1041, at 1049.

The 'right', then, 'is exercisable by the state against those with the power to deny or constrain the capacity of the state to formulate national development policies that benefit the people within the state'.[34] While this is consistent with the role of the state as an agent of the people, it presupposes that the state is representing the interests of the people—which necessarily includes, for example, that adequate and timely information is made available for the purposes of public scrutiny, and that there is effective participation of affected communities in the elaboration and implementation of any development policy or programme—all criteria identified by the Task Force, and endorsed by the Working Group as essential to human-rights based partnerships for development.[35]

While developing states have the duty to formulate development policies (in line with human rights principles and standards), in a globalized world they can also be said to have a right exercisable against the international community, because they face constraints that can be removed only by the cooperation of the international community; for example, through market access, debt relief,[36] and modifying the asymmetries in global governance and the exercise of foreign power.[37] As Chapter 2 made clear, international cooperation can take many forms, and is not limited to financial assistance. International obligations include the requirement that states acting singly respect the enjoyment of human rights in other countries, and acting collectively as part of international organizations, take due account of human rights.[38] International cooperation could include challenging what the World Commission on the Social Dimension of Globalization has concluded is a 'system of rules governing the global economy that has been prejudicial to the interests of most developing countries, especially the poor within them', and thus 'to put in place a coherent set of international economic and social policies to achieve a pattern of globalization that benefits all people'.[39]

The right to development as proclaimed by the community of states is, as such, conditioned by international cooperation in the creation of an international environment conducive to the elimination of poverty, and the realization of human rights. The recent complementary principle of a shared responsibility recognizes that the ability of a developing state to formulate, and execute, human rights policies for its people cannot be disassociated from the influence, and cooperative role, of certain members of the international community of states

[34] Orford, 'Globalization and the Right to Development', 127, at 137.
[35] See the Recommendations in the *Report of the High-Level Task Force* (2005, 2nd) and the *Report of the Working Group* (2006).
[36] A Sengupta, *Fourth Report of the Independent Expert on the Right to Development* (Working Group on the Right to Development, 3rd session, 2002) UN Doc E/CN4/2002/WG18/2, para 43.
[37] *Report of the High-Level Task Force* (2005, 2nd), paras 75 and 92.
[38] For example, CESCR, General Comment no 14, The Right to the Highest Attainable Standard of Health (Art 12), (22nd session, 2000) UN Doc E/C12/2000/4, para 39.
[39] *A Fair Globalization*, Report of the World Commission on the Social Dimension of Globalization, (ILO, 2004), para 353.

acting collectively. The right to development is a human right that is largely exercised by a state on behalf its people; but in the final analysis its fulfillment means that each individual person becomes capable of living a life free from poverty—the life she or he has chosen, in short, a life in larger freedom.

3.3 The Right to Development as a Particular Process of Development

3.3.1 The indivisibility and interdependence of all human rights and the conditioning of economic policy

The preamble of the Declaration on the Right to Development has the General Assembly '[r]ecognizing that the human person is the central subject of the development *process* . . .'.[40] It is a process aimed at constantly improving human well-being;[41] its objective being commensurate with the expansion of the capabilities or freedoms of individuals to realize what they value; 'development as freedom' in the seminal words of Amartya Sen,[42] 'development as a right' when translated into the language of law. Drawing on the eloquent depiction provided by O'Manique, Obiora describes the right to development as a process that allows for the exercise of the full range of rights, and has as its goal the pursuit of self-actualization of people, in conditions of dignity, through the exercise of their rights.[43] The elements of the particular process necessary for giving effect to the right to development are vital, so much so that Sengupta characterizes the right to development as the '*right* to a *particular* process of development'.[44]

This particular process of development requires that all rights will be considered in an indivisible and interdependent manner. Both the instrumental (as a means to the realization of other rights), and the substantive importance of rights (as intrinsically valuable in the achievement of human dignity), and the mutually reinforcing relationship between the two sets of rights (civil and political/ economic, social and cultural), were reaffirmed by states in the Vienna Declaration on Human Rights of 1993. Despite this recognition by the international community, the ideological split that saw the creation of two covenants from the compendium of rights in the UDHR has made it difficult to enforce systematically this doctrine of indivisibility and interdependence. The Declaration on the Right

[40] DRD, preambular para 13, emphasis added; art 8(1) refers in particular to the importance of undertaking effective measures 'to ensure that women have an active role in the development process'.

[41] Ibid, preambular para 2 and art 2(3); see also preambular para 12.

[42] A Sen, *Development as Freedom* (Oxford University Press, 1999).

[43] Obiora, 'Beyond the Rhetoric of a Right to Development', 366, at 389.

[44] A Sengupta, *Second Report of the Independent Expert on the Right to Development* (Working Group on the Right to Development, 1st session, 2000) UN Doc E/CN4/2000/WG18/CRP1, paras 15–25.

to Development, however, advances a process of recognizing all human rights as indivisible and interdependent, whereby '... equal attention and urgent consideration [...] be given to the civil, political, economic, social and cultural rights.'[45]

In the context of development, considering human rights as indivisible and interdependent has several implications for domestic policy. First, rights are not to be postponed for pronounced greater objectives, for example, an increase in national wealth or for benefits anticipated at some indeterminate time in the future. The argument made for sacrificing distributional equity in favour of rapid accumulation is rejected.[46] The right to development disallows any economic policy prescription (whether formulated by the state or at the behest of the international financial institutions (IFIs)) that proposes a sacrifice of human rights for some people, for some undetermined period of time, until growth and a rise in income levels will enable people to claim their human rights. This is an approach still common among libertarian economists,[47] and the official trade policy community.[48] At the international level, the right to development could be understood as requiring that developing states, claiming the right to development on behalf of their people, do not sacrifice their rights—for example to food, and food security, to education and to health, all rights threatened under the WTOs intellectual property regime[49]—for membership in a club that binds them to respond to the demands of the market, and for promises of future gains.[50]

Second, the notion of indivisibility and interdependence rejects the prioritization of certain rights over others based on their value as instrumental means

---

[45] DRD, art 6(2); preambular para 10; art 6(3).

[46] Donnelly refers to this as the 'equity trade-off'. J Donnelly, 'Human Rights, Democracy and Development' 21 *HRQ* 3 (1999) 608, at 626–7.

[47] See the transcript for the debate E Lucas (chair), 'Is Respect for Human Rights Essential to Economic Development?', London School of Economics, London, 13 October 2005.

[48] R Howse, *Mainstreaming the Right to Development into International Trade Law and Policy at the World Trade Organization*, UN Doc E/CN4/Sub2/2004/17, para 14. Howse notes that: 'This manner of understanding development remains influential in the official trade policy community; it often underlies the rejection of linkage of environmental and labour standard to trade policies'.

[49] Concern over the negative impact on developing countries relates to, for example, issues pertaining to lack of food security, and access to medicines, and to knowledge under the WTO's Agreement on Trade-Related Aspects of Intellectual Property Rights (TRIPS). Bilateral and regional trade deals in this area (TRIPS Plus) strengthen, and extend, existing multilateral provisions, and further reduce the limited flexibilities provided for in TRIPS. The current intellectual property regime generally is criticized for striking the wrong balance between the interests of technology-holders and the wider public interest, and for leaving developing countries limited space to determine national policies. See, UNDP, *Human Development Report 2005: International Cooperation at a Crossroads: Aid, Trade and Security in an Unequal World* (Oxford University Press, 2005) Ch 4, at 135.

[50] In her compelling exposition equating the demands of the international trade regime to the blind sacrifice that underpins Christian theology, Orford explains: 'Translated into the language of international economic law, the harmonization agreements require decision-makers to understand themselves as bound to respond to the demands of the market, to sacrifice (their citizens, their public obligations) in expectation of the reward of the righteous in the future by the Father (God/Market) who sees in secret'. A Orford, 'Beyond Harmonization: Trade, Human Rights and the Economy of Sacrifice' 18 *LJIL* (2005) 179, at 198.

for achieving economic policy objectives. Favouring certain rights in this way ignores the comprehensive and balanced set of human rights provided for under the international human rights regime, holistically represented—for good reason—in the Declaration on the Right to Development. It disregards the existing system provided for within human rights law for prioritizing rights, and potentially for limiting rights, which are to be determined through the principles of legality, necessity and proportionality. Moreover, the singling out of certain rights by international actors motivated by particular priorities, and devoted to certain institutional creeds, gives rise to the possibility that human rights will be misappropriated to achieve other objectives. The UN Committee on Economic, Social and Cultural Rights drew attention to this concern recently when it sought to distinguish between the rights of authors under international human rights law (ICESCR, Article 15 (1)(c)), and intellectual property rights. The Committee noted: 'Human rights are fundamental, inalienable and universal entitlements belonging to individuals and, under certain circumstances, groups of individuals and communities. Human rights are fundamental as they are inherent to the human person ... In contrast, intellectual property rights are generally of a temporary nature ... [and the] intellectual property regime primarily protects business and corporate interests and investments'.[51]

Third, no *set* of rights is to be favoured. The right to development rejects any argument that the right to vote, to take part in the conduct of public affairs, and rights related to an independent media and an impartial judiciary (political and civil rights), can be limited in the name of development. There can be no sacrificing of civil and political rights in the name of efficiency in addressing underdevelopment;[52] although advocating that human rights need not be respected until an adequate level of development is reached is an approach often favoured by undemocratic regimes. Likewise, a focus on good governance to the exclusion of economic, social and cultural rights, the approach favoured by most donors,[53] does not ensure that the improvement of any one set of rights is not at the expense of a deterioration in the other set of rights. The sacrifice of certain

---

[51] CESCR, General Comment no 17, The Right of Everyone to Benefit from the Protection of the Moral and Material Interests Resulting from any Scientific, Literary or Artistic Production of which he is the Author, (art 15(1)(c)), (35th session, 2005) UN Doc E/C12/GC/17 (2005), paras 1–2.

[52] Donnelly refers to this as the 'liberty trade-off': Donnelly, 'Human Rights, Democracy and Development', 608, at 626–7. The DRD at Art 6(3) recognizes that the failure to observe civil and political rights poses an obstacle to development.

[53] A study commissioned by the Organization For Economic Co-operation and Development (OECD) (Development Assistance Committee Network on Governance) on donor approaches concluded that: 'Governance is the sector most closely associated with human rights, and this is where the majority of aid agencies locate the issue institutionally .... The majority of human rights interventions have addressed civil and political rights issues, often under a governance heading, linked to democracy and the rule of law .... A contradiction seems to remain in a number of agencies between the rhetorical commitment to the indivisibility of all human rights, and the prominence given to civil and political rights programming'. L-H Piron with T O'Neil, *Integrating Human Rights into Development: A Synthesis of Donor Approaches and Experiences* (Overseas Development Institute, 2005) 13 and 25.

rights subjectively determined can only be avoided when the two sets of rights are considered as an integrated whole, in a manner that takes into account their effects on each other, on the allocation of resources, and on the sustainability of the whole development process.[54]

The recognition of resource constraints that gives rise to the notion of progressive realization of economic, social and cultural rights, however, reflects the likelihood that policy-makers will have to make trade-offs among rights, since it may not be possible for all rights to be fulfilled at the same time, and to the same degree. Where these rights cannot be realized immediately due to resource constraints, states acting 'individually and through international assistance and cooperation' are required to 'take steps' towards achieving the full realization of economic, social and cultural rights.[55] In undertaking this procedural obligation however, the human rights principle of indivisibility requires that no particular human rights be considered intrinsically of lesser merit than others, requiring that the basis for the prioritization of certain types of interventions be determined on practical grounds—e.g. because a certain right remains comparatively under-realized, or because it is likely to act as a catalyst towards the fulfillment of other rights.[56] Consistent with the human rights principle of non-retrogression, no state, group, or person has a right to engage in any activity or perform any act aimed at the destruction or limitation of codified rights and freedoms.[57] Any measures that result in the retrogression of economic, social and cultural rights, would require a full justification by reference to the totality of human rights, and would need to be weighed against the standards that oblige the full use of the maximum available resources,[58] which include those available from the international community.[59] Finally, the recognition of resource constraints notwithstanding, the international human rights system specifies core obligations that require states to ensure, with immediate effect, certain minimum levels of enjoyment of each economic, social and cultural right.[60] 'Core obligations must be treated as binding constraints to the allocation of resources, i.e. no trade-offs are permitted with regard to them.'[61] All actors in a position to influence domestic

[54] On the right to development as a vector of integrated (and not merely aggregated) rights, see, Sengupta, *Fourth Report*, paras 2–4. On the rights of minorities and indigenous peoples as part of the right to development see, Salomon with Sengupta, *The Right to Development*.

[55] ICESCR, art 2(1).

[56] P Hunt, M Nowak and S Osmani, *Principles and Guidelines for a Human Rights Approach to Poverty Reduction Strategies* (OHCHR, 2005), para 59.

[57] For example, ICCPR, art 5 and CESCR, General Comment no 18, The Right to Work (art 6), (35th session, 2005) UN Doc E/C12/GC/18 (2005), paras 21 and 34.

[58] CESCR, General Comment no 3 on Art 2(1) (The Nature of States Parties' Obligations), (5th session, 1990) UN Doc E/1991/23 annex III, para 9.

[59] Ibid, para 13.

[60] Ibid, para 10; and see for example, CESCR, General Comment no 15, The Right to Water (arts 11 and 12), (29th session, 2002) UN Doc E/C12/2002/11, para 37. Civil and political rights are not subject to progressive realisation.

[61] Hunt, Nowak and Osmani, *Principles and Guidelines*, para 61.

policy, be they the developing states, developed states, or international institutions, should be seeking to see these minimum standards reached as a priority. Notably, the Committee on Economic, Social and Cultural Rights has concluded that these basic obligations form part of customary international law,[62] thereby also providing an authoritative view as to the obligations of international organizations.

International human rights law has standards of assessment against which any interference with, or limitation of, a person's human rights must be justified. Where rights conflict with other rights, or with policy objectives that are directed at 'promoting the general welfare',[63] the test seeks to strike a fair balance between the fundamental rights of the person or persons, and the general interest of the community or of another group. Non-arbitrariness and legality (i.e. is the interference provided for in law), whether the restriction is in order to pursue a (specified) legitimate aim, and whether that aim is proportionate to the objectives sought (i.e. *necessary* in a democratic society to address a pressing social need with the interference no greater than is necessary to meet that need) all figure prominently in the just determination of any limitations on rights.[64] According to the European Court of Human Rights, which has done the most to develop the judicial reasoning with regard to qualified rights, a legitimate aim may still result in an unacceptable interference with rights if that aim could have been achieved through less severe means.[65] The CESCR has pursued a similar line of reasoning on limitations, emphasizing that measures deemed 'necessary for the promotion of the general welfare in a democratic society' are to be strictly construed.[66] International human rights law also requires that there be a remedy where rights are violated, including in the context of policy-making,[67] and that in any process of trading-off no one should fall below the

---

[62] CESCR, Concluding Observations: Israel (30th session, 2003) UN Doc E/C12/1/Add9 (2003), para 31.

[63] ICESCR, art 4: 'The States Parties to the present Covenant recognize that, in the enjoyment of those rights provided by the State in conformity with the present Covenant, the State may subject such rights only to such limitations as are determined by law only in so far as this may be compatible with the nature of these rights and solely for the purpose of promoting the general welfare in a democratic society'.

[64] ME Salomon, 'Towards a Just Institutional Order: A Commentary on the First Session of the UN Task Force on the Right to Development' 23 *NQHR* 3 (2005) 409, at 428–432; and generally, Y Arai-Takahashi, *The Margin of Appreciation Doctrine and the Principle of Proportionality in the Jurisprudence of the European Court of Human Rights* (Intersentia, 2002).

[65] See further, C Ovey and R White, *Jacob's and Whites The European Convention on Human Rights* (4th edn, Oxford University Press, 2006) 218–40.

[66] CESCR, General Comment no 14, The Right to Health, paras 28–9.

[67] The right to a remedy is expressly guaranteed in both global and regional human rights instruments. It contains two separate concepts: the procedural aspect of effective access to a fair hearing and the substantive aspect of relief afforded to a successful claimant. D Shelton, *Remedies in International Human Rights Law* (2nd edn, Oxford University Press, 2005) 9; 'While the general approach of each legal system needs to be taken into account, there is no Covenant right which could not, in the great majority of systems, be considered to possess at least some significant justiciable dimensions. It is sometimes suggested that matters involving the allocation of resources should be left to the political authorities rather than the courts. While the respective competences

minimum essential level of rights[68] required to live in conditions of dignity.[69] To these ends, the Working Group on the Right to Development suggested that 'the right to development should guide in setting priorities and resolving trade-offs in resource allocations and policy frameworks'.[70]

The IMF (along with other relevant institutions) has shown its willingness to participate in human rights fora such as the Task Force on the Right to Development, where these issues have been debated. As Marks concludes though, they do this 'because they are attentive to the priorities of their member states ... while maintaining a core concern for macroeconomic stability and market efficiency'.[71] The IMF, for example, has taken the public position that trade-offs require only that the concerns of the 'losers' are addressed as best as can be,[72] a far cry from seeing that the formulation and implementation of law and policy '... ensure[s] the full exercise and progressive enhancement of the right to development'.[73]

While the human rights model does not offer perfect solutions to complex and diverse problems in this area,[74] it conditions economic reasoning in significant

---

of the various branches of government must be respected, it is appropriate to acknowledge that courts are generally already involved in a considerable range of matters which have important resource implications. The adoption of a rigid classification of economic, social and cultural rights which puts them, by definition, beyond the reach of the courts would thus be arbitrary and incompatible with the principle that the two sets of human rights are indivisible and interdependent. It would also drastically curtail the capacity of the courts to protect the rights of the most vulnerable and disadvantaged groups in society.': CESCR, General Comment no 9, The Domestic Application of the Covenant (19th session, 1998) UN Doc E/C12/1998/24, para 10.

[68] CESCR, General Comment no 3, The Nature of States Parties' Obligations, para 10.

[69] *The Government of the Republic of South Africa* v *Irene Grootboom and Ors* (October 2000) Constitutional Court of South Africa, Case CCT11/00, para 83; *Minister of Health and Ors* v *Treatment Action Campaign and Ors* (July 2002) Constitutional Court of South Africa, Case CCT 8/02, para 28. The international community has recognized extreme poverty as constituting a 'violation of human dignity': Vienna Declaration and Programme of Action, Pt I, art 25.

[70] *Report of the Open-ended Working Group on the Right to Development* (6th session, 2005) UN Doc E/CN4/2005/25, para 43.

[71] SP Marks, 'Misconceptions about the Right to Development', Special Report, Human Rights and Development, (guest eds), D Freestone and JK Ingram, 8 *Development Outreach* (The World Bank Institute, October 2006) 9, at 10.

[72] Task Force on the Right to Development (2005, 1st). Notes on file with author. See, further, Salomon, 'Towards a Just Institutional Order' 409, at 428–32. This view, while unacceptable from a human rights perspective, does serve to emphasize the importance of identifying the effects of policies on the poor and vulnerable, the need for the provision of special measures including in the form of social safety nets and targeted transfers and subsidies, and the role of multilateral trade and development institutions in supporting national efforts in this regard (*Report of the High-Level Task Force* (2005, 1st), paras 24 and 38). Nonetheless, the categorical approach expressed by the representative of the IMF—that anticipates economic policy winners and policy losers in a system requiring trade-offs—gives rise to grave concerns from the standpoint of international human rights law.

[73] DRD, art 10 states: 'Steps should be taken to ensure the full exercise and progressive enhancement of the right to development, including the formulation, adoption and implementation of policy, legislative and other measures at the national and international levels'.

[74] See, P Uvin, *Human Rights and Development* (Kumarian Press, 2004) 184–94; R Archer, 'The Strengths of Different Traditions: What Might be Gained and What Might be Lost by Combining Rights and Development?' 3 *SUR International Journal on Human Rights* 4 (2006) 81.

ways. As Uvin concludes, '… a human rights approach demands that we question the status quo, render explicit the concerns of the oppressed and the poor when thinking through policies, and not take resource constraints as natural givens but to treat them as the results of past choices. In practical terms, then, a strong human rights approach seems to lend strong credence to a significant national and international redistribution of incomes and assets, whereas a strong economist approach does the opposite, almost always disfavouring any form of redistribution'.[75]

That rights taken together reflect more than the sum of their parts can be an important policy tool, serving to emphasize the value of norm coherence, and increasing sensitivity to legitimate means of determining any trade-offs in rights that may come about as a result of resource constraints, while highlighting the requirement to minimize the negative impact of policy choices on the vulnerable. The focus on this indivisibility of norms transcends the human rights arena, addressing also the need for coherence in state policies generally, both nationally, and in their application internationally.

The final point on the Declaration's focus on indivisibility and interdependence, pertains to its articulation of linking, not only all rights, but all *aspects* of the Declaration. Article 9 (1) states that: 'All the aspects of the right to development set forth in the present Declaration are indivisible and interdependent and each of them should be considered in the context of the whole'. Drawing attention to the importance of international peace and security to development,[76] the Declaration recognizes the tension that exists between security and development in the allocation of resources internationally. It aims to ensure that, even while attempting to maintain international peace and security, sufficient resources are allocated towards the development of poor countries.[77] A point reaffirmed by the Task Force.[78] This approach not only recognizes the interrelationship between development, security and human rights, but also seeks to ensure that the foreign policy objectives of wealthy and powerful countries are conducive to furthering this comprehensive agenda. Almost 20 years after the adoption of the DRD, the UN Secretary-General endorsed this approach when he offered his counsel regarding

---

[75] Uvin, *Human Rights and Development*, 191–2.

[76] DRD, preambular para 11: 'Considering that international peace and security are essential elements for the realization of the right to development'.

[77] DRD, art 7: 'All States should promote the establishment, maintenance and strengthening of international peace and security and, to that end, should do their utmost to achieve general and complete disarmament under effective international control, as well as to ensure that the resources released by effective disarmament measures are used for comprehensive development, in particular that of the developing countries.'; preambular para 12: '… and that resources released through disarmament measures should be devoted to the economic and social development and well-being of all peoples and, in particular, those of the developing countries.'

[78] The Task Force on the Right to Development concluded that the periodic evaluation of aid from a right to development perspective requires: 'Sustaining the levels of ODA, notwithstanding requirements of emergency aid and aid for the purposes of national security'. *Report of the High-Level Task Force* (2005, 2nd), para 58 (d).

UN reform: 'we will not enjoy development without security, we will not enjoy security without development, and we will not enjoy either without respect for human rights. Unless all these causes are advanced, none will succeed'.[79]

3.3.2 Rights-based economic growth

The integration of human rights standards and principles, both in the process and outcome of development interventions, is reflected in the 'human rights-based approach to development'. Under this approach, human rights standards and principles, as provided for in international law, should underscore development processes at all levels, and development should be aimed at furthering human rights. The tools of development—economic growth, technical assistance and any policies and programmes—are meant to play an instrumental role designed to further the realization of human rights. The language of human rights—one of rights, obligations, and accountability based on international law—is meant to provide 'both the tools and the essential references'.[80]

Consistent with the views of human rights scholars on the Task Force, but not of the representatives of the international financial institutions, at its 6th session in 2005 the Working Group on the Right to Development 'recognized the multi-faceted nature of the right to development [and] agreed that a rights-based approach to economic growth and development contributes to the realization of the right to development while it does not exhaust its implications and requirements at both the national and international levels'.[81] The right to development, while sensitive to human development and inclusive of the rights-based approach, takes the development formula one step further by treating all rights as an integrated whole, and the right to development as a comprehensive process for their achievement. A development process that takes account of the objectives that must be met to realize the right to development would include, as we have

[79] Report of the UN Secretary-General, *In Larger Freedom: Towards Development, Security and Human Rights for All*, UN Doc A/59/2005, para 17.

[80] P van Weerelt, 'A Human-Rights-Based Approach to Development Programming in UNDP—Adding the Missing Link' (UNDP, 2001). See generally, *The Second UN Interagency Workshop on Implementing a Human Rights-Based Approach in the Context of UN Reform*, 5–7 May 2003, Stamford, USA, Attachment 1: The Human Rights-Based Approach to Development Cooperation: Towards a Common Understanding Among UN Agencies, 17–8.

[81] *Report of the Working Group* (2005), para 46. The Task Force could not reach a common position on this matter. In the end, it could only accept that '[f]or some [members], the terminology of a human rights-based approach was a sufficient reference; for others, the concept of the right to development, as defined in the Declaration on the Right to Development, embraced and exceeded a rights-based approach': *Report of the High-Level Task Force* (2005, 1st), para 28. Reflecting support for the Working Group's approach, see, SP Marks, *The Human Rights Framework for Development: Seven Approaches* (2003) 16 <http://www.hsph.harvard.edu/fxbcenter>; Sengupta also sees the right to development as broader than the rights-based approach. In his work, economic growth with equity is a constituent element of the right: A Sengupta, *Fifth Report of the Independent Expert on the Right to Development* (Working Group on the Right to Development, 4th session, 2003) UN Doc E/CN4/2002/WG18/6, paras 8–12.

seen; consideration of whether rights are protected and promoted with attention to their indivisibility and interdependence; whether states acting at the national and international levels are contributing to the fulfilment of human rights; and, whether relevant procedures, including those undertaken at the international level, are consistent with the rights-based approach to development.

So, if economic growth is shedding its moniker as synonymous with development, and if it is to be rights-based, the question begged is the degree to which favoured methods for achieving growth are consistent with human rights, and their function as an instrument in the realization of human rights. On the first point, the DRD, notably, reflects this normative shift of moving our understanding of development well beyond that which can be measured purely in terms of economic growth, and physical infrastructure, to a multidimensional definition of development linked specifically to the exercise and fulfilment of human rights. From the start, this thinking provided the conceptual basis of the drafting of the Declaration. In the course of the general discussion held at the first session of the Working Group of Governmental Experts in 1982, there was 'general agreement that development is a concept reaching far beyond the notion of economic growth and that accordingly the discussion should relate to the political, economic, social, cultural, legal and ethical aspects of the right to development'.[82]

Thus a requirement posed by this particular process of development is that it must be carried out in a manner consistent with human rights; considerations of equity, justice and respect for human rights are to determine the strategies for growth and the beneficiaries of it.[83] Rights-based economic growth is meant to integrate fairness into the traditional process of the expansion of wealth, and allocation of resources, focusing on distributional aspects i.e. ensuring minimum quality of life throughout the population, and widespread poverty reduction. A focus merely on aggregate growth as the poverty panacea has lost its power of persuasion,[84] it

---

[82] *Report of the Working Group of Governmental Experts on the Right to Development*, (1st–3rd sessions, 25 January 1982) UN Doc E/CN4/1489 (1982), para 8.

[83] Policies adopted to increase economic growth and in connection with the reallocation of existing resources must be consistent with human rights principles, so as not to negate policies aimed at the realization of rights. They are also to be equitable, non-discriminatory, participatory and transparent, and pursued within a system of accountability. A Sengupta, Independent Expert on the Right to Development, *Statement to the 58th session of the Commission on Human Rights*, 22 March 2002 <http://www.unhchr.ch>; Sengupta, *Fifth Report*, paras 8–12; and further, J Donnelly, *Universal Human Rights: Theory and Practice* (Cornell University Press, 2003) 201.

[84] Jerve remarks that most governments emphasise aggregate growth as key to their poverty reduction goals, while others stress distributional aspects as well, the latter perspective dominating the policies of both bilateral and multilateral development agencies today: AM Jerve, 'Social Consequences of Development in a Human Rights Perspective: Lessons from the World Bank', in I Kolstad and H Stokke (eds), *Writing Rights* (Fagbokforlaget, 2005) 98, at 100. Still, according to the Leader of the UNDP's Poverty Group: 'Poverty reduction continues to be seen as an automatic by-product of economic growth and macroeconomic stability. Governments and their partners find it difficult to translate the concept of "pro-poor growth" into practice. Equity continues to be the big absentee in most anti-poverty strategies': J Vandemoortele, *The MDG's and Pro-Poor Policies: Related but not Synonymous*, UNDP International Policy Centre, Working Paper no 3 (2004) 1.

accepts too readily a system of winners and losers, of short-term disadvantage to some, based on claims that benefits from the greater supply in goods and services will be made available through growth to 'everyone'. The danger, as Donnelly points out, is that '"everyone" does not mean each (every) person' but rather refers to the 'average individual, an abstract collective entity. And even "he" is assured gains only in the future'.[85] This is not the same 'everyone' with recognized rights under the International Covenant on Economic, Social and Cultural Rights.[86]

The improvement of the lot of some, or even many, may also deprive others. Those who suffer any 'adjustment costs'– lost jobs, higher food prices, user fees on health care and education—tend to be the poor, and those already less advantaged or politically influential. The justification is derived from an attachment to a fictional notion of the 'collective good' or 'aggregate benefit' an approach wholly inconsistent with the universality of human rights to which every person is entitled.[87] This utilitarianism, based on the greatest good for the greatest number, is rejected by the human rights paradigm which is rigorous in its endorsement of equal rights for all, and of just and consistent methods of reconciling tensions, for example, between the rights of particular groups and the interests of society as a whole. As Howse concludes, 'the right to development, in requiring that development be pursued through and along with the respect for and furtherance of all internationally recognized human rights, stipulates the categorical rejection of one of the most prominent narratives about the nature of development and growth ... that "you cannot make an omelet without breaking a few eggs"'.[88]

The Task Force on the Right to Development emphasized that the right to development framework made it an imperative that social impact assessments should result in the identification of dislocative effects of adopted policies on the poor and most vulnerable, and that there be the provision of special measures including in the form of social safety nets, such as well-targeted transfers and subsidies—particularly in the context of addressing the effects of external shocks on the well-being of people.[89] UNCTAD had earlier highlighted its concern that 'an unfavourable international economic and political environment has exacerbated the poverty trap in poor countries', noting that the causal factors include 'gaps between policy prescriptions sponsored by the international financial institutions in the form of adjustment programmes and support measures required to implement them'.[90] Given this international dimension, the multilateral trade

---

[85] Donnelly, *Universal Human Rights*, 201.

[86] 'The States Parties to the present Covenant recognize the right of everyone to ... social security... to an adequate standard of living ... to be free from hunger ... to the highest attainable standard of physical and mental health ... to education ... to take part in cultural life ...'.

[87] Donnelly, *Universal Human Rights*, 201–2.

[88] Howse, *Mainstreaming the Right to Development*, para 13.

[89] *Report of the High-Level Task Force* (2005, 1st), para 24.

[90] *The Right to Development: The Importance and Application of the Principle of Equity at Both the National and International Levels*, UN Doc E/CN4/2003/25 (OHCHR, 2003), para 48. A World Bank sponsored independent assessment on its 'contribution to freer trade' for the period

and development institutions 'had to take steps in support of national efforts to facilitate and sustain such measures'.[91]

Insofar as economic growth is necessary for the sustained realization of human rights, the right to development requires '... equality of opportunity for all in access to basic resources, education, health services, food, housing, employment and the fair distribution of income ... [and that] [a]ppropriate economic and social reforms should be carried out with a view to eradicating all social injustices'.[92] This has several implications: the search for growth, or any economic or social reforms, must not violate any human right; it must target people or groups with unequal opportunity to access the minimum essential level of rights, for example the poor, minorities, indigenous peoples, children, women, people in rural areas; and it must have as its objective the elimination of injustices characterized by unfulfilled human rights.

The emphasis on growth with equity aims to ensure that growth serves as a means to the greater goal of overall well-being measured in terms of the realization of human rights for all. As the Working Group has agreed, respect for human rights must determine the strategies for growth.[93] This approach moves away from earlier prescriptions that viewed development purely in terms of increased national income based on the 'trickle down approach', with inadequate attention being given to concurrent increases in intra-state inequality and regional disparities, or to exploitive conditions of employment. Under the 2004 Task Force consensus, agreed among the representatives of development, finance and trade institutions and human rights experts, the primary utilization of growth is as an instrument in ensuring the right to development and the eradication of poverty.[94] The conclusions and recommendations as adopted by the Task Force

1987–2004, concluded that, 'it has been least effective in helping countries manage external shocks and adjustment costs related to trade liberalization', recommending thus that the Bank give greater attention to addressing poverty and distributional outcomes, and cushioning shocks associated with trade policies: *Assessing World Bank Support for Trade*, Executive Summary, Independent Evaluation Group (World Bank, 2006) xviii, xx.

[91] *Report of the High-Level Task Force* (2005, 1st), paras 24, 38. The Task Force also reminded the Working Group that from the human rights perspective, the concept of social safety nets corresponds to the right to an adequate standard of living, including social security as defined in human rights treaties, at para 39. While the World Bank itself would seem to support the idea of safety nets, it lays the responsibility at the door of the national government. 'Safety nets ... are often an essential element of a strategy to ensure that market expansion leads to more equal opportunities ... trade opening creates winners and losers. How this affects equity depends partly on how governments can offer support to the losers': World Bank, *World Development Report 2006: Equity and Development* (World Bank/Oxford Univsersity Press, 2006) 197.

[92] DRD, art 8(1). As mentioned, this art refers specifically to the need for special measures to ensure that women have an active role in the development process.

[93] *Report of the Working Group* (2005), at para 46.

[94] This emphasis on the instrumental role of income can be seen in the way in which poverty itself is defined. It is no longer understood as constituting only a lack of income, but includes deprivations in capability, choice, security and power. CESCR, Statement on Poverty and the International Covenant on Economic, Social and Cultural Rights (25th session, 2001) UN Doc E/C12/2001/10, para 8.

recognized 'that development had to be grounded in sound economic policies that fostered growth with equity ...'.[95] To these ends, the Working Group subsequently adopted the view that economic policies that foster growth cannot be distinct from social justice,[96] and that 'a rights-based approach to economic growth and development contributes to the realization of the right to development ...'.[97] The Declaration's intergovernmental drafting group recalled, on a number of occasions during its work in the first half of the 1980s, that the provisions being worked out 'reflect, inter alia, the general recognition of the interdependence of economic growth and social and cultural development in the wider process of growth and change and of the promotion and observance of human rights as a fundamental principle'.[98]

3.3.3 Obligations of conduct at the international level

Human rights law establishes a binary relationship between right-holders and duty-bearers. It exists not only to protect people from abuse of power (initially foreseen at the hands of the state), but to secure a normative framework within which the individual is understood to have a claim on the conduct of the state. The right to development with its focus on global institutional arrangements conducive to securing human rights, harnesses this element of the human rights framework, emphasizing process over outcome, conduct over result. The component of the human rights agenda attentive to conduct, is thus also concerned with suitable *international* arrangements that will increase the likelihood of furthering human rights, i.e. that will reduce world poverty and create conditions in which people in poor countries can exercise their rights. Indicators related to obligations of cooperation, for example, focus on international and institutional conduct (of intergovernmental organizations), that is, on the adequacy of state policy and decisions.[99] When considering obligations of conduct, an overt responsibilities approach is adopted, whereby the minimum entitlement to economic, social and cultural rights entails corresponding action required of various actors, including those acting at the international level, the absence of which may be considered a violation of that right.

---

[95] *Report of the High-Level Task Force* (2005, 1st), para 31.
[96] *Report of the Working Group* (2005), at para 42.
[97] Ibid, para 46.
[98] *Report of the Working Group of Governmental Experts on the Right to Development (Open-ended Drafting Group)* (4th session, 9 July 1982) UN Doc E/CN4/AC39/1982/11 art 7; *Report of the Working Group of Governmental Experts on the Right to Development* (5th session, 9 December 1982) UN Doc E/CN4/1983/11, annex IV, para 7.
[99] See, 2.4 above and, S Fukuda-Parr, *Millennium Development Goal 8: Indicators for Monitoring Implementation* UN Doc E/CN4/2005/WG18/TF/CRP2, para 18 *passim*, and *Report of the High-Level Task Force* (2005, 2nd), para 51.

In the course of its work on the responsibility of states for international wrongful acts, the International Law Commission (ILC)[100] noted the distinction between 'obligations of conduct and obligations of result'—terms which have gained currency in international law.[101] Obligations of conduct are referred to as 'best efforts obligations', whereas obligations of result are 'tantamount to guarantees of outcome'.[102] The importance of distinguishing between obligations of conduct, and of result, with regard to international cooperation in the progressive realization of economic, social and cultural rights, has been addressed by CESCR. In its interpretation of ICESCR Article 2(1) on the nature of states parties obligations, including their international obligations of assistance and cooperation, the Committee explicitly states that '[t]hose obligations include both what may be termed (following the work of the International Law Commission) obligations of conduct and obligations of result'.[103] The ILC itself has also specifically recognized the applicability of the terms in relation to the provisions of ICESCR, stating: 'An instance of a case where the distinction was of value ... was provided by Article 2, paragraph 1 [which addresses the nature of States parties' obligations] of the International Covenant on Economic, Social and Cultural Rights, which contained a delicate mix of obligations of conduct and obligations of result'.[104]

The initial distinction in international law was borrowed from French law in which the obligations of result tend to be stronger than that of conduct, in that 'the mere fact of non-materialization of the result constitutes a violation of the obligation, rather than an obligation to make a bone fide effort with a view to achieving the result, but without guaranteeing its materialization'.[105] In this work of the ILC on the subject, however, obligations of conduct tend to be more stringent than obligations of result.[106] The obligation to put in place a process for

---

[100] The ILC was established by the UN General Assembly in 1947 to promote the progressive development of international law and its codification. It is composed of 34 independent members elected by the General Assembly.

[101] *Report of the International Law Commission* (51st Session, 1999) UN Doc A/54/10 (1999), para 132. The ILC further observes that 'the distinction between obligations of result and obligations of conduct had become commonplace in international legal discourse, not only at the academic level but also at that of inter-State relations' (para 146). See also *Gabčíkovo-Nagymaros Project* (Hungary v Slovakia) ICJ Rep (1997) 7, at para 135: 'In order to achieve these objectives the parties accepted obligations of conduct, obligations of performance, and obligations of result'.

[102] *Report of the International Law Commission*, para 132.

[103] CESCR, General Comment no 3, The Nature of States Parties' Obligations, para 1. In the domestic context see also the expert *Maastricht Guidelines on Violations of Economic, Social and Cultural Rights*, reproduced in 20 *HRQ* 3 (1998) 691, at para 7.

[104] *Report of the International Law Commission*, para 152.

[105] G Abi-Saab, 'The Legal Formulation of a Right to Development' in R-J Dupuy (ed), *The Right to Development at the International Level, Workshop of the Hague Academy of International Law 1979* (Sijthoff & Noordhoff, 1980) 173–4.

[106] *Report of the International Law Commission*, para 133. The ILC explains that in French law the obligation of result is considered the more stringent of the two because it is concerned with risk, whereas under the work of the ILC the obligation of conduct is the more stringent, given its emphasis is on the determinacy of the conduct. Explicit reference to obligations of conduct and obligations of result does not appear, however, in the Articles on the Responsibility of States for

the progressive realization of rights might also invite more rigorous requirements than those entailing an immediate result. In the words of CESCR, 'the principal obligation [is] to take steps to achieve progressively the full realization of the [ESC] right ... it [i]mposes an obligation to move as expeditiously as possible towards the goal'[107] and '[s]uch steps should be deliberate, concrete and targeted as clearly as possible towards meeting the obligations ...'.[108] As Alston and Quinn have remarked, the undertaking 'to take steps'—language that appears throughout the ICESCR—is akin to assuming an obligation of conduct.[109]

Obligations of conduct for rights that may entail progressive realization require that action be 'reasonably calculated' to realize the enjoyment of a particular right.[110] Certainly, then, with regard to the right to development, which entails a particular process that necessarily includes different variables and agents, and for which therefore there may be less control over the outcome, the obligation of conduct, aimed at the process of realizing the right, can be understood as imposing a more exacting obligation than that of result. While states acting internationally maintain human rights obligations of result, which include, for example, meeting internationally set targets to satisfy detailed substantive standards,[111] obligations of conduct require the implementation of policies conducive to the realization of human rights. The collective responsibilities of states are triggered for failure to put in place suitable policies that would avoid exacerbating world poverty, and would actively reduce the existing deprivation.[112] With its responsibilities approach, and focus on international duties to address poverty

---

Internationally Wrongful Acts (2001). The Articles are concerned with the codification and progressive development of secondary rules and thus as Crawford and Bodeau elucidate, the reference to obligations of conduct and of result as applied to the question of a breach, the existence of which relies upon the specific content of the primary rule, 'lacked consequence within the framework of the Draft articles'. The ILC Articles do refer to the 'character of an obligation'. The reference to 'character' is to ensure recognition of the continued value of the terms as they relate to obligations. An overview of the second reading further recognizes their 'currency in international law', despite the explicit reference being dropped: J Crawford and P Bodeau, *Second Reading of the ILC Draft Articles on State Responsibility: Further Progress* <http://www.law.cam.ac.uk/rcil/ILCSR/Forum2.doc>. The ILC has also specifically referred to their significance in relation to the effects of reservations under the Vienna Convention on the Law of Treaties, and with regard to the nature of states parties' obligations under the ICESCR, as mentioned. It was further remarked that courts had also found the distinction useful. See *Report of the International Law Commission*, paras 152–3; See further, *Articles on the Responsibility of States for Internationally Wrongful Acts with commentaries* (2001) art 12.

[107] CESCR, General Comment no 12, The Right to Adequate Food (art 11), (20th session, 1999) UN Doc E/C12/1999/5, para 14.

[108] CESCR, General Comment no 3, The Nature of States Parties' Obligations, para 2.

[109] P Alston and and G Quinn, 'The Nature and Scope of States Parties' Obligations under the International Covenant on Economic, Social and Cultural Rights' 9 *HRQ* 2 (1987) 156, at 167.

[110] *Maastricht Guidelines*, 691, at 694.

[111] 'We urge developed countries that have not done so to make concrete efforts towards the target of 0.7% of gross national product (GNP) as ODA to developing countries'. Monterrey Consensus, paras 41–2.

[112] See further, Ch 5.

and underdevelopment, the right to development posits international cooperation as a central element in determining the scope of necessary conduct.

The distinction between obligations of conduct, and of result, may also assist in ascertaining when a breach of an international obligation has occurred,[113] and as the ILC has clarified, a failure to exercise due diligence in meeting the legal obligations of conduct could trigger responsibility.[114] In fact the ILC has recognized that the failure of a state to take the necessary steps to avoid a breach is enough to be considered a breach of the obligation. Whether or not the threat was realized as a result of the inaction is not the deciding factor.[115] The European Court of Human Rights has also distinguished situations whereby the duty of the Contracting State is to take measures rather than to guarantee the achievement of desirable results.[116] This places the notion of process at the centre of determining the content of responsibility, whereby conduct (or lack thereof), in and of itself , can constitute a violation of the primary right. Conversely, the obligation of result is not discharged if the particular process is not respected in reaching a given outcome. So for example, forced privatization of public goods,[117] while it may successfully increase public revenue in a given developing country, can be in contravention of the right to development (among other rights) if the process of boosting national wealth results in certain people or groups within the country being rendered unable to afford clean water, healthcare or primary education.[118]

The requirement to adjust the rules of operation of trading and financial institutions would seem to offer a consensus on the specific content of obligations of international conduct.[119] Repeated reports condemn the lack of influence developing countries exercise at the international level for example, suggesting that the

---

[113] ILC Commentary on the articles on state responsibility addressing the 'character' of a breach under art 12. *Articles on Responsibility of States for Internationally Wrongful Acts with commentaries*, 2001, 130.

[114] *Report of the International Law Commission*, para 154.

[115] Ibid, para 162.

[116] *Plattform 'Ärzte Für das Leben' v Austria*, ECtHR App no 10126/82, judgment of 21 June 1988, para 34.

[117] The UK only recently decided to stop imposing policy choices on partner countries as a condition of aid, including in the area of privatisation: *Partnerships for Poverty Reduction: Rethinking Conditionality*, UK Policy Paper, March 2005, para 5.13. Oxfam reports that Norway and the European Commission also 'now publicly reject the inclusion of privatisation as a condition for aid. However, all three continue to channel resources to World Bank projects that actively promote private sector solutions, or link their aid to conditions imposed by the World Bank and the IMF.': B Emmet, *In the Public Interest* (Oxfam, 2006) 65.

[118] On the impact of the IFI-mandated privatization of the veterinary services in Niger and the consequential exacerbation of food insecurity, see J Ziegler, *Report to the General Assembly of the Special Rapporteur on the Right to Food* UN Doc A/60/350, para 43. Ziegler further reports that in a country where at a minimum one in four children die before the age of five due to malnutrition, cost recovery policies (i.e. user fees for drugs and services that can render them unaffordable) imposed on health centres by the IFIs have resulted in children not being treated for malnutrition (paras 15 and 42).

[119] For a detailed consideration of what international cooperation may entail see, Ch 2.4.

reversal of the status quo is essential if we seek to modify the rules that keep them impoverished.[120] Writing on international trade, the UNDP concludes in its 2005 *Human Development Report* that within the existing rules-based multilateral system 'costs and benefits have been unevenly distributed across and within countries, perpetuating a pattern of globalization that builds prosperity for some amid mass poverty and deepening inequality for others'.[121] The rules arranged to benefit developed countries at the impoverishment of the people in low-income countries are based on a foundation of 'hypocrisy and double standards',[122] '... [t]he critical challenge for a multilateral system is to provide a framework in which the voices of the weaker members carry weight',[123] in which policy advice given to developing countries better recognizes that the global markets are inequitable and are based on rules that do not favour them.[124]

Yet, the international institutions responsible for global economic policy are composed of Members States that have human rights obligations born of conventions, custom, and general principles of international law. The majority of states belonging to the international financial institutions, for example, have ratified the major human rights conventions, including the ICESCR, and are thereby bound to honour their human rights obligations, including when entering into bilateral agreements with other states, and through their actions in international organizations. The CESCR has made it clear that should a state party fail to take into account its legal obligations when entering into bilateral or multilateral agreements with other states or international organizations, it is in breach of its human rights obligations under the Covenant.[125] Where states parties are entering into agreements with another state party to the Covenant, there is a further duty not to induce them to breach the obligations they have undertaken under the Covenant by adopting measures inconsistent with those obligations. The CESCR has drawn attention to this on several occasions, noting with regard to the right to health that:

... States parties have an obligation to ensure that their actions as members of international organizations take due account of the right to health. Accordingly, States parties which

---

[120] Recent studies calling for the democratization of the WTO, IMF and World Bank include: *Final Report and Recommendations Derived from the Multi-Stakeholder Consultations Organized by the New Rules for Global Finance Coalition*, November 2004-September 2005; *On Addressing Systemic Issues, Section F, Monterrey Consensus Document, Financing For Development/New Rules for Global Finance* (2005); UNDP, *Human Development Report 2005: International Cooperation at a Crossroads; Investing in Development: A Practical Plan to Achieve the Millennium Development Goals* (UNDP, 2005); *Our Common Interest, Report of the Commission for Africa* (2005) <http://www.commissionforafrica. org>; *EU Heroes and Villains: Which Countries are Living up to their Promises on Aid, Trade, and Debt?* Joint NGO Briefing Paper, Action Aid, Eurodad and Oxfam (2005); *A Fair Globalization*.
[121] UNDP, *Human Development Report 2005: International Cooperation at a Crossroads*, Ch 4, at 113.
[122] Ibid.
[123] Ibid, Ch 4, at 146.
[124] World Bank, *World Development Report 2006: Equity and Development*, 16.
[125] CESCR, General Comment no 14, The Right to Health, para 50; CESCR, General Comment no 12, The Right to Food, para 19.

are members of international financial institutions, notably the International Monetary Fund, the World Bank and the regional development banks, should pay greater attention to the protection to the right to health in influencing lending policies, credit agreements and international measures of these institutions.[126]

The Committee makes a similar point, for example, with regard to the right to food,[127] the right to work,[128] and in its Concluding Observations on states' reports.[129] Similarly, the Declaration on the Right to Development imposes a duty on states to take steps '*individually and collectively* to formulate international development policies with a view to facilitating the full realization of the right to development'.[130] The joint action of states to cooperate in the protection of human rights is also a pledge of UN Member States as codified in the Charter.[131]

As some of the most commanding formulations of development policies occur through the collective decisions of (wealthy) states as members of the World Bank and IMF, it falls to these states to uphold their human rights obligations in relation to the execution of their collective decisions as members of the IFIs. As highlighted in Chapter 2, an important trend in decisions from the European Court of Human Rights reflects that the human rights responsibilities of Member States continue even after the transfer of competences to international organizations,[132] and they may thus be accountable—singly and jointly—for any human rights violations of the international organizations of which they are a member. This is separate from the convention-based obligations that the organization would have were it to be a signatory to the human rights treaty,[133] and distinct from the obligations of an international organization to abide by customary international law.[134]

---

[126] CESCR, General Comment no 14, The Right to Health, para 39.

[127] CESCR, General Comment no 12, The Right to Food, para 41.

[128] CESCR, General Comment no 18, The Right to Work, para 30.

[129] CESCR, Concluding Observations: Japan (26th session, 2001) UN Doc E/C12/1/Add67 (2001), para 37; CESCR, Concluding Observations: Morocco (24th session, 2000) UN Doc E/C12/1Add55 (2000), para 38; CESCR, Concluding Observations: Belgium (24th session, 2000) UN Doc E/C12/1/Add 54 (2000), para 31; CESCR, Concluding Observations: Italy (23rd session, 2000) UN Doc E/C12/1/Add43 (2000), para 20.

[130] DRD, art 4(1), (emphasis added); see, *Report of the Working Group* (2006), para 36.

[131] UN Charter, art 56.

[132] *Matthews* v *United Kingdom*, ECtHR App no 24833/94, Grand Chamber judgement of 18 February 1999, paras 29, 32, and 34; *Bosphorus Airways* v *Ireland*, ECtHR App no 45036/98, Grand Chamber judgment of 30 June 2005, paras 152–6; *Waite and Kennedy* v *Germany*, ECtHR App no 26083/94, Grand Chamber judgment of 18 February 1999, para 67; see also A Reinisch, 'The Changing International Legal Framework for Dealing with Non-State Actors' in P Alston (ed), *Non-State Actors and Human Rights* (Oxford University Press, 2005) 37, at 67 and 81–4.

[133] Reinisch remarks on the renewed interest by EU member states on possible EC accession to the ECHR triggered by their desire to avoid being held accountable for the acts of international organization which they cannot fully control. Reinisch, 'The Changing International Legal Framework', 37, at 83–4.

[134] The international organization as an international legal person is subject to the rules of international law, including conventional (where they have consented) and customary rules and principles

During its 2005 session, the Task Force on the Right to Development, as mandated by the intergovernmental Working Group, elaborated right to development criteria for the evaluation of Millennium Development Goal 8 on Global Partnerships for Development.[135] In suggesting criteria for improving the effectiveness of global partnerships from the perspective of the right to development, the Task Force addressed decision-making, and norm-setting, in international trade and finance concerned by the fact that it heavily favours the interests of developed countries. It remarked in this regard that institutional asymmetries in global governance are found in the formal 'voting structures of the World Bank and IMF [which are] heavily weighted towards developed countries. [And] WTO rules give equal votes to each country but decision-making is by consensus, which, in practice, does not allow for significant agreement that would benefit many developing or least developed countries at the expense of more developed ones'.[136] In order to further the right to development, the Task Force recommended revision of the governance structures and procedures of the international financial institutions, and WTO, to ensure better representation of developing countries;[137] a demand high on the agenda of civil society, expert commissions, and certain Northern governments, for some time. Yet, as highlighted during the Task Force discussions, the universally endorsed MDGs offer little by way of a system for monitoring powerful countries under MDG 8. Goal 8 is silent on the need to increase the voices of poor countries in international decision-making, and there is no timetable for the required policy changes necessary to achieve the broad objectives under the Goal.[138]

Consideration of international obligations of conduct is relevant to the international trading system. The trading system is criticized for representing an end in itself, for reflecting few calculated linkages to the improvement of human well-being, and for all too often having a deleterious impact on the human rights of people in the poorest countries. Rich-country trade policies see the highest trade barriers erected against some of the poorest countries, with the barriers faced by developing countries three to four times higher than those faced by rich countries when they trade with each other.[139] In agricultural trade, rich country subsidies (e.g. US cotton subsidies, EU farm subsidies) coupled with high tariffs, directly undermine the livelihoods—the rights to an adequate standard of living and to food, including food security—of the two-thirds of all people living on less than US$1 a day in developing countries who live and work in rural areas.[140] It would seem that the

---

of general international law: P Sands and P Klein, *Bowett's Law of International Institutions* (5th edn, Sweet & Maxwell Ltd, 2001) 456 and 458.

[135] CHR res 2005/4, The right to development (61st session, 2005), para 5.
[136] *Report of the High-Level Task Force* (2005, 2nd), para 74.
[137] Ibid, para 92.
[138] These weaknesses regarding the implementation of MDG 8 were raised by the UNDP: *Report of the High-Level Task Force* (2005, 2nd), para 23.
[139] UNDP, *Human Development Report 2005: International Cooperation at a Crossroads*, Ch 4, 127.
[140] Ibid, 10. Notably, 80% of all farmers in Africa are women. *Fast Facts: The Faces of Poverty*, UN Millennium Project (2005).

international trading system is rigged in favour of the rich countries; in a world where there is enough food to feed everyone, more than 40 per cent of Africans do not even have the ability to obtain sufficient food on a day-to-day basis.[141]

Trade-related intellectual property rights under the intellectual property regime covering patents, trademark, and copyright are known to favour the richest countries.[142] The regime under TRIPS threatens access by the people of developing countries to essential medicines, including HIV treatment, by limiting the domestic ability of developing countries to produce, or pay for, pharmaceuticals. While the (WTO Ministerial) Doha Declaration on TRIPS and Public Health (2001)[143] authoritatively reaffirms that all WTO members can use the flexibilities provided by the TRIPS agreement (notably compulsory licensing and parallel importation) to ensure access to affordable medicines, concerns remain as to whether the Declaration will be interpreted as intended, including whether 'TRIPS Plus' provisions in other trade agreements will serve to undermine the Declaration's objectives.[144] Currently, there is a disproportionate focus on diagnostic tools, and research and development related to ailments that affect people in developed countries, such as obesity, over those that affect people in developing countries, such as, Chagas' disease, sleeping sickness, or river blindness, demonstrating how disease prevention and cures are favoured or neglected based on market justifications.[145] The intellectual property regime also raises concerns in the areas of access to food, and food security, of people in developing countries,[146]

---

[141] *Fast Facts: The Faces of Poverty.*

[142] TRIPS establishes a global regime for intellectual property based on the level of protection provided in the most developed countries. Yet a one-size-fits-all approach to intellectual property protection is criticized for not taking into consideration the needs of developing countries and for undermining poverty reduction. *Report of the Commission on Intellectual Property Rights: Integrating Intellectual Property Rights and Development Policy,* UK (2002). The TRIPS Agreement, which provides monopoly rights for 20 years, enables drug prices to be set high and stay high, while stifling competition. As noted earlier, firms in developed countries currently account for 96% of royalties from patents, or US$71 billion a year: UNDP, *Human Development Report 2005: International Cooperation at a Crossroads,* Ch 4, at 135.

[143] WT/MIN(01)/DEC/2, 20 November 2001; on WTO rulings conducive to the right to health, see, *Report of the High-Level Task Force* (2005, 2nd), para 66 (supporting the right of countries to safeguard public health and promote access to essential medicines; regarding the easing of restrictions on the importation of generic drugs by the poorest countries for the treatment of rapidly spreading diseases; and on the decision to extend the transition period for least developed countries to provide protection for intellectual property under TRIPS).

[144] '[TRIPS Plus] provisions explicitly strengthen the protection afforded to pharmaceutical companies beyond WTO provisions and circumscribe the policy space for governments': UNDP, *Human Development Report 2005: International Cooperation at a Crossroads,* Ch 4, at 136; see also P Hunt, *Report of the Special Rapporteur on the Right of Everyone to the Highest Attainable Standard of Health: Mission to the WTO,* UN Doc E/CN4/2004/49/Add1.

[145] I Sample, 'Doctors who Put Lives Before Profits', *The Guardian,* 4 January 2006; P Hunt, *Report of the Special Rapporteur on the Right of Everyone to the Highest Attainable Standard of Health,* UN Doc E/CN4/2004/49, para 76.

[146] For example, patents and other means of intellectual property protection on plants and their genes prevent farmers from saving and reusing seeds and may undermine agricultural diversity, negatively impacting on food security.

access to education and knowledge,[147] including traditional knowledge of indigenous peoples,[148] and regarding environmental protection and the conservation and sustainable use of biological diversity.[149] Notably, this list is not exhaustive, and other areas of international trade are also being challenged for their negative impact on human development.[150] The threat to the exercise of rights in these areas saw the Task Force express concern.[151]

Despite the apparent 'equality' among WTO members in terms of the consensus principle and 'one-country-one-vote', the differential in wealth and power between developed and developing states has provoked some effort to build up the capacity of least developed countries to develop trade policy, to support financially the teams required to represent their interests in international trade negotiations, and to provide technical assistance in implementing the law contained in WTO treaties in domestic regulations.[152] Linked to this deficit in meaningful representation and knowledge but of *prior* concern though, are the values and objectives of the international trading system itself, and the impact this has on the exercise of economic, social and cultural rights in poor countries. Howse doubts whether the technical assistance provided to assist developing countries

[147] Education through access to information available on the internet (copyright resulting in costly subscription-only databases); radio broadcasts (criticism levelled against the proposed WIPO broadcasting treaty); affordable and up to date school textbooks. Notably, the cultural rights provided for in Art 15 of the ICESCR while seeking to protect the interests of authors (ICESCR, art 151.c.), explicitly balances these rights against the interests of the wider community, for example, to enjoy the benefits of scientific progress (ICESCR, art 15.1.b.). See generally, Background note, *Intellectual Property, Human Rights and the Drafting of the General Comment on article 15.1.c ICESCR*, January 2005; and, CESCR, General Comment no 17, The Right to Protection of Moral and Material Interests.

[148] Of particular significance to indigenous peoples are also the rights 'to take part in cultural life' (ICESCR art 15.1.a) and '[t]o benefit from the protection of the moral and material interests resulting from any scientific, literary or artistic production' authored by them (ICESCR, art 15.1.c). See generally, F Mackay, 'Cultural Rights' in ME Salomon (ed), *Economic, Social and Cultural Rights: A Guide for Minorities and Indigenous Peoples* (MRG, 2005) 83.

[149] See generally, *Indigenous Peoples and the International and Domestic Protection of Traditional Knowledge*, Working paper prepared for the UN Working Group on Indigenous Populations by the Secretariat of the Convention on Biological Diversity, UN Doc E/CN4/Sub2/AC4/2005/CRP2 (reporting on the loss of traditional knowledge and the scarcity of measures to reverse this trend, and noting the CBD's Memorandum of Understanding with WIPO aimed at furthering cooperation on intellectual property issues such as enhancing genetic resources, benefit sharing and environmental sustainability).

[150] The WTO's Agreement on Trade-Related Investment Measures (TRIMS) is roundly criticized for prohibiting tools that would maximize the local benefits of foreign investment (e.g. technology transfer, local employment)—tools that were earlier used by developed countries. The UNDP concludes that: '... the current regime is entirely out of step with what is required to strengthen the links between trade and human development. The starting point for reform should be a recognition that the purpose of multilateralism is not to impose common rules or a free market blueprint on countries with different approaches and different levels of development, but to accept the case for diverse public policies.' UNDP, *Human Development Report 2005: International Cooperation at a Crossroads*, Ch 4, at 135. On concerns over Non-Agricultural Market Access and human development see, Ch 4, at 126–9.

[151] *Report of the High-Level Task Force* (2005, 2nd), para 67.

[152] Howse, *Mainstreaming the Right to Development*, para 31.

is consistent with the normative concerns of the right to development. He questions, for example, whether the emphasis when training government officials from developing countries in WTO law favours a 'maximally trade-liberalizing version or interpretation [of WTO law, rather than giving] equal or greater emphasis to interpretations and legal strategies that would maximize the flexibilities and limiting dimensions of trade-liberalizing obligations ...'.[153]

Other elements relevant to meeting international obligations of conduct apply to aid, debt relief, and the regulation and contribution of the private sector. Improving the quality and increasing the quantity of aid, while important, particularly for certain countries, does not address the global structural disadvantages that contribute to the continued impoverishment of developing countries, and further, aid is underpinned by a relationship based on dependency. The debt burden still represents an obstacle for many countries in fulfilling economic, social and cultural rights, including via the achievement of the Millennium Development Goals. While the Task Force deems it necessary 'to define debt sustainability within a State context with a view to attaining a level of debt that allows countries to achieve the goals and avoid an increase in debt ratios by 2015'[154] the need to look beyond assessing the sustainability of debt servicing, to the legitimacy of certain debts themselves, is also receiving considerable attention.[155]

Regarding the private sector, transnational corporations are the subject of considerable focus given their ability directly, and indirectly, to violate human rights.[156] While they may have a positive effect on the development efforts of host (developing) countries, contributing to the enjoyment of human rights through, for example, investment, employment creation, just and equitable working conditions, the stimulation of economic growth, and community development,[157] they operate in a climate of soft regulation, and of impunity for their negative impact

[153] Ibid, para 32.
[154] *Report of the High-Level Task Force* (2005, 2nd), para 62; On the need to align the IMF monetary policies imposed on debtor governments with the MDGs, see the case studies from 13 countries undertaken by ActionAid International highlighting the fundamental contradiction between the need to scale-up social spending (e.g. to tackle HIV/AIDS) and what can actually be spent under the IMF's low inflation monetary policy. The Secretary-General's UN Millennium Project report similarly noted that: 'IMF program design has paid almost no systematic attention to the [Millennium Development] Goals when considering a country's budget or macroeconomic framework': *Square Pegs, Round Holes* and *Contradicting Commitments: How the Achievement of Education for All is Being Undermined by the International Monetary Fund* (Action Aid International, 2005); *Investing in Development: A Practical Plan to Achieve the Millennium Development Goals* (UNDP, 2005).
[155] J Hanlon, *Defining Illegitimate Debt*, Norwegian Church Aid (2002) <http://english.nca.no/article/view/2381/?TreeMenu=109>; Lutheran World Federation, Statement to the Commission on Human Rights (61st session, 2005) <http://www.lutheranworld.org/News/LWI/EN/1660.EN.html>; TW Pogge, 'Priorities of Global Justice' in TW Pogge (ed), *Global Justice* (Blackwell Publishers, 2001) 6, at 20.
[156] See generally, J Ruggie, *Interim Report of the UN Special Representative of the Secretary-General on the issue of human rights and transnational corporations and other business enterprise*, UN Doc E/CN4/2006/97.
[157] *Report of the High-Level Task Force* (2005, 2nd), para 70.

on the exercise of rights.[158] All the while transnational corporations (TNCs) account for over 70 per cent of world trade, form 51 of the world's 100 largest economies, and of the 200 largest TNCs none maintains headquarters outside of North America, Europe, Japan or South Korea.[159] As a preliminary measure, the periodic evaluation of the right to development would require, according to both the Task Force and Working Group, the monitoring of TNCs from the perspective of human rights.[160] However, steps to circumscribe appropriately the private sector, to ensure that they have responsibilities consistent with the freedoms they enjoy, and to further the responsible allocation of access to global wealth, would need to be considerable:

> ... [T]hese corporations control much of the world's investment capital, technology, and access to international markets. ... These giant firms and their global strategies have become major determinants of trade flows, the location of industries, and other economic activities around the world. As a consequence, TNCs have become extremely important players that influence the economic, political and social welfare of many nations.[161]

As Pogge has similarly emphasized, dealing with the impact of TNCs on the exercise of human rights would need to address the features of the global order itself that help to explain the persistence of poverty.[162]

The skewed playing field that makes a fair international economic system unworkable, and the systemic features of global arrangements that benefit the rich at the expense of the poor, lead to the conclusion that conduct at the international level has been 'reasonably calculated' not to encourage the progressive realization of economic, social and cultural rights, but to violate them. This is despite the fact that the General Assembly has recently recognized the 'systemic' impediments to a just form of development,[163] highlighting the need for international cooperation in achieving the 'fundamental role' of the

---

[158] Thus notably, the Secretary-General's Special Representative on the Issue of Human Rights and Transnational Corporations and Other Business Enterprises has been mandated to begin his work by addressing the issues of 'complicity' and 'sphere of influence'.

[159] MB Steger, *Globalization: A Very Short Introduction* (Oxford University Press, 2003) 48–9.

[160] *Report of the High-Level Task Force* (2005, 2nd), para 89; *Report of the Working Group* (2006), para 56: 'TNCs should operate in a manner consistent with the domestic and international human rights obligations of the host countries and the countries of origin. The Working Group, therefore, considers that the elaboration of criteria should be considered for periodic evaluation of the effects of TNC activities. Such criteria may contribute to ensure their compliance with human rights laws and regulations, and the effectiveness of the enforcement of these laws and regulations, taking into account the degree of influence exercised by many TNCs'.

[161] Steger, *Globalization: A Very Short Introduction*, 48 and 51.

[162] Pogge remarks that '... oppression and corruption are very substantially encouraged and sustained by global factors such as ... the still poorly policed bribe-paying practices of multinational corporations, and the international arms trade'. TW Pogge, 'The First UN Millennium Development Goal: A Cause for Celebration?' 5 *Journal of Human Development* 3 (2004) 377, at 392.

[163] The General Assembly reflects its concern regarding the systemic issues that impact on underdevelopment such as global governance and international economic decision-making, as well as, inter alia, the external debt problem, and market access: 2005 World Summit Outcome, Values and Principles, paras 35–9.

UN in promoting the:

coherence, coordination and implementation of the development goals, and the resolve of its member states to strengthen coordination within the United Nations system in close cooperation with all other multilateral financial trade and development institutions in order to support sustained economic growth, poverty eradication and sustainable development.[164]

The distinction between obligations of conduct and those of result can be a useful one, in that it prescribes certain conduct even if the outcome remains uncertain. It is through the meeting of obligations of conduct that progressive realization, where necessary, is implemented, and responsibility and accountability can be attributed. The likelihood of achieving appropriate results can be linked to the degree to which conduct consistent with international human rights has been planned, and given effect, and to the failure to abstain from international policies that are likely to contribute to human rights violations.

The global character of the modern world has largely limited the possibility of any individual developing state putting in place a sustainable process for the fulfilment of the right to development. The domestic implementation of the right to development cannot be pursued in isolation, only in cooperation, and thus the meeting of obligations of conduct by powerful members of the international community is a prerequisite to its realization.

3.3.4 Principles of the right to development

The Working Group recalls 'the principles that underlie the right to development, namely, equality, non-discrimination, participation, transparency and accountability, as well as international cooperation. It also attaches particular importance to the principle of equity, as was stressed by the independent expert on the right to development, and the rule of law and good governance, at all levels, as being central to the right to development'.[165] While of course not limited to the international level, when taken together, and applied at the international level, the principles serve as a tool to appraise our system of international governance, and to highlight certain weaknesses.

3.3.4.1 *Equality and non-discrimination*

World poverty today suggests that what we are witnessing under this international economic system is domestic discrimination writ large: the creation and perpetuation of a global 'underclass' at the hands of a powerful and rich elite.[166]

---

[164] Ibid, para 38.
[165] *Report of the Working Group* (2006), para 40.
[166] See generally, J Oloka-Onyango, *Globalization in the Context of Increased Incidents of Racism, Racial Discrimination and Xenophobia* (Sub-Commission, 51st session, 1999) UN Doc E/CN4/Sub2/1999/8.

The trade principle of non-discrimination is primarily directed towards reducing trade protectionism, and improving international competitive conditions, rather than achieving substantive equality, which lies at the heart of the human rights regime, including when applied in the context of globalization.[167] In human rights terms, equality and non-discrimination 'provide the foundations for the free and equal enjoyment of human rights. The equality referred to is not restricted to formal equality but extends to achieving substantive equality. This is illustrated by the fact that States carry obligations under human rights treaties to take positive measures to redress the structural biases that lead to discrimination'.[168]

The principle of non-discrimination under international human rights law can also be violated when there is a failure to treat differently persons whose situations are significantly different.[169] By expecting of developing countries that which industrialized countries would not have undertaken when they were developing, are they being 'discriminated' against? Trade rules are criticized for advancing a single recipe for economic growth, failing to allow for diverse national institutions and standards and for the preferences citizens might have for the role of government regulation or provision of social welfare.[170] By comparison, as Townsend's research has pointed out, during their development to present conditions of prosperity, some OECD member countries steadily increased the percentage of national income invested annually in universal social services and social security.[171] Under current conditions developing countries are unlikely to be able to exercise this degree of autonomy.

The argument for asymmetric international rules, and greater domestic autonomy, that take into consideration a country's level of development is a strong one. This call for asymmetry might be understood as a form of positive discrimination in favour of human development, in ensuring that trade becomes a means to a greater good.[172] The Declaration on the Right to Development recognizes

---

[167] In trade policy terms non-discrimination applies to a principle that is meant normally not to allow countries to discriminate between their trading partners or between imported and locally-produced goods, known respectively as the 'Most-Favoured-Nation' (MFN) treatment and 'National' treatment, which constitute the non-discrimination principle. Today, the trade principle deals not only with discrimination against goods, but also—since the inclusion of rules concerning trade in services and intellectual property—with the regulation of service suppliers (individuals or corporations) and intellectual property rights holders (individuals or corporations), respectively; *Analytical Study of the High Commissioner for Human Rights on the Fundamental Principle of Non-Discrimination in the Context of Globalization*, UN Doc E/CN4/2004/40, para 25.

[168] Ibid, para 26.

[169] *Thlimmenos* v *Greece*, ECtHR App no 34369/97, Grand Chamber judgment of 6 April 2000, para 44.

[170] UNDP et al, *Making Global Trade Work for People* (UNDP, 2003) 67.

[171] P Townsend, *The Right to Social Security and National Development: Lessons from OECD Experience for Low-Income Countries*, Discussion Paper 18 (ILO, 2007) viii.

[172] 'The asymmetry must favour development. It is not a question of favouring one country over another or certain workers over others. But there must be, if you like, positive discrimination in favour of human development. If the rules need to be asymmetric or different for different countries to enable that outcome, so be it. ... I think [using tariffs for selective infant industry protection] is a case where you cannot argue that industrialized countries that have had 200–300 years to develop, under high industrial tariffs until very recently, should ask for symmetry with developing countries. But there are many other examples': K Malhotra, *Promoting Human Development through*

fully the need for a global approach to development to complement national action, and international cooperation directed at allowing diversity of development strategies and standards, perhaps conceived of as a form of affirmative action in favour of developing countries, might thus form an important way of giving effect to this right.[173] There are grave concerns over the 'one size fits all' approach to trade rules when 'that "one size" doesn't fit the vast majority of [the WTO's] member states'.[174]

3.3.4.2 Participation

International human rights law does not prescribe a certain economic system, nor any particular form of government beyond that which is democratic, and thereby (generally) respects human rights. As such, a meaningful application of the principle of participation is essential to shape and direct any system in a manner that is consistent with human rights.[175] The CESCR 'reaffirms that the rights recognized in the Covenant are susceptible of realization within the context of a wide variety of economic and political systems, provided only that the interdependence and indivisibility of the two sets of human rights, as affirmed inter alia in the preamble to the Covenant, is recognized and reflected in the system in question. The Committee also notes the relevance in this regard of other human rights and in particular the right to development'.[176] Participation is a key tenet of the Declaration on the Right to Development, featuring in its first article. Article 1 provides that by virtue of their inalienable right to development 'every human person and all peoples' are entitled to participate in, and contribute to, and enjoy, development.[177]

Trade, Address at the Carnegie Council on Ethics and International Affairs, 5 April 2006 <http://www.globalpolicy.org/socecon/trade/2006/0405humandev.htm>.

[173] Salomon with Sengupta, *The Right to Development*, at 30.

[174] Malhotra, *Promoting Human Development through Trade*. A WTO solution to asymmetry in the multilateral trading system is to apply the concept of special and differential treatment (SDT). As regards Uruguay Round Agreements such as TRIMS and TRIPS, SDT typically translates to longer transitional periods for developing and least-developed countries to come into compliance with the obligations under the agreements in question. Another method to address some of the imbalances of the multilateral trading system has been to propose a system of finer 'calibration' between WTO members whereby the actual stage of development (and needs) would be duly reflected in the commitments of a given WTO member. Apparently, resistance has come from stronger developing countries who have more to gain by maintaining their 'developing country' status. Trachtman remarks 'that this concept [of SDT] seems to mask the fact that the international system has done little specifically intended to alleviate poverty; it is not special and differential enough': JP Trachtman, 'Legal Aspects of a Poverty Agenda at the WTO: Trade Law and "Global Apartheid"', 6 *JIEL* 1 (2003) 3, at 10–11.

[175] 'The Committee notes that the undertaking "to take steps ... by all appropriate means including particularly the adoption of legislative measures" neither requires nor precludes any particular form of government or economic system being used as the vehicle for the steps in question, provided only that it is democratic and that all human rights are thereby respected. Thus, in terms of political and economic systems the Covenant is neutral and its principles cannot accurately be described as being predicated exclusively upon the need for, or the desirability of a socialist or a capitalist system, or a mixed, centrally planned, or laisser-faire economy, or upon any other particular approach ... .' CESCR, General Comment no 3, The Nature of States Parties' Obligations, para 8.

[176] Ibid.

[177] DRD, art 1(1). Notably, the Declaration qualifies the legitimacy of state development policies also with reference to participation. At art 2(3) the DRD recognizes that States have the right

At the international level, appeals for equal participation among states speak to a call for functional equality, not merely sovereign equality. But developed states realize that, being outnumbered by less developed states, international democracy would not serve their interests. The World Bank and IMF formally subscribe to a system of weighted voting based on the percentage of shares a member country holds—with the largest shares being held by the US, at 16.4 per cent of the vote in the World Bank (IBRD) (17.08 per cent in the IMF), followed by Japan, Germany, France and the United Kingdom.[178] At the WTO, the governing principle—as under the GATT—is one of consensus. However, there is a history of leaving the vast majority of developing/least-developed countries out of the negotiations and consultations, which determine the decisions. While majority-voting can be used, based on 'one country one vote', it rarely is.[179] And while on some issues certain groupings of developing countries are on the offensive,[180] and we are apparently witnessing an increase in negotiating leverage of middle-income developing countries as well as the poorest among the developing countries,[181] a WTO Deputy Director-General speaking after the 2005 Doha Development Round offered a long list of imbalances that would need to be corrected if the multilateral trading system were to be fair to developing countries.[182] As noted by Howse, '[u]nderstood in terms of the right to development, many of the [WTO] meta-structures leave much to be desired. They narrow the possibilities for individual WTO members to shape and reshape their trade rights and obligations in order to pursue development through and within the fulfilment of all internationally recognized human rights'.[183] This concern was high on the agenda of certain states from the first session of the Working Group on the Right to Development. They called for developing countries to be given 'the possibility to participate in general [in a range of aspects related to international trade], and in particular to be given a more important role in discussions at the WTO'.[184]

---

and the duty to formulate national development, but that these policies are conditional upon peoples' 'active, free and meaningful participation'.

[178] World Bank, *World Development Report 2006: Equity and Development*, 66–7. Similarly, in the IMF, each member country is assigned a quota, based broadly on its relative size in the world economy. A member's quota determines its maximum financial commitment to the IMF and its voting power.

[179] See, BL Das, 'Why the WTO Decision-Making System of "Consensus" Works Against the South', <http://www.twnside.org.sg/title/bgl3-cn.htm>. The author was formerly India's Ambassador and Permanent Representative to the General Agreement on Tariffs and Trade (GATT).

[180] For example, advanced developing countries regarding non-agricultural market access. V Sendanyoye-Rugwabiza, 'Is the Doha Development Round a Development Round?', London School of Economics, London, 31 March 2006.

[181] The Deputy Director-General of the WTO explained in 2006 that G20 countries such as Brazil, China and India 'have completely changed the architecture of negotiations' while the G90 'may be poor but reflect power in framing negotiations'. Ibid, 9, checked against delivery.

[182] Ibid, 4.

[183] Howse, *Mainstreaming the Right to Development*, para 38.

[184] *Report of the Open-ended Working Group on the Right to Development* (1st and 2nd sessions, 2001) UN Doc E/CN4/2001/26, para 148.

Yet, the quest for democracy at the international level, that is rule of law and good governance in international decision-making, does not address what Orford refers to as 'a secret relationship to the market'. So, membership and participation in the wholly imperfect democratic polity of the WTO occurs:

only *after* [states] have responded to the demands of the market . . . . For "developing" and "least-developed" country members, . . . these states in general have already responded to detailed prescriptions requiring an openness to global economic integration and removal of barriers to market access. These conditions are imposed as part of conditions for use of funds dispersed by international financial institutions or in order to be entitled to "preferential" treatment from developed countries permitted under GATT.[185]

Thus in a system predicated on, and delineated by, market freedoms a focus on the international rule of *law* begs the question what law? And, with a focus on *rule* of law in a rules-based system like the WTO, the question becomes whose rules? Orford incisively draws attention to the limits of greater international participation, and increased transparency, in democratic governance that does not challenge the 'pre-democratic' *form of law* as established by trade agreements, and the sacrifice it engenders. What is required is more than an open and transparent, rather than secretive, declaration of the decisions that sacrifice lives.[186] A just form of economic globalization requires, in the first instance, settling questions about democratic versus authoritarian control of production and distribution.[187] And this would include power asserted through coercive agreements secured outside of the (imperfect) multilateral system.[188]

Given the commitments under multilateral agreements in trade and related areas, and their impact on the ability of developing countries to give effect to their human rights obligations in the area of socio-economic rights, the Task Force on the Right to Development (is one of many bodies) to have raised concerns as to the lack of domestic autonomy or 'policy space' available to developing countries.[189] Although keen to avoid any implication that this recognition suggested a diminished set of responsibilities for developing states, the Task Force reaffirmed the Declaration's recognition that 'the creation of conditions favourable to the development of peoples and individuals is the primary responsibility of *their* States'.[190]

This issue of space for national economic policy in the implementation of the right to development figured among the topics targeted by the Working Group

---

[185] Orford, 'Beyond Harmonization', 179, at 207.
[186] Ibid, 179, at 204 and 208.
[187] N Chomsky, 'Free and Fair Trade' *Global Agenda* (2006) 111.
[188] 'Even when each country has equal representation in an international body such as . . . the WTO, powerful forces can chisel away at developing country interests (through separate bilateral agreements, for example). And the capacity for developing countries to make decision can be limited': World Bank, *World Development Report 2006: Equity and Development,* 66.
[189] *Report of the High-Level Task Force* (2005, 1st), para 33; UNCTAD, *World Investment Report,* 2003, Ch 5.
[190] DRD, preambular para 14 (emphasis added).

to guide future work,[191] although it was a point of considerable tension along traditional North-South lines, with Northern states voicing concern that the vaguely defined notion of national policy space leaves wide open the possibility for it to be used by developing states as a blanket waiver on trade issues.[192]

3.3.4.3 Accountability

The current international economic order falls short of securing basic human rights for a vast number of people. It is lacking in just processes, it produces profoundly inequitable outcomes, and we are bearing witness to nothing short of gross and systematic violations of socio-economic rights that are necessarily produced as a result. The most powerful states have, so far, failed to address adequately problems of power-sharing in the management of global governance, protectionist trade barriers, poorly designed rules for intellectual property, and the supply of insufficient development assistance. They are criticized for leaving little scope for alternative approaches to managing the global economy,[193] and thus for preventing 'the low-income world from climbing up the rungs of development.'[194] Most crucially, they have, so far, failed to address, in the words of Townsend: 'how the ladder was constructed or why the distance between the rungs has been getting wider ... [we have not spelled out] the determining structural faults at the apex of power'.[195] Despite the fact that human rights are concerned with challenging abuse of power at all levels—preventing it, protecting people from it, providing for claims against its coercive use, ensuring a system of accountability, and remedying the violations brought about by its occurrence—the global system offers no meaningful method for attributing responsibility, and determining accountability, within an order that provides for yet another person from a developing country to die of starvation every 3.6 seconds, the large majority of whom are children under the age of five.[196]

Accountability failures that undermine the attainment of the Millennium Development Goals, that seek to address world poverty and its manifestations, were listed among the challenges to the implementation of the MDGs identified by the Task Force,[197] a view subsequently adopted by the Working Group.[198] Among the major challenges, as identified by the Task Force, was to put into

[191] *Report of the Working Group* (2005), para 55(a). See also para 41 in which the Working Group '... urges States, in pursuing the discussion [on national economic policy space], to bear in mind its relevance to the realization of the right to development'.

[192] See, Salomon, 'Towards a Just Institutional Order', 409, at 426–7.

[193] For a range of suggestions see, P Townsend and D Gordon (eds), *World Poverty: New Policies to Defeat an Old Enemy* (The Policy Press, 2002) Appendix A, Manifesto: international action to defeat poverty.

[194] J Sachs, *The End Of Poverty* (2005) as cited in P Townsend, 'An End to Poverty or More of the Same?' *The Lancet*, April 2005, 1379.

[195] Townsend, 'An End to Poverty or More of the Same?', 1379.

[196] *Fast Facts: The Faces of Poverty*.

[197] *Report of the High-Level Task Force* (2005, 1st), para 40.

[198] *Report of the Working Group* (2005), para 51.

practice several distinctive features of human rights, including the need for human rights accountability to inform the MDG process, and the need 'to establish and make use of clearly defined accountability mechanisms at the national and international levels which are participatory in nature, accessible, transparent and effective and are based on identification of rights-holders, duty-bearers and procedures for claiming human rights through judicial or other means'.[199]

Focusing on global governance in particular, the Working Group endorsed the Task Force's position that 'States, while adopting agreements and making commitments in international fora, such as in the context of the WTO ... remain accountable for their human rights obligations'.[200] In his final report to the joint World Bank/IMF, Development Committee former World Bank President James Wolfensohn, highlighted the need to 'strengthen' the Bank's governance system. The aims would be, inter alia, '... to reflect modern practices, with clear accountability and benchmarks, and with appropriate representation of all stakeholders. [The] ... issues of voice and participation .... are crucial to address if in the longer run the institution is to retain the accepted legitimacy that is so important to its effectiveness'.[201]

The principle of international cooperation has been reaffirmed by the Working Group as representing a responsibility pivotal to the realization of the right to development, and essential to the promotion of economic, social and cultural rights under the Covenant. These are calls for international cooperation premised on humanitarian objectives as provided for under the UN Charter. Other forms of international cooperation that interfere with the promotion of social progress, higher standards of living, and universal respect for, and observance of, human rights and fundamental freedoms—objectives of a higher 'constitutional' order—do not trump international cooperation for human rights. So, for example, the European Court of Human Rights has held that, while Contracting Parties to the European Convention on Human Rights are not prohibited from transferring sovereign power to an international organization in order to pursue international cooperation in certain fields of activity,[202] '[t]he State is considered to retain Convention liability in respect of treaty commitments subsequent to the entry into force of the Convention'.[203] In cases where equivalent substantive guarantees and mechanisms controlling their observance to that afforded under the Convention are not provided by the IGO, the interest of international cooperation would be outweighed by the Convention's role as a 'constitutional instrument of European public order' in the field of human rights.[204] As noted in Chapter 1, international

---

[199] *Report of the High-Level Task Force* (2005, 1st), para 37.
[200] *Report of the Working Group* (2006), para 41.
[201] J Wolfensohn, *Note from the President of the World Bank to the Joint Ministerial Development Committee of the Board of Governors of the Bank and the Fund*, 12 April 2005 DC 2005–0005, para 61.
[202] This case dealt with the European Community. *Bosphorus Airways* v *Ireland*, ECtHR App no 45036/98, Grand Chamber judgment of 30 June 2005, para 152.
[203] *Bosphorus Airways* v *Ireland*, para 154.
[204] Ibid, para 156.

cooperation, while increasingly important in many areas of contemporary international relations, is not necessarily a positive force, unless and until it shows itself to be consistent with international human rights principles and standards.

3.4 The Current Incongruence of International Legal Regimes

A range of factors have resulted in ever-greater pressure being put on decision-makers to ensure a cross-fertilization of legal regimes as well as coherence in international policy: the growth in influence of international human rights law, facilitated by an increase in the number of monitoring mechanisms; the expansion of global civil society movements around issues of rights and justice, resulting in a worldwide focus as to the negative effects of international economic policies on social and developmental issues.[205]

The international free trade regime,[206] with its commitment to a form of globalization that often serves to undermine the rights of people in poor countries, and the poorest within those countries,[207] gives rise to concerns over conflicts with international human rights law, for example, the human rights to food,

---

[205] *Finland's Report on the Millennium Development Goals 2004*: 'According to the Government Resolution on Development Policy of February 2004, coherence in all sectors of international cooperation and national policy that have an impact on developing countries is a key prerequisite for achieving the objectives of Finnish development policy (at 17) ... At the multilateral level, strengthening cooperation between the United Nations, international financing institutions and the WTO, is a key tool to improve coherence in the management of globalization (at 18) ... Finland will increasingly take into account the interests of developing countries in its trade policy' (at 29) <http://www.undp.org/mdg/donorcountryreports.html>. See also, the ILO's Policy Coherence Initiative aimed at 'strengthening partnerships within the multilateral system (para 9) ... The objective would be to develop progressively integrated policy proposals that appropriately balance economic, social and development concerns ...' (para 12): ILO, Governing Body, *Working Party on the Social Dimension of Globalization*, BG292/WP/SDG/1 (2005). Oxfam estimates that 'the costs of EU market restrictions for Ethiopia, Mozambique, and Malawi amount to total losses since the inception of the Everything But Arms initiative in 2000 [market-access rights are severely restricted in the area of sugar] to US$238m. Projected losses for 2004 are US$38m for Mozambique and US$32m for Malawi. The figures highlight a shameful lack of coherence between EU aid and trade policies. For every US$3 that the EU gives Mozambique in aid, it takes back US$1 through restrictions on access to its sugar market'. K Watkins, *Dumping on the World: How EU Sugar Policies Hurt Poor Countries*, Oxfam International briefing paper 61, March 2004, 2; see also OECD, *Agriculture and Development. The Case for Policy Coherence* (OECD, 2005).

[206] The UNDP notes that the idea of 'free trade ... is fallacious, for it involves trade between unequal partners'. UNDP, *Asia-Pacific Human Development Report 2006: Trade on Human Terms* (MacMillan India Ltd, 2006) Ch 7, at 146.

[207] Chomsky laments that: 'Globalization ... has been appropriated by advocates of the investor-rights style of integration that is built into the so-called "free-trade agreements", with their complex mixture of liberalization, protectionism, and the undermining of popular democratic control over policy. ... Globalization that does not prioritize the rights of people will very likely degenerate into a form of tyranny ... .': Chomsky, 'Free and Fair Trade', 111. Recent work by the UNDP addresses its concern that '... [F]ree trade will not embrace the poor unless countries pursue a bold new policy agenda harnessing economic growth to promote human development': See, UNDP, *Asia-Pacific Human Development Report 2006*.

health, work, and an adequate standard of living.[208] Lawyers point out that the preamble to the WTO Agreement has free trade as an objective of a system aimed at the fulfilment of basic human values.[209] The preambular references to raising standards of living, ensuring full employment, and to sustainable development, reflect the objective that human development and well-being is (formally) a central concern of the trade regime under the WTO.[210] This position was, in fact, endorsed by the WTO representative at the first session of the Working Group on the Right to Development in 2000, when she claimed that the WTO shared the same objectives for development as those set out in the UN Charter, and the Universal Declaration of Human Rights.[211] While it may be the case that in the twenty-first century social and economic rights can only be met through international trade, as the speaker seemed to suggest, it has to be harnessed if it is to serve human development. In asserting the primacy of human rights within our international legal order, CESCR has been clear in its position that trade liberalization, 'must be understood as a means, not an end. The end which trade liberalization should serve is the objective of human well-being to which the international human rights instruments give legal expression'.[212]

Despite the impact international trade has on the realization of fundamental human rights the world over, the international trade and international human rights regimes have developed in isolation, and their relationship remains undefined.[213] After ruling in its first decision in 1996 that WTO rules are not to be interpreted in 'clinical isolation' from other rules of general public international law,[214] the Appellate Body of the WTO has considered other normative sources in international law and policy. In the *Shrimp/Turtle* dispute, it relied on

---

[208] The concerns regarding the negative impact on human rights of the agenda for trade, financial and investment liberalization pursued by the WTO came to the fore in the aftermath of the Uruguay Round of the GATT trade negotiations of 1994. The Uruguay Round significantly expanded the range of activities brought within the scope of the GATT regime to include trade-related aspects of intellectual property rights, trade in services and trade-related investment measures. It also increased the enforcement powers of the regime through the establishment of the WTO: Orford, 'Globalization and the Right to Development', 127, at 158.

[209] Agreement Establishing the World Trade Organization (1994), entered into force 1 January 1995, 1867 UNTS 31874 (Marrakesh Agreement) preambular para 1.

[210] See, R Howse and M wa Mutua, *Protecting Human Rights in a Global Economy: Challenges for the World Trade Organization*, International Centre for Human Rights and Democratic Development (ICHRDD, 2000) <http://www.ichrdd.ca>.

[211] *Report of the Open-ended Working Group on the Right to Development* (1st session, 18–22 September 2000) UN Doc E/CN4/2001/26, para 112.

[212] CESCR, Statement to the Third Ministerial Conference of the World Trade Organization (21st session, 1999) UN Doc E/C12/1999/9, para 6.

[213] Howse and wa Mutua, *Protecting Human Rights in a Global Economy*. The authors note: 'Both trade and human rights have been codified in highly developed legal regimes, negotiated by governments since the end of World War II. These two legal regimes have developed however in splendid isolation from one another. Both trade law and human rights law narrow the range of policy options that are available to governments. And yet, it seems that the question of whether the two legal regimes are contradictory has rarely been asked'.

[214] *United States—Standards for Reformulated and Conventional Gasoline*, Report of the Appellate Body, WT/DS2/AB/R, Panel Report adopted by the DSB 20 May 1996 at 17.

various international instruments when it sought to determine the meaning of 'exhaustible natural resources', and endorsed the concept of sustainable development found in the preamble to the WTO Agreement.[215] However, commentators criticize the limited degree to which conflicts between substantive norms of different legal regimes have been addressed: 'Substantive aspects have, at best, been applied as part of the interpretation and application of trade rules, with environmental concerns and the legal arrangements devoted to their solution merely justifying an exception from the principles of free trade. As of now, no provision of environmental law has been applied side by side—or even overruling— the substantive law of the WTO'.[216] The same conclusion can be drawn with regards to reconciling international trade law with international human rights law.[217] And, although certain dispute settlement decisions might find a certain compatibility with a human rights approach to the same issue,[218] this unintended reconciliation provides for no meaningful convergence of legal regimes, nor does it address fundamentally the lack of coherence between international policies, for instance EU development aid on the one hand, and its agricultural trade policies that so undercut anti-poverty initiatives in poor countries on the other.[219]

In a later dispute, the Appellate Body relied exclusively on the judgement of the IMF in determining that India would not have to change its development policies since it could address the consequences of removing its balance-of-payment-based import restrictions through macroeconomic policies.[220] Here the Appellate Body has been criticized for relying on an understanding of development offered by one particular institution, and failing to solicit the views of a broader range of relevant actors mandated to work on development, such as UNCTAD and

[215] *United States—Import Prohibition of Certain Shrimp and Shrimp Products*, Report of the Appellate Body WT/DS58/AB/R (and DS61), Panel Report adopted by the DSB 6 November 1998.

[216] A Lindroos and M Mehling, 'Dispelling the Chimera of "Self-Contained Regimes": International Law and the WTO' 16 *EJIL* 5 (2005) 857, at 877.

[217] The footnote in the Appellate Body's Report in the *EC-Hormones* dispute drives home the point. Here the Appellate Body held that even if scientific evidence concerning the risk to women of (imported) meat from animals treated with growth hormones was correct, it would only effect 371 women in the EU out of a total population of 371 million. This utilitarianism is, in principle and in practice, anathema to human rights. As Orford remarks: 'By implication, the deaths of this number of women would not justify enacting measures that could constrain the operation of the market or inhibit progress towards economic integration …'. Orford, 'Beyond Harmonization', 179, at 191. Harrison's research has shown that '[r]eferences to human rights, at all, in any of the dispute settlement proceedings of the WTO, are extremely rare and none relates to the exceptions clauses': J Harrison, *Human Rights and World Trade Agreements* (OHCHR, 2005) 6. And note Lindroos and Mehling's' point above on non-trade norms, at best, constituting exceptions.

[218] W Vandenhole, 'Third State Obligations under the ICESCR: A Case Study of EU Sugar Policy' 76 *NordJInt'lL* 1 (2007) 73.

[219] The UNDP asks: 'If the developed countries are so keen on free trade why, for example, do the EU and US persist with huge market-distorting subsidies on agriculture?' UNDP, *Asia-Pacific Human Development Report 2006*, Ch 7, at 146.

[220] *India—Quantitative Restrictions on Imports of Agricultural, Textile and Industrial Products*, Report of the Appellate Body, WT/DS90/AB/R, Panel Report adopted by the DSB on 22 September 1999, paras 125–30.

the UNDP. Criticism has also centred around the failure at adequately linking macroeconomic and related policies, revenue, and the availability of government funds, to the fulfilment of social and economic rights.[221]

Fittingly, the Working Group on the Right to Development has encouraged the further development, and use, of national and international social impact assessments as a tool to avoid the negative repercussions of trade and development policies on the exercise of human rights.[222] In its 2006 report, it included them as part of the criteria for assessing whether global partnerships for development under MDG 8 are consistent with human rights requirements.[223] One of the shortcomings of protecting human rights through, for example, the general exceptions provisions raised at the dispute settlement stage, is that it does not serve the wider purpose of reconciling human rights with trade and economic development which places the realization of human rights *among the very objectives* of trade rules.[224] Thus human rights/social impact assessments seek a human rights approach to trade reform, whereby human rights will be promoted in the process of *negotiating* and *implementing* trade rules.[225]

In a dispute in which Mexico argued that the WTO dispute settlement mechanism should decline jurisdiction in a case that also fell under the regulation of the North American Free Trade Agreement (NAFTA), and to which a NAFTA Panel was, according to Mexico, more appropriate,[226] the Appellate Body, while rejecting Mexico's argument on a number of grounds, restated its position that it needed to be careful to 'avoid becoming adjudicators of non-WTO disputes'. In doing so, it dismissed the implication that the WTO dispute settlement system could be used to determine rights and obligations outside the covered agreements.[227] However, a mandate limited to resolving disputes under WTO law should not preclude the dispute settlement system from seeking a reading, and application, of WTO law consistent with the human rights obligations of the parties through a good faith interpretation of the provisions of the WTO,

---

[221] Howse, *Mainstreaming the Right to Development*, paras 46–9.

[222] *Report of the Working Group* (2005), para 52; see also para 54(e). The Task Force on the Right to Development notes the importance of *ex ante* assessment and analysis of policy reforms and agreements. *Report of the High-Level Task Force* (2005, 1st), para 41.

[223] *Report of the Working Group* (2006), para 67(i). This represents a more progressive line on social impact assessment than the Working Group was prepared to adopt at its sixth session when it considered the use of social impact assessments by the WTO.

[224] So, for example, general exceptions will be considered in a dispute only once there has been a determination of a violation of other WTO provisions (the general exceptions providing the grounds for a possible justification for the violation), and the state invoking human rights will always need to defend its position with the burden of proof being on that state: Harrison, *Human Rights and World Trade Agreements*, 15.

[225] Ibid.

[226] *Mexico—Tax Measures on Soft Drinks and Other Measures*, Report of the Appellate Body, WT/DS308/AB/R, Panel Report adopted by the DSB on 24 March 2006, para 54.

[227] Ibid, para 78 art 3.2 of the Dispute Settlement Understanding states that the WTO's dispute settlement system 'serves to preserve the rights and obligations of Members under the covered agreements, and to clarify the existing provisions of those agreements'.

including its exceptions provisions. This position was publicly defended also by a Counsellor for the Legal Affairs Division of the WTO Secretariat.[228] The WTO rules do not form part of a 'self-contained' regime in the sense of treaty regimes that are completely isolated from all rules of general international law,[229] yet it cannot be said that the human rights obligations of its Member States are being systematically reconciled with WTO law or policy.[230] Howse and wa Mutua note in this regard that: 'Human rights norms should always be taken into account when interpreting international trade and investment obligations ... [t]rade law is basically treaty law. Its interpretation must be taken into account and be consistent with the hierarchy of norms in international law, reflecting for instance the status of some human rights as preemptory norms, *erga omnes*'.[231]

Since giving weight to human rights norms and standards by the WTO adjudicating bodies (Panels and Appellate Body) may require them to determine whether the trade restriction can find justification in the exception provisions of the WTO,[232] the WTO legal regime would thus, de facto, be placing trade law above other norms, and further would leave it to the WTO judge to thereby decide on the relative hierarchical value of the two sets of norms. The capacity, and suitability, of the WTO Panels or the Appellate Body to interpret, and define, the content of substantive human rights obligations that arise from international human rights standards and norms presents a further concern.[233] Having the WTO dispute settlement system draw on human rights experts and bodies when taking a decision related to human rights, for example, under the general exceptions

[228] G Marceau, 'WTO Dispute Settlement and Human Rights' 13 *EJIL* 4 (2002) 753.

[229] J Pauwelyn, 'The Role of Public International Law in the WTO: How Far Can We Go' 95 *AJIL* (2001) 535, at 539; M Koskenniemi. 'Study on the Function and Scope of the Lex Specialis Rule and the Question of "Self-Contained Regimes"' UN Doc ILC (LVI)/SG/FIL/CRD1/Add1 (2004), para 134.

[230] See further, K Dawkins, *International Treaties/International Law: A Hierarchy of Values* (Institute for Agriculture and Trade Policy, 2005).

[231] Howse and wa Mutua, *Protecting Human Rights in a Global Economy*.

[232] WTO agreements that contain general exceptions clauses are: the General Agreement on Tariffs and Trade (GATT), General Agreement on Trade in Services (GATS) and the Agreement on Government Procurement (GPA). General exceptions with particular importance for human rights allow states to take measures to protect 'public morals', 'human ... life or health' and 'public order'. There are WTO provisions (i.e. not 'exceptions') that have the potential to protect human rights, such as those allowing for 'compulsory licensing' and 'parallel importation' in the TRIPS Agreement. Compulsory licensing allows countries in certain circumstances to use a patented invention without the patentee's permission serving, for example, to reduce the cost of anti-retroviral therapy for HIV/AIDS sufferers in a way that is compliant with TRIPS and human rights obligations. Parallel importation provides for a less stringent application of the international exhaustion of intellectual property rights which can allow for the 'parallel importation' of cheaper patent products than might be produced domestically: Harrison, *Human Rights and World Trade Agreements*.

[233] Harrison, *Human Rights and World Trade Agreements*, 16; Human rights advocates have heeded the warning from the environmental movement around the risks of the WTO dispute settlement mechanism 'intruding' into areas outside of its expertise. See, *Fédération Internationale des ligues des Droits de l'Homme (FIDH), Understanding Global Trade and Human Rights*, Report no 423/2, July 2005.

clauses, may offer one solution. And as a complement to the integration of human rights standards into trade law, redressing this normative disequilibrium between regimes would require strengthening the human rights enforcement system, a point also recognized by the Director-General of the WTO.[234]

Today, human rights are understood as universal, codified internationally and regionally, and entrenched nationally—a pillar of our contemporary international system.[235] The widespread interest in having the UN Commission on Human Rights strengthened through its transformation into a more effective Human Rights Council, including through consideration by the General Assembly of elevating it in due time to a principal organ of the UN alongside the Security Council and General Assembly, reflects the centrality and ascendance of the place of human rights in the new international legal order established under the UN Charter. Kofi Annan noted that the creation of the Council accords human rights a more authoritative position, 'which corresponds to the primacy of human rights in the Charter of the United Nations',[236] a view adopted by the international community in 1993 when it reaffirmed that 'human rights and fundamental freedoms are the birthright of all human beings; their protection and promotion is the *first* responsibility of governments'.[237]

Yet, despite the post-1945 trend towards establishing an international order based on the centrality of universal human rights, as well on the premise that respect for, and observance of, human rights impose *erga omnes* obligations on all states,[238] the WTO's powerful enforcement mechanism (and the comparatively weaker human rights mechanisms) would seem to be giving international trade de facto supremacy. There is a need to redress what the Director-General of the WTO has also referred to in this regard as an 'imbalance' in our international legal order.[239] While it can be argued that all states benefit, at least potentially, from the existence of a rules-based multilateral trading system, the question remains: whose rules, and how are they reconciled with other international legal obligations?[240]

---

[234] P Lamy, 'The Place and Role of the WTO (WTO Law) in the International Legal Order', Address to the European Society of International Law, Paris, 19 May 2006.

[235] On the UDHR's considerable influence on domestic legislation and courts, as elsewhere, see, H Hannum, 'The Status of the Universal Declaration of Human Rights in National and International Law' 12 *Interights Bulletin* (1998/9) 3; and note UN Charter, art 103.

[236] Report of the UN Secretary-General, *In Larger Freedom: Towards Development, Security and Human Rights for All*, UN Doc A/59/2005, para 183.

[237] Vienna Declaration and Programme of Action, Pt I, art 1 (emphasis added).

[238] This theme is developed in Ch 4.

[239] Lamy, *The Place and Role of the WTO*.

[240] 'Mainstreaming the right to development, with its focus on values such as inclusiveness, participation and interconnectedness of rights in development, requires considerable attention to what might be called the "meta-structures" of WTO, some formal and explicitly stated in WTO rules and some informal but nevertheless with revealed normative influence . . . Many of the meta-structures of the WTO leave much to be desired. They narrow the possibilities for individual WTO members to shape and reshape their trade rights and obligations in order to pursue development through and within the fulfilment of all internationally recognized human rights. They also may limit the kind

This preoccupation with harmonizing the regimes of human rights and international trade is found throughout the work of the Task Force. In encouraging states to undertake assessments of the impact of trade agreements on poverty, human rights and other social matters, it reminded them that the use of such assessments would be consistent with WTO objectives in so far as the preamble of the Marrakesh Agreement refers to 'the need for positive efforts designed to ensure that developing countries, and especially the least developed among them, secure a share in the growth in international trade commensurate with the needs of their economic development'. Significantly though, the Task Force remarked that undertaking these assessments, and having them influence trade negotiations, would 'also be consistent with human rights standards and principles'.[241]

3.5 Conclusion

In recent years, the figures on world poverty have given rise to a surge of concern regarding the operation, and priorities, of our global order, and the place of human rights within it. The concentration of poverty in developing countries along with the ascent of human rights, has strengthened demands at the international level to better reconcile international trade law and international human rights law, which so far seem to characterize contradictory trends. Inequality has highlighted the need to reconcile conflicting ideologies and practices around what constitutes acceptable strategies for the generation of wealth internationally, and domestically, and the approach to its distribution. The right to development with its focus on the person as the centrepiece of development, and on just processes in addressing underdevelopment, has a contribution to make in guiding a rights-based approach to globalization generally, and to economic growth specifically.

First off, it is highly problematic from a human rights perspective to assess gains from a policy such as trade liberalization in terms of whether trade itself has been expanded or whether it has contributed to aggregate increases in national or global wealth or income.[242] Success is to be judged according to the positive contribution made to human well-being, which can be measured in terms of securing basic human rights. This includes broader acceptance that laws and policies aimed at economic development be devised, and assessed, in terms of their enhancement of human development. The responsibility of states, and of

---

of voice that smaller or poorer countries have in collectively shaping or reshaping the rules. As a general matter, these meta-structures are the product of the mindset that trade liberalization is an end in itself, not a means, and that WTO rules and structures should favour linear progress in that direction, even if tolerating some straggling by countries that are in any case on the margins of the global economy': Howse, *Mainstreaming the Right to Development*, at paras 37–8.

[241] *Report of the High-Level Task Force* (2005, 1st), para 51.

[242] Howse, *Mainstreaming the Right to Development*, para 15.

states acting collectively through multilateral institutions, is to people, not to the market as an end in itself. People are not merely playing an instrumental role in the achievement of economic policy objectives;[243] through the right to development the notion that human rights exist to serve instrumental functions in the achievement of economic ends is being subordinated.[244]

Second, international human rights law does not prescribe a particular economic system; it is neutral in so far as its principles do not favour one economic model over another. It does, however, contain both principles and standards that seek to ensure that the methods for achieving economic growth are just, and that its benefits are fairly distributed. At its most basic, human rights are egalitarian, all individuals are equal. The dominant market-based strategies for growth, on the other hand, tend to be maximizing and collectivizing: they seek activities that are likely to bring the highest growth rate, and are justified in terms of aggregate benefit. In addressing the implications of the right to development for trade law and policy, it has been noted that quite the opposite to this human-centred development approach is influential in the official trade policy community, that is, the idea that 'development' often entails the sacrifice of human rights, the welfare state and environmental protection.[245]

While the right to development is conceptually and practically allied to the familiar human rights-based approach to development, it may be understood as extending beyond it. Based on the language of the Declaration on the Right to Development, it advances an anti-poverty ethos premised on a rigorous application of the doctrine of the indivisibility and interdependence of rights. A central aim of this approach, is to challenge dominant theories that too easily accept trading-off the human rights of some people, for some greater good, whether it be domestically in terms of growth strategies, or internationally, in terms of participation in a global regime that promises future gains. Thus, the objective of the right to development is to contribute to processes and outcomes of development which are consistent with, and further, human rights protection and promotion both domestically and internationally. As the Declaration makes clear, and as the Task Force and Working Group saw fit to reiterate, the DRD posits explicitly a responsibilities approach: '[s]tates have the primary responsibility for the creation of the national and international conditions favourable to the realization of the right to development and they have the duty to take steps, individually and collectively, at the national and the international levels, to formulate policies and practices with a view to facilitating the full realization of the right to development.'[246]

---

[243] Orford, 'Beyond Harmonization', 179, at 184 and 201; P Alston, 'Resisting the Merger and Acquisition of Human Rights by Trade Law: A Reply to Petersmann' 13 *EJIL* 4 (2002) 815, at 843.

[244] Salomon, 'The Significance of the Task Force on the Right to Development', 27, at 28.

[245] Howse, *Mainstreaming the Right to Development*, paras 13–14.

[246] *Report of the High-Level Task Force* (2005, 1st), para 26; *Report of the Working Group* (2005), para 40; DRD, art 3(1).

One key requirement in achieving the objective of reconciling competing tendencies, not just between domestic policies and the exercise of human
rights, but in the practice of global governance, is to have states that are negatively affected by the rules and policies that direct globalization secure stronger
voices. It would also require that decision-makers in developing countries are
sufficiently autonomous with adequate policy space in order to prioritize their
national and international human rights obligations.[247] Currently, the concern is
that decision-makers from developing countries understand themselves as bound
to respond to the demands of the market, to sacrifice their citizens, and their public obligations, in the expectation of being rewarded in the future.[248]

Pascal Lamy, the WTO Director-General remarked recently in a speech to the
European Society of International Law that he 'believe[d] that efforts of international coherence are the only way to ensure the peaceful evolution of international relations and our international legal system. But international coherence
is also crucial to ensuring the legitimacy of the WTO and the effectiveness of
trade rules'.[249] If there is support for the idea that this integration of norms is
the way forward, as Lamy has stated, it is not yet obvious when, and how, this
important evolution will take shape (or whether his view is shared more broadly
by e.g. trade ministers). When the Vice-President for External Affairs at the
World Bank was asked recently how the rich countries are doing on trade, he
replied: 'Trade remains the most damaging of policies, the most economically
illiterate, the most politically short-sighted, the most environmentally destruc-
tive, and the most socially ineffective form of intervention of the rich countries
in the economy'.[250] While the Vice-President is not alone in holding this view,
he may have also pointed out that past and present policies of the Bank (and
the IMF) are also known to have caused adverse affects on the poor, including
through the use of trade conditionality. And he might have raised the fact that
the Marrakesh Agreement establishing the WTO explicitly foresees cooperation between the WTO, the World Bank and the IMF 'with a view to achieving
greater coherence'.[251]

Responsibilities have become more complex. The traditional thinking that
has development limited to international economic issues discretely constituting
international trade, finance, and investment, is under increasing pressure to give

[247] In some instances this requirement is not entirely straightforward. While certain industrialized members of the WTO have been advocating a linkage between trade and the observance
of certain core labour standards, developing countries question whether the linkage of trade and
labour standards is prompted by genuine concern regarding non-observance of such standards, or
whether it is a protectionist ploy aimed at shutting out exports from certain developing countries.

[248] Orford, 'Beyond Harmonization', 179, at 198; See further, Salomon, 'The Significance of
the Task Force on the Right to Development', 27, at 28.

[249] Lamy, *The Place and Role of the WTO.*

[250] I Goldin, 'Meeting the Challenge of Development—An Action Agenda to Achieve the
Millennium Development Goals', London School of Economics, London, 3 February 2005.

[251] Marrakesh Agreement, art III, 5.

way to a more holistic view of the development process which includes human rights standards and principles, with internationally recognized minimum standards being applicable globally. This integrated view of development recognizes that human rights, and economic aspects of international transactions, are too intertwined to be treated separately.[252] As Bradlow has pointed out, and as this chapter has sought to detail, the Declaration on the Right to Development constitutes an important document for this 'modern' approach.[253]

Challenges to addressing world poverty can be framed within the human rights system that has been accurately characterized as an evolving and dynamic system of safeguards intended to respond to our growing understanding of particular techniques of repression, and of different systems of oppression.[254] Considering the responsibilities derived from a contemporary application of the right to development is but an attempt to do what the international law of human rights is meant to do: impose obligations on actors that limit their ability to oppress, and that advance their contribution to creating an environment in which human rights can be realized, for all.

[252] DD Bradlow, 'Development Decision-Making and the Content of International Development Law' 27 *BCInt'l & CompLRev* 2 (2004) 195, at 213.

[253] Ibid, 195, at 211 *et seq.*

[254] M Winston, 'On the Indivisibility and Interdependence of Human Rights', Paper delivered at the World Congress of Philosophy PADAEIA (1998) <http://www.bu.edu/wcp/Papers/Huma/HumaWins.htm>.

4

A Doctrine of Basic Universal Rights
and Supra-positive Obligations

4.1 Introduction

An assessment of the legal responsibility of the international community regarding world poverty—as this book seeks to provide—invites consideration as to the status of rights to which this global responsibility corresponds. This chapter harnesses jurisprudential and doctrinal developments in support of the existence of a general principle of international law to respect and observe human rights in the main. It then advances the premise that the basic rights of the human person of which this principle consists, today, must include socio-economic rights.

The idea that there are obligations owed to the international community as a whole is well-developed in international law, as is juridical acceptance that there are, for example, rules fundamental to the respect of the human person, and to elementary considerations of humanity. As customary international law, the obligations corresponding to this principle to protect human rights universally, triggers the 'legal interest' of the international community of states. However, the way in which these obligations, as a global responsibility, are owed to the international community, and how the 'legal interest' of states is triggered to protect human rights by virtue of such obligations, is considerably neglected in the sphere of socio-economic rights.

The expectation that there exists a collective interest in relation to securing globally a range of human rights has been shown recently with regard to the rights enshrined in the International Covenant on Civil and Political Rights (ICCPR). These community requirements, pertaining to the legal interest of every state party in the performance by every other state party of its obligations regarding rights that are found in treaties with clauses limiting jurisdiction,[1] only strengthens the claim for a rigorous application of collective obligations in treaties for which the fulfillment of the rights are foreseen as requiring international cooperation,

---

[1] HRC, General Comment no 31 on Art 2 (The Nature of the General Legal Obligation Imposed on States Parties to the Covenant), (80th session, 2004) UN Doc CCPR/C/21/Rev1/Add13 (2004), para 2.

such as the International Covenant on Economic, Social and Cultural Rights (ICESCR).

Socio-economic rights are entrenched in a range of treaties, with very high levels of ratification, and they have been repeatedly endorsed by the international community of states as requiring urgent action, most recently in the form of the Millennium Development Goals (MDG). That no single person should be deprived of 'essential foodstuffs, of essential primary health care, of basic shelter and housing, or of the most basic forms of education' constitutes a core obligation, in the first instance of states parties to the ICESCR.[2] But we are not limited to state consent when considering sources of international law, and there can be said to exist a legal obligation to protect basic human rights, which undoubtedly entails in the present day the responsibility to protect all people from starvation, and related privations constituting the ravages of poverty. This doctrine of basic universal rights that includes socio-economic rights is borne of the UN Charter, and is consistent with the theory of human rights law premised on the essential requirement that each and every person is entitled to live in conditions of dignity.

4.2 Beyond Legal Positivism

The *South-West Africa* cases in which the International Court of Justice (ICJ) was to address the alleged contravention of the League of Nations mandate for South-West Africa by South Africa were quelled by a ruling in 1966 that the applicant states lacked standing.[3] The deciding vote was cast by the president, and some of the judges, in response to the ruling, declared that they were entitled, if not judicially bound, to examine the merits of the issues raised by the parties in the course of the proceedings.[4] The result was the renowned dissenting opinion of Judge Tanaka in which he provides an exposition on the concept of equality, and the prohibition of racial discrimination, and in so doing addresses the general theory of law, and norms of international law in relation to human rights.

In his dissenting opinions Judge Tanaka referred to the category of the norm of *jus cogens*,[5] stating that 'surely the law concerning the protection of human

---

[2] CESCR, General Comment no 3 on Art 2(1) (The Nature of States Parties' Obligations), (5th session, 1990) UN DocE/1991/23, annex III (1990), para 10.

[3] *South-West Africa (Second Phase)* (Ethiopa v South Africa; Liberia v South Africa) ICJ Rep (1966) 6.

[4] 'The majority opinion cannot be conceived to establish any limits to the separate opinions of individual judges.': *South-West Africa*, Judge Tanaka (diss op) 6, at 262. Judge Jessup wrote that he considered it to be his 'judicial duty to examine the legal issues in this case which has been before the Court for six years'. *South-West Africa*, Judge Jessup (diss op) 6, at 325. See further, M Ragazzi, 'International Obligations *Erga Omnes*: Their Moral Foundation and Criteria of Identification in Light of Two Japanese Contributions' in GS Goodwin-Gill and S Talmon (eds), *The Reality of International Law: Essays in Honour of Ian Brownlie* (Oxford University Press, 1999) 455, at 465.

[5] At the time, *jus cogens* had recently been examined and soon after incorporated into the Vienna Convention on the Law of Treaties (1969).

rights may be considered to belong to *jus cogens*'.[6] The concept of *jus cogens* was accepted by the International Law Commission (ILC), and incorporated into the Vienna Convention on the Law of Treaties (VCLT) adopted in 1969, in the form of Article 53. *Jus cogens* is a peremptory norm of general international law defined for the purposes of the VCLT as 'a norm accepted and recognized by the international community of States as a whole as a norm from which no derogation is permitted and which can be modified only by a subsequent norm of general international law having the same character'. *Jus cogens*, then, refers to the non-derogable quality of the norm.[7] In affirming the status of human rights, the protection of which can be invoked as a rule under international law, Judge Tanaka also proclaimed that 'the concept of human rights and [of] their protection is included in the general principles mentioned in Article [38(1)(c) of the ICJ Statute]'.[8]

Article 38(1) of the ICJ Statute lists the sources of international law upon which the Court can draw when determining disputes. The Court may apply 'the general principles of law recognized by civilized nations,[9] separate and independent of international conventions,[10] and international custom.[11] General principles derive from a wide base of legal principles elaborated both in domestic, as well as in international, fora.

In addressing the effect of general principles of law as a source of international law, Waldock takes the view that legal policy and principles at the domestic level are adapted to the solution of international problems through the application at the international level of the general concepts of law that underlie them; their application does not lie in the 'concrete manifestations' as presented domestically.[12]

---

[6] *South-West Africa*, Judge Tanaka (diss op) 6, at 298.

[7] R Higgins, *Problems and Process: International Law and How We Use It* (Oxford University Press, 1998) 167.

[8] *South-West Africa*, Judge Tanaka (diss op) 6, at 298. The Statute of the International Court of Justice (1945) art 38(1)(c): 'The Court, whose function is to decide in accordance with international law such disputes as are submitted to it, shall apply ... (c) the general principles of law recognized by civilized nations; ...'.

[9] See, O Schachter, *International Law in Theory and Practice* (Martinus Nijhoff, 1991) 50, where he notes that: 'The fact that the sub-paragraph was distinct from those on treaty and custom indicated an intent to treat general principles as an independent source of law, and not as a subsidiary source'. See also, I Brownlie, *Principles of Public International Law* (5th edn, Clarendon Press, 1998) 15, who likewise states that art 38(1)(c) is a source which comes after those that depend on state consent 'yet escapes classification as a "subsidiary means" in paragraph (d)'.

[10] ICJ Statute, art 38(1)(a).

[11] Ibid, art 38(1)(b).

[12] H Waldock, 'General Course on Public International Law' 106 *Rec des Cours* 54 (1962 II) in DJ Harris, *Cases and Materials on International Law* (5th edn, Sweet and Maxwell, 1998) 49: 'The intention in using it [the phrase civilised nations], clearly, was to leave out of account undeveloped legal systems so that a general principle present in the principal legal systems of the world would not be disqualified from application in international law merely by reason of its absence from, [undeveloped legal systems] ... Accordingly, we are quite safe in construing that "the general principles of law recognised by civilised nations" as meaning to-day simply the general principles recognised in the legal systems of independent States'.

Brownlie notes that there was no consensus on the precise significance of the phrase in the Committee of Jurists which prepared the Statute, with the Belgian jurist interpreting the provision as providing for 'the rules of international law recognized by the legal conscience of civilized peoples'.[13]

Although the dominant legal view sees general principles of law as those developed in domestic fora, some legal scholars argue that this presents too narrow and restrictive a perspective, which seeks simply to provide validation of general principles in a reliable way, and ignores the fact that acceptance or recognition may also be effected on the international plane.[14] The defining element for the drafters of the ICJ Statute was that the principles are not derived from 'mere speculation' but rather 'made objective through some sort of general acceptance or recognition by States'.[15] It can be argued, in light of the practice of the ICJ, to regard the sources of custom under Article 38(1)(b)(c) of the ICJ Statute as forming a single corpus of law, treated as 'common law'. And, while the body of customary international law is more readily applied by the Court, and tends to predominate over the application of general principles, Harris concludes that 'paragraph (c) adds to this corpus—very much in the way actually intended by its authors—a flexible element which enables the Court to give greater completeness to customary international law and in some limited degree to extend it'.[16]

The processes that determine the existence of general principles of law, and norms of customary international law respectively, provide some noteworthy distinctions. A particular characteristic of the former, it has been argued, is that 'the concept of a "recognized" general principle seems to conform more closely than the concept of custom to the situation where a norm invested with strong inherent authority is widely accepted even though widely violated'.[17] Furthermore, although the two principal sources of international law—treaty and custom—reflected in Articles 38(1)(a) and 38(1)(b) of the ICJ Statute respectively, exist as a result of the consent of the majority of states, general principles of law in the area of human rights rely on other sources for their formation, and do not require the consent of states as a condition of their recognition. Consequently, it may also be

---

[13] Brownlie, *Principles of Public International Law*, at 15.

[14] B Simma and P Alston, 'The Sources of Human Rights Law: Custom, *Jus Cogens*, and General Principles' 12 *Aust YBIL* (1988–9) 82, at 102.

[15] Ibid 82 at 102.

[16] Harris, *Cases and Materials*, at 48.

[17] Committee on the Formation of Customary International Law, International Law Association (American Branch): 'The Role of State Practice in the Formation of Customary International Law' (19 January 1987) 10, as cited in Simma and Alston, 'The Sources of Human Rights Law', 82, at 102. Similarly, in the case of customary international law, compliance is not necessarily required for the retention of its normative quality: '[I]f a state acts in a way prima facie incompatible with a recognized rule, but defends its conduct by appealing to exceptions and justifications contained within the rule itself, then whether or not the State's conduct is in fact justifiable on that basis, the significance of that attribute is to confirm rather than to weaken the rule': *Military and Paramilitary Activities in and against Nicaragua* (Merits) (Nicaragua v United States of America) ICJ Rep (1986) 14, at para 186.

concluded that the persistent objector rule[18] neither affects the development of 'general principles of law', nor detracts from them acquiring this status.[19] There is a limit to legal positivism with reference to the global responsibility to protect human rights that can arise from the strategic application of 'general principles of law' in international law.

On the limits of legal positivism Judge Tanaka unequivocally deduces:

[I]t is undeniable that in Article 38(1)(c), some natural law elements are inherent. It extends the concept of the source of international law beyond the limit of legal positivism according to which, the States being bound only by their own will, international law is nothing but the law of the consent and auto-limitation of the State. But this viewpoint, we believe, was clearly overruled by Article 38, paragraph 1 (c), by the fact that this provision does not require the consent of States as a condition of the recognition of the general principles. States which do not recognize this principle or even deny its validity are nevertheless subject to its rule. From this kind of source international law could have the foundation of its validity extended beyond the will of States, that is to say, into the sphere of natural law and assume an aspect of its supra-national and supra-positive character.[20]

The fact that the drafters of the ICJ Statute included general principles of law as a source of international law reflects the compromise between the positivist and naturalist schools of legal thought. Proponents of both concepts made up the Committee of Jurists who eventually agreed on the provision, and as Brierly remarked back in 1963, 'its inclusion is important as a rejection of the positivistic doctrine, according to which international law consists solely of rules to which States have given their consent'.[21] General principles of law therefore can be said to reflect consensus, they do not, however, require the fulfillment of the formal criteria reserved for other sources. What some commentators refer to as the natural law roots of human rights[22] are reflected in, for example, the common preambular paragraphs to the International Covenant on Civil and Political Rights,

---

[18] 'If whilst a practice is developing into a rule of general law, a State persistently and openly dissents from the rule, it will not be bound by it.': *Report of the Committee on Customary International Law*, International Law Association (2000) 27; *Anglo-Norwegian Fisheries* case ICJ Rep (1951) 131.

[19] Thus, the rejection by the United States of economic, social and cultural rights, and of the right to development, would not influence the development of a general principle to respect and observe human rights, including basic socio-economic rights.

[20] *South-West Africa* (diss op) at 298.

[21] JL Brierly, *The Law of Nations: An Introduction to the International Law of Peace* (6th edn,Oxford University Press, 1963) 63, as cited by Judge Tanaka in *South-West Africa*, 6, at 299.

[22] On the contested foundation of international law see, Dimitrijevic, in which he argues that morals form the basis of international law, promptly rejecting any theory of natural law. Dimitrijevic states that: 'The most formidable logical objection to the theory of natural law has been that there can be no rule without will, and that nature can furnish only facts. Nature contains no inherent preferences, upon which legal norms can be based'. V Dimitrijevic, 'A Natural or Moral Basis for International Law' in A Grahl-Madsen and J Toman (eds), *The Spirit of Uppsala, Proceedings of the Joint UNITAR-Uppsala University Seminar on International Law and Organization for a New World Order* (Walter de Gruyter, 1984) 383, at 383. Reisman concurs stating: '... I regret the use of the words "natural law". As Professor Dimitrijevic observed, nature *is*, while law involves *choices* about how it is to be used'. W M Reisman, 'Sovereignty and Humanity', Interventions at Plenary Session

and the International Covenant on Economic, Social and Cultural Rights which recognize that 'these rights derive from the inherent dignity of the human person'.[23]

4.3 The Universal Principle to Respect and Observe Human Rights

Reflecting on the jurisprudence of the International Court of Justice back in 1988, Alston and Simma concluded that, 'the Court has unambiguously accepted that the obligation to respect fundamental human rights is an obligation under general international law'.[24] The Court has, on repeated occasions, spoken of international principles that create obligations meant to bind all states, and in so doing established that states are expected to observe basic human rights as a matter of custom.[25] Contemporary international law for the protection of human rights is evolving to address the scope of corresponding obligations within what has been referred to as an objective international legal order.[26]

In the *Barcelona Traction, Light and Power Co Ltd* case (1970) the International Court of Justice addressed the matter of obligations owed 'towards all.' The case dealt with the protection of companies and shareholders in relation to a company established under Canadian law which developed electricity supplies in Spain. The claim was brought by Belgium, on behalf of its shareholders, in respect of the injury to its nationals when the company went bankrupt. Although the position of all states in respect of a breach of an obligation towards the international community as a whole was not actually at stake in this case (in contrast with the position of an injured state in the context of diplomatic protection), the Court took the opportunity 'to clearly indicate that for the purposes of State responsibility certain obligations are owed to the international community as a whole, and that by reason of the importance of the rights involved, all States have a legal interest in their protection'.[27] This underlies both the global responsibility to protect

on 'A Natural or Moral Basis for International Law' in Grahl-Madsen and Toman, *The Spirit of Uppsala*, 449, at 450.

[23] Preambular para 2.
[24] Simma and Alston, 'The Sources of Human Rights Law', 82, at 105.
[25] C Beyani, 'The Legal Premises for the International Protection of Human Rights' in Goodwin-Gill and Talmon (eds), *The Reality of International Law*, 21, at 34.
[26] Y Saito, 'International Law as a Law of the World Community: World Law as Reality and Methodology' in Grahl-Madsen and Toman (eds), *The Spirit of Uppsala*, 233, at 243; see J Delbrück, 'Prospects for a "World (Internal) Law"? Legal Developments in a Changing International System' 9 *IJGLS* (2002) 401, at 415–17.
[27] *Articles on the Responsibility of States for Internationally Wrongful Acts with commentaries* (2001) Chapter III, Serious breaches of obligations under peremptory norms of general international law (at 278). It has been suggested that in order to make up for the face-losing ruling in the *South-West Africa* case where, as was previously mentioned, the ICJ failed to rule on the merits of the dispute because it found, on the casting vote of its president, that the applicant states lacked standing, the ICJ took the *Barcelona Traction* case as an opportunity to address the previously neglected

human rights, and the duty in customary law for states to cooperate towards that end.

The celebrated obiter dictum on obligations *erga omnes* can be found in two paragraphs in the *Barcelona Traction* judgment:

[A]n essential distinction should be drawn between the obligations of a State owed towards the international community as a whole, and those arising vis-à-vis another State in the field of diplomatic protection. By their very nature the former are the concern of all States. In view of the importance of the rights involved, all States can be held to have a legal interest in their protection; they are obligations *erga omnes*.

Such obligations derive, for example, in contemporary international law, from the outlawing of acts of aggression, and of genocide, *as also from the principles and rules concerning basic rights of the human person* including protection from slavery and racial discrimination. Some of the corresponding rights of protection have entered into the body of general international law (*Reservations to the Convention on the Prevention and Punishment of the Crime of Genocide, Advisory Opinion*, ICJ Reports 1951, p 23); others are conferred by international instruments of a universal or quasi-universal character.[28]

While the *Barcelona Traction* case was the first to refer to obligations *erga omnes*, the idea of universal fundamental principles of well-being in peace time, from which obligations would necessary flow, was pronounced in the 1949 *Corfu Channel* case in which the ICJ referred to obligations based on 'general and well-recognized principles', among them 'elementary considerations of humanity'.[29] The Court cited its *Corfu Channel* dictum in the *Nicaragua* decision of 1986 when it evaluated action taken by the United States in light of obligations resulting from 'fundamental general principles of humanitarian law'.[30] In the *Reservations to the Genocide Convention* advisory opinion, the ICJ observed that 'the principles underlying the Convention are principles which are recognized by civilized nations as binding on States, even without any conventional obligation', a reference cited in its *Bosnia* case of 1996 to which the Court affirmed, 'the rights and obligations enshrined by the Convention are rights and obligations *erga omnes*. The Court notes that the obligation each State thus has to prevent and to punish the crime of genocide is not territorially limited by the Convention'.[31] In repeated cases the ICJ affirmed that this objective is derived from '*a common interest*, namely the accomplishment of those high purposes which are the raison d'être of the Convention'.[32]

issue of obligations *erga omnes* in relation to human rights protection. See Ragazzi, 'International Obligations *Erga Omnes*', 455, at 464–5.

[28] *Barcelona Traction, Light and Power Company Limited (Second Phase)* (Belgium v Spain) ICJ Rep (1970) 3, at paras 33–4 (emphasis added).

[29] *Corfu Channel* case (Merits) (United Kingdom v Albania) ICJ Rep (1949) 4, at 22.

[30] *Nicaragua*, 14, at para 218.

[31] *Case Concerning Application of the Convention on the Prevention and Punishment of Genocide* (Bosnia-Herzegovina v Yugoslavia) ICJ Rep (1996) 595, at para 31.

[32] *Reservations to the Convention on the Prevention and Punishment of the Crime of Genocide*, Adv Op, ICJ Rep (1951) 14, at 23, (emphasis added); *Application of the Genocide Convention* (Bosnia-Herzegovina v Yugoslavia) 595, at para 32.

In the *Nuclear Weapons* case we see revisited this notion that there are rules fundamental to respect of the human person and to elementary consideration of humanity,[33] with the ICJ taking the view in its advisory opinion on the *Legal Consequences of the Construction of a Wall in the Occupied Palestinian Territory*, that rules of international humanitarian law 'incorporate obligations which are essentially of an *erga omnes* character'.[34] In reaffirming the principles underlying the Genocide Convention, the Court in the *DRC v Rwanda* judgment of 2006 noted that '...a consequence of that conception is "the universal character both of the condemnation of genocide and of the co-operation required in order to liberate mankind from such an odious scourge (Preamble to the Convention)" (*Reservations to the Convention on the Prevention and Punishment of the Crime of Genocide, Advisory Opinion ...*). It follows that "the rights and obligations enshrined by the Convention are rights and obligations *erga omnes*" (*Application of the Convention on the Prevention and Punishment of the Crime of Genocide (Bosnia and Herzegovina v Yugoslavia), Preliminary Objections, Judgment ...*).'[35]

In the *Tehran Hostages* case the Court referred more specifically to human rights principles as derived from the UN Charter and Universal Declaration of Human Rights when stating that '[w]rongfully to deprive human beings of their freedom and to subject them to physical constraint in conditions of hardship is in itself manifestly incompatible with the principles of the Charter of the United Nations, as well as with the fundamental principles enunciated in the Universal Declaration of Human Rights'.[36] In the *East Timor* case, the Court recognized the 'irreproachable' *erga omnes* character of the principle of self-determination of peoples as evolved from the UN Charter,[37] as it did in its 2004 advisory opinion on the *Construction of a Wall in the Occupied Palestinian Territory*,[38] a position consistent with its view on the principle taken in previous cases.[39] Thus, the

---

[33] 'A great many rules of humanitarian law applicable in armed conflict are so fundamental to the respect of the human person and "elementary considerations of humanity" ...', that they are 'to be observed by all States whether or not they have ratified the conventions that contain them, because they constitute intransgressible principles of international customary law': *Legality of the Threat or Use of Nuclear Weapons*, Adv Op, ICJ Rep (1996) 226, at para 79.

[34] *Legal Consequences of the Construction of a Wall in the Occupied Palestinian Territory*, Adv Op ICJ Rep (2004) 136, at para 157.

[35] *Armed Activities on the Territory of the Congo* (New Application 2002) (Jurisdiction and Admissibility) (Democratic Republic of Congo v Rwanda) ICJ (2006), para 64.

[36] *United States Diplomatic and Consular Staff in Tehran* (Merits) (United States of America v Iran) ICJ Rep (1980) 3, at para 91.

[37] *Case Concerning East Timor* (Judgment) (Portugal v Australia) ICJ Rep (1995) 90, at para 29.

[38] 'The Court would observe that the obligations violated by Israel include certain obligations *erga omnes*. As the Court indicated in the *Barcelona Traction* case, such obligations are by their very nature "the concern of all States" and, "In view of the importance of the rights involved, all States can be held to have a legal interest in their protection."': (*Barcelona Traction*, 32, at para 33). The obligations *erga omnes* violated by Israel are the obligation to respect the right of the Palestinian people to self-determination, and certain of its obligations under international humanitarian law: *Legal Consequences of the Construction of a Wall*, 136, at paras 155–156.

[39] *Legal Consequences for States of the Continued Presence of South Africa in Namibia (South-West Africa) notwithstanding Security Council Resolution 276 (1970)* Adv Op, ICJ Rep (1971) 16, at paras 52–53; *Western Sahara*, ICJ Adv Op (1975) 12, at paras 54–59.

notion that there are obligations owed to the international community as a whole is today incontestable. They attend to fundamental principles that require international cooperation, transcending bilateral or multilateral obligations of states in the area of human rights, addressing rather every state of the international community as duty-bearer, and the international community as a whole as the holder of basic rights.

The non-conventional status in international law of a particular principle to respect and observe human rights in the main attracts considerable support from eminent legal scholars. Verdross and Simma assert that 'nowadays certain obligations to respect and ensure human rights derive from "general" international law',[40] and Beyani concludes that 'the obligation to respect and observe human rights in the Charter of the United Nations is a fundamental norm now accepted into the corpus of customary international law'.[41] Meron remarks that even non-state parties to the ICCPR may not derogate from basic human rights,[42] and Bossuyt argued back in 1978 that '... no State could maintain that it had the right to violate human rights and fundamental freedoms, as long as the Covenant [ICCPR] was not in force, or as long as it had not ratified the Covenant, once it has entered into force. *The obligation to respect human rights is a general principle of law recognized by all civilized nations*'.[43] Describing the aim of a human rights convention, Bossuyt explains that it is not to constitute new rights, or to establish a previously non-existent obligation to respect those rights, but rather to enumerate the definition of rights and freedoms. These norms will then be further refined by the interpretation, and application, provided by the implementing organ which in turn will add precision to the obligations imposed on states parties to it. So, although the entry into force of such an international instrument is necessary to set in motion the new international monitoring machinery, and to create the obligation upon states parties to cooperate with it, 'it is not necessary to establish the obligation of States parties to respect the rights recognized in it'.[44] This view echoes that taken earlier by Judge Tanaka when he provided that: 'A State or States are not capable of creating human rights by law or by convention; they can only confirm their existence and give them protection. The role of the State is no more than declaratory'.[45]

Human rights treaties, binding under international law for those states that have ratified or acceded to them, provide the most evident basis for the responsibility to respect and observe the human rights articulated in those treaties. However, the widespread recognition within human rights treaties of states'

---

[40] A Verdross and B Simma, 'Universelles Volkerrechte: Theorie und Praxis' as cited in Simma and Alston, 'The Sources of Human Rights Law', 82 at 85.

[41] Beyani, 'The Legal Premises', 21, at 33.

[42] T Meron, *Human Rights Law Making in the United Nations* (Clarendon, 1986) 198.

[43] M Bossuyt, 'The United Nations and Civil and Political Rights in Chile' 27 *ICLQ* 2 (1978) 462, at 467.

[44] Ibid, 462, at 467.

[45] *South-West Africa*, Judge Tanaka (diss op) 6, at 297.

obligations to cooperate in ensuring the respect and observance of human rights *generally,* strengthens claims as to the non-conventional status of this principle. This principle is referred to in the universally ratified UN Charter and repeatedly endorsed within human rights instruments.[46]

The purposes of the UN include, as per Article 1(3) of the UN Charter, 'promoting and encouraging human rights', and Articles 55 and 56 entrench the obligations of the UN to cooperate internationally in the promotion of 'universal respect for, and observance of human rights'. This key point is reaffirmed in preambular paragraph 6 of the Universal Declaration of Human Rights, which states: 'Whereas Member States have pledged themselves to achieve, in cooperation with the United Nations, the promotion of universal respect for and observance of human rights and fundamental freedoms'. Moreover, virtually every major international and regional human rights treaty restates the overarching need for states to cooperate internationally in the achievement of this broad objective.[47] In conventions addressing economic, social and cultural rights— notably the International Covenant on Economic, Social and Cultural Rights with 155 states parties,[48] and the Convention on the Rights of the Child with near universal ratification[49]—it forms part of the specific obligations undertaken by contracting states and is provided for in operative paragraphs.[50] The consistent references to the obligation to respect and observe human rights found in human rights treaties, along with the very patterns of the standard-setting of human rights treaties which reflect the progress of human rights in international law,[51] strengthens the claims as to the non-conventional status of this universal principle.

[46] See Ch 2.

[47] See for example, the International Convention on the Elimination of All Forms of Racial Discrimination, preambular para 1, which refers explicitly to the language in the UN Charter: 'Considering that … all Member States have pledged themselves to take joint and separate action, in co-operation with the Organization, for the achievement of one of the purposes of the United Nations which is to promote and encourage universal respect for and observance of human rights and fundamental freedoms for all, without distinction as to race, sex, language or religion,'. Both the ICCPR and the ICESCR, which form the bedrock of the human rights treaty regime, share the common preambular para 4 which reflects the importance given to the respect and observance of human rights. It states: 'The States Parties to the Present Convention…Considering the obligation of States under the Charter of the United Nations to promote universal respect for, and observance of human rights and freedoms … Agree upon the following articles …' The Convention on the Rights of the Child at preambular para 2 refers to the Charter's commitment to fundamental human rights, and in preambular para 13 relates this directly to 'the importance of international cooperation in improving the living conditions of children in every country, in particular in developing countries'. See also preambular para 2 of the European Convention on Human Rights; preambular para 4 of the African Charter on Human and Peoples' Rights; and preambular para 2–4 of the American Convention on Human Rights.

[48] At 6 December 2006.

[49] 193 states parties at 6 December 2006, with Somalia and the United States as signatories.

[50] For coverage of the legal sources of international cooperation for human rights see Ch 2, including on the issue of the anachronistic reference to 'international cooperation based on free consent' in Article 11(1) of the ICESCR regarding the right of everyone to an adequate standard of living.

[51] On the latter point, Beyani, 'The Legal Premises', 21, at 32–3.

The existence of an objective international legal order recognized in the Barcelona Doctrine is an order in which legal positivism loses its influence,[52] in which law moves beyond the sum of rules to which states have consented to be bound.[53] It is an order which exists in conformity with a contemporary appreciation of considerations of humanity and the dictates of public conscience,[54] and in turn, judges positive international law by these standards. While international cooperation in the respect for and observance of human rights finds its legal foundations in the UN Charter's consecration of the principle, it has now taken on a 'supra-positive character',[55] crystallizing within a process of globalization. The result today, as the ILC has noted, is that '[e]very state by virtue of its membership in the international community, has a legal interest in the protection of certain basic rights and the fulfillment of certain essential obligations'.[56]

4.4 What Constitutes Basic Rights Today?

In addition to a range of specific human rights obligations owed towards all, including those derived from the prohibition of genocide, slavery and racial discrimination, the ICJ, in its *Barcelona Traction* dictum refers explicitly, in paragraph 34, to 'principles and rules concerning basic rights of the human person'. Although the Court did not elaborate as to what those basic rights might consist,[57] the case was decided prior to the codification of most international human rights law, and thus the basis for the obligations owed to all where drawn largely from

---

[52] Saito, 'International Law as a Law of the World Community', 233, at 243. While recognizing that the 'Barcelona Doctrine' provides the court's strongest articulation of 'the objectivity of the international legal order', Saito refers to other rulings in which the ICJ has reflected a similar position, beginning with the *Reparation for Injuries Suffered in the Service of the United Nations*, Adv Op, ICJ Rep (1949) 174. Saito observes that prominent internationalists, in pointing out the 'transnational phenomenon in international relations', adopted expression such as 'transnational law' (Jessup), 'common law of mankind' (Jenks), and 'world law' (Tanaka). They all deliberately avoided the use of the term 'international' which would thus exclusively apply to inter-state relations consequently failing to represent *jus gentium* (at 234).

[53] Saito, 'International Law as a Law of the World Community', 233, at 235. Saito cites Brierly in reference to the use of the term 'consensual theory', i.e. the theory that international law is exclusively the sum of rules to which a state has given its consent to be bound.

[54] Judge Weeramanty dissenting in the *Nuclear Weapons* case recognized the role of the human rights movement in shaping 'the dictates of public conscience.' In its oral submission in the same case, Australia argued that 'international standards of human rights must shape conceptions of humanity and have an impact on the dictates of public conscience', further remarking that '[i]nternational concern for human rights has been one of the most characteristic features of this era of international law': T Meron, 'The Martens Clause, Principles of Humanity, and Dictates of Public Conscience' 94 *AJIL* 1 (2000) 78, at 84.

[55] *South-West Africa*, Judge Tanaka (diss op) 6, at 298.

[56] *Articles on the Responsibility of States for Internationally Wrongful Acts with commentaries* (2001) Commentary to art 1, at 66.

[57] Reference is made generally to 'corresponding rights of protection hav[ing] entered into the body of general international law [. . .]; others are conferred by international instruments of a universal or quasi universal character'. *Barcelona Traction*, 3, at para 33.

international humanitarian law. By contrast, today there are a wide range of international human rights conventions and declarations which specifically, and in considerable detail, enumerate basic rights; the list of rights considered fundamental to the respect of the human person, and to elementary consideration of humanity, that therefore engage the responsibility of the international community of states was always going to evolve over time.[58] According to the ICJ, the principles and rules concerning basic rights of the human person are '[b]y their very nature' the concern of all states and thus impose obligations *erga omnes* upon them.[59] The reference to nature, as opposed to conventional obligations as the starting point, reaffirms that the 'rationale for the universal opposability of obligations *erga omnes* is not to be found in extrinsic principles, such as the presumed or effective predominance of the will of the majority of states or the more powerful states over a dissenting minority, but in the universal validity of the moral values that these obligations are meant to protect'.[60]

What, then, might these 'basic rights' of the human person be? Some contend that they consist wholesale of those rights within the Universal Declaration or the International Bill of Human Rights.[61] O'Manique takes the view rather that there are 'fundamental rights'—those that are required for 'good human development.'[62] These are, according to O'Manique, 'food, shelter, non-threatening physical environment, security, health, knowledge, work, freedom of conscience, freedom of expression, freedom of association, and self-determination'.[63] He explains that although these rights are interrelated to some extent, none of these can be reduced to another, and each is a foundation for a whole range of requirements. He further explains that those rights appearing in the Covenants that are excluded from his list are rights that are 'derived' from fundamental rights, and in many instances are ways of protecting the exercise of fundamental rights.[64] He adds that the 'fundamental rights' to which he refers are not rooted in the same logic

[58] For example, the Commentary to the Articles on State Responsibility: '... [It is not the] function of the Articles to provide a list of those obligations which under existing international law are owed to the international community as a whole ... in any event, such a list would be only of limited value, as the scope of the concept will necessarily evolve over time. The Court [ICJ in the *Barcelona Traction* case] itself has given useful guidance: in its 1970 judgment it referred by way of example to the outlawing of acts of aggression, and of genocide, and to the principles and rules concerning the basic rights of the human person, including protection from slavery and racial discrimination. In its judgment in the *East Timor* case, the Court added the right of self-determination of peoples to this list'. *Articles on the Responsibility of States for Internationally Wrongful Acts with commentaries* (2001) Commentary to Art 48, at 331–2.

[59] *Barcelona Traction*, 3, at paras 33–4.

[60] Ragazzi, 'International Obligations *Erga Omnes*', 455, at 466.

[61] For example, JP Humphrey, 'The Universal Declaration of Human Rights: Its History, Impact and Juridical Character' in BG Ramcharan, *Human Rights: Thirty Years After the Universal Declaration* (Martinus Nijhoff, 1979). See also, V Kartashkin, *Observance of Human Rights by States which are Not Parties to the United Nations Human Rights Conventions* (Sub-Commission, 51st session, 1999) UN Doc E/CN4/Sub2/1999/29, para 4.

[62] J O'Manique, 'Human Rights and Development' 14 *HRQ* 1 (1992) 78, at 84–85.

[63] Ibid, 78, at 84.

[64] Ibid, 78, at 84–5.

as the 'basic rights' referred to by Henry Shue, defined as those rights which are claims necessary for basic survival.[65] A concept of 'basic rights' was proposed by Shue in the early 1980s to describe certain rights, the enjoyment of which are essential to the enjoyment of all other rights.[66] These 'basic rights' are to physical security, subsistence and liberty.

Drawing a distinction between 'basic rights', and 'non-basic rights', Shue proposed that non-basic rights may be sacrificed if necessary to secure 'basic rights'. The division, according to Shue, is not to suggest that one set of rights has a greater intrinsic value than another set, but to recognize that certain rights can only be enjoyed (non-basic rights) if basic rights are enjoyed, and thus basic rights need to be firmly established before other rights can be secured.[67] Müllerson prefers to see the prioritization of rights—that is the attribution of a 'special value'—determined on a case by case basis depending on concrete circumstances and, significantly, on the levels of development of a society.[68] Hunt, Nowak and Osmani in their *Principles and Guidelines for a Human Rights Approach to Poverty Reduction Strategies*, produced for the Office of the United Nations High Commissioner for Human Rights (OHCHR), take the position that while the human rights approach (in allowing for the progressive realization of economic, social and cultural rights) recognizes that priorities will need to be set, this approach also imposes certain conditions on the conduct of progressive realization, and therefore on the act of prioritizing rights. The Guidelines explain that 'the international human rights system specifies some core obligations that require States to ensure, with immediate effect, certain minimum levels of enjoyment of various rights'.[69] This is close to the position of CESCR, which as we saw in Chapter 3 in our consideration of resource constraints and the prioritization of rights, refers in its Statement on Poverty to all economic, social and cultural rights as imposing certain core obligations which '... establish an international minimum threshold ... [and] are non-derogable'.[70]

At least, since the adoption of the Vienna Declaration on Human Rights in 1993, emphasis has been placed on the value of recognizing rights as universal, indivisible, interdependent and interrelated.[71] Although suggesting formulations from which we might derive a collection of 'basic rights' to which there is universal entitlement, and thus a legal interest of all states in ensuring their protection,

[65] Ibid, 78, at 84, fn 20.

[66] H Shue, *Basic Rights: Subsistence, Affluence and U.S Foreign Policy* (Princeton University Press, 1980) 19.

[67] Ibid, 18–20.

[68] Müllerson, *Ordering Anarchy*, 256.

[69] P Hunt, M Nowak and S Osmani, *Principles and Guidelines for a Human Rights Approach to Poverty Reduction Strategies* (OHCHR, 2005), para 61.

[70] CESCR, Statement on Poverty and the International Covenant on Economic, Social and Cultural Rights (25th session, 2001) UN Doc E/C12/2001/10, paras 17–18; see also CESCR, General Comment no 3, The Nature of States Parties' Obligations, para 10.

[71] Vienna Declaration and Programme of Action (1993), Pt I, art 5.

none of the models above challenged that tenet. That the various human rights are mutually reinforcing does not negate the fact that there can be many reasons to have to make choices about which rights to prioritize.

The rights which constitute norms of customary international law within the framework of the Third Restatement of United States Foreign Relations Law provide additional insight into what might comprise the 'basic' rights referred to by the ICJ requiring the interest of all states,[72] including through the modernizing of this 1987 proclamation, which is now undoubtedly required.

Along the lines of the dictum in the *Barcelona Traction* case, the Third Restatement of United States Foreign Relations Law in the area of customary international human rights law, recognizes the responsibility of all states (*erga omnes*) in the area of human rights, and proposes that '[v]iolations of the rules stated in this section [e.g. (a)–(g)] are violations of obligations to all other states and any state may invoke the ordinary remedies available to a state when its rights under customary international law are violated'.[73] The Restatement refers specifically to (a) genocide; (b) slavery or the slave trade; (c) the murder or causing the disappearance of individuals; (d) torture or other cruel, inhuman or degrading treatment; (e) prolonged arbitrary detention; (f) systematic racial discrimination, or (g) *a consistent pattern of gross violations of internationally recognized human rights.*

In addition to the rights enumerated above, the commentary to the Restatement cites a range of other civil and political rights covered by the clause including: systematic harassment, invasion of the privacy of the home, arbitrary arrest and detention (even if not prolonged); denial of fair trial in criminal cases; grossly disproportionate punishment; denial of freedom to leave the country; denial of the right to return to one's country; mass uprooting of a country's population; denial of freedom of conscience and religion; denial of personality before the law; denial of basic privacy such as the right to marry and raise a family; and invidious racial or religious discrimination. Even at the time, however, authoritative commentators vociferously challenged the selective focus of the rights listed, remarking that as the wording of the clause 'a consistent pattern of gross violations of internationally recognized human rights' was taken from a UN procedure under the Economic and Social Council 1503, which the UN has stated to be equally applicable to economic, social and cultural rights as to civil and political rights, it would be expected that recognition would also be given, inter alia, to rights such as: the right to be free from hunger, the right to adequate housing, the

---

[72] 'Restatement of the Law (Third), Foreign Relations Law of the United States', 2 *ALI* (1987) 165.

[73] Ibid, sec 702, Comment o. Unlike for the acts enumerated in clauses (a)–(f), which are violations of customary international law even if the practice is not consistent or part of a pattern, in the case of clause (g), i.e. regarding human rights violations, the restatement declares that a consistent pattern of gross violations must be shown in order to constitute a violation of customary international law.

right to access basic health care, and the right to primary education.[74] While the Restatement serves to assert the supra-positive status of human rights, its interpretation excludes those rights which the United States fails to recognize in its domestic law, and which then, as today, receive widespread international support.[75] Alston and Simma rightly query:

> In the final resort it must be asked whether any theory of human rights law which singles out race but not gender discrimination, which condemns arbitrary imprisonment but not capital punishment for crimes committed by juveniles or death by starvation and which finds no place for a right of access to primary health care, is not flawed in terms both of the theory of human rights and the United Nations doctrine.[76]

Today, any list of basic rights with an elevated normative status would be considered incomplete without the inclusion of, at least, the minimum essential levels of certain rights provided for in the ICESCR. Alston has recently argued that the selection and content of socio-economic rights that are reflected in the MDGs, and have been frequently endorsed by states internationally and nationally, are contenders for customary international law status.[77] He points out that this approach of drawing out a narrow core of rights is consistent with what occurred regarding the formation of customary international law in the case of civil and political rights.[78]

4.5 Basic Rights and Community Obligations

There are several elements central to the concept of obligations *erga omnes*. One prominent characteristic which has been given considerable attention is that of 'solidarity', which relates to the aspect that every state is deemed to have a legal interest in the furtherance of these obligations. Another characteristic of obligations *erga omnes* is that of universality—that obligations *erga omnes* are binding on all states without exception. Other elements include broad issues of enforcement and legal standing.[79] Yet these defining features tell us little as to

---

[74] Simma and Alston, 'The Sources of Human Rights Law', 82, at 94–5.

[75] Ibid, 82, at 95; see Ch 1: The Continued Predominance of Cooperative Internationalism in the 21st century.

[76] Simma and Alston, 'The Sources of Human Rights Law', 82, at 95.

[77] Freedom from hunger, universal primary education, eliminating gender disparities in education, addressing child mortality and maternal mortality, and aspects of the right to health e.g. combating HIV/AIDS and other major diseases.

[78] 'By insisting on what is truly a bare minimum selection of those rights, the approach would be in line with what has occurred in relation to civil and political rights—the more expansive and broad-ranging of these rights are generally assumed not to be part of customary law, while a narrow core has taken on that status': P Alston, 'Ships Passing in the Night: The Current State of the Human Rights and Development Debate Seen Through the Lens of the Millennium Development Goals,' 27 *HRQ* 3 (2005) 755, at 773–4.

[79] Higgins, *Problems and Process*, 167. See also, ALI Restatement (Third), sec 703, which states that with regard to 'remedies for violation of human rights obligations . . . (2) Any state may pursue

who the holder of the substantive ('basic' or 'minimum') human rights is that may trigger *erga omnes* obligations. In all cases states (at a minimum) are subject to the resulting legal obligations related to the protection of human rights, but who has the procedural right to enforce them? As Meron points out, it is not entirely clear whether 'the individual is a subject of international law so that he or she has these legal rights, although enforceable perhaps only by states as agents? Or is he or she just the third party beneficiary of an obligation which each state owes to all other states (*erga omnes*) ... ?'.[80] This issue has resonance when considering obligations of international cooperation in the context of world poverty, and the right to development assists in clarifying the distinction between rights holders and duty-bearers within a system whereby international duties are owed to people in countries other than a state's own, and are the basis of claims against states as members of the international community. As developed in section 3.2 above on 'The "right-holder" of the right to development', it is Meron's former proposition that provides the preferred interpretation in which claimants and beneficiaries may be distinct. While a state may need to claim the right to development from the international community before it can be exercised by the people to whom it belongs, the government is acting on behalf of the people who are holders of the rights, the realization of which requires the cooperation of the international community.

This is consistent with the ILC's Articles on State Responsibility which provides that the community interest is exercised in the interest of the injured state *or the beneficiaries of the obligation*.[81] With regard to a community interest derived of convention human rights, the ILC notes that '... a State's responsibility for the breach of an obligation under a treaty concerning the protection of human rights may exist towards all the other parties to the treaty, but the individuals concerned should be regarded as the ultimate beneficiaries and in

---

international remedies against any other state for a violation of the customary law of human rights ...' . Notably, whether derived of customary international law or international agreement, a violation gives rise to international remedies against the violating state, for example resorting to the ICJ or another international tribunal. With regard to remedies for violations of customary law of human rights the Restatement provides that: 'Since obligations of the customary law of human rights are *erga omnes* (obligations to all states), any state may pursue remedies for their violations, even if the individual victims were not nationals of the complaining state and the violations did not affect any other particular interest of that state ...'. Regarding remedies of individual victims: 'In general individuals do not have direct international remedies against a state for violating their human rights, except where provided by international agreement. ... International human rights agreements generally require a state party to provide such remedies': ALI Restatement (Third), sec 703 and Comments (a) and (b) and (c), as cited in Harris, *Cases and Materials*, 729.

[80] T Meron, *Human Rights and Humanitarian Norms as Customary Law* (Clarendon Press, 1989) 95–98.

[81] Draft Articles on the Responsibility of States for Internationally Wrongful Acts, *Report of the International Law Commission on the work of its 53rd session*, UN Doc A/56/10 (2001) art 48(1)(b) (emphasis added).

that sense as the holders of the relevant rights'.[82] Distinguishing between the procedural limitations regarding the enforcement of state responsibility in the area of human rights, and the existence of substantive rights held by people, the ILC remarked that '... certain provisions, for example in various human rights treaties, allow invocation of responsibility by *any* State party. In those cases where they have been resorted to, a clear distinction has been drawn between the capacity of the applicant State to raise the matter and the interests of the beneficiaries of the obligation'.[83]

As we have seen there has been a discernable shift in international law towards the idea of community interest in human rights protection, as well as the mutual responsibility of states to secure compliance by other states with their human rights obligations. This view has also been advanced by the Human Rights Committee (HRC) regarding the interpretation of treaty provisions. In its general comment on the *Nature of the General Legal Obligation Imposed on States Parties*, the HRC emphasizes the shared nature of the Covenant obligations. The language employed suggests that the Committee is interpreting the scope of the ICCPR to reflect a broad interpretation of states parties' interests in the performance by other states parties of its obligations under the Covenant, through an appreciation of the universal values and interests of human rights that today may increasingly impose obligations, on all states, towards all people. At paragraph 2, the Committee notes that:

[w]hile article 2 is couched in terms of the obligations of States Parties towards individuals as the right-holders under the Covenant, every State Party has a legal interest in the performance by every other State Party of its obligations. This follows from the fact that the 'rules concerning the basic rights of the human person' are *erga omnes* obligations, and that, as indicated in the fourth preambular paragraph of the Covenant, there is a United Nations Charter obligation to promote universal respect for, and observance of, human rights and fundamental freedoms.[84]

---

[82] *Articles on the Responsibility of States for Internationally Wrongful Acts with commentaries* (2001) Commentary to art 33, at 234. 'In cases where the primary obligation is owed to a non-State entity, it may be that some procedure is available whereby that entity can invoke the responsibility on its own account and without the intermediation of any State. This is true, for example, under human rights treaties which provide a right of petition to a court or some other body for individuals affected.': *Articles on the Responsibility of States for Internationally Wrongful Acts with commentaries* (2001) Commentary to art 48, at 234.

[83] *Articles on the Responsibility of States for Internationally Wrongful Acts with commentaries* (2001) Commentary to art 48, at 323. Indeed there may be factors—mere willingness being one—other than capacity that influence the preparedness of a state to complain against another state for human rights breaches particularly when it does not affect its nationals, as the very limited number of such complaints would attest. An individual complaint mechanism under the ICESCR could in principle allow for right-holders to invoke the responsibility of a state party or states parties for a violation of Covenant rights as a result of their failure to meet their obligations of international assistance and cooperation.

[84] HRC, General Comment no 31, The Nature of the Legal Obligation, para 2.

Further, in an attempt to encourage states parties that have made the declaration under Article 41 to make use of the Covenants inter-state complaint mechanism, the Committee reassures states parties that drawing attention to breaches of the Covenant obligations is an act reflecting 'legitimate community interest'.[85]

Encouraging community responses under a human rights treaty that is primarily concerned with acts or omissions that violate the rights of individuals within the (territorial) jurisdiction of a state party, such as the ICCPR, is an important development, not least for the reasons described above. It further suggests that the community requirement is fortified in human rights treaties addressing economic, social and cultural rights the fulfillment of which are not jurisdictionally circumscribed, but rather are *premised* on an obligation of international cooperation, i.e. obligations of states to people in other countries, and whereby the states parties recognize the 'rights of everyone' to, inter alia, an adequate standard of living, to be free from hunger, to the highest attainable standard of health, to work etc. As has elsewhere been noted, the absence of an explicit clause limiting jurisdiction along the traditional lines, has human rights treaty obligations generally regarded as extending to all acts of contracting states irrespective of where they may be taken as having effect.[86] This is also the case with the Geneva Conventions addressing the laws of war, due to common Article 1.[87] The ICJ, in that regard, has emphasized 'that every State party to that Convention, whether or not it is a party to a specific conflict, is under an obligation to ensure that the requirements of the instruments in question are complied with'.[88]

The CESCR for its part has repeatedly advanced the interpretation that international obligations of cooperation flowing from the UN Charter and the Covenant are essential to development, and to the full realization of Covenant rights, and require joint and separate action.[89] The Declaration on the Right to Development had also earlier provided that: 'All States should cooperate with

---

[85] Ibid. In his separate opinion on the *DRC* v *Uganda* case, Judge Simma makes a similar point, when he remarks that: 'The obligations deriving from the human rights treaties cited above and breached by the DRC are instances par excellence of obligations that are owed to a group of States, including Uganda, and are established for the protection of a collective interest of the States parties to the Covenant: *Armed Activities on the Territory of the Congo* (Democratic Republic of the Congo v Uganda) Judge Simma (sep op) ICJ (2005), para 35. See also, H Duffy, 'Towards Global Responsibility for Human Rights Protection: A Sketch of International Developments' 15 *Interights Bulletin* 3 (2006) 104.

[86] M Craven 'Human Rights in the Realm of Order: Sanctions and Extraterritoriality' in F Coomans and MT Kamminga (eds), *Extraterritorial Application of Human Rights Treaties* (Intersentia, 2004) 233, at 251.

[87] 'The High Contracting Parties undertake to respect and to ensure respect for the present Convention in all circumstances.'

[88] *Legal Consequences of the Construction of a Wall*, 136, at para 158. For an exposition on this point see, *Armed Activities on the Territory of the Congo,* Judge Simma (sep op), paras 32–4.

[89] CESCR, General Comment no 14, The Right to the Highest Attainable Standard of Health (art 12),(22nd session 2000) UN Doc E/C12/2000/4, para 38; CESCR, General Comment no 3, The Nature of States Parties' Obligations, para 14.

a view to promoting, encouraging and strengthening universal respect for and observance of all human rights and fundamental freedoms ... .'[90] This idea that human rights provide rules laying down a 'community obligation' ('that is either a customary obligation *erga omnes* protecting such fundamental values as ... human rights ... or an obligation *erga omnes contractantes* laid down in a multilateral treaty safeguarding those fundamental values') is captured also in Cassese's notion of a legal regime of 'aggravated responsibility' i.e. 'generalized responsibility for gross and systematic violations of human rights'.[91] He further concludes that under the treaty system, the protection of the community values entrenched in human right conventions 'provides for a "public interest" in their implementation', prioritizing collective remedial action.[92]

The ILC Articles on State Responsibility provide that a breach of obligations pertaining to gross and systematic peremptory norms of international law[93] may trigger an *entitlement* among states to act,[94] and it also imposes an obligation to cooperate with other states to bring an end to the breach.[95] Preferring flexibility of measures, the Commentary to the ILC Articles for its part does not specify the form this cooperation should take, except that the choice will 'depend on the circumstances of the given situation' (and be lawful),[96] emphasizing that '[w]hat is called for in the face of serious breaches is a joint and coordinated effort by all states to counteract the effects of these breaches'. The call to cooperate in Article 41(1), 'seeks to strengthen existing mechanisms of cooperation, on the basis that all states are called upon to make an appropriate response'.[97]

4.6 Conclusion

This chapter argues that the status of a universal principle to respect and observe human rights has been elevated to a level where it legally binds all states. An appreciation that there are fundamental rules regarding respect of the human

[90] DRD, art 6(1).

[91] A Cassese, *International Law* (2nd edn, Oxford University Press, 2005) 262.

[92] Ibid, 276. See also Cassese's elaboration of 'special aggravated responsibility' for minor or sporadic breaches of community obligations.

[93] ILC Articles on State Responsibility, art 40.

[94] Ibid, arts 48(2)(a) and (b).

[95] Ibid, art 41(1). Under the articles on state responsibility, cooperation would be a secondary obligation, whereas under the ICESCR, for example, it is a primary one. A similar development can be seen in the doctrine of the 'responsibility to protect' in which the international community endorsed its collective *responsibility* to protect people in any country from certain human rights violations. This approach has superceded a doctrine that frames such intervention as a *right*. 2005 World Summit Outcome, UN Doc A/60/L1 (2005), paras 138–9. For a fuller consideration, see, *Report of the International Commission on Intervention and State Sovereignty, The Responsibility to Protect* (International Development Research Centre, 2001).

[96] *Articles on the Responsibility of States for Internationally Wrongful Acts with commentaries* (2001) Commentary to art 41, at 287.

[97] Ibid.

person, and thus the protection of human rights has, since the adoption of the UN Charter and the subsequent strengthening of a common commitment to human rights, entered into the body of customary international law.

Today it can hardly be said that socio-economic rights so central to survival, and to the ability of people to live in conditions of dignity, and widely supported by the international community of states, do not form part of these 'basic rights of the human person' that demand universal respect, and engage community legal interest. Moreover, it may become increasingly difficult to defend the view that the scale of poverty and hunger in the world, which affects half the global population, does not constitute gross and systematic violations of socio-economic rights giving rise to a common responsibility of all states. While state consent is the condition historically deemed necessary for any 'demonstration of rule legitimacy', it was never deemed necessarily sufficient, and recent legal developments would support this contention.[98] As Lukashuk concludes, '[t]he significance of universal legal relations, of *erga omnes* legal relations is growing ... '.[99]

However, the fact that international cooperation is essential today to securing the basic rights of everyone to be free from hunger, to have sufficient and safe water,[100] and access to healthcare and to the underlying determinants of a healthy life,[101] etc should not obscure the fact that state responsibilities are individual. It is to the complex task of determining state responsibility for global structural impediments to the exercise of basic socio-economic rights that we will now turn.

---

[98] See, T Franck, *Fairness in International Law and Institutions* (Oxford University Press, 1995) 29.

[99] II Lukashuk, 'The Law of the International Community' in *International Law on the Eve of the Twenty-First Century: Views from the International Law Commission* (United Nations, 1997) 51, at 68.

[100] 'The human right to water entitles everyone to sufficient, safe, acceptable, physically accessible and affordable water for personal and domestic uses'. CESCR, General Comment no 15, The Right to Water (arts 11 and 12), (29th session, 2002) UN Doc E/C12/2002/11, para 2.

[101] CESCR, General Comment no 14, The Right to Health, para 11.

5

Attributing Global Legal Responsibility

5.1 Introduction

This chapter will offer several bases for disaggregating global responsibility pertaining to collective state conduct, for violations of socio-economic rights, manifested as world poverty. The proposals draw from legal doctrine and interpretive guidelines in the area of human rights, and consider them in light of what are routinely shown to be structural obstacles to the realization of socio-economic rights. The focus is on the attribution of responsibility within a global environment legally inhospitable to individualizing the human rights responsibilities of developed states due to the extent of economic interdependence, the many actors implicated, and the enduring nature of hunger and other deprivations in poor countries. While the fulfilment of human rights has undoubtedly been recognized by the entire international community as requiring international cooperation,[1] and the basic rights of the human person that demand universal respect can be said legally to bind all states,[2] insufficient advances in remedying world poverty have so far been made on a claim all too often required of an 'undifferentiated international community'. This inquiry is part of a reasonably new, yet growing, doctrinal as well as judicial trend towards delineating the parameters of external human rights obligations.

Only in the late 1990s did the legal community begin to devote significant attention to the idea that our contemporary world order requires revisiting the nature and scope of the human rights obligations owed by states.[3] The UN Sub-Commission had only just mandated two Rapporteurs to undertake their first of several studies on globalization and human rights;[4] the current Working Group

---

[1] Ch 2.

[2] Ch 4.

[3] It still took a number of years for research pertaining to this concern to be prioritized, even after Asbjorn Eide, as Special Rapporteur on the Right to Food, remarked in his 1987 report on the subject that: '... the fact that no other studies have been undertaken within the framework of the human rights organs of the United Nations on any one of the specific rights proclaimed in the International Covenant on Economic, Social and Cultural Rights makes such a general consideration all the more necessary.': A Eide, *Report on the Right to Adequate Food as a Human Right* (39th session, 1987) UN Doc E/CN4/Sub2/1987/23, para 39.

[4] Sub-Commission on the Promotion and Protection of Human Rights res 2000/102, Globalization and its impact on the full enjoyment of all human rights (52nd session, 2000).

on the Right to Development—where obligations of international cooperation are hotly debated—had not yet held its first session,[5] its Independent Expert on the Right to Development had not yet crafted the first of many working papers in which the law of international cooperation was addressed in each subsequent report with increased prominence.[6] And, while today there are a number of scholarly papers inquiring into the human rights obligations of international organizations, most notably, the World Bank, the International Monetary Fund (IMF) and the World Trade Organization (WTO), at that time there seemed to be but a handful.[7]

An early and notable exception to the previously limited focus on this subject, was the 1987 working paper on *The Right to Adequate Food as a Human Right* submitted to the (then) UN Sub-Commission on the Prevention of Discrimination and Protection of Minorities by Sub-Commission expert Asbjørn Eide. Mandated to address the right to food in relation to 'the establishment of a new international economic order' Eide was explicit in endorsing the existence of international responsibilities for human rights to people outside of a state's jurisdiction. In the section of his report entitled, 'International Obligations', he began by asking: 'Do States have obligations, with regard to livelihood rights, to the international community and to the people of other States? This was clearly envisaged from the earliest drafting of the Charter of the United Nations'. He also referred to 'the building blocks of international responsibility' as including more than '... the fulfilment of national obligations held by Governments towards those living under their jurisdiction'. He observed that '[p]eoples and States interact with each other with increasing intensity; self-sufficiency is often impossible in modern times ... [t]here is a high level of interdependence .... Freedom from want, like other human rights, cannot be achieved only through the fulfilment of national obligations held by Governments towards those living under their jurisdiction'. Eide drew the conclusion towards the end of his report that: 'States

---

[5] Although this intergovernmental Working Group had been preceded by various UN bodies established in an attempt to advance the right, such as, a Working Group of Intergovernmental Experts on the Implementation and Promotion of the Right to Development (1996–7), and a Working Group of Governmental Experts (1981–9).

[6] Further, the mandate of the Independent Expert on structural adjustment policies, now the post of Independent Expert on the Effects of Economic Reform Policies and Foreign Debt on the full enjoyment of Human Rights, particularly Economic, Social and Cultural Rights, was only established in 1998. The resolution establishing the post of Independent Expert on the question of human rights and extreme poverty was also adopted in 1998.

[7] P Alston, 'The International Monetary Fund and the Right to Food' 30 *How LJ* 2 (1987) 473; M Lucas, 'The International Monetary Fund's Conditionality and the International Covenant on Economic Social and Cultural Rights' 25 *RBDI* 1 (1992) 104; and M Cogen, 'Human Rights, Prohibition of Political Activities and the Lending Policies of the World Bank and the International Monetary Fund' in SR Chowdhury et al (eds), *The Right to Development in International Law* (1992) 379; P Klein, '*La Responsabilité des Organisations Financières Internationales et les Droits de la Personne*' 32 *RBDI* (1999) 97. It was the 2nd edn, published in 2000, of Steiner and Alston's human rights compendium, *International Human Rights in Context: Law, Politics and Morals*, which included a section on 'Globalization, Human Rights and Development' for the first time.

have obligations also to the peoples of other States and to the international community. These can be derived from provisions found within human rights law and from a set of principles of international law'.[8] Recognizing the critical importance of making human rights law relevant to the nature of contemporary human rights violations, the current Special Rapporteur on the Right to Food of the Human Rights Council has begun to consider 'current discussions that push the boundaries of human rights beyond their traditional boundaries ...' within the context of his mandate to examine 'emerging issues'.[9]

In response to deprivations inadequately addressed by the current global institutional system, ensuring human rights today might increasingly be understood as having (at least) two quite clearly defined legal dimensions: that of the extraterritorial obligations of states (i.e. the negative effects of a state's policies and activities on the people in another country); and the obligations of international cooperation more broadly (i.e. responsibilities of states in their collective capacities for example, as members of international organizations,[10] and in relation to their influence over the global order as a whole).[11] The collective obligations of the international community of states forms the focus of this book, and pertain to obligations to ensure arrangements that are just, and thereby conducive to the fulfilment of the socio-economic rights of all people.

5.2 The Due Diligence Requirement and the Global Standard of Care

While the responsibility for human rights falls to the state as duty-bearer, under international human rights law, the occurrence of violations does not presuppose that the state is the perpetrator of human rights abuses, nor that the state or its agents are directly responsible for breaches.[12] State responsibility also exists where

---

[8] Eide, *Report on the Right to Adequate Food as a Human Right*, paras 182, 194, 201, and 279.
[9] J Zeigler, *Report of the Special Rapporteur on the Right to Food*, UN Doc E/CN4/2005/47 2.
[10] See generally, SI Skogly, *The Human Rights Obligations of the World Bank and the International Monetary Fund* (Cavendish Publishing, 2001); M Darrow, *Between Light and Shadow: The World Bank, The International Monetary Fund and International Human Rights Law* (Hart, 2003).
[11] This doctrinal distinction is emerging quite consistently. See R Künnemann, *Report to ICESCR on the Effect of German Policies on Social Human Rights in the South* (The Foodfirst Information and Action Network, 2001) <http://www.fian.org>; S I Skogly and M Gibney, 'Transnational Human Rights Obligations' 24 *HRQ* 3 (2002) 781; *Duties sans Frontières: Human Rights and Global Social Justice* (International Council on Human Rights Policy, 2003). These are not wholly discrete areas, and as Künnemann has pointed out '... well-defined cooperation of states ... is necessary to ensure ... extraterritorial obligations ....': R Künnemann, 'Extraterritorial Application of the International Covenant on Economic, Social and Cultural Rights' in F Coomans and MT Kamminga (eds), *Extraterritorial Application of Human Rights Treaties* (Intersentia, 2004) 201, at 227.
[12] *Velasquez Rodriguez* v *Honduras*, Inter-AmCtHR (Ser C) No 4 (1988), judgment of 29 July 1988, para 172.

the perpetrator cannot be identified.[13] Further, acts or omissions that have the *effect* of impairing the enjoyment or exercise of rights are as stringent a determinant of state responsibility as intent.[14] What might this tell us about the attribution of responsibility under international human rights law for the 500,000 women a year who die in pregnancy and childbirth while these deaths are 100 times more likely to occur in sub-Saharan Africa than in high income countries,[15] and for the 30,000 children, coming almost exclusively from developing countries, who die each day of preventable diseases?[16] While focusing on the issue of international responsibility we can still acknowledge, in full, the responsibilities of developing states acting at the national level,[17] and the positive impact of domestic initiatives on poverty reduction.[18] Domestic factors in developing countries play an important role in the increase or reduction of their poverty,[19] however, global factors are also extremely relevant. Global factors are linked to concerns in many, if not most, areas that impact on the exercise of socio-economic rights, for example: initiatives to integrate and deregulate markets around the world that favour economically powerful countries;[20] externally imposed requirements to privatize

[13] Ibid.

[14] See, art 1(1) International Convention on the Elimination of All Forms of Racial Discrimination, entered into force 4 January 1969, General Assembly res A/RES/2106 (XX), 660 UNTS 195; art 1(1) Convention on the Elimination of All Forms of Discrimination Against Women (1979), entered into force 3 September 1981, General Assembly res A/RES/34/180, 1249 UNTS 20378.

[15] UNDP, *Human Development Report 2003: Millennium Development Goals*, 8.

[16] Ibid.

[17] For consideration of domestic policies and programmes on poverty reduction, see for example, the UNDP National Human Development Reports.

[18] The microfinance Grameen bank in Bangladesh has lent US$5.7bn, in a country where almost half the country's 140 million people live in poverty. Today the bank has 6.5 million borrowers in Bangladesh, 97% of whom are women. 'Mr Yunus [the bank's founder] has recently pointed out that Bangladesh has been reducing poverty by 2% a year since the turn of the millennium. If sustained this rate of poverty reduction will see the country halve the number of poor people by 2015.' R Ramesh, 'Banker to the world's poor wins Nobel peace prize', *The Guardian*, 14 October 2006.

[19] For example, according to an Oxfam report on public services for the delivery of basic needs, we see that, despite the fact that more than a third of Sri Lanka's population lives on £1 a day, its maternal mortality rate is among the lowest in the world. And, while Kazakhstan has an income 60% higher than Sri Lanka, children are nearly five times more likely to die in their first five years, and are far less likely to go to school, drink clean water or have the use of a toilet: A Balakrishnan, 'Public services: The revolutionary way to deliver health and education, says Oxfam', *The Guardian*, 1 September 2006; B Emmet, *In the Public Interest* (Oxfam, 2006). Jeffrey Sachs remarks that domestic impediments said to undermine poverty alleviation may include lack of irrigation and drought (resulting in insufficient food production), insufficient disease control, and physical isolation/lack of connectivity: J Sachs, *The End Of Poverty: Economic Possibilities for Our Time* (Penguin Books, 2005). However, these may not be wholly domestic issues. We can see quite easily how the international community may be implicated in, for example, distorting weather patterns that cause drought due to CO_2 emissions—of which the United States is by far the largest emitter both absolutely and per head. On the matter of insufficient disease control, it is important to recognize that only 3% of the research and development expenditure of the pharmaceutical industry is directed towards diseases that plague the developing world, while 90% of the disease burden falls on the developing world.

[20] M B Steger, *Globalization: A Very Short Introduction* (Oxford University Press, 2003) 103.

public services;[21] the skills drain;[22] and even the worsening weather.[23] And while it is the state acting domestically that has the primary responsibility for the realization of human rights when it comes to the people within its territory, this does not weaken what is essentially a complementary duty of the international community to remedy the violation of minimum essential levels of economic, social and cultural rights. We will return to this central point.

In addition to the negative requirement to abstain from certain courses of action, it is widely accepted that a state's failure in meeting its positive obligations to exercise due diligence in preventing and adequately responding to human rights violations determines whether its responsibility is triggered, and not only whether the act that caused the violation was shown to have been committed by its agents and is thereby directly imputable to it.[24] Applying the familiar due diligence standard to the actions taken by the international community that impact negatively on the world's poor, we would ask whether the actors ought to have acted differently and thus are wholly or partly at fault for the current state of affairs; could the 'agents' acting together have *foreseen* that their conduct and decisions would lead to these outcomes; and could they have reasonably averted the harm[25] without substantial costs to themselves?[26] There is no shortage of authoritative literature detailing particular global policies and their debilitating impact on people in poor countries. This is matched by widespread

---

[21] While privatization may offer the preferred policy consistent with poverty reduction plans that take account of the views, concerns and rights of poor people, the UK government now points out that 'in the 1980s and 1990s donors pushed for the introduction of [these] reforms, regardless of whether they were in the countries' best interests.' The UK has only recently decided not to impose privatization as a condition of aid. United Kingdom Department for International Development (DFID), *Partnerships for Poverty Reduction: Rethinking Conditionality*, UK Policy Paper, March 2005, paras 1.6 and 4.5.

[22] The skills shortage in developing countries is exacerbated by the emigration of key workers from developing countries to Northern countries, constituting what the UN Special Rapporteur on the Right to Health, and others, note is a 'perverse subsidy': P Hunt, *Report of the Special Rapporteur on the Right of Everyone to the Highest Attainable Standard of Health* UN Doc A/60/348 (2005).

[23] See United Kingdom Department for International Development, *Eliminating World Poverty: Making Governance Work for the Poor*, White Paper, July 2006, 93. To drive the point home, Pogge adds that 'even if country-specific factors fully explain the observed variations in the economic performance of developing countries, global factors may still play a major role in explaining why they did not on the whole do much better or much worse than they did in fact'. TW Pogge, 'The First UN Millennium Development Goal: A Cause for Celebration?' 5 *Journal of Human Development* 3 (2004) 377, at 391.

[24] HRC, General Comment no 31 on Art 2 (The Nature of the General Legal Obligation Imposed on States Parties to the Covenant), (80th session, 2004) UN Doc CCPR/C/21/Rev1/Add13 (2004), para 8. In *Osman v UK*, responsibility hinged on the fact that the authorities knew, or ought to have known of, the existence of the immediate risk to life of a person, and failed to take measures which judged reasonably, might have been expected to avoid said risk: *Osman v UK*, ECtHR App no 87/1997/871/1083, judgment of 28 October 1998, para 116. See further, *Mastromatteo v Italy*, ECtHR App no 37703/97, Grand Chamber judgment of 24 October 2002, para 68; *Velasquez Rodriguez v Honduras*, paras 172 and 174.

[25] *Velasquez Rodriguez v Honduras*, paras 172 and 174.

[26] See, TW Pogge, 'What is Global Justice?' in A Follesdal and TW Pogge (eds), *Real World Justice* (Springer, 2005) 2.

awareness as to what needs to be done to address them, as reflected in the multitude of international commitments and calls to address systemic imbalances in the international trading system;[27] to eliminate external debt, including odious debt incurred by previous undemocratic regimes; to regulate transnational corporations (TNCs) in the area of human rights;[28] to ensure responsible foreign investment;[29] to increase the quality and quantity of aid; and to reform global governance.[30] Hunger concentrated in developing countries is not a result of there being not enough food globally, but rather of certain people just not having enough to eat—this raises serious questions of distribution, access, responsibility and accountability.[31] The due diligence requirement—providing, in the first instance, a positive 'duty to prevent' the violation of human rights[32]—is a

---

[27] The Doha Round outcome benchmarks are the production of rules addressing unbalanced trade practices by improving access to markets, reducing agricultural subsidies and revisiting agreements and negotiations that limit the policy space available to developing countries to further human development. The UNDP points out that the issues raised by the WTO rules on, for example, investment and intellectual property demonstrate the problem. UNDP, *Human Development Report 2005: International Cooperation at a Crossroads: Aid, Trade and Security in an Unequal World* (Oxford University Press, 2005) 126.

[28] See for example, CHR res 2005/69, establishing the post of the UN Special Representative of the Secretary-General on Human Rights and Transnational Corporations and Other Business Enterprises.

[29] See the recent concerns of the Task Force and Working Group on the Right to Development regarding foreign direct investment: 'The right to development implies that foreign direct investment (FDI) should contribute to local and national development in a responsible manner, that is, in ways that are conducive to social development, protect the environment, and respect the rule of law and fiscal obligations in the host countries. The principles underlying the right to development, as mentioned above, further imply that all parties involved, i.e. investors and recipient countries, have responsibilities to ensure that profit considerations do not result in crowding out human rights protection ... .': *Report of the Working Group on the Right to Development* (7th session, 2006) UN Doc E/CN4/2006/26, para 59; and *Report of the High-Level Task Force on the Implementation of the Right to Development* (2nd session, 2005) UN Doc E/CN4/2005/WG18/TF/3, para 73.

[30] As noted in Ch 3, there are no shortage of recent studies calling for the democratization of the WTO, IMF and World Bank, see for example: *Final Report and Recommendations Derived from the Multi-Stakeholder Consultations Organized by the New Rules for Global Finance Coalition*, November 2004–September 2005); *On Addressing Systemic Issues, Section F, Monterrey Consensus Document, Financing For Development/New Rules for Global Finance* (2005); UNDP, *Human Development Report 2005: International Cooperation at a Crossroads*; *Investing in Development: A Practical Plan to Achieve the Millennium Development Goals* (UNDP, 2005); *Our Common Interest, Report of the Commission for Africa* (2005) <http://www.commissionforafrica.org>; *EU Heroes and Villains: Which Countries are Living up to their Promises on Aid, Trade, and Debt?*, Joint NGO Briefing Paper, Action Aid, Eurodad and Oxfam (2005); *A Fair Globalization*.

[31] In developing countries, more than 850 million people, 300 million of whom are children, go to bed hungry every night. Of these 300 million children, 90% are suffering long-term malnourishment and six million children die annually of malnourishment. More than 40% of Africans do not even have the ability to obtain sufficient food on a day-to-day basis. All the while, the international trading system is 'rigged' in favour of the rich countries. *Fast Facts: The Faces of Poverty*, UN Millennium Project (2005); UNDP, *Human Development Report 2005: International Cooperation at a Crossroads*, at ch 1.

[32] *Velasquez Rodriguez v Honduras*, para 174.

rule of customary international law,[33] including in the context of extraterritorial obligations where states exercise jurisdiction through effective control abroad.[34] In light of these facts, it is suggested that the standard of due diligence has an important role to play in determining parameters for the disaggregated appraisal of collective state conduct in order to facilitate the attribution of responsibility to otherwise undifferentiated state players of the global institutional order. Its effective application at the international level would seek to render imperfect obligations—obligations that do not clearly belong to any particular agent (by belonging to many agents)—perfect.[35]

In an era of international economic interdependence, actions and decisions within the global order cannot easily be disaggregated and attributed to a particular state or states for purposes of state responsibility.[36] However, responsibility need not be limited to the establishment of a *direct causal* relationship between people suffering from poverty and the actions and omissions of specific states. World poverty is also attributable to the existing global system, elements of which *by design* cause and/or fail to remedy this widespread deprivation. The failure of

---

[33] See, for example, A Reinisch, 'The Changing International Legal Framework for Dealing with Non-State Actors' in P Alston (ed), *Non-State Actors and Human Rights* (Oxford University Press, 2005) 37, at 79; Y Ertürk, *Report of the Special Rapporteur on Violence Against Women, Its Causes and Consequences: The Due Diligence Standard as a Tool for the Elimination of Violence against Women*, UN Doc E/CN4/2006/61, para 29.

[34] See, Ertürk, *Report of the Special Rapporteur on Violence Against Women*, para 34. On due diligence, see generally, A Gattini, 'Smoking/No Smoking: Some remarks on the Current Place of Fault in the ILC Draft Articles on State Responsibility' 10 *EJIL* 2 (1999) 397, at 399.

[35] The Independent Expert on the Right to Development applied this Kantian notion (familiar in the work of Amartya Sen) to emphasize the importance of identifying agents responsible for the realization of rights. Once a right is subject to a corresponding 'perfect' obligation, the possibility is created whereby it can be made legally enforceable: A Sengupta, *Second Report of the Independent Expert on the Right to Development* (Working Group on the Right to Development, 1st session, 2000) UN Doc E/CN4/2000/WG18/CRP1, paras 8–9.

[36] Commentators have suggested ways in which to advance a system of 'disaggregated' international decision-making for the purposes of ensuring human rights and attributing responsibility. Künnemann, for example, argues that where states parties to the ICESCR do not form the majority of a governing body, and therefore cannot ensure that the outcome of a vote will be consistent with their obligations under the Covenant, the states parties must not be part of such authorities. He goes on to make the point that: 'If a violation by an international authority [such as the governing board of the World Bank or IMF] is based on explicit voting it should be clear which states parties are in violation. If a violation is not based on explicit voting it can be said that the governing community of states parties is implied [sic] in a violation of ICESCR'. Künnemann, 'Extraterritorial Application of the International Covenant', 201 and 215. In his paper on the EU's sugar regime, Vandenhole concludes that 'EU Member States, all of which are states parties to the ICESCR, are in violation of their third state obligation to respect the right to an adequate standard of living of small sugar producers in the South by support for or condoning of the sugar regime of subsidies for surplus production and export dumping to the South'. To these ends he notes that the (intergovernmental) European Council explanations and votes are made public on legislative matters and 'it is therefore possible to identify a country's position and voting behaviour, which allows establishing the co-responsibility of a particular state for legislative acts': W Vandenhole, 'Third State Obligations under the ICESCR: A Case Study of EU Sugar Policy' 76 *Nord J Int'l L* 31–4 (2007) 73.

influential states to remedy the causes of ongoing breaches through reform of the system perpetuates this deprivation.

The first challenge we face is to define clearly the obligations to cooperate of the 'undifferentiated international community' required to address the structural impediments to the realization of fundamental human rights.[37] This is a somewhat distinct exercise from determining the responsibilities of differentiated duty-bearers where causation might be easier to demonstrate, such as when states are acting extraterritorially. The application of this due diligence standard globally eliminates the requirement to establish a causal link between the actions of the powerful members of the international community and the persistence of world poverty (i.e. human rights violations). Instead, it becomes a tool against which policies, agreements and actions internationally are tested for human rights compliance. This would seem an appropriate standard of care when the harm of world poverty is both ongoing and bound up with the activities of myriad actors, and the specific content of the obligation to cooperate internationally, while emerging, is not entrenched. Since world poverty is a product of a system that *structurally* benefits some and disadvantages others, establishing causal relationships between harms experienced elsewhere in the world and the actions of states acting internationally can be extremely complex. A question worth posing is therefore: to what degree is the global order *in its entirety* to blame for the current state of affairs, and all states—to greater and lesser degrees—are thereby responsible for 'causing' the harm?

Given the perpetuation of world poverty and the dramatic difference between the affluence of people in developed countries and the deprivation in developing countries, any burden of proof should lie with the powerful and wealthy countries. It should be for those who benefit disproportionately from the global economic system to demonstrate that they have done all they can to redress world poverty, and to prevent its continuation. In the language of the International Covenant on Economic, Social and Cultural Rights (ICESCR), the requirement is that of 'international assistance and cooperation' to the 'maximum available resources' of states, with this duty attaching itself 'in particular to States parties that are in a position to assist',[38] as well as other 'actors in

---

[37] In considering the 'internationalization of responsibility', Alston takes the view that while it can be argued that there exists an obligation of international cooperation based on repeated commitments by the international community of states, this obligation is 'at best, a generic one which attaches to the undifferentiated international community': P Alston, 'Ships Passing in the Night: The Current State of the Human Rights and Development Debate Seen Through the Lens of the Millennium Development Goals' 27 *HRQ* 3 (2005) 755, at 777. But see 2.4.3: 'The Structural content of international cooperation'.

[38] For example, CESCR, General Comment no 17, The Right of Everyone to Benefit from the Protection of the Moral and Material Interests Resulting from any Scientific, Literary or Artistic Production of which he is the Author (art 15(1)(c)), (35th session, 2005) UN Doc E/C12/GC/17 (2005), para 37. Craven points out, that while under the Covenant, conditions of deprivation will not in themselves be evidence of non-compliance given that the obligations can be progressively implemented, this does not do away with the question 'as to whether [one] state[s] can and should

a position to assist'.[39] The general aim of the obligation of international assistance and cooperation is to allow for an environment whereby developing countries are in a position to fulfil their human rights obligations under the Covenant.[40]

Yet, the positive duty to assist only partially addresses the demands of world poverty. While it is a norm consistent with the objective of international human rights law, which seeks to ensure *minimum* standards, it is an inadequate basis upon which to attempt equitable access to, and a just distribution of, global wealth. It is help-based rather than redistributive (of power or wealth), it is a 'threshold norm' rather than a 'maximizing-norm',[41] and some have argued strongly that it does not address the first need of the global poor, that is the more stringent (negative) duty not to hamper development and not to design and uphold arrangements that aggravate world poverty.[42]

It is suggested here that the due diligence requirement facilitates placing responsibility for, inter alia, the premature deaths of children in developing countries, due to lack of having their basic and essential needs met, at the door of developed countries. So for example, while the international obligation 'to assist' found in the Covenant requires help in line with a state parties' 'maximum available resources' (rather than based on what it would take to lift the poorest out of poverty):[43]

[t]he 2,735 million people the World Bank counts as living below its more generous US$2 per day international poverty line consume only 1.3 per cent of the global product, and

---

be held responsible for failing to take adequate steps to address conditions of deprivation experienced in the territory of other states parties': M Craven, 'Human Rights in the Realm of Order: Sanctions and Extraterritoriality' in Coomans and Kamminga (eds), *Extraterritorial Application of Human Rights Treaties*, 233, at 252.

[39] CESCR, Statement on Poverty and the International Covenant on Economic, Social and Cultural Rights (25th session, 2001) UN Doc E/C12/2001/10, para 16; CESCR, General Comment no 17, The Right to Benefit from Protection of Moral and Material Interests, para 40.

[40] CESCR, General Comment no 17, The Right to Benefit from Protection of Moral and Material Interests, para 40.

[41] See, W Hinsch, 'Global Distributive Justice' in TW Pogge (ed), *Global Justice* (Blackwell, 2001) 55, at 64. A maximizing principle, in line with Rawls' Difference Principle, whereby 'a just global distribution of wealth would maximize the wealth of the economically least privileged society in the global society'.

[42] TW Pogge, 'Severe Poverty as a Violation of Negative Duties: A Reply to the Critics' 19 *Ethics and International Affairs* 1 (2005) 55, at 75. We face the problem that states acting internationally are not merely assisting too little but are also preventing development too much through actions and arrangements that contribute to world poverty. See ME Salomon, 'Addressing Structural Obstacles and Advancing Accountability for Human Rights: A Contribution of the Right to Development to MDG 8,' Briefing Note to the 2nd session of the UN High-Level Task Force on the Right to Development, November 2005 <http://www.ohchr.org/english/issues/development/taskforce.htm>.

[43] The international commitment of developed states to providing 0.7% of GNI to poverty reduction under the Millennium Development Goals comes closer to this latter approach, although Goal 1 is aimed only at lifting half of the world's poor out of poverty by 2015. The CESCR considers part of a state party's obligations of international assistance and cooperation to include meeting this financial requirement (and it thereby provides the basis as to what constitutes 'maximum

would need just 1 per cent more to escape poverty so defined. The high-income countries, with 955 million citizens by contrast, have about 81 percent of the global product.[44]

The failure of the rich countries to shift that one per cent—reasonably assumed to be within their collective 'available resources'—when it is foreseen that not to do so will result in severe deprivation and death of much of the global population, speaks to their responsibility for those deaths. And a global arrangement that structurally provides for such advantage and disadvantage attributes responsibility to the drivers (and primary beneficiaries) of that system, first and foremost, for being able to anticipate the repercussions of their actions, yet allowing that system to be maintained.

5.3 A Typology for World Poverty: International Obligations to Remedy and to Prevent Human Rights Violations

Obligations of international cooperation for the realization of human rights are understood to have both negative (obligations of abstention) and positive (obligations of action) dimensions. The negative international obligation 'to respect' Covenant rights is, in the work of the Committee, as well as politically, the least contentious.[45] Regarding positive international obligations, in particular 'to fulfil' Covenant rights elsewhere, the Committee on Economic, Social and Cultural Rights (CESCR) has gone only some way in delineating the international obligations of states parties.[46] Its focus on a generalized duty to assist and to cooperate

available resources' under the Covenant). See, for example, CESCR, Concluding Observations: Norway (34th session, 2005) UN Doc E/C12/1/Add109 (2005), para 3: 'The Committee appreciates the State party's commitment to international cooperation as reflected in the volume of official development assistance, standing at 0.92% of the gross national income'. See also, at 2.4.2: 'Maximum available resources'.

[44] TW Pogge, 'World Poverty and Human Rights' 19 *Ethics and International Affairs* 1 (2005) 1, at 1.

[45] 'To comply with their international obligations in relation to the right to water, States parties *have to* respect the enjoyment of the right in other countries ...'. CESCR, General Comment no 15, The Right to Water (arts 11 and 12), (29th session, 2002) UN Doc E/C12/2002/11, para 31 (emphasis added).

[46] With regard to international cooperation in the realization of economic, social, and cultural rights, the CESCR considers states parties to have negative international obligations to respect the enjoyment of rights in other countries (CESCR, General Comment no 14, The Right to the Highest Attainable Standard of Health (art 12), (22nd session, 2000) UN Doc E/C12/2000/4, para 39) which entails refraining from actions that interfere, directly or indirectly, with the enjoyment of Covenant rights (CESCR, General Comment no 15, The Right to Water, para 31). But it also recognizes positive obligations to protect the rights of people in other countries against violations at the hands of third parties over which they have influence (CESCR, General Comment no 14, The Right to Health, para 39). 'Depending on the availability of resources', positive obligations to facilitate (fulfil) the realization of rights include, for example, facilitating access to goods and services in other countries (CESCR, General Comment no 14, The Right to Health, para 39), and the obligation to provide (fulfil) aid. (CESCR, General Comment no 14, The Right to Health, para 39; CESCR,

internationally provides the basis of the obligation to fulfil.[47] Overall, the work of the Committee in this area has in some ways been dynamic, as we saw in Chapter 1,[48] however the language adopted by it in the elaboration of positive international obligations can also be hortatory,[49] and over-qualified.[50]

In terms of the nature of states parties' obligations generally, the Covenant provides for progressive realization and acknowledges constraints based on limits of available resources (Article 2(1)), while also imposing various obligations that are of an immediate effect, including meeting core obligations (i.e. to ensure satisfaction of the minimum essential levels of each right). Steps taken to fulfil obligations must be 'deliberate, concrete and targeted' towards the full realization of Covenant rights, and progressive realization still requires, according to the Committee, a 'specific and continuing obligation to move as expeditiously and effectively as possible towards the full realization' of the rights. While developed to affirm the normative force and strengthen the implementation of Covenant rights by the state when acting domestically,[51] there is no reason to conclude that this explanation, specifying the nature of states parties' obligations, is limited to domestic obligations, although little has so far been done to apply the benchmarks in the international context.

In an international legal system that seeks primarily to regulate the relationship between a state and the people within its territory, determining the nature and parameters of the human rights obligations of external states, including in their collective capacities, gives rise to vexing questions. The notion of simultaneous

General Comment no 12, The Right to Food, para 36; CESCR, General Comment no 15, The Right to Water, paras 30–36). The obligation to promote (fulfil) rights includes, for example, the request that states parties endeavour to promote the right to work in other countries as well as in bilateral and multilateral negotiations (CESCR, General Comment no 18, The Right to Work (art 6), (35th session, 2005) UN Doc E/C12/GC/18 (2005), para 30).

[47] CESCR, General Comment no 3 on Art 2(1) (The Nature of States Parties' Obligations), (5th session, 1990) UN DocE/1991/23, annex III (1990), para 14; CESCR, General Comment no 17, The Right to Benefit from Protection of Moral and Material Interests, para 36.

[48] Section 1.4.2 on the position of treaty bodies addresses the Committee's work on outlining structural obstacles to the realization of economic, social and cultural rights and, to some degree, the corresponding collective obligations of states parties, as well as of the international community more broadly.

[49] 'States parties *should* ensure that their actions as members of international organizations take due account of the right to water.': CESCR, General Comment no 15, The Right to Water, para 36. 'To comply with their international obligations in relation to article 6, States parties *should endeavour* to promote the right to work ... in bilateral and multilateral negotiations'. CESCR, General Comment no 18, The Right to Work, para 30 (emphasis added). This language is not a reflection of the non-binding nature of general comments since, when specifying the content of positive Covenant obligations at the domestic level, the Committee (rightly) uses mandatory terms such as 'obligated' and 'required'. See, CESCR, General Comment no 18, The Right to Work, paras 26–8.

[50] '*Depending on the availability of resources*, States should facilitate realization of the right to water in other countries, for example through provision of water resources, financial and technical assistance, and provide the necessary aid *when required*.' CESCR, General Comment no 15, The Right to Water, para 34, emphasis added.

[51] CESCR, General Comment no 3, The Nature of States Parties' Obligations, paras 1–2, 9.

negative obligations undertaken by the domestic state and the external state(s) when they pertain to abstaining from taking action inconsistent with human rights or to positive action in the regulation of third parties, such as TNCs, would seem to be a sound proposition. However, this duty-sharing model is replaced by one that has the external state(s) as the holders of *secondary* obligations to those of the domestic state, when applied to positive obligations to fulfil economic, social and cultural rights elsewhere. A widely endorsed position, including by CESCR, is that external states' obligations 'to fulfil' human rights are triggered if the domestic state is unable, for reasons beyond its control, to fulfil the rights concerned by the maximum use of available means at its disposal.[52] Jean Ziegler, the UN Special Rapporteur on the Right to Food, frames the obligation similarly, as one to 'support to fulfill',[53] which, importantly, includes the creation of an enabling international environment that would allow for the realization of the right to food in all countries.[54] But such a qualified obligation, as reflected in the obligation merely to 'support' to fulfil, offers that which is necessary, but when faced with structural obstacles and gross violations of socio-economic rights globally, can it be said to provide that which is sufficient?

While the relative weakness reflected in the language elaborating international obligations of a positive nature is likely to be indicative of the Committee's sensitivity to the political predispositions of Northern states,[55] it does not go nearly far enough in providing a normative response to world poverty. This is certainly the case with regard to positive obligations, and no doubt some, such as Pogge, would be inclined to argue, with regard to the vast negative obligations to stop imposing the existing global order too. But there is a separate question to consider beyond whether positive obligations of international cooperation have been sufficiently elaborated, and that is whether the negative/positive framework (including the tripartite typology), so familiar when considering obligations pertaining to economic, social and cultural rights domestically, is well-suited to the consideration of obligations of international cooperation in this area.

The tripartite typology of obligations to respect, protect and fulfil human rights[56] has functioned to highlight the negative and positive components present in both sets of rights—economic, social and cultural, as well as civil and political.

---

[52] W Vandenhole, *A Partnership for Development: International Human Rights Law as an Assessment Instrument*, Submission to the 2nd session of the UN High-Level Task Force on the Right to Development, November 2005, paras 6 and 14. <http://www.ohchr.org/english/issues/development/taskforce.htm>.

[53] J Ziegler, *Report of the Special Rapporteur on the Right to Food,* UN Doc E/CN4/2005/47, para 47. See notably, the valuable work in this area undertaken by the FoodFirst Information and Action Network (FIAN).

[54] Ziegler, *Report of the Special Rapporteur on the Right to Food*, para 57.

[55] See, ME Salomon, 'Towards a Just Institutional Order: A Commentary on the First Session of the UN Task Force on the Right to Development', 23 *NQHR* 3 (2005) 409, at 424 and note 84.

[56] H Shue, *Basic Rights: Subsistence, Affluence and U.S Foreign Policy* (Princeton University Press, 1980); A Eide, 'Realization of Social and Economic Rights and the Minimum Threshold Approach' 10 *HRLJ* 1–2 (1989) 35.

Its consistent application by CESCR in its more recent general comments has served to transcend a somewhat exaggerated distinction that traditionally held progressively realized, often resource-reliant, rights to be exclusively positive (with civil and political rights, subject to immediate implementation, without cost, and largely negative). While the typology has contributed to bridging the divide between the initial normative assumptions pertaining to each set of rights, as well as reinforcing an appreciation as to their indivisibility, interdependence and interrelatedness, it likewise relies on an elaboration of obligations based on the requirements of abstention (negative) and those of action (positive). The tripartite typology does not challenge this method of configuring human rights obligations, but rather advances a general appreciation of the equal significance, force and justiciability of socio-economic rights vis-a-vis civil and political rights.

However, perhaps the negative/positive distinction so familiar to international human rights law is not the most suitable approach to take in addressing existing human rights deprivations linked to the structure of the global order. Human rights violations are structurally provided for through a failure of the creators, controllers, and primary beneficiaries of the global order to offer a feasible alternative,[57] and their failure to exercise due diligence, which could reasonably avoid the continuation of widespread world poverty. The obligations of states to respect and observe human rights owed to people everywhere[58] might impose negative obligations in so far as they are required to abstain from any act that would violate the human rights of people anywhere in the world. However, *if basic rights have already been violated in a global context,* and, for example, people are starving, then the obligation imposed is also positive—that is, every state, to a greater or lesser degree, is under an obligation to take action to remedy that violation and to prevent its continuation. Adequate implementation of the legal framework of international cooperation either through a rigorous application of negative obligations to *stop* imposing a structural economic arrangement that sees poverty continue,[59] or by moving beyond anodyne positive obligations of 'assistance', is compounded by the application of the negative/positive division. This division has become devoid of any meaning when the first obligation has

[57] Pogge makes the significant point that that even if world poverty was in decline it does not follow that the global order is not harming the poor, since world poverty might be going down despite the global order and not because of it. And, even if the global institutional order were having a poverty-reducing affect, it might still be harming the global poor severely. Moreover, as he explains, the basis for relieving the international community of its duties to address world poverty is not to be determined by a 'diachronic comparison with an earlier time, but on a counterfactual comparison with its feasible institutional alternatives': Pogge, 'The First UN Millennium Development Goal', 377, at 390–1. In any event, in 2005, the then World Bank President James Wolfensohn noted that poverty in the 47 countries of sub-Saharan Africa is, in fact, increasing: J D Wolfensohn, 'Some Reflections on Human Rights and Development' in P Alston and M Robinson (eds), *Human Rights and Development: Towards Mutual Reinforcement* (Oxford University Press, 2005) 19, at 22–3.

[58] See ch 4.

[59] TW Pogge, 'Priorities of Global Justice' in Pogge (ed), *Global Justice,* 22; TW Pogge, 'The International Significance of Human Rights' *Journal of Ethics* 4 (2000) 45.

become the obligation *to remedy* the violation of existing minimum essential socio-economic rights globally. The subsequent obligation would be to prevent the further deterioration of rights.

Drawing a rigid distinction between the negative/positive nature of obligations when it comes to international cooperation and world poverty loses much of its value for another reason. While in part the primary international obligation is to stop imposing a structural economic arrangement that sees poverty continue, and in this sense the obligation is negative, reform requires action, so a positive obligation to act is derived from the negative obligation.[60] The duties corresponding to the right to development provide an example. The scope of the duty of states acting at the international level in the realization of the right to development provides for both a negative duty to ensure that they abstain from actions that inhibit the right to development, and a positive duty based on a collective responsibility to ensure an international enabling environment, within which the right to development can be realized. Thus, under the conditions of interdependence and international cooperation within the global order, negative and positive obligations cannot be fully separated.

While all states are to cooperate in order to contribute to the common objective of eradicating world poverty, the responsibility of a state for the creation of a just institutional economic order should be in accordance largely with its weight and capacity in the world economy.[61] The content of this principle of common but differentiated responsibilities in the context of international cooperation for human rights provides the basis for four indicators that may assist in determining responsibility for world poverty. First, responsibility may be determined as a result of the contribution that a state has made to the emergence of the problem;[62] second, as a result of the relative power it wields at the international level that is manifested as influence over the direction of finance, trade, and development (effective control);[63] third, responsibility may be determined based on whether the given state is in a position to assist;[64] and fourth, responsibility can be determined on the basis of those states that benefit most from the existing distribution of global wealth and resources.

---

[60] Pogge, 'What is Global Justice?', 2.

[61] For example, the Final Act of the United Nations Conference on Trade and Development VII (1987), as cited in Analytical Compilation of Comments and Views on the Implementation and Further Enhancement of the Declaration on the Right to Development, UN Doc E/CN4/AC39/1989/1 22.

[62] New Delhi Declaration of Principles of International Law Relating to Sustainable Development, 70th Conference of the International Law Association, res 3/2002, para 3.

[63] See, ME Salomon, 'International Human Rights Obligations in Context: Structural Obstacles and the Demands of Global Justice' in B-A Andreassen and SP Marks (eds), *Development as a Human Right: Legal, Political and Economic Dimensions* (Harvard School of Public Health—Harvard University Press, 2006) 96, at 107–11.

[64] CESCR, Statement on Poverty, para 16.

5.4 Conclusion

This chapter has addressed the current need to determine means of attributing responsibility for world poverty. It began by proposing that the responsibility of powerful states acting together can be ascertained based on whether they could have foreseen and averted the deleterious effects of their decisions. The due diligence standard as regards state responsibility is an important legal tool when the damaging act is not directly imputable to the state, as we see with regard to the jurisprudence on private violence perpetrated against women,[65] and violations by non-state actors or unidentified agents generally.[66] Applying the established due diligence standard in order to disaggregate collective state responsibility for world poverty is a natural extension of its use to a situation where direct imputability of individual states for the repercussions of an asymmetrical economic global order may be difficult to deduce. This application of the due diligence doctrine represents the deployment of the tools and techniques of international law to the realities that we face today.

In determining responsibilities of the international community of states we need to release ourselves from the instinct to identify a causal chain from international state behaviour to violations of socio-economic rights. First, the global institutional system, as currently *designed*, allows for the perpetuation of poverty or, at a minimum, has failed sufficiently to relieve poverty, and the situation is worsening. Second, the multiplicity of actors can make it extremely difficult to track and attribute individual state responsibility. Third, as a result of this key characteristic of the structure of the global system, every actor within that system is implicated, with obligations determined through the system of weighted responsibility described above. In so far as effective action to address world poverty is beyond the capability of any one state in an interdependent world, the obligation of each state to contribute to this objective through international cooperation—with its obligations dosed accordingly—is strengthened.[67]

In an effort to determine state responsibility for global structural impediments to the exercise of basic socio-economic rights, we might summarize this chapter as follows: due diligence as the global standard of care applied at the international level can play a significant role in attributing international legal responsibilities for poverty to undifferentiated duty-bearers. Second, based on a series of indicators, collective responsibility can be disaggregated, according to: the contribution a state

---

[65] Committee on the Elimination of Discrimination against Women, General Recommendation no 19 (Violence against Women), (11th session, 1992) UN Doc A/47/38 (1993) at 1 para 9.
[66] For an overview of the subject see Reinisch, 'The Changing International Legal Framework', 37, at 78–82.
[67] G Abi-Saab, 'The Legal Formulation of the Right to Development' in R-J Dupuy (ed), *The Right to Development at the International Level*, Workshop of the Hague Academy of International Law 1979 (Sijthoff & Noordhoff, 1980) 170–1.

has made to the conditions of world poverty; the power and influence it wields over the direction of the institutional economic order; its capability to contribute to changing the present state of affairs; and notably, the degree to which a state benefits from the distribution of global wealth. Third, the *existence* of world poverty informs the parameters of the obligation of international cooperation, delineating a primary requirement of the international community to *remedy* related violations of economic, social, and cultural rights, and to *prevent* further violations. The familiar system of distinguishing negative from positive obligations becomes subsumed by this typology which prioritizes the remedying of existing violations and the prevention of further violations, regardless of whether that would require abstention or action.

The logic of the Declaration on the Right to Development epitomizes this reorientation of international law. The DRD requires a synchronal set of duties applied to developing states acting domestically, and developed states acting internationally.[68] While by no means affirming that states acting domestically are in any way relieved of their traditional primary responsibility for the realization of human rights,[69] the right to development invites a claim by developing states against the international community for the fulfilment of its complementary duty to give effect to this right. The right to development exists as a result of, and in relation to, the international community, and can only be achieved through the shared effort of that community.[70]

---

[68] See further, at 1.4.1 and ch 3.

[69] DRD, preambular para 15.

[70] H Gros Espiell, 'Community-Oriented Rights: Introduction' in M Bedjaoui (ed), *International Law: Achievements and Prospects* (Martinus Nijhoff Publishers, 1991) 1167, at 1170. See also, SP Marks, 'Emerging Human Rights: A New Generation for the 1980's?' 33 *Rutgers L Rev* 2 (1981) 435.

6

Concluding Remarks: Latter-day Tyranny and the Future of Human Rights

The influence of international economic organizations, the impact of external actors advancing the requirements of a global free-market, and the corresponding diminution in domestic autonomy that limits the ability of states independently to decide their own economic and social policies, is a contemporary reality, particularly among poor and less influential states. The World Trade Organization (WTO) is the main international economic institution for the regulation of international trade and trade-related issues. Within the organization, the more powerful members press for the terms under which the opening of markets will take place. The lead international financial institutions (IFI)—the World Bank and International Monetary Fund (IMF)—in seeking to achieve coherence with the WTO regime,[1] influence greatly the domestic policies in borrowing countries that will best serve these market-oriented objectives. The 'holy trinity' made up of these three international institutions is directed to a very considerable degree by the wealthy and powerful states, with repeated findings showing that the ideological priorities and policies pursued by the organizations favour those countries disproportionately. The pervasive impact of these preferences on the exercise of basic economic, social and cultural rights in developing countries is enormous, focusing attention on the very design of the political-economic order itself as a substantial factor contributing to the perpetuation of world poverty. With the locus of economic power internationalized, a fundamental reconfiguration of the duty-bearers of human rights is elicited, matched by a requirement to determine the 'perfect obligations' of these new duty-bearers.

If the right to self-determination was the meta-right of the twentieth century, then the right to self-determined development is that of the twenty-first century. The commitment to independent political status during the period of decolonization preoccupied the United Nations (UN) in its early years of standard-setting, and today the sovereign equality of every state has been given its due recognition, with its internal dimension—the right to democratic governance—accepted as a universal good. However, the professed commitment to sovereign equality on the

---

[1] Marrakesh Agreement, art III, 5.

international stage has yet to translate into functional equality. All states are not equal in their ability to determine international policies that impact on securing basic economic needs. Today, all states are equal, but some states are more equal than others.[2]

Cast in the language of human rights, the failure to see these needs met constitutes a violation of the right of everyone to an adequate standard of living, including adequate food, clothing and housing, and rights to health and education. Just as international economic arrangements favour developed states that influence their substance and direction, ongoing deprivation adversely affects the 2.7 billion people concentrated in developing countries. In the words of the UN Committee on Economic, Social and Cultural Rights (CESCR) the existence of world poverty reflects a 'massive and systemic breach' of international human rights law.[3] The fulfilment of these rights through the observance of corresponding legal obligations of international cooperation would signal the beginning of the end of poverty. Addressing global injustices relies in no small measure on the legal regime for the protection and promotion of human rights, and the demands it places on the form and exercise of state power today.

These great disparities exist alongside an international community of states that has shown the universal values of human rights to be reflective of the interests of states organized as a collective. The principle of international cooperation has been recognized as a legal requirement in order to achieve in our interdependent world that which states cannot achieve unilaterally; to share in the responsibility to manage the global order equitably. In instruments starting with the UN Charter, international cooperation for human rights has been understood as critical to a stable and just international order, complemented in recent law-making fora by the principle of shared responsibility for managing worldwide economic and social development. The prominence given to human rights since the founding of the United Nations, and their widespread acceptance as an articulation of common interests and agreed values of the international community, implies that decisions and actions of states at the international level can only be granted legitimacy in relation to them.

But as is clear, legal (and political) commitments to cooperate in ensuring human rights have not consistently been followed by practice, and responsibilities under international human rights law have not fully shifted from the classical focus on violations of individuals at the hands of their own states, to the responsibilities of states acting internationally. But important legal developments have been taking place. This book has charted the progressive development of international law pertaining to obligations among states to address poverty-related human rights violations globally, and delineated progress still required if effective

---

[2] 'All animals are equal, but some animals are more equal than others': G Orwell, *Animal Farm* (Secker & Warburg, 1945).

[3] CESCR, Statement on Poverty and the International Covenant on Economic, Social and Cultural Rights (25th session, 2001) UN Doc E/C12/2001/10, para 4.

meaning is to be given to the commitment of international cooperation in the respect for, and observance of, human rights for all people. As was anticipated in the UN Charter, human rights obligations would need also to apply to relations among states when it comes to alleviating world poverty and underdevelopment, but today, great store is placed in this particular formulation. The challenges posed to the exercise of basic human rights as a result of economic globalization as currently practiced, necessitates more than national or even extraterritorial human rights obligations. It demands a global responsibility for human rights under international law for the structural impediments to the realization of basic socio-economic rights of half the people in the world.

The crystallization of an international law of cooperation in the realization of human rights within this era of globalization advances what may be referred to as a rights-based approach to globalization. It seeks to ensure that human rights are recognized, protected and promoted within any economic system for the creation of, and access to, wealth, and that the means and ends of this globalization be consistent with them. This is not merely a moral appeal, it is reflective of an obligation upon states rooted in international law, which has evolved, and must continue to develop, in relation to the world it seeks to regulate.[4] Given the structure of our current global order, claims regarding violations of basic socio-economic rights can be understood as against, not only (certain) states acting collectively, but also the global order as a whole, over which the affluent and powerful states exercise effective control.

The UN Declaration on the Right to Development (DRD) is an important document for this new approach to the way in which we understand contemporary obligations in relation to world poverty and underdevelopment. It places people and their human rights at the centre of the processes and outcomes of national and international development strategies. The way in which duties are framed in the Declaration, is to require, on the one hand, that attention be focused nationally on all human rights thereby seeking to furnish a domestic environment in which equitable development can be realized. But central to its logic is the need for international cooperation in order to ensure that the external environment is conducive to this human-centred development process. Critically, responsibilities are understood also to devolve upon states acting at the international level, and developing states are endowed with the prerogative to invoke this right as against the public international order on behalf of their people.[5]

The UN High-Level Task Force on the Implementation of the Right to Development as an advisory body to the Working Group on the Right to Development faces an important challenge in its current mandate of improving the effectiveness, from a right to development perspective, of 'global partnerships

---

[4] R Higgins, *Problems and Process: International Law and How We Use It* (Oxford University Press, 1998) 10: ('… law as process encourages interpretation and choice that is more compatible with values we seek to promote and objectives we seek to achieve.').

[5] DRD, preambular para 16, art 2(3).

for development' under the eighth UN Millennium Development Goal (MDG). Reaffirming the particular role of Northern states in the persistence of world poverty, the 'partnerships' referred to in Goal 8, as its targets and indicators would suggest, are left to the rich and powerful states to set in motion, and it is those states that are expected to report against the Goal. The fact that Goal 8 is recognized as necessary for the achievement of the other seven Goals, underscores the role played by the external environment regarding the alleviation of world poverty.

While all countries, including poor and middle-income countries, have human rights obligations both domestically and internationally, certain responsibilities in the alleviation of world poverty—the cornerstone of the right to development—apply exclusively to developed countries and constitute an 'essential complement' to domestic efforts at fulfilling socio-economic rights.[6] With regard to economic, social and cultural rights specifically, positive obligations of external states 'to fulfil' socio-economic rights elsewhere tend to be understood as secondary obligations i.e. when the developing state is unable to fulfil the rights on its own with the maximum use of its available resources. The primary obligations for the fulfilment of economic, social and cultural rights are thus largely understood as belonging to the developing state acting in its domestic capacity. However, considering the responsibilities of states in the context of economic globalization, whereby the external arrangements against which these developing countries are meant to fulfil the rights to food, water, education etc of their people structurally disadvantages them (and structurally advantages developed countries), challenges the traditional way in which the sharing of obligations is conceived under international human rights law. The Declaration on the Right to Development advances this latter perspective. It demands a reorientation in the determination of responsibilities by recognizing that the efforts to address the manifestations of world poverty and underdevelopment cannot be disassociated from the role and responsibilities of the powerful states of the international community. As is proposed herein, since poverty-related violations already exist, a typology based on an international obligation, in the first instance, to remedy chronic hunger and related deprivations, and subsequently, to prevent their continuation, offers a better model than one which frames international obligations in terms of negative and positive obligations (i.e. to refrain from doing harm and to support developing states in achieving their obligations, respectively). The existence of a customary international legal obligation to respect and observe the human rights of people everywhere, constituting a doctrine of basic universal rights, supports this model insofar as every state—to varying degrees—has an obligation to cooperate in order to address these existing violations.

As has been discussed in this work, indicators to determine the particular states responsible for contributing to the creation of a just institutional economic order,

---

[6] Ibid, art 4(2).

and the level of their obligation to cooperate, is based on the principle of common but differentiated responsibilities and can be derived from a number of factors. These include the state's weight and capacity in the world economy; its relative power and influence over the direction of finance, trade, and development; and the degree to which it benefits from the existing distribution of global wealth and resources. What is required then, for MDG 8 to be consistent with the right to development, is international cooperation in removing structural obstacles to the realization of human rights, a reorganization of the governance and priorities of the global economic system that sustain gross and systemic inequalities, and mechanisms for ensuring international accountability related to the exercise of basic socio-economic rights.

The MDGs have been criticized by the Task Force for failing to include any system of accountability.[7] It is clear that where benchmarks pertaining to global partnerships for development are not achieved, contributing considerably to any failure to meet the Goals 'to eradicate extreme poverty and reduce hunger' etc, no international actors are formally implicated. Yet, speaking after the 2005 Doha Development Round a WTO Deputy Director-General confirmed that a long list of imbalances would need to be corrected if the multilateral trading system were to be fair to developing countries.[8] Still, there is no accountability for the repercussions of those 'imbalances' that are likely to impact on the exercise of human rights in the South.

Similarly, the World Bank recently acknowledged that despite the fact that 'the global markets are far from equitable, and the rules governing their functioning have a disproportionately negative effect on developing countries', the policies it, and other international lenders, advocated for poor countries to adopt over the last several decades have nonetheless emphasized the advantages of participating in the global economy.[9] While the adoption of this policy advice is often required by the international financial institutions given that it forms part of debt relief and loan conditionality, there is no accountability for the repercussions on human rights that may ensue as a result of unsuitable advice.[10] Another example might be offered. In deciding to cease imposing privatization as a condition of aid in 2005, the United Kingdom publicly acknowledged that 'in the 1980s and 1990s donors pushed for the introduction of [privatization and trade] reforms,

---

[7] *Report of the High-Level Task Force on the Implementation of the Right to Development* (1st session, 2004) UN Doc E/CN4/2005/WG18/2, para 40.

[8] V Sendanyoye-Rugwabiza, 'Is the Doha Development Round a Development Round?', London School of Economics, London, 31 March 2006.

[9] World Bank, *World Development Report 2006: Equity and Development* (World Bank/Oxford University Press, 2006) 16.

[10] Addressing the more recent focus of the IFIs on a 'country-driven national ownership' approach to poverty reduction strategies, the representative of Bosnia-Herzegovina remarked that: 'the IFIs used to tell us what to do; now we tell them what they want to hear'. Presentation by Bosnia-Herzegovina, Ministry of Foreign Trade and Economic Relations, UN High-Level Seminar on the Right to Development: Global Partnership for Development, UN Doc HR/GVA/SEM/RTD/2004/1 (Agenda), Geneva, 9–10 February 2004. Notes on file with author.

regardless of whether they were in the [developing] countries' best interests.'[11] This begs the question as to whether there has been any form of donor accountability to the people whose basic rights to water or healthcare may have been affected as a result of injurious externally imposed economic policies. Where deliberate policy prescriptions can be shown to have lead or contributed to the violation of human rights, a public acknowledgement, and even a change of policy (while not without merit), is hardly sufficient by the standards of international human rights law.[12] As CESCR has made clear, ensuring a system of accountability and providing for remedies is a fundamental requirement under international human rights law, including at the international level.[13]

In discussing the elaboration of systems of international accountability during an exchange with the Task Force at its 2nd session in 2005, CESCR member Eibe Riedel questioned whether obligations of 'international assistance and cooperation' under Article 2(1) of the Covenant are not best suited to an interstate complaint mechanism, rather than one providing for individual petition. These are issues currently being considered by a UN Working Group drafting an optional protocol to ICESCR.[14] (Riedel queried the prospect, for example, of an individual or group from a developing country claiming a violation of Covenant rights on the basis of a Northern state not meeting official development assistance (ODA) targets set by the international community).[15] A complementary

---

[11] *Partnerships for Poverty Reduction: Rethinking Conditionality*, UK Policy Paper, March 2005, para 4.5. The Policy Paper also recognizes the general concern around the 'social impact of privatization policies in the area of public services' and notes that there are 'examples where privatization has not benefited the poor' (para 4.6). In 2005–2006, £272 million of the UK's Gross Public Expenditure on Development was channelled through the World Bank Group <http://www.dfid.gov.uk/aboutdfid/statistics.asp>, which continues to impose privatization measures. On privatization and the international financial institutions, see, B Emmet, *In the Public Interest* (Oxfam, 2006) ch 4.

[12] Fukuda-Parr reminds us that: 'States have the obligation to put in place procedures for remedying violations, and for holding responsible parties accountable. In the national context, procedures exist for legal and administrative recourse, and the effectiveness of these procedures can be monitored. In the international context, such procedures are exceptional ....'. S Fukuda-Parr, *Millennium Development Goal 8: Indicators for Monitoring Implementation*, UN Doc E/CN4/2005/WG18/TF/CRP2, para 40.

[13] CESCR, General Comment No 9, The Domestic Application of the Covenant (19th session, 1998) UN Doc E/C12/1998/24, para 4 ('The existence and further development of international procedures for the pursuit of individual claims is important ...'); see also inter alia, CESCR, General Comment no 12, The Right to Adequate Food (art 11), (20th session, 1999) UN Doc E/C12/1999/5, para 32 ('Any person or group who is a victim of a violation of the right to adequate food should have access to effective judicial or other appropriate remedies at both national and international levels. All victims of such violations are entitled to adequate reparation, which may take the form of restitution, compensation, satisfaction or guarantees of non-repetition ....').

[14] Task Force notes on file with author; see also *Report of the Open-ended Working Group to consider options regarding the elaboration of an optional protocol to the International Covenant on Economic, Social and Cultural Rights* (2nd session, 2005) UN Doc E/CN4/2005/52, para 79. HRC res 1/3, Open-ended Working Group on an optional protocol to the International Covenant on Economic, Social and Cultural Rights (1st session, 2006).

[15] Importantly, Riedel has emphasized that 'the distinction had to be made between international cooperation and assistance—which was a legal obligation under article 2, para 1, of the

inquiry procedure under the protocol is also being discussed, and has support among some states,[16] with non-governmental organizations (NGOs) having suggested that this type of procedure would also provide an impartial accountability mechanism for evaluating the effectiveness of international cooperation and assistance.[17] The absence of an international mechanism established to receive complaints from private persons against either individual states or groups of states concerning the implementation of MDGs and related rights has been elsewhere noted,[18] and as Chinkin observes, there are areas that remain unexplored in terms of human rights enforcement mechanisms at the international level for redress of structural violations, such as the notion of class actions.[19]

Further consideration to advancing human rights accountability for structural obstacles to the exercise of human rights, can be found in the recent work of the Task Force on the Right to Development. The Task Force is a new international body mandated to scrutinize the human rights performance of international organizations by evaluating, from the perspective of the right to development, the relationships between, inter alia, international organizations and developing countries. At its recently concluded third session, the European Union proposed that the Partnership Agreement between the EU and African, Caribbean and Pacific (ACP) states (Cotonou Agreement), be subject to evaluation against the right to development criteria for global partnerships for development.[20] The Cotonou Agreement, which involves more than 100 states, encompasses aid, trade (assistance for trade arrangements to be made WTO-compatible) and a range of other policy fields.[21] The Task Force has also proposed that the Working Group consider mandating it to evaluate a forthcoming World Bank plan for Africa.[22] To these ends, the Task Force noted that: 'Given the preponderant role of the World Bank in the development of Africa and the influence of its thinking and operations on the donor community at large, its partnership should be critically scrutinized. Accordingly, the Bank should therefore be invited by the

---

Covenant—and development cooperation': *Report of the Open-ended Working Group to consider options regarding the elaboration of an optional protocol to the International Covenant on Economic, Social and Cultural Rights* (3rd session, 2006) UN Doc E/CN4/2006/47, para 88.

[16] Ibid, para 70.

[17] Ibid, para 87.

[18] ME Salomon, 'Addressing Structural Obstacles and Advancing Accountability for Human Rights: A Contribution of the Right to Development to MDG8', Briefing Note to the 2nd session of the UN High-Level Task Force on the Right to Development, November 2005, 5 <http://www. ohchr.org/english/issues/development/taskforce.htm>.

[19] C Chinkin, 'The United Nations Decade for the Elimination of Poverty: What Role for International Law?' 54 *CLP* (2001) 553, at 587.

[20] *Report of the High-Level Task Force on the Implementation of the Right to Development* (3rd session, 2007) UN Doc A/HRC/4/WG2/TF/2, paras 15 and 92.

[21] Ibid, paras 84–5.

[22] Ibid, paras 86–7 and 92. The Task Force Report underlines that the World Bank's Africa Action Plan is: 'a comprehensive strategic framework for supporting the development of the continent's poorest countries. … Implementation of the Plan will be reviewed by the Development Committee during the IMF/World Bank Spring Meetings in April 2007'.

Working Group to allow the African Action Plan and its partnerships with governments of Sub-Saharan African to be evaluated against the criteria on the right to development'.[23]

This nascent development reflects not only progress in providing for a system of international human rights monitoring of international organizations and the impact of their conduct on poverty-related human rights violations, but also supports the thesis advanced herein: that today there can be said to exist a general principle of international law to respect and observe human rights in the main. This doctrine of basic universal rights owed to all, imposes obligations on states—as was discussed—as well as on other participants in the international legal system capable of impacting on the exercise of human rights. The way in which human rights obligations are conceptualized is necessarily undergoing change, and these initial steps in providing for corresponding international mechanisms of accountability reflect attempts to address an unsustainable gap in the current system of human rights procedural safeguards.

Because human rights are violated also as a result of the very structure of our global order, the attribution of responsibility and ultimately accountability becomes very difficult. While important advances both normatively, and to some degree procedurally, have taken place, and continue to do so, giving effect to human rights obligations at the international level remains unsatisfactory. While there is enough food to feed everyone on the planet, one in three (640 million) children in developing countries are malnourished.[24] Ten per cent of the world's health resources service the needs of 90 per cent of the global population.[25] A third of all children in developing countries live without adequate shelter.[26] There is inadequate progress on addressing the structural imbalance of our world order, and the real calculations of our global interdependence. In light of these facts, the first legal responsibility of the powerful members of the international community of states can only be to remedy the existing state of affairs, and to ensure their conduct is likely to prevent any further human rights violations that these figures on world poverty reflect.

The right to development, while at times contentious, and somewhat unconventional in its approach to human rights, might in our present climate be recognized as a right without which a range of other rights cannot be enjoyed. In this era of economic globalization that seeks to provide for an international environment conducive to the further accumulation of wealth by the wealthy through the expansive tendencies of global capital, this right demands international

[23] Ibid, para 87.
[24] WHO, *Removing Obstacles to Healthy Development*, World Health Organization Report on Infectious Diseases, (WHO, 1999).
[25] 'An aspirin for Juelly is no longer good enough', *Financial Times*, 25 January 2005. See further, P Hunt, *Report of the Special Rapporteur on the Right of Everyone to the Highest Attainable Standard of Physical and Mental Health: Mission to Uganda*, UN Doc E/CN4/2006/48/Add2, para 63.
[26] UNICEF, *The State of the World's Children 2005* (UNICEF, 2004).

cooperation under law for the creation of a structural environment conducive to the realization of basic rights, for everyone.

The legal challenges posed by the human rights regime to the deficiencies in the institutional economic order remain forthcoming though. And as the proceedings of a Nobel Symposium on the right to development recently concluded, while grounded in international law, the ability of this right to constrain states legally is only in the process of evolution.[27] Obiora reminds us however, that the legal status of human rights is not determined by the fact that 'the actual level of protection of many human rights remains problematic, or the machinery for their enforcement is in most cases inadequate, or because there are still important areas of uncertainty about the content and application of rights. These realities are taken nowadays ... as reasons for improving the articulation and enforcement of international human rights standards ... '.[28]

Changes in international society in the area of economic affairs are making particular demands on international law for the protection and promotion of human rights. Given the extent and features of world poverty today, to limit the discourse to the human rights obligations of states at the domestic level, or to narrowly-framed external obligations of states, is far too insignificant a gesture to confront the task at hand. While these methods of human rights protection are of critical importance, there is a more cumbersome responsibility to be met: nothing short of healing the world entire.

---

[27] B-A Andreassen and SP Marks, 'Conclusions' in B-A Andreassen and SP Marks (eds), *Development as a Human Right: Legal, Political and Economic Dimensions* (Harvard School of Public Health—Harvard University Press, 2006) 304, at 305.

[28] LA Obiora, 'Beyond the Rhetoric of a Right to Development' 18 *Law & Pol* 3–4 (1996) Special Issue on the Right to Development, M wa Mutua, LA Obiora and RJ Krotoszynski Jr (eds), 366, at 380.

Bibliography

PUBLICATIONS

Abi-Saab, G, 'The Legal Formulation of a Right to Development' in R-J. Dupuy (ed), *The Right to Development at the International Level, Workshop of the Hague Academy of International Law 1979* (Alphen aan den Rijn: Sijthoff & Noordhoff, 1980).

—— 'Whither the International Community?' 9 *European Journal of International Law* 2 (1998) 248.

Action Aid, Eurodad, Oxfam International, *EU Heroes and Villains: Which Countries are Living Up to their Promises on Aid, Trade and Debt*, Briefing Paper, Action Aid, Eurodad, Oxfam International (2005).

ActionAid International, *Square Pegs, Round Holes* and *Contradicting Commitments: How the Achievement of Education for All is Being Undermined by the International Monetary Fund* (Action Aid/ActionAid International, 2005).

Allott, P, 'The True Function of Law in the International Community' 5 *Indiana Journal of Global Legal Studies* 2 (1998) 391.

Alston, P., 'The Shortcomings of a 'Garfield the Cat' Approach to the Right to Development' 15 *California Western International Law Journal* 3 (1985) 510.

—— 'The International Monetary Fund and the Right to Food' 30 *Howard Law Journal* 2 (1987) 473.

—— 'Introduction' in P Alston (ed), *Peoples' Rights* (Oxford: Oxford University Press, 2001).

—— 'Peoples' Rights: Their Rise and Fall' in P Alston (ed), *Peoples' Rights* (Oxford: Oxford University Press, 2001) 259.

—— 'Resisting the Merger and Acquisition of Human Rights by Trade Law: A Reply to Petersmann' 13 *European Journal of International Law* 4 (2002) 815.

—— 'Ships Passing in the Night: The Current State of the Human Rights and Development Debate Seen through the Lens of the Millennium Development Goals' 27 *Human Rights Quarterly* 3 (2005) 755.

—— and G Quinn, 'The Nature and Scope of States Parties' Obligations under the International Covenant on Economic, Social and Cultural Rights' 9 *Human Rights Quarterly* 2 (1987) 156.

Alvarez, J, 'The Rule (and Role) of Law in the International Community', 72nd International Law Association Conference, Toronto, 4–8 June 2006.

—— 'The Promise and Perils of International Organizations', London School of Economics, London, 6 December 2006.

Alves, J, 'The Declaration of Human Rights in Post Modernity' 22 *Human Rights Quarterly* (2000) 478.

Amarasinha, S D, and J. Kokott, 'The Long and Winding Road towards Multilateral Investment Rules' in P Muchlinski and F Ortino (eds), *Oxford Handbook of International Law of Foreign Investment* (forthcoming, Oxford: Oxford University Press, 2008).

Andreasson, B-A, 'Article 22' in G Alfredsson and A Eide (eds), *The Universal Declaration of Human Rights: A Common Standard of Achievement* (Dordrecht: Martinus Nijhoff, 1999) 453.

—— and S P Marks, 'Conclusions' in B-A Andreassen and S P Marks (eds), *Development as a Human Right: Legal, Political and Economic Dimensions* (Cambridge, MA: Harvard School of Public Health—Harvard University Press, 2006) 304.

Annan, K, United Nations Secretary-General, Address to the General Assembly, New York, 9 September 2006.

Arai-Takahashi, Y, *The Margin of Appreciation Doctrine and the Principle of Proportionality in the Jurisprudence of the European Court of Human Rights* (Antwerp: Intersentia, 2002).

Archer, R, 'The Strengths of Different Traditions: What Might be Gained and What Might be Lost by Combining Rights and Development?' 3 *SUR International Journal on Human Rights* 4 (2006) 81.

Aréchaga, E J, de, 'Sovereignty and Humanity: Interventions at Plenary and Group Sessions' in A Grahl-Madsen and J Toman (eds), *The Spirit of Uppsala, Proceedings of the Joint UNITAR-Uppsala University Seminar on International Law and Organization for a New World Order* (Berlin: Walter de Gruyter, 1984) 449.

Balakrishnan, A, 'Public services: The revolutionary way to deliver health and education, says Oxfam', *The Guardian*, 1 September 2006.

Barsh, R L, 'The Right to Development as a Human Right: Results of the Global Consultation' 13 *Human Rights Quarterly* (1991) 322.

Beattie, A, 'Dipak and the Goliaths', *Financial Times Magazine*, 10–11 December 2005.

Bedjaoui, M, 'Are the World's Food Resources the Common Heritage of Mankind?' 24 *The Indian Journal of International Law* (1984) 459.

—— 'General Introduction' in M Bedjaoui (ed), *International Law: Achievements and Prospects* (Dordrecht: Martinus Nijhoff, 1991) 1.

—— 'The Right to Development' in M Bedjaoui (ed), *International Law: Achievements and Prospects* (Dordrecht: Martinus Nijhoff, 1991) 1177.

Bengoa, J, *The Relationship Between the Enjoyment of Human Rights, in particular Economic, Social and Cultural Rights, and Income Distribution*, Final Report (Sub-Commission, 49th session, 1997) UN Doc E/CN 4/Sub 2/1997/9.

—— *The Relationship Between the Enjoyment of Human Rights, in particular Economic, Social And Cultural Rights, and Income Distribution/Poverty, Income Distribution and Globalization: A Challenge For Human Rights*, Addendum to the Final Report (Sub-Commission, 50th session, 1998) UN Doc E/CN 4/Sub 2/1998/8.

—— *Implementation of Existing Human Rights Norms and Standards in the Context of the Fight Against Extreme Poverty*, Preliminary working paper by the ad hoc group of Experts (Sub-Commission, 55th session, 2003) UN Doc E CN 4/Sub 2/2003/17.

—— *Report of the Chairperson/Rapporteur, UN Social Forum* (Sub-Commission, 57th session, 2005) UN Doc E/CN 4/Sub 2/2005/21.

Beyani, C, 'The Legal Premises for the International Protection of Human Rights' in G S Goodwin-Gill and S Talmon (eds), *The Reality of International Law: Essays in Honour of Ian Brownlie* (Oxford: Oxford University Press, 1999) 21.

Bhabha, J, 'Enforcing the Human Rights of Citizens and Non-Citizens in the Era of Maastricht: Some Reflections on the Importance of States' 29 *Development and Change* (1998) 697.

Blair, T, Address by the Prime Minister to the Economic Club, Chicago, 24 April 1999.

—— 'Let Us Re-Order the World Around Us', Prime Minister's Address to the Labour Party Conference, Brighton, 2 October 2001.

Bolton, J, Letter from the Representative of the United States of America on the Millennium Development Goals, 13 August 2005 <http://www.unreform.org>.

—— Letter from the Representative of the United States of America to the General Assembly (Development Chapter) 30 August 2005 <http://www.unreform.org>.

Bond, P, 'NEPAD: Breaking or Shining the Chains of Global Apartheid?', Columbia University, New York, 22 April 2003.

Bossuyt, M, 'The United Nations and Civil and Political Rights in Chile' 27 *International and Comparative Law Quarterly* 2 (1978) 462.

Bradlow, D D, 'Development Decision-Making and the Content of International Development Law' 27 *Boston College International and Comparative Law Review* 2 (2004) 195.

Brierly, J L, *The Law of Nations: An Introduction to the International Law of Peace* (Oxford: Oxford University Press, 6th edn, 1963).

Brown, C, 'From International to Global Justice?' in J. Dryzek, B Honig and A Phillips (eds), *Oxford Handbook of Political Theory* (Oxford: Oxford University Press, 2006) 621.

Brownlie, I, *'The Human Right to Development'*, Commonwealth Secretariat (1989) 1.

—— 'International Law and the Fiftieth Anniversary of the United Nations' *Recueil des Cours* (1995) 21.

—— *Principles of Public International Law* (Oxford: Clarendon Press, 5th edn, 1998).

Bull, H, *The Anarchical Society: A Study of Order in World Politics* (Basingstoke: MacMillan, 2nd edn, 1995).

Cassese, A, *International Law* (Oxford: Oxford University Press, 2nd edn, 2005).

Chapman, A R, *Approaching Intellectual Property as a Human Rights: Obligations Related to Article 15(1)(c)*, (24th session, 2000) UN Doc E/C 12/2000/12 (2000).

Chinkin, C, 'The UN Decade on the Eradication of Poverty: What Role for International Law', Current Problems in International Law Series, University College London, 22 February 2001.

—— 'The United Nations Decade on the Elimination of Poverty: What Role for International Law', 54 *Current Legal Problems* (2001) 553.

Chomsky, N, 'Free and Fair Trade', *Global Agenda* (2006) 111.

Clapham, A, *'Globalization and the Rule of Law'* 61 *The Review of the International Commission of Jurists* (1999) 17.

—— and S Danailov, *Whither the State of Human Rights Protection? (New Ways to Hold Non-State Actors Accountable), Mapping Paper* (Versoix: The International Council on Human Rights Policy, 1998).

Cogen, M, 'Human Rights, Prohibition of Political Activities and the Lending Policies of the World Bank and the International Monetary Fund' in S R Chowdhury, E Denters and P J I M Waart (eds), *The Right to Development in International Law* (Dordrecht: Martinus Nijhoff, 1992) 379.

Commission for Africa (UK), *Our Common Interest* (London: 2005). <http://www.commissionforafrica.org>.

Commission on Intellectual Property Rights (UK), *Integrating Intellectual Property Rights and Development Policy* (London: 2002). <http://www.iprcommission.org>

Conference on the Human Dimension of the Conference on Security and Cooperation, Conclusions of the Moscow Meeting, 30 *International Legal Materials* (1991) 1670.

Coopération Internationale pour le Développement et la Solidarité, *Europe: A True Global Partnership for Development?: CIDSE Shadow Report on European Progress towards Millennium Development Goal 8* (Brussels: CIDSE, 2005).

Costello, C., 'The Bosphorus Ruling of the European Court of Human Rights: Fundamental Rights and Blurred Boundaries in Europe' 6 *Human Rights Law Review* 1 (2006) 87.

Craven, M.,*The International Covenant on Economic, Social and Cultural Rights: A Perspective on its Development* (Oxford: Oxford University Press, 2002).

—— 'Human Rights in the Realm of Order: Sanctions and Extraterritoriality' in F. Coomans and M.T. Kamminga (eds), *Extraterritorial Application of Human Rights Treaties* (Antwerp: Intersentia, 2004) 233.

Crawford, J., 'Some Conclusions' in J. Crawford (ed), *The Rights of Peoples* (Oxford: Clarendon Press, 1988) 159.

—— and P. Bodeau, *Second Reading of the ILC Draft Articles on State Responsibility: Further Progress.* <http://www.law.cam.ac.uk/rcil/ILCSR/Forum2.doc>.

Cumaraswamy, D.P., 'The Universal Declaration of Human Rights—Is it Universal?' 58–59 *The Review of the International Commission of Jurists* (1997) 120.

Dañino, R., *Legal Opinion on Human Rights and the Work of the World Bank*, 27 January 2006 (Washington: World Bank, 2006).

Darrow, M., *Between Light and Shadow: The World Bank, The International Monetary Fund and International Human Rights Law* (Oxford: Hart, 2003).

Das, B.L., 'Why the WTO Decision-Making System of "Consensus" Works Against the South', <http://www.twnside.org.sg/title/bgl3-cn.htm>.

Dawkins, K., *International Treaties/International Law: A Hierarchy of Values* (Minneapolis: Institute for Agriculture and Trade Policy, 2005).

De Schutter, O., 'Transnational Corporations as Instruments of Development' in P. Alston and M. Robinson (eds), *Human Rights and Development: Towards Mutual Reinforcement* (Oxford: Oxford University Press, 2005) 403.

Delbrück, J., 'Prospects for a "World (Internal) Law"? Legal Developments in a Changing International System' 9 *Indiana Journal of Global Legal Studies* (2002) 401.

Dimitrijevic, V., 'A Natural or Moral Basis for International Law' in A. Grahl-Madsen and J. Toman (eds), *The Spirit of Uppsala, Proceedings of the Joint UNITAR-Uppsala University Seminar on International Law and Organization for a New World Order* (Berlin: Walter de Gruyter, 1984) 383.

Dixon, M., *Textbook on International Law* (London: Blackstone Press, 3rd edn, 1990).

Donnelly, J., 'Human Rights, Democracy and Development' 21 *Human Rights Quarterly* 3 (1999).

—— 'In Search of the Unicorn: The Jurisprudence and Politics of the Right to Development' 15 *California Western International Law Journal* 3 (1985) 473.

—— *Universal Human Rights: Theory and Practice* (Ithaca NY: Cornell University Press, 2003).

Duffy, H., 'Towards Global Responsibility for Human Rights Protection: A Sketch of International Developments' 15 *Interights Bulletin* 3 (2006) 104.

Eide, A., *Report on the Right to Adequate Food as a Human Right* (Sub-Commission, 39th session, 1987) UN Doc. E/CN.4/Sub.2/1987/23.

—— 'Realization of Social and Economic Rights and the Minimum Threshold Approach' 10 *Human Rights Law Journal* 1–2 (1989) 35.

—— 'Article 28' in G. Alfredsson and A. Eide (eds), *The Universal Declaration of Human Rights: A Common Standard of Achievement* (Dordrecht: Martinus Nijhoff, 1999) 597.

—— *Report on the Right to Adequate Food and to be Free from Hunger* (Sub-Commission, 51st session, 1999) UN Doc. E/CN.4/Sub.2/1999/12.

Emmet, B., *In the Public Interest* (Oxford: Oxfam, 2006).

Ertürk, Y., *Report of the Special Rapporteur on Violence Against Women, Its Causes and Consequences: The Due Diligence Standard as a Tool for the Elimination of Violence against Women*, UN Doc. E/CN.4/2006/61.

Evans, G., '2005: Make or Break for Global Governance', London School of Economics, London, 18 February 2005.

Falk, R., 'The Making of Global Citizenship' in J. Brecher, J.B. Childs and J. Cutler (eds), *Global Visions: Beyond the New World Order* (Cambridge, MA: South End Press, 1993) 39.

—— *Predatory Globalization: A Critique* (Malden MA: Polity Press, 1999).

Farer, T., 'Sovereignty and Humanity: The Suppression of Tyranny' in A. Grahl-Madsen and J. Toman (eds), *The Spirit of Uppsala, Proceedings of the Joint UNITAR-Uppsala University Seminar on International Law and Organization for a New World Order* (Berlin: Walter de Gruyter, 1984) 422.

Fassbender, B., 'The United Nations Charter As Constitution of the International Community' 36 *Columbia Journal of Transnational Law* 3 (1998) 529.

Finland's Report on the Millennium Development Goals 2004. <http://www.undp.org/mdg/donorcountryreports.html>.

Franck, T., *Fairness in International Law and Institutions* (Oxford: Oxford University Press, 1995).

Friedmann, W., *The Changing Structure of International Law* (New York NY: Columbia University Press, 1964).

Gros Espiell, H., 'Human Welfare and International Law: Reordering Priorities' in W. Friedmann, L. Henkin and O. Lissitzyn (eds), *Transnational Law in a Changing Society: Essays in Honor of Philip C. Jessup* (New York NY: Columbia University Press, 1972) 113.

—— 'Sovereignty, Independence and Interdependence of Nations' in A. Grahl-Madsen and J. Toman (eds), *The Spirit of Uppsala, Proceedings of the Joint UNITAR-Uppsala University Seminar on International Law and Organization for a New World Order* (Berlin: Walter de Gruyter, 1984) 277.

—— 'Introduction: Community-Oriented Rights' in M. Bedjaoui (ed), *International Law: Achievements and Prospects* (Dordrecht: Martinus Nijhoff, 1991) 1167.

Frowein, J.A., 'Reactions by Not Directly Affected States to Breaches of Public International Law', 274 *Recueil des Cours* (1994 IV) 245.

Fukuda-Parr, S., *Millennium Development Goal 8: Indicators for Monitoring Implementation*, UN Doc. E/CN.4/2005/WG.18/TF/CRP.2. <http://www.ohchr.org/english/issues/development/taskforce.htm>

Gattini, A., 'Smoking/No Smoking: Some Remarks on the Current Place of Fault in the ILC Draft Articles on State Responsibility' 10 *European Journal of International Law* 2 (1999) 397.

Gearty, C.A., 'Human Rights' in A. Kuper and J. Kuper (eds), *The Social Science Encyclopedia* (Routledge, 3rd edn, 2004) Vol. I, 468.

Ghandhi, P.R., 'The Universal Declaration of Human Rights at Fifty Years: Its Origins, Significance and Impact' 41 *German Yearbook of International Law* (1998) 207.

Gianviti, F., 'Economic, Social and Cultural Rights and the International Monetary Fund' in P. Alston (ed), *Non-State Actors and Human Rights* (Oxford: Oxford University Press, 2005) 113.

Goldin, I., 'Meeting the Challenge of Development—An Action Agenda to Achieve the Millennium Development Goals', London School of Economics, London, 3 February 2005.

—— and K. Reinert, *Globalization for Development: Trade, Finance, Aid, Migration, and Policy* (Washington/London: World Bank/Palgrave MacMillan, 2006).

Greig, D., 'International Community—Theory or Reality?' British Institute of International and Comparative Law, London, 22 October 2001.

—— '"International Community", "Interdependence" and All That … Rhetorical Correctness?' in G. Kreijan, M. Brus, J. Duursma, E. de Vos and J. Dugard (eds), *State, Sovereignty, and International Governance* (Oxford: Oxford University Press, 2002) 521.

Grossman, C., and D.D. Bradlow, 'Are we Being Propelled Towards a People-Centred Transnational Legal Order?' 9 *American University Journal of International Law and Policy* 1 (1993) 1.

Gunning, R., 'Modernizing Customary International Law: The Challenge of Human Rights' 31 *Virginia Journal of International Law* 2 (1991) 211.

Hanlon, J., *Defining Illegitimate Debt*, Norwegian Church Aid (2002), http://english.nca.no/article/view/2381/?TreeMenu=109.

Hannum, H., 'The Status of the Universal Declaration of Human Rights in National and International Law' 12 *Interights Bulletin* 1 (1998/9) 3.

Harris, D.J., *Cases and Materials on International Law* (London: Sweet and Maxwell, 5th edn, 1998).

Harrison, J., *Human Rights and World Trade Agreements* (Geneva: OHCHR, 2005).

Henkin, L., *The Age of Rights* (New York NY: Columbia University Press, 1990).

—— 'The United Nations and Human Rights' 19 *International Organization* (1965) 504.

—— 'The Universal Declaration at 50 and the Challenge of Global Markets' 25 *Brooklyn Journal of International Law* 1 (1999) 17.

Higgins, R., *Problems and Process: International Law and How We Use it* (Oxford: Oxford University Press, 1998).

Hildyard, N., *The World Bank and the State: A Recipe for Change?* (Bretton Woods Project: The Corner House, UK, 2000).

Hinsch, W., 'Global Distributive Justice' in T.W. Pogge (ed), *Global Justice* (Oxford/Malden, MA: Blackwell, 2001).

Honoré, A, 'Causation in the Law', *Stanford Encyclopedia of Philosophy* (2005) <http://plato.stanford.edu/entries/causation-law/#2>

Hossain, K, 'Introduction' in K Hossain (ed), *Legal Aspects of the New International Economic Order* (London: Frances Pinter Publishers, 1980).

Howse, R, *Mainstreaming the Right to Development into International Trade Law and Policy at the World Trade Organization*, UN Doc E/CN 4/Sub 2/2004/17.

—— *Social Impact Assessment in the Areas of Trade and Development at the National and International Levels* (Geneva: OHCHR, 2004).

—— and M wa Mutua, *Protecting Human Rights in a Global Economy: Challenges for the World Trade Organization* (International Centre for Human Rights and Democratic Development, 2000). <http://www.ichrdd.ca>.

Hudson, M, 'Integrity of International Instruments' 42 *American Journal of International Law* (1948) 105.

Humphrey, J, 'The Universal Declaration of Human Rights: Its History, Impact and Juridical Character' in B G Ramcharan (ed), *Human Rights: Thirty Years After the Universal Declaration* (Dordrecht: Martinus Nijhoff, 1979) 21.

Hunt, P, 'Relations between the UN Committee on Economic, Social and Cultural Rights and the International Financial Institutions' in W van Genugten, P Hunt and S Mathews (eds), *World Bank, IMF and Human Rights* (Nijmegen: Wolf Legal Publishers, 2003) 139.

—— *Report of the Special Rapporteur on the Right of Everyone to the Highest Attainable Standard of Physical and Mental Health: Mission to the WTO*, UN Doc E/CN 4/2004/49/Add 1.

—— *Report of the Special Rapporteur on the Right of Everyone to the Highest Attainable Standard of Physical and Mental Health*, UN Doc A/60/348 (2005).

—— Special Rapporteur on the Right of Everyone to the Enjoyment of the Highest Attainable Standard of Physical and Mental Health, *Statement to the Third Committee of the General Assembly*, 8 October 2005.

—— *Report of the Special Rapporteur on the Right of Everyone to the Highest Attainable Standard of Physical and Mental Health: Mission to Uganda*, UN Doc E/CN 4/2006/48/Add 2.

——, M Nowak, and S Osmani, *Principles and Guidelines for a Human Rights Approach to Poverty Reduction Strategies* (Geneva: OHCHR, 2005). <http://www.unhchr.ch>

Ignatieff, M, 'Introduction: American Exceptionalism and Human Rights' in M Ignatieff (ed), *American Exceptionalism and Human Rights* (Princeton NJ: Princeton University Press, 2005) 1.

ILO, *A Fair Globalization, Report of the World Commission on the Social Dimension of Globalization* (Geneva: International Labour Organization, 2004).

IMF Press Release, No. 05/210 (24 September, 2005); "World Bank, IMF Strike Debt Deal, Shift Sights to WTO" *Bridges Weekly Trade News Digest*, 28 September, 2005.

International Council on Human Rights Policy, *Taking Duties Seriously: Individual Duties in International Human Rights Law* (Versoix: International Council on Human Rights Policy, 1999).

—— *Duties sans Frontières: Human Rights and Global Social Justice* (Versoix: International Council on Human Rights Policy, 2003).

International Law Association, *New Delhi Declaration of Principles of International Law Relating to Sustainable Development*, 70th Conference, res 3/2002.

International Law Association, *Report on the Accountability of International Organizations* (International Law Association, 2004).

International Law Commission, *Report of the International Law Commission* (51st Session, 1999) UN Doc A/54/10 (1999).

—— *Articles on the Responsibility of States for Internationally Wrongful Acts with commentaries* (2001).

—— *Draft Articles on the Responsibility of States for Internationally Wrongful Acts, Report of the International Law Commission on the work of its 53rd session*, UN Doc. A/56/10 (2001).

Investing in Development: A Practical Plan to Achieve the Millennium Development Goals (The UN Millennium Project Report, 2005).

Jackson, W D, 'Thinking about the International Community and its Alternatives' in K W Thompson (ed), *Community, Diversity and the New World Order* (Lanham MD: University Press of America, 1994) 4.

Jenks, C.W., *Law, Freedom and Welfare* (London: Longman, 1963).

Jennings, R, and A Watts (eds), *Oppenheim's International Law* (London: Longman, 9th edn, 1992).

Jerve, A M, 'Social Consequences of Development in a Human Rights Perspective: Lessons from the World Bank' in I. Kolstad and H. Stokke (eds), *Writing Rights* (Bergen: Fagbokforlaget, 2005).

Kagan, R, *Paradise and Power: America and Europe in the New World Order* (London: Atlantic Books, 2003).

Kamminga, M T, *Inter-State Accountability for Violations of Human Rights* (Pennsylvania PA: Penn Press, 1992).

Kartashkin, V., *Observance of Human Rights by States which are not Parties to the United Nations Human Rights Conventions* (Sub-Commission, 51st session, 1999) UN Doc E/CN 4/Sub 2/1999/29.

Keck, A, and P Low, *Special and Differential Treatment in the WTO: Why, When and How?*, WTO Economic Research and Statistics Division, Staff Working Paper ERSD-2004–03, May 2004.

Klein, L, 'La Responsabilité des Organisations Financières Internationales et les Droits de Personnes' 32 *Revue Belge de Droit International* (1999) 97.

Koh, H K, 'America's Jekyll and Hyde Exceptionalism' in M. Ignatieff (ed), *American Exceptionalism and Human Rights* (Princeton NJ: Princeton University Press, 2005) 111.

Koskenniemi, M, *From Apology to Utopia: The Structure of International Legal Argumentation* (Helsinki: Finnish Lawyer's Publishing Company, 1989).

—— '*Study on the Function and Scope of the Lex Specialis Rule and the Question of "Self-Contained Regimes"*'. UN Doc ILC(LVI)/SG/FIL/CRD 1/Add 1 (2004).

Kritsiotis, D, 'Imagining the International Community', 13 *European Journal of International Law* 4 (2002) 961.

Künnemann, R, *Report to ICESCR on the Effect of German Policies on Social Human Rights in the South* (The Foodfirst Information and Action Network, 2001). <http://www.fian.org>.

—— 'Extraterritorial Application of the International Covenant on Economic, Social and Cultural Rights' in F Coomans and M T Kamminga (ed.), *Extraterritorial Application of Human Rights Treaties* (Antwerp: Intersentia, 2004) 201.

Lamy, P, *The Place and Role of the WTO (WTO Law) in the International Legal Order*, WTO Director-General's Address to the European Society of International Law, Paris, 19 May 2006.

Landau, J-P, *Group de Travail sur Les Nouvelles Contributions Financieres Internationales* (France), (Landau Report, 2004).

Lauterpacht, H, *International Law and Human Rights* (London: Stevens & Sons, 1950).

Lennox, C, and M E Salomon, 'Negotiating the Right to Development for Minorities' 4 *McGill International Review* 1(Winter 2003) 4.

Lillich, R B, 'Sovereignty and Humanity: Can they Converge?' in A Grahl-Madsen and J Toman (eds), *The Spirit of Uppsala, Proceedings of the Joint UNITAR-Uppsala University Seminar on International Law and Organization for a New World Order* (Berlin: Walter de Gruyter, 1984) 406.

Lindholm, T, 'Art. 1' in G Alfredsson and A Eide (eds), *The Universal Declaration of Human Rights: A Common Standard of Achievement* (Dordrecht: Martinus Nijhoff, 1999) 41.

Lindroos, A, and M Mehling, 'Dispelling the Chimera of "Self-Contained Regimes": International Law and the WTO' 16 *European Journal of International Law* 5 (2005) 857.

Lucas, E, (chair), Panel, 'Is Respect for Human Rights Essential to Economic Development?', London School of Economics, London, 13 October 2005.

Lucas, M, 'The International Monetary Fund's Conditionality and the International Covenant on Economic, Social and Cultural Rights: An Attempt to Define the Relations' 25 *Revue Belge de Droit International* 1 (1992) 104.

Lukashuk, I I, 'The Law of the International Community' in *International Law on the Eve of the Twenty-First Century: Views from the International Law Commission* (New York NY: United Nations, 1997) 51.

Maastricht Guidelines on Violations of Economic, Social and Cultural Rights, reproduced in 20 *Human Rights Quarterly* 3 (1998) 691.

Mackay, F, 'Cultural Rights' in M E Salomon (ed), *Economic, Social and Cultural Rights: A Guide for Minorities and Indigenous Peoples* (London: Minority Rights Group International, 2005) 83.

Malhotra, K, *Promoting Human Development through Trade*, Address at the Carnegie Council on Ethics and International Affairs, 5 April 2006 <http://www.globalpolicy.org/socecon/trade/2006/0405humandev.htm>.

Manigat, L F, 'Independence and Interdependence (Interventions at Plenary and Group Sessions)' in A Grahl-Madsen and J Toman (eds), *The Spirit of Uppsala, Proceedings of the Joint UNITAR-Uppsala University Seminar on International Law and Organization for a New World Order* (Berlin: Walter de Gruyter, 1984) 351.

Manokha, I, 'Terrorism and Poverty: Is there a Causal Relationship?' in M E Salomon, A Tostensen and W Vandenhole (eds), *Casting the Net Wider: Human Rights, Development and New Duty-Bearers* (forthcoming, Antwerp: Intersentia, 2007).

Mansell, W, and J Scott, 'Why Bother about the Right to Development?' 21 *Journal of Law and Society* (1994) 171.

Marceau, G, 'WTO Dispute Settlement and Human Rights' 13 *European Journal of International Law* 4 (2002) 753.

Marks, S P, 'Emerging Human Rights: A New Generation for the 1980s?' 33 *Rutgers Law Review* 2 (1981) 435.

Marks, S P, *The Human Rights Framework for Development: Seven Approaches* (2003). <http://www.hsph.harvard.edu/fxbcenter>.

—— 'The Human Right to Development: Between Rhetoric and Reality' 17 *Harvard Human Rights Journal* (2004) 137.

—— 'Misconceptions about the Right to Development' Special Report, Human Rights and Development, D Freestone and J K Ingram (guest eds), 8 *Development Outreach* (Washington: The World Bank Institute, October 2006) 9.

Maxwell, S, *The Washington Consensus is Dead! Long Live the Meta-Narrative*, Overseas Development Institute, Working Paper 243 (2005).

Mbaye, K, 'Le Droit du Développement comme un Droit de l'Homme' *Revue des Droits de l'Homme* 5 (1972) 503.

—— 'Introduction' to (Part Four) 'Human Rights and Rights of Peoples' in M Bedjaoui (ed), *International Law: Achievements and Prospects* (Dordrecht: Martinus Nijhoff, 1991) 1041.

McCorquodale, R, and R Fairbrother, 'Globalization and Human Rights' 21 *Human Rights Quarterly* 3 (1999) 735.

McDougal, M S, and W M Reisman, *International Law in Contemporary Perspective: The Public Order of the World Community* (Mineola NY: Foundation Press, 1981).

McWhinney, E, 'The Concept of Co-operation' in M Bedjaoui (ed), *International Law: Achievements and Prospects* (Dordrecht: Martinus Nijhoff, 1991) 425.

Meron, T, *Human Rights Law Making in the United Nations* (Oxford: Clarendon Press, 1986).

—— *Human Rights and Humanitarian Norms as Customary Law* (Oxford: Clarendon Press, 1989).

—— 'The Martens Clause, Principles of Humanity, and Dictates of Public Conscience' 94 *American Journal of International Law* 1 (2000) 78.

Mesquita, J. Bueno de, *International Covenant on Economic, Social and Cultural Rights: Obligations of International Assistance and Cooperation, Background briefing submitted to the Committee on Economic, Social and Cultural Rights* (Unpublished, 2003).

Mills, K, 'Reconstructing Sovereignty: a Human Rights Perspective' 15 *Netherlands Quarterly of Human Rights* 3 (1997) 267.

'Mind the Gap between the US and its Allies: Today's Differences Turn on Values instead of Geopolitics', *Financial Times*, 10 December 2005.

Montealegre, H, 'Sovereignty and Humanity', Report of the Working Group III, in A Grahl-Madsen and J Toman (eds), *The Spirit of Uppsala, Proceedings of the Joint UNITAR-Uppsala University Seminar on International Law and Organization for a New World Order* (Berlin: Walter de Gruyter, 1984) 58.

Morsink, J, *Universal Declaration of Human Rights: Origins, Drafting and Intent* (Philadelphia PA: University of Pennsylvania Press, 1999).

Mosler, H, 'The International Society as a Legal Community' 140 *Recueil des Cours* (1974 IV) xv.

Mudho, B, *Report of the Independent Expert on the Effects of Structural Adjustment Policies and Foreign Debt on the full Enjoyment of Human Rights, particularly Economic, Social and Cultural Rights* (Commission, 61st session, 2005) UN Doc E/CN 4/2005/42.

Müllerson, R, *Human Rights Diplomacy* (Oxford: Routledge, 1997).

—— *Ordering Anarchy: International Law in International Society* (Dordrecht: Martinus Nijhoff, 2000).

Multi-Stakeholder Consultations Organized by the New Rules for Global Finance Coalition, Final Report and Recommendations (November 2004–September 2005).

Nastase, A, 'The Right to Peace' in M Bedjaoui (ed), *International Law: Achievements and Prospects* (Dordrecht: Martinus Nijhoff, 1991) 1217.

Nayer, M G K., 'Human Rights: United Nations and United States Foreign Policy' 19 *Harvard International Law Journal* (1978) 813.

Nolte, G, 'Chapter 1, Article 2(7)' in B Simma (ed), *The Charter of the United Nations: A Commentary* (Oxford: Oxford University Press, 2nd edn, 2002) Vol I, 171.

Nowrot, K, 'Legal Consequences of Globalization: The Status of Non-Governmental Organizations Under International Law' 6 *Indiana Journal of Global Legal Studies* 2 (1999) 579.

O'Manique, J, 'Development, Human Rights and the Law' 14 *Human Rights Quarterly* 3(1992) 383.

—— 'Human Rights and Development' 14 *Human Rights Quarterly* 1 (1992) 78.

Obiora, L A, 'Beyond the Rhetoric of a Right to Development' 18 *Law and Policy* 3–4 (1996) 366. Special Issue on the Right to Development, M wa Mutua, L A Obiora and R J Krotoszynski Jr, (eds).

OHCHR, *Definitions on Poverty*, UN Doc. HR/GVA/POVERTY/SEM/2001/2 (2001).

—— *The Impact of the Agreement on Trade-Related Aspects of Intellectual Property Rights on Human Rights*, UN Doc E/CN 4/Sub 2/2001/13.

—— *Globalization and its Impact on the full Enjoyment of Human Rights (World Trade Organization Agreement on Agriculture)* UN Doc E/CN 4/2002/54.

—— *Liberalization of Trade in Services and Human Rights*, UN Doc E/CN 4/ Sub 2/2002/9.

—— *Human Rights, Trade and Investment*, UN Doc E/CN 4/Sub 2/2003/9.

—— *The Right to Development: The Importance and Application of the Principle of Equity at Both the National and International Levels*, UN Doc E/CN 4/2003/25 (2003).

—— *Analytical Study of the High Commissioner for Human Rights on the Fundamental Principle of Non-Discrimination in the Context of Globalization*, UN Doc E/CN 4/2004/40.

—— *Analytical Study of the High Commissioner for Human Rights on the Fundamental Principle of Participation and its Application in the Context of Globalization*, UN Doc E/CN4/2005/41.

—— *Report on the Responsibilities of Transnational Corporations and related Business Enterprises with regard to Human Rights*, UN Doc E/CN 4/2005/91.

Oloka-Onyango, J, *Globalization in the Context of Increased Incidents of Racism, Racial Discrimination and Xenophobia* (Sub-Commission, 51st session, 1999) UN Doc E/CN 4/ Sub 2/1999/8.

—— 'Poverty, Human Rights and the Quest for Sustainable Human Development in Structurally-Adjusted Uganda' 18 *Netherlands Quarterly Of Human Rights* 1 (2000) 23.

—— *Globalization and its Impact on the Full Enjoyment of Human Rights* (Sub-Commission, 53rd session, 2001) UN Doc E/CN 4/Sub 2/2001/10.

—— *Globalization and its Impact on the Full Enjoyment of Human Rights* (Sub-Commission, 55th session, 2003) UN Doc E/CN 4/Sub 2/2003/14.

—— and D Udagama, *Globalization and its Impact on the Full Enjoyment of Human Rights* (Sub-Commission, 52nd session, 2000) UN Doc E/CN 4/Sub 2/2000/13.

Opsahl, T and V Dimitrijevic, 'Article 29 and 30' in G Alfredsson and A Eide (eds), *The Universal Declaration of Human Rights: A Common Standard of Achievement* (Dordrecht: Martinus Nijhoff, 1999) 633.

Orford, A, 'Globalization and the Right to Development' in P Alston (ed), *Peoples' Rights* (Oxford: Oxford University Press, 2001) 127.

—— 'Beyond Harmonization: Trade, Human Rights and the Economy of Sacrifice' 18 *Leiden Journal of International Law* (2005) 179.

Ouguergouz, F, *The African Charter on Human and Peoples' Rights: A Comprehensive Agenda for Human Dignity and Sustainable Democracy in Africa* (Dordrecht: Martinus Nijhoff, 2003).

Ovey, C, and R White, *Jacob's and Whites The European Convention on Human Rights* (Oxford: Oxford University Press, 4th edn, 2006).

Pauwelyn, J, 'The Role of Public International Law in the WTO: How Far Can We Go' 95 *American Journal of International Law* 3 (2001) 535.

Perry, R W, 'Rethinking the Right to Development: After the Critique of Development, After the Critique of Rights' 18 *Law and Policy* (1996) 225. Special Issue on the Right to Development, M wa Mutua, L A Obiora and R J Krotoszynski Jr, (eds).

Piron, L H, and T O'Neil, *The Right to Development: A Review of the Current State of the Debate for the UK Department for International Development* (London: Overseas Development Institute, 2002).

—— *Integrating Human Rights into Development: A Synthesis of Donor Approaches and Experiences*, Report for the OECD Development Assistance Committee Network on Governance (London: Overseas Development Institute, 2005).

Pogge, T W, 'The International Significance of Human Rights' *The Journal of Ethics* 4 (2000) 45.

—— 'Priorities of Global Justice' in T W Pogge (ed), *Global Justice* (Oxford/Malden MA: Blackwell Publishers, 2001).

—— *World Poverty and Human Rights* (Malden MA: Polity Press, 2002).

—— Severe Poverty as a Human Rights Violation (2003) 20 <http://www.etikk.no/globaljustice>.

—— 'The First UN Millennium Development Goal: A Cause for Celebration?' 5 *Journal of Human Development* 3 (2004) 377.

—— 'Severe Poverty as a Violation of Negative Duties: A Reply to the Critics' 19 *Ethics and International Affairs* 1 (2005) 55.

—— 'What is Global Justice?' in A Follesdal and T W Pogge (eds), *Real World Justice* (Berlin: Springer, 2005) 2.

—— 'World Poverty and Human Rights' 19 *Ethics and International Affairs* 1 (2005) 1.

—— 'Reward Pharmaceutical Innovators in Proportion to the Health Impact of their Invention' (Carnegie Council on Ethics and International Affairs, 2006) <http://www.policyinnovations.org>.

—— '"Assisting" the Global Poor' in D.K. Chatterjee (ed), *The Ethics of Assistance: Morality and the Distant Needy* (Cambridge: Cambridge University Press, 2004) 260.

—— and S Reddy, *How Not to Count the Poor* (2003) <http://www.columbia.edu/~sr793/techpapers.html>.

Ragazzi, M, 'International Obligations *Erga Omnes*: Their Moral Foundation and Criteria of Identification in Light of Two Japanese Contributions' in G S Goodwin-Gill and S Talmon (eds), *The Reality of International Law: Essays in Honour of Ian Brownlie* (Oxford: Oxford University Press, 1999) 455.

—— *The Concept of International Obligations Erga Omnes* (Oxford: Oxford University Press, 2000).

Rajagopal, B 'The Violence of Development' *The Washington Post*, 8 August 2001.

Ramcharan, B G, 'The Universality of Human Rights' 58 *The Review of the International Commission of Jurists* (1997) 105.

Ramesh, R, 'Banker to the World's Poor Wins Nobel Peace Prize', *The Guardian*, 14 October 2006.

Ramphal, S, 'Globalism and Meaningful Peace: A New World Order Rooted in International Community' 23 *Security Dialogue* (1992) 81.

—— Panellist, 'Lawless World: The US, Britain and the Making and Breaking of Global Rules', The Royal Institute of International Affairs (Chatham House), London, 9 March 2005.

Randelzhofer, A, 'Chapter I: Purposes and Principles, Article 2' in B. Simma (ed), *The Charter of the United Nations: A Commentary* (Oxford University Press, 2nd edn, 2002) Vol. I, 64.

Riedel, E, 'Chapter IX: International Economic and Social Co-operation, Article 55(c)' in B Simma (ed), *The Charter of the United Nations: A Commentary* (Oxford: Oxford University Press, 2nd edn, 2002) Vol II, 917.

Reinisch, A, 'The Changing International Legal Framework for Dealing with Non-State Actors' in P Alston (ed), *Non-State Actors and Human Rights* (Oxford: Oxford University Press, 2005) 37.

Reisman, W M, 'Sovereignty and Humanity, Interventions at Plenary Session on 'A Natural or Moral Basis for International Law' in A Grahl-Madsen and J Toman (eds), *The Spirit of Uppsala, Proceedings of the Joint UNITAR-Uppsala University Seminar on International Law and Organization for a New World Order* (Berlin: Walter de Gruyter, 1984) 449.

—— 'Sovereignty, Interdependence and Independence', Interventions at Plenary Session' in A Grahl-Madsen and J Toman (eds), *The Spirit of Uppsala, Proceedings of the Joint UNITAR-Uppsala University Seminar on International Law and Organization for a New World Order* (Berlin: Walter de Gruyter, 1984) 351.

—— 'Sovereignty and Human Rights in Contemporary International Law' 84 *American Journal of International Law* (1990).

Report of the High-Level Task Force on the Implementation of the Right to Development (1st session, 2004) UN Doc E/CN 4/2005/WG 18/2.

Report of the High-Level Task Force on the Implementation of the Right to Development (2nd session, 2005) UN Doc E/CN 4/2005/WG 18/TF/3.

Report of the High-Level Task Force on the Implementation of the Right to Development (3rd session, 2007) UN Doc A/HRC/4/WG 2/TF/2.

Report of the International Commission on Intervention and State Sovereignty, The Responsibility to Protect (Ottawa: International Development Research Centre, 2001).

Report of the Open-ended Working Group on the Right to Development (1st and 2nd sessions 2001) UN Doc E/CN 4/2001/26.

Report of the Open-ended Working Group on the Right to Development (3rd session, 2002) UN Doc E/CN 4/2002/28/Rev 1 [not adopted].

Report of the Open-ended Working Group on the Right to Development (4th session, 2003) UN Doc E/CN 4/2003/26.

Report of the Open-ended Working Group on the Right to Development (5th session, 2004) UN Doc E/CN 4/2004/23.

Report of the Open-ended Working Group on the Right to Development (6th session, 2005) UN Doc E/CN 4/2005/25.

Report of the Open-ended Working Group on the Right to Development (7th session, 2006) UN Doc E/CN 4/2006/26.

Report of the Open-ended Working Group to consider options regarding the elaboration of an optional protocol to the International Covenant on Economic, Social and Cultural Rights (1st session, 2004) UN Doc E/CN 4/2004/44.

Report of the Open-ended Working Group to consider options regarding the elaboration of an optional protocol to the International Covenant on Economic, Social and Cultural Rights (2nd session, 2005) UN Doc E/CN 4/2005/52.

Report of the Open-ended Working Group to consider options regarding the elaboration of an optional protocol to the International Covenant on Economic, Social and Cultural Rights (3rd session, 2006) UN Doc E/CN 4/2006/47.

Report of the Secretary-General, In Larger Freedom: Towards Development, Security and Human Rights for All, 21 March 2005, UN Doc A/59/2005.

Report of the UN High-Level Panel on Threats, Challenges and Change, A More Secure World: Our Shared Responsibility, 29 November 2004, UN Doc A/59/565 (2004).

Report of the Working Party on the Social Dimension of Globalization, (ILO) GB 292/15, March 2005.

'Restatement of the Law (Third), Foreign Relations Law of the United States' 2 *American Law Institute* (1987) 165.

Ruggie, J G, 'American Exceptionalism, Exemptionalism and Global Governance' in M Ignatieff (ed), *American Exceptionalism and Human Rights* (Princeton NJ: Princeton University Press, 2005) 304.

—— *Interim Report of the UN Special Representative of the Secretary-General on the issue of human rights and transnational corporations and other business enterprise*, UN Doc E/CN 4/2006/97.

Sachs, J, *The End Of Poverty: Economic Possibilities for Our Time* (London: Penguin Books, 2005).

—— *The End of Poverty: Economic Possibilities for Our Time* (Transcript), Carnegie Council on Ethics and International Affairs, 30 March 2005 <http://www.carnegiecouncil.org>.

Saito, Y., 'International Law as a Law of the World Community: World Law as Reality and Methodology' in A Grahl-Madsen and J Toman (eds), *The Spirit of Uppsala, Proceedings of the Joint UNITAR-Uppsala University Seminar on International Law and Organization for a New World Order* (Berlin: Walter de Gruyter, 1984) 233.

Salama, I., *The Right to Development: Towards a New Approach?* Annual Meeting of the Academic Council on the United Nations System (Ottawa, 16–18 June 2005).

—— H.E Ambassador, Chair, Working Group on the Right to Development, *Statement to the Third Committee of the General Assembly*, 25 October 2005.

Salomon, M.E. *The Nature of a Right: The Right to a Process in the Right to Development'* in Reflections on the First Four Reports of the Independent Expert on the Right to Development (Geneva: Franciscans International, 2003) 82.

—— *Addressing Structural Obstacles and Advancing Accountability for Human Rights: A Contribution of the Right to Development to MDG8*, Submission to the 2nd session of the UN High-Level Task Force on the Right to Development (November 2005) <http://www.ohchr.org/english/issues/development/taskforce.htm>.

—— 'Towards a Just Institutional Order: A Commentary on the First Session of the UN Task Force on the Right to Development' 23 *Netherlands Quarterly of Human Rights* 3 (2005) 409.

—— 'International Human Rights Obligations in Context: Structural Obstacles and the Demands of Global Justice' in B-A Andreassen and S P Marks (eds), *Development as a Human Right: Legal, Political and Economic Dimensions* (Cambridge MA: Harvard School of Public Health—Harvard University Press, 2006) 96.

—— 'The Significance of the Task Force on the Right to Development', Special Report, Human Rights and Development, D Freestone and J K Ingram (guest eds), 8 *Development Outreach* (Washington: The World Bank Institute, October 2006) 27.

—— 'International Economic Governance and Human Rights Accountability' in M E Salomon, A Tostensen and W Vandenhole (eds), *Casting the Net Wider: Human Rights, Development and New Duty-Bearers* (forthcoming, Antwerp: Intersentia, 2007).

—— and A Sengupta, *The Right to Development: Obligations of States and the Rights of Minorities and Indigenous Peoples* (London: Minority Rights Group International, 2003).

Sample, I, 'Doctors who Put Lives Before Profits', *The Guardian*, 4 January 2006.

Sands, P, 'International Law: Alive and Kicking', *The Guardian*, 17 May 2005.

—— *Lawless World: America and the Making and Breaking of Global Rules* (London: Penguin Books, 2005).

—— and P Klein, *Bowett's Law of International Institutions* (London: Sweet & Maxwell Ltd, 5th edn, 2001).

Sarnoff, I (ed), *International Instruments of the United Nations: A Compilation of Agreements, Charters, Conventions, Declarations, Principles, Proclamations, Protocols, Treaties adopted by the General Assembly of the United Nations, 1945–1995* (New York: United Nations, 1997).

Saxena, J N, 'Sovereignty, Independence and Interdependence of Nations' in A Grahl-Madsen and J Toman (eds), *The Spirit of Uppsala, Proceedings of the Joint UNITAR-Uppsala University Seminar on International Law and Organization for a New World Order* (Berlin: Walter de Gruyter, 1984) 289.

Schachter, O, *International Law in Theory and Practice* (Dordrecht: Martinus Nijhoff, 1991).

Schram, G G, 'Independence and Interdependence (Interventions at Plenary and Group Sessions)' in A Grahl-Madsen and J Toman (eds), *The Spirit of Uppsala, Proceedings of the Joint UNITAR-Uppsala University Seminar on International Law and Organization for a New World Order* (Berlin: Walter de Gruyter, 1984) 351.

Schwelb, E, 'The Law of Treaties and Human Rights' in W M Reisman and B H Weston, *Towards World Order and Human Dignity: Essays in Honour of Myres S McDougal* (London: Collier MacMillan, 1976) 262.

Secretariat of the Convention on Biological Diversity, *Indigenous Peoples and the International and Domestic Protection of Traditional Knowledge, Working paper prepared for the UN Working Group on Indigenous Populations*, UN Doc E/CN 4/Sub 2/ AC 4/2005/CRP 2.

Sen, A, *Development as Freedom* (Oxford: Oxford University Press, 1999).

—— 'Consequential Evaluation and Practical Reason' 27 *The Journal of Philosophy* (2000) 477.

——, 'Law and Human Rights', The Paul Sieghart Memorial Lecture, British Institute of Human Rights, London, 6 July 2005.

Sendanyoye-Rugwabiza, V, 'Is the Doha Development Round a Development Round?' London School of Economics, London, 31 March 2006.

Sengupta, A, *First Report of the Independent Expert on the Right to Development* (General Assembly, 55th session, 2000) UN Doc A/55/306.

—— *Second Report of the Independent Expert on the Right to Development*, (Working Group on the Right to Development, 1st session, 2000) UN Doc E/CN4/2000/ WG 18/CRP 1.

—— *Third Report of the Independent Expert on the Right to Development* (Working Group on the Right to Development, 2nd session, 2001) UN Doc E/CN 4/2001/ WG 18/2.

—— *Fourth Report of the Independent Expert on the Right to Development* (Working Group on the Right to Development, 3rd session, 2002) UN Doc E/CN 4/2002/WG 18/2.

—— *Fourth Report of the Independent Expert on the Right to Development: Mission to the Organization for Economic Cooperation and Development, the United Kingdom of Great Britain and Northern Ireland, the International Monetary Fund, the World Bank, the United States of America and the Netherlands* (Working Group on the Right to Development, 3rd session, 2002) UN Doc E/CN 4/2002/WG 18/2/Add.1

—— Independent Expert on the Right to Development, *Statement to the 58th session of the Commission on Human Rights*, 22 March 2002.

—— 'On the Theory and Practice of the Right to Development' 24 *Human Rights Quarterly* 4 (2002) 837.

—— *Fifth Report of the Independent Expert on the Right to Development* (Working Group on the Right to Development, 4th session, 2003) UN Doc E/CN 4/2002/WG 18/6.

—— *Preliminary Study of the Independent Expert on the Right to Development, on the Impact of International Economic and Financial Issues on the Enjoyment of Human Rights*, (Working Group on the Right to Development, 4th session, 2003) UN Doc E/ CN 4/2003/WG 18/2.

—— *Sixth Report of the Independent Expert on the Right to Development: Implementing the Right to Development in the Current Global Context* (Working Group on the Right to Development, 5th session, 2004) UN Doc E/CN 4/2004/WG 18/2.

—— *Human Rights and Extreme Poverty, Report of the Independent Expert on the question of human rights and extreme poverty.* UN Doc E/CN 4/2005/49.

Shelton, D, *Remedies in International Human Rights Law* (Oxford: Oxford University Press, 2nd edn, 2005).

Shihata, I, 'Foreign Investment, Human Rights and Development' International Law Association, 69th Conference, London, 25–27 July 2000.

Shue, H, *Basic Rights: Subsistence, Affluence and U.S Foreign Policy* (Princeton NJ: Princeton University Press, 1980).

Sieghart, P, *The Lawful Rights of Mankind: An Introduction to the International Legal Code of Human Rights* (Oxford: Oxford University Press, 1985).

Simma, B, and P Alston, 'The Sources of Human Rights Law: Custom, Jus Cogens, and General Principles' 12 *Australian Yearbook of International Law* (1988–89) 82.

—— and A L Paulus, 'The International Community: Facing the Challenge of Globalization. General Conclusions' 9 *European Journal of International Law* 2 (1998) 266.

Skogly, S I, *The Human Rights Obligations of the World Bank and International Monetary Fund* (London: Cavendish, 2001).

—— 'The Obligation of International Assistance and Co-operation in the International Covenant on Economic, Social and Cultural Rights' in M Bergsmo (ed), *Human Rights and Criminal Justice for the Downtrodden: Essays in Honour of Asbjørn Eide* (London: Kluwer Law International, 2004) 403.

—— 'Beyond National Borders: States' Human Rights Obligations in International Cooperation* (Antwerp: Intersentia, 2006).

—— and Gibney, M, 'Transnational Human Rights Obligations' 24 *Human Rights Quarterly* 3 (2002) 781.

Sloan, B, 'General Assembly Resolutions Revisited (Forty Years Later)' 58 *British Yearbook of International Law* (1987) 39.

Steger, M B, *Globalization: A Very Short Introduction* (Oxford: Oxford University Press, 2003).

Stiglitz, J, *Globalization and its Discontents* (London: Penguin Press, 2002).

—— Distant Voices, *The Guardian*, 12 March 2004.

Suy, E, 'A New International Law for a New World Order' in A Grahl-Madsen and J Toman (eds), *The Spirit of Uppsala, Proceedings of the Joint UNITAR-Uppsala University Seminar on International Law and Organization for a New World Order* (Berlin: Walter de Gruyter, 1984) 92.

Tesón, F R, 'Interdependence, Consent, and the Basis of International Obligation' 83 *American Society of International Law Proceedings* (1989) 558.

Tomuschat, C, 'Obligations Arising for States Without or Against their Will' 241 *Recueil des Cours* (1993) 199.

—— 'International Law: Ensuring the Survival of Mankind on the Eve of a New Century' 281 *Recueil des Cours* (1999) 23.

Townsend, P 'Poverty, Social Exclusion and Social Polarisation: the Need to Construct an International Welfare State' in P Townsend and D Gordon (eds), *World Poverty: New Policies to Defeat an Old Enemy* (Bristol: The Policy Press, 2002) 3.

—— 'An End to Poverty or More of the Same?' *Lancet* (April 2005) 1379.

—— *The Right to Social Security and National Development: Lessons from OECD Experience for Low-Income Countries*, Discussion Paper 18 (International Labour Organization, 2007).

—— and D Gordon, 'Introduction: the Human Condition is Structurally Unequal' in P Townsend and D Gordon (eds), *World Poverty: New Policies to Defeat an Old Enemy* (Bristol: The Policy Press, 2002) xi.

Trachtman, J P, 'Legal Aspects of a Poverty Agenda at the WTO: Trade Law and "Global Apartheid"' 6 *Journal of International Economic Law* 1 (2003) 3.

Udombana, N, 'A Question of Justice: The WTO, Africa and Countermeasures for Breaches of International Trade Obligations' 38 *The John Marshall Law Review* (2005) 1153.

UNCTAD, *World Investment Report 2003* (New York/Geneva, 2003).

UNDP, *Human Development Report 1999: Globalization with a Human Face* (Oxford: Oxford University Press, 1999).

—— *Human Development Report 2000: Human Rights and Human Development* (Oxford: Oxford University Press, 2000).

—— *Human Development Report 2003: Millennium Development Goals, A Compact Among Nations to End Human Poverty* (Oxford: Oxford University Press, 2003).

—— *Human Development Report 2005: International Cooperation at a Crossroads: Aid, Trade and Security in an Unequal World* (Oxford: Oxford University Press, 2005).

—— *Asia-Pacific Human Development Report 2006: Trade on Human Terms* (New Delhi: Macmillan India Ltd, 2006).

UNDP et al., *Making Global Trade Work for People* (New York: UNDP, 2003).

United Kingdom, *Partnerships for Poverty Reduction: Rethinking Conditionality*, UK Policy Paper (March 2005).

United Kingdom Department for International Development, *Eliminating World Poverty: Making Governance Work for the Poor*, White Paper (July 2006).

United Kingdom, 'G8 Finance Ministers' Conclusions on Development', Press Release, 11 June 2005.

United Kingdom, Statement on behalf of the European Union (High-Level Task Force on the Right to Development, 2nd session, 2005).

UNICEF Statistics: Child Mortality (May 2006). <http://childinfo.org/areas/childmortality>.

—— *The State of the World's Children 2005* (New York: UNICEF, 2004).

United Nations Division for the Advancement of Women, *The Feminization of Poverty*, <http://www.un.org/womenwatch/daw>.

United Nations High-Level Seminar on the Right to Development: *Global Partnership for Development*, Geneva, 9 February 2004 (notes unpublished at the time of publication of this book).

United Nations Interagency Workshop on Implementing a Human Rights-Based Approach in the Context of UN Reform (the Second), Attachment 1: *The Human Rights-Based Approach to Development Cooperation: Towards a Common Understanding Among UN Agencies*, Stamford, USA (May 2003).

United Nations Millennium Project (2005) *'Fast Facts: The Faces of Poverty'*. <http://mirror.undp.org/unmillenniumproject/facts/index.htm>.

UNRISD, *'The Sources of Neoliberal Globalization'* Report of UNRISD Seminar on Improving Knowledge on Social Development in International Organizations II (2002) <http://www.unrisd.org>.

Ustor, E, 'Independence and Interdependence' (Oral presentation of the Report of the Working Group II) in A Grahl-Madsen and J Toman (eds), *The Spirit of Uppsala,*

Proceedings of the Joint UNITAR-Uppsala University Seminar on International Law and Organization for a New World Order (Berlin: Walter de Gruyter, 1984) 375.

—— 'Independence and Interdependence' (Report of the Working Group II) in A Grahl-Madsen and J Toman (eds), *The Spirit of Uppsala, Proceedings of the Joint UNITAR-Uppsala University Seminar on International Law and Organization for a New World Order* (Berlin: Walter de Gruyter, 1984) 52.

Uvin, P, *Human Rights and Development* (Bloomfield CT: Kumarian Press, 2004).

Vandemoortele, J, *The MDG's and Pro-Poor Policies: Related but not Synonymous*, UNDP International Policy Centre, Working Paper No 3 (2004).

Vandenhole, W, *A Partnership for Development: International Human Rights Law as an Assessment Instrument*, Submission to the 2nd session, of the UN High-Level Task Force on the Right to Development (November 2005). <http://www.ohchr.org/english/issues/development/taskforce.htm>.

—— 'Third State Obligations under the ICESCR: A Case Study of EU Sugar Policy' 76 *Nordic Journal of International Law* 1(2007) 73.

van Dijk, P, 'A Common Standard of Achievement: About Universal Validity and Uniform Interpretation of International Human Rights Norms' 13 *Netherlands Quarterly Of Human Rights* 2 (1995) 105.

van Weerelt, P, *A Human-Rights-Based Approach to Development Programme in the UNDP: Adding the Missing Link*, Briefing Note (UNDP, 2001).

wa Mutua, M 'Editor's Introduction' 18 *Law & Policy* 3–4 (1996) 366 . Special Issue on the Right to Development, M wa Mutua, L A Obiora and R J Krotoszynski Jr, (eds).

Waldock, H, 'General Course on Public International Law', 106 *Recueil des Cours* 54 (1962 II).

Watkins, K, *Globalisation and Liberalization: Implications for Poverty, Distribution and Inequality*, Occasional Paper 12 (UNDP 1997). <http://hdr.undp.org/publications/papers.cfm>.

—— *Dumping on the World: How EU Sugar Policies Hurt Poor Countries*, International Briefing Paper 61 (Oxfam 2004).

Weiler, J H H, 'Fin-de Siècle World Law: Taking Democracy Seriously' International Law Association (British Branch), Committee on Theory and International Law, Beyond the Kosovo Crisis: Fundamental Questions and Enquiries for the Discipline of International Law, London, 25 July 2000.

Weissbrodt, D, Statement on Humanizing Globalization, Item 4 (Sub-Commission, 55th session, 2003).

WHO, *Removing Obstacles to Healthy Development*, World Health Organization Report on Infectious Diseases (Geneva: World Health Organization, 1999).

Winston, M., *'On the Indivisibility and Interdependence of Human Rights'*, Paper delivered at the World Congress of Philosophy PADAEIA (1998). <http://www.bu.edu/wcp/Papers/Huma/HumaWins.htm>.

Woicke, P, 'Putting Human Rights Principles into Development Practice through Finance: The Experience of the International Finance Corporation' in P Alston and M Robinson (eds), *Human Rights and Development: Towards Mutual Reinforcement* (Oxford: Oxford University Press, 2005) 327.

Wolfensohn, J D, *Note from the President of the World Bank to the Joint Ministerial Development Committee of the Board of Governors of the Bank and the Fund*, 12 April 2005, DC 2005–0005.

—— 'Some Reflections on Human Rights and Development' in P Alston and M Robinson, (eds), *Human Rights and Development: Towards Mutual Reinforcement* (Oxford: Oxford University Press, 2005) 19.

Wolfrum, R, 'Chapter IX: International Economic and Social Co-operation, Article 55(a) and 55(b)' in B Simma (ed), *The Charter of the United Nations: A Commentary* (Oxford: Oxford University Press, 2nd edn, 2002) Vol II, 897.

Woods, N, 'What Kind of Banker Does the World Need?' London School of Economics, London, 4 May 2005.

World Bank, Independent Evaluation Group, *Assessing World Bank Support for Trade 1987–2004* (Washington: World Bank, 2006).

—— *Pro-Poor Growth in the 1990s: Lessons and Insights from 14 Countries* (Washington/NY: World Bank, 2005).

—— *World Development Report 2000–2001: Attacking Poverty—Opportunity, Empowerment and Security* (New York: Oxford University Press, 2000).

—— *World Development Report 2006: Equity and Development* (New York: Oxford University Press, 2006).

Ziegler, J, *Report of the Special Rapporteur on the Right to Food* (Commission on Human Rights, 61st session, 2005) UN Doc E/CN 4/2005/47.

—— *Report of the Special Rapporteur on the Right to Food* (General Assembly, 60th session, 2005) UN Doc A/60/350.

INTERNATIONAL AND REGIONAL TREATIES AND DECLARATIONS

African Charter on Human and Peoples' Rights (1981), entered into force 21 October 1986, Organization of African Unity (OAU) Doc CAB/LEG/67/3 rev. 5.

Agreement Establishing the World Trade Organization (1994), entered into force 1 January 1995, 1867 UNTS 31874 (Marrakesh Agreement).

Agreement on Trade-Related Aspects of Intellectual Property Rights (TRIPS), entered into force 15 April 1994. Agreement Establishing the World Trade Organization (1994), Annex 1C.

American Convention on Human Rights (1969), entered into force 18 July 1978, Organization of American States (OAS) Treaty Series No. 36, 1144 UNTS 123.

Charter of the United Nations (1945), entered into force 24 October 1945, 59 Stat 1031, TS 993, 3 Bevans 1193.

Convention on the Elimination of All Forms of Discrimination Against Women (1979), entered into force 3 September 1981, General Assembly res A/RES/34/180, 1249 UNTS 20378.

Convention on the Prevention and Punishment of the Crime of Genocide (1948), entered into force 12 January 1951, 78 UNTS 277.

Convention on the Rights of the Child (1989), entered into force 2 September 1990, General Assembly res A/RES/44/25, annex 44, UN GAOR Supp (No 49) at 167, UN Doc A/44/49 (1989).

Covenant of the League of Nations (1919), entered into force 10 January 1920, 225 Consolidated Treaty Series (CTS) 195.

Declaration of the World Food Summit: Five Years Later, WSF: fyl 2002/3 (FAO, 2002).

Declaration on the Occasion of the Fiftieth Anniversary of the United Nations, General Assembly res 3201, 24 October 1995, UN GOAR, 50th session, Resolutions Supp (A/50/49, vol 1) at 13, UN Doc A/RES/50/6 (1995).

Declaration on the Principles of International Law concerning Friendly Relations and Cooperation among States in accordance with the Charter of the United Nations, General Assembly res A/RES/2625 (XXV), 24 October 1970, UN Doc A/RES/8082 (1970).

Declaration on Social Progress and Development, General Assembly res A/RES/2542 (XXIV), 11 December 1969, 24 UN GAOR Supp (No 30) at 49, UN Doc A/7630 (1969).

Declaration on the Right to Development, General Assembly res A/RES/41/128, 4 December 1986, annex, 41 UN GAOR Supp (No 53) 186, UN Doc A/RES/41/53 (1986).

Declaration on the Right and Responsibility of Individuals, Groups and Organs of Society to Promote and Protect Universally Recognized Human Rights and Fundamental Freedoms, 8 March 1999, General Assembly res A/RES/53/144, annex, 53, UN Doc A/RES/53/144 (1999).

Declaration of the United Nations Conference on the Human Environment, UN Doc A/CONF 48/14/Rev 1 (1973).

Declaration on the Use of Scientific and Technological Progress in the Interests of Peace and for the Benefit of Mankind, General Assembly res. 3384 (XXX), 10 November 1975, 30 UN GAOR Supp (No 34) at 86, UN Doc A/10034 (1975).

European Convention on Human Rights (1950), entered into force 3 September 1953, European Treaty Series 005.

Food and Agriculture Organization of the United Nations, Voluntary Guidelines to Support the Progressive Realization of the Right to Adequate Food in the Context of National Food Security (127th session, FAO Council, 2004).

International Convention on the Elimination of All Forms of Racial Discrimination (1965), entered into force 4 January 1969, General Assembly res A/RES/2106 (XX), 660 UNTS 195.

International Convention on the Suppression and Punishment of the Crime of Apartheid (1973), entered into force 18 July 1976, General Assembly res A/RES/3068 (XXVIII), UN GAOR Supp (49) at 192, UN Doc A/48/49 (1993).

International Covenant on Civil and Political Rights (1966), entered into force 23 March 1976, General Assembly res A/RES/2200A (XXI), 999 UNTS 171.

International Covenant on Economic, Social and Cultural Rights (1966), entered into force 3 January 1976, General Assembly res A/RES/2200A (XXI), 993 UNTS 3.

New Partnership for Africa's Development (NEPAD, 2001), African Union Summit, Heads of State and Government, 23 October 2001.

Rome Statute of the International Criminal Court (1998), entered into force 1 July 2002, UNTS vol 2187, p 3, UN Doc A/CONF/9.

Statute of the International Court of Justice (1945), entered into force 24 October 1945, UN Charter, annex I.

United Nations Conference on Environment and Development (1992), Rio Declaration on Environment and Development, UN Doc A/CONF 151/26.

United Nations Fourth World Conference on Women: Action for Equality, Development and Peace, Beijing Declaration and Platform for Action, (1995),UN Doc A/Conf 177/29 and A/Conf 177/20/add 1.

United Nations International Conference on Financing for Development, Outcome of the International Conference on Financing for Development (Monterrey Consensus), (2000), UN Doc A/CONF 198/3.

United Nations Millennium Declaration (2000), UN Doc A/55/2.

United Nations World Conference Against Racism, Racial Discrimination, Xenophobia and Related Intolerance, Durban Declaration and Programme of Action (2001), UN Doc A/CONF 189/12.

United Nations World Conference on Human Rights, Proclamation of Teheran (1968), UN Doc A/CONF 32/41.

United Nations World Conference on Human Rights, Vienna Declaration and Programme of Action (1993), UN Doc A/CONF 157/23.

United Nations World Conference on Sustainable Development (2002), WSSD Declaration and Plan of Implementation, UN Doc A/CONF 199/20.

United Nations World Summit for Social Development, Copenhagen Declaration and Programme of Action (1995) UN Doc A/CONF 166/9.

United Nations World Summit for Social Development and Beyond: Achieving Social Development for All in a Globalizing World (Copenhagen +5, 2000), General Assembly res A/RES/S-24/2 (24th special session, 1 July 2000).

United Nations World Summit Outcome 2005, UN Doc A/60/L 1, 15 September 2005.

Universal Declaration of Human Rights, General Assembly res 217A (III), 10 December 1948, UN GAOR, 3rd Session Resolutions, pt 1, at 71, UN Doc A/810 (1948).

Vienna Convention on the Law of Treaties (1969), entered into force 27 January 1980, 1166 UNTS 331.

World Trade Organization Ministerial Declaration on the TRIPS Agreement and Public Health (2001) WT/MIN(01)/DEC/2, 20 November 2001 (Doha Declaration).

UNITED NATIONS RESOLUTIONS

Commission on Human Rights res. 1998/25, Human rights and extreme poverty, UN Doc E/CN 4/1998/L 29.

Commission on Human Rights res 1998/33, The right to education, UN Doc E/CN4/1998/34.

Commission on Human Rights res 1998/72, The right to development, UN Doc E/CN4/1998/L 19.

Commission on Human Rights res 2000/5, The right to development, UN Doc E/CN4/2000/L 14.

Commission on Human Rights res 2000/9, Question of the realization in all countries of the economic, social and cultural rights contained in the Universal Declaration of Human Rights and in the International Covenant on Economic, Social and Cultural Rights, and study of special problems which the developing countries face in their efforts to achieve these human rights, UN Doc E/CN 4/2000/L17.

Commission on Human Rights res 2000/10, The right to food, UN Doc E/CN 4/2000/L 19.

Commission on Human Rights res 2000/82, Effects of structural adjustment policies and foreign debt on the full enjoyment of all human rights, particularly economic, social and cultural rights, UN Doc E/CN 4/2000/L20.

Commission on Human Rights res 2001/9, The right to development, UN Doc E/CN4/2001/L 15.

Commission on Human Rights res 2002/31, The right of everyone to the enjoyment of the highest attainable standard of physical and mental health, UN Doc E/CN 4/2002/L 47.

Commission on Human Rights res 2003/18, Question of the realization in all countries of the economic, social and cultural rights contained in the Universal Declaration of Human Rights and in the International Covenant on Economic, Social and Cultural Rights, and study of special problems which the developing countries face in their efforts to achieve these human rights, UN Doc E/CN 4/2003/L 11/Add 3.

Commission on Human Rights res 2003/27, Adequate housing as a component of the right to an adequate standard of living, UN Doc E/CN 4/2003/L 30/Rev 1.

Commission on Human Rights res 2003/35, Strengthening of popular participation, equity, social justice, and non-discrimination as essential foundations of democracy, UN Doc E/CN 4/2003/L 11/Add 4.

Commission on Human Rights res 2003/36, Interdependence between democracy and human rights, UN Doc E/CN 4/2003/L 11/Add 4.

Commission on Human Rights res 2003/63, Promotion of a democratic and equitable international order, UN Doc E/CN 4/2003/L 11/Add 6.

Commission on Human Rights res 2003/83, The right to development, UN Doc E/CN4/2003/L 14/Rev 1.

Commission on Human Rights res 2004/7, The right to development, UN Doc E/CN4/2004/L 17.

Commission on Human Rights res 2005/4, The right to development, UN Doc E/CN4/2005/L 10/Add 7.

Commission on Human Rights res 2005/69, Human rights and transnational corporations and other business enterprises, UN Doc E/CN 4/2005/L 10/Add.17.

Commission on Human Rights res 2005/24, The right of everyone to the enjoyment of the highest attainable standard of physical and mental health, UN Doc E/CN 4/2005/L28.

General Assembly res A/RES/ 616 A and B (VII), Question of Race Conflict in South Africa Resulting from the Policies of Apartheid of the Government of the Union of South Africa, 5 December 1952.

General Assembly res A/RES/2871 (XXVI), Question of Namibia, 20 December 1971.

General Assembly res A/RES/3201 (S-VI) and A/RES/3202 (S-VI) Declaration on the Establishment of a New International Economic Order, 1 May 1974.

General Assembly res A/RES/3281 (XXIX) Charter on the Economic Rights and Duties of States, 12 December 1974.

General Assembly res A/RES/49/179 (1994) Human rights and extreme poverty, 23 December 1994.

General Assembly res A/RES/51/97 (1996) Human rights and extreme poverty, 12 December 1996.

General Assembly res A/RES/53/146 (1998) Human rights and extreme poverty, 9 December 1998.

General Assembly res A/RES/55/96 (2000) Promoting and consolidating democracy, 4 December 2000.

General Assembly res A/RES/55/106 (2000) Human rights and extreme poverty, 4 December 2000.

General Assembly res A/RES/57/211 (2002) Human rights and extreme poverty, 18 December 2002.

General Assembly res A/RES/59/186 (2004) Human rights and extreme poverty, 20 December 2004.

General Assembly res A/RES/61/157 (2006) Human rights and extreme poverty, 19 December 2006.

Human Rights Council res 1/3, Open-ended Working Group on an optional protocol to the International Covenant on Economic, Social and Cultural Rights (1st session, 2006).

International Labour Organization Governing Body, GB 292/WP/SDG/1, Policy Coherence Initiative, Working Party on the Social Dimension of Globalization (292nd session, 2005).

TRAVAUX PREPARATOIRES (RIGHT TO DEVELOPMENT)

Report of the Working Group of Governmental Experts on the Right to Development (1st-3rd sessions, 25 January 1982) UN Doc E/CN 4/1489 (1982).

Working Group of Governmental Experts on the Right to Development (1st session, 10 June 1982) UN Doc E/CN 4/AC 39/1982/1 (Provisional Agenda).

Working Group of Governmental Experts on the Right to Development (4th session, 29 June 1982) UN Doc E/CN 4/AC 39/1982/3 (List of relevant United Nations documents).

Working Group of Governmental Experts on the Right to Development (4th session, 2 July 1982) UN Doc E/CN 4/AC 39/1982/4 (Proposals submitted by the Netherlands).

Working Group of Governmental Experts on the Right to Development (4th session, 2 July 1982) UN Doc E/CN 4/AC 39/1982/5 (Proposals submitted by the USSR).

Working Group of Governmental Experts on the Right to Development (4th session, 2 July 1982) UN Doc E/CN 4/AC 39/1982/6 (Proposals submitted by Iraq).

Working Group of Governmental Experts on the Right to Development (4th session, 6 July 1982) UN Doc E/CN 4/AC 39/1982/7 (Proposals submitted by Yugoslavia).

Working Group of Governmental Experts on the Right to Development (4th session, 6 July 1982) UN Doc E/CN 4/AC 39/1982/8 (Working Paper submitted by the Drafting Committee).

Working Group of Governmental Experts on the Right to Development (4th session, 6 July 1982) UN Doc E/CN 4/AC 39/1982/10 (Proposals submitted by Senegal).

Report of the Working Group of Governmental Experts on the Right to Development (4th session, 9 July 1982) UN Doc E/CN 4/AC 39/1982/11.

Report of the Working Group of Governmental Experts on the Right to Development (4th session, 9 December 1982) UN Doc E/CN 4/1983/11.

Report of the Working Group of Governmental Experts on the Right to Development (6th and 7th sessions, 14 November 1983) UN Doc E/CN 4/1984/13.

Report of the Working Group of Governmental Experts on the Right to Development (8th session, 24 January 1985) UN Doc E/CN 4/1985/11.

Analytical compilation of comments and views on the implementation and further enhancement of the Declaration on the Right to Development prepared by the Secretary-General (12th session, Working Group of Governmental Experts on the Right to Development, 21 December 1988) UN Doc E/CN 4/AC 39/1989/1.

UNITED NATIONS TREATY-BODY GENERAL
COMMENTS/RECOMMENDATIONS AND
CONCLUDING OBSERVATIONS

Committee on Economic, Social and Cultural Rights, General Comment No 1, Reporting by States Parties (3rd session, 1989) UN Doc Doc E/1989/22.

Committee on Economic, Social and Cultural Rights, General Comment No 2, International Technical Assistance Measures (Article 22), (4th session, 1990) UN Doc E/1990/23, annex III at 86 (1990).

Committee on Economic, Social and Cultural Rights, General Comment No 3, The Nature of States Parties' Obligations (Article 2(1), (5th session, 1990) UN Doc UN Doc E/1991/23, Annex III.

Committee on Economic, Social and Cultural Rights, General Comment No 4, The Right to Adequate Housing (Article 11(1)), (6th session, 1991) UN Doc E/1992/23.

Committee on Economic, Social and Cultural Rights, General Comment No 5, Persons with Disabilities, (11th session, 1994) UN Doc E/1995/22 at 19.

Committee on Economic, Social and Cultural Rights, General Comment No 6, The Economic, Social and Cultural Rights of Older Person (13th session, 1995) UN Doc E/1996/22 at 20 (1996).

Committee on Economic, Social and Cultural Rights, General Comment No 7, The Right to Adequate Housing: Forced Evictions (Article 11(1)), (16th session, 1997) UN Doc E/1998/22, annex IV at 113 (1997).

Committee on Economic, Social and Cultural Rights, General Comment No 8, The Relationship between Economic Sanctions and Respect for Economic, Social and Cultural Rights (17th session, 1997) UN Doc E/C 12/1997/8.

Committee on Economic, Social and Cultural Rights, General Comment No 9, The Domestic Application of the Covenant (19th session, 1998) UN Doc E/C 12/1998/24.

Committee on Economic, Social and Cultural Rights, General Comment No 10, The Role of National Human Rights Institutions in the Protection of Economic, Social and Cultural Rights (19th session, 1998) UN Doc E/C 12/1998/25.

Committee on Economic, Social and Cultural Rights, General Comment No 11, Plans of Action for Primary Education (Article 14), (20th session, 1999) UN Doc E/C 12/1999/4.

Committee on Economic, Social and Cultural Rights, General Comment No 12, The Right to Adequate Food (Article 11), (20th session, 1999) UN Doc E/C 12/1999/5.

Committee on Economic, Social and Cultural Rights, General Comment No 13, The Right to Education (Article 13), (21st session, 1999) UN Doc E/C 12/1999/10.

Committee on Economic, Social and Cultural Rights, General Comment No 14, The Right to the Highest Attainable Standard of Health (Article 12), (22nd session, 2000) UN Doc E/C 12/2000/4.

Committee on Economic, Social and Cultural Rights, General Comment No 15, The Right to Water (Articles 11 and 12), (29th session, 2002) UN Doc E/C 12/2002/11.

Committee on Economic, Social and Cultural Rights, General Comment No 16, The Equal Right of Men and Women to the Enjoyment of all Economic, Social and Cultural Rights (Article 3), (34th session, 2005) UN Doc E/C 12/2005/4.

Committee on Economic, Social and Cultural Rights, General Comment No 17, The Right of Everyone to Benefit from the Protection of the Moral and Material Interests Resulting from any Scientific, Literary or Artistic Production of which he is the Author (Art 15(1)(c)), (35th session, 2005) UN Doc E/C 12/GC/17 (2005).

Committee on Economic, Social and Cultural Rights, General Comment No 18, The Right to Work (Article 6), (35th session, 2005) UN Doc E/C 12/GC/18 (2005).

Committee on Economic, Social and Cultural Rights, Decision on Globalization and its Impact on the Enjoyment of Economic, Social and Cultural Rights (18th session, 1998) UN Doc E/1999/22.

Committee on Economic, Social and Cultural Rights, Statement to the Third Ministerial Conference of the World Trade Organization (21st session, 1999) UN Doc E/C 12/1999/9.

Committee on Economic, Social and Cultural Rights, Statement on Poverty and the International Covenant on Economic, Social and Cultural Rights (25th session, 2001) UN Doc E/C 12/2001/10.

Committee on Economic, Social and Cultural Rights, Statement on Human Rights and Intellectual Property (27th session, 2001) UN Doc E/C 12/2001/15.

Committee on Economic, Social and Cultural Rights and the UN Commission on Human Rights' Special Rapporteurs on Economic, Social and Cultural Rights, Joint Statement on: The Millennium Development Goals and Economic, Social and Cultural Rights, 29 November 2002.

Committee on Economic, Social and Cultural Rights Concluding Observations: Israel (19th session, 1998) UN Doc E/C 12/1/Add 27 (1998).

Committee on Economic, Social and Cultural Rights, Concluding Observations: Italy (23rd session, 2000) UN Doc E/C 12/1/Add 43 (2000).

Committee on Economic, Social and Cultural Rights, Concluding Observations: Belgium (24th session, 2000) UN Doc E/C 12/1/Add 54 (2000).

Committee on Economic, Social and Cultural Rights, Concluding Observations: Morocco (24th session, 2000) UN Doc E/C 12/1Add 55 (2000).

Committee on Economic, Social and Cultural Rights, Concluding Observations: Japan (26th session, 2001) UN Doc E/C 12/1/Add 67 (2001).

Committee on Economic, Social and Cultural Rights, Concluding Observations: Ireland (28th session, 2002) UN Doc E/C 12/1/Add 77 (2002).

Committee on Economic, Social and Cultural Rights, Concluding Observations: United Kingdom of Great Britain and Northern Ireland—Dependent Territories (28th session, 2002) UN Doc E/C 12/1/Add 79 (2002).

Committee on Economic, Social and Cultural Rights, Concluding Observations: Solomon Islands, (29th session, 2002) UN Doc E/C 12/1/Add 84 (2002).

Committee on Economic, Social and Cultural Rights, Concluding Observations: Israel (30th session, 2003) UN Doc E/C 12/1/Add 9 (2003).

Committee on Economic, Social and Cultural Rights, Concluding Observations: Ecuador (32nd session, 2004) UN Doc E/C 12/1/Add.100 (2004).

Committee on Economic, Social and Cultural Rights, Concluding Observations: Chile (33rd session, 2004) UN Doc E/C 12/1/Add 105 (2004).

Committee on Economic, Social and Cultural Rights, Concluding Observations: Norway (34th session, 2005) UN Doc E/C 12/1/Add 109 (2005).

Committee on Economic, Social and Cultural Rights, General Day of Discussion on: Substantive issues arising out of the implementation of the ICESCR on the Right of everyone to benefit from the protection of the moral and material interests resulting from any scientific, literary or artistic production of which he is the author, Article 15(1)(c), (24th session, 2000) UN Doc E/C 12/2000/12.

Committee on the Elimination of Discrimination Against Women, General Recommendation No 19 (Violence against Women), (11th session, 1992) UN Doc A/47/38 at 1 (1993).

Committee on the Elimination of Racial Discrimination, General Recommendation No 21, Right to Self-Determination (48th session, 1996) UN Doc A/51/18, annex VIII at 125 (1996).

Committee on the Elimination of Racial Discrimination, General Recommendation No 27, Discrimination against Roma (57th session, 2000) UN Doc A/55/18, annex V (2000).

Committee on the Rights of the Child, General Comment No 5, General Measures of Implementation of the Convention on the Rights of the Child (Arts 4, 42 and 44, para 6), (34th session, 2003) UN Doc CRC/GC/2003/5 (2003).

Committee on the Rights of the Child, Concluding Observations: Germany (35th session, 2004) UN Doc CRC/C/15/Add 226 (2004).

Committee on the Rights of the Child, Concluding Observations: Botswana (37th session, 2004) UN Doc CRC/C/15/Add 242 (2004).

Committee on the Rights of the Child, Concluding Observations: Philippines (39th session, 2005), UN Doc CRC/C/15/Add 258 (2005).

Human Rights Committee, General Comment No 31, The Nature of the General Legal Obligation Imposed on States Parties to the Covenant (Article 2)), (80th session, 2004) UN Doc CCPR/C/21/Rev 1/Add 13 (2004).

Human Rights Committee, Concluding Observations: USA (53rd session, 1995) UN Doc CCPR/C/79/Add 50 (1995).

Human Rights Committee, Concluding Observations: Israel (63rd session, 1998) UN Doc CCPR/C/79/Add 93 (1998).

Human Rights Committee, Concluding Observations: Israel (78th session, 2003) UN Doc CCPR/CO/78/ISR (2003).

Human Rights Committee, Concluding Observations: Belgium (81st session, 2004) UN Doc CCPR/CO/81/BEL (2004).

Index

Introductory Note

Titles of books and papers are presented in italics, as are terms in Latin and French. References in the form '18 n 25' indicate footnote 25 on page 18, whilst those in the form '40–1' indicate continuous discussion of a topic over the pages in question, and 'nn' without a note number is used in cases where a topic is referred to in multiple notes on a single page. In the rare cases where more than six references are provided without division into subheadings, the most significant discussions of the topic are presented in bold (e.g. 'extraterritoriality 6, 76, 83 n 90, 110, 177 n 86, 182, **186–8**'). Where a heading is followed by *'(key discussion)'*, this indicates a topic referred to with great frequency throughout the book which would have been difficult to split into suitable subheadings. In these cases, only a limited number of key references are provided.